San Antonio
7 November 1997

THE DEAD SEA SCROLLS

The
DEAD SEA SCROLLS

by
MILLAR BURROWS

ⵑⵑⵑⵑⵑⵑⵑⵑⵑⵑⵑⵑⵑⵑⵑⵑⵑⵑⵑⵑⵑⵑ

With Translations
by the Author

GRAMERCY PUBLISHING COMPANY

New York

This 1986 edition is published by Gramercy Publishing Company, distributed by Crown Publishers, Inc., 225 Park Avenue South, New York, New York 10003, by arrangement with Viking Penguin, Inc.

Printed and Bound in the United States of America

Library of Congress Cataloging in Publication Data

Burrows, Millar, 1889-
  The Dead Sea scrolls.

  Bibliography: p. 419
  1. Dead Sea scrolls—Criticism,
interpretation, etc.   I. Title.
BM487.B78   1986   296.1'55   86-19323

    Plates I, II, VII, and map of the Qumran Caves Expedition are reproduced by permission of Professor W. L. Reed; Plates III, V, VI, VIII, and IX by the courtesy of the Palestine Archeological Museum of Jerusalem; Plate IV by the courtesy of the American Schools of Oriental Research.

ISBN 0-517-62535-0

h g f e d c

To

CHARLES CUTLER TORREY

ספרא די מתאלף למלכות שמיא דָמֵא לגברא
מר ביתא די מפיק מבית גנווהי חדתָן ועתיקָן

A "man of letters who has received the teaching of
the kingdom of heaven" and "is like a householder
who brings forth from his storehouse things new and
old."   (Matthew 13:52)

Contents

PART FOUR: THE COMMUNITY OF QUMRAN

PART FIVE: THE IMPORTANCE
OF THE DEAD SEA SCROLLS

PART SIX: TRANSLATIONS

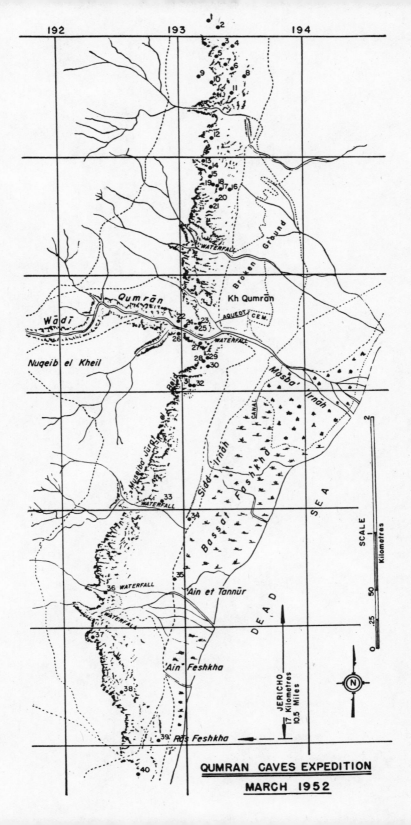

QUMRAN CAVES EXPEDITION

MARCH 1952

Preface

〰〰〰〰〰〰〰〰〰〰〰〰〰〰〰〰〰〰〰〰〰〰〰〰〰

It would be unprofitable to apologize for the shortcomings of this book, which reviewers and readers will detect all too easily. A word of explanation is in order, however, concerning the omission of a few features that might be expected in a book about ancient manuscripts.

Scholars will note the absence of footnotes and an index. These have been left out in order to keep the size and cost of the volume within reasonable bounds, and to avoid encumbering it with matter for which most readers would have no use. It is hoped that students who wish to pursue the subject further will find some compensation for these omissions in the rather extensive bibliography. To facilitate reference to the works of scholars whose views are mentioned in the course of the book, the bibliography is given in alphabetical order instead of being classified by subjects.

It is a pleasure to acknowledge the kind assistance of many friends, by which this book has quite literally been made possible. The scholars whose industry, learning, and insight have provided most of its substance, especially those who have generously sent me their books and articles, cannot even be named here. I can only express my obligation and gratitude to them all.

The quotation of Matthew 13:52 in the dedication to Professor Torrey is taken from his own translation, *The Four Gospels,* used by permission of Harper and Brothers. He is not, of course, responsible for my Aramaic.

For permission to use photographs of the excavation of Khirbet Qumran and objects found there I am grateful to Mr. G. Lankester Harding, Director of the Department of Antiquities of the Hashimite Kingdom of Jordan, to Father R. de Vaux, Director of the French Dominican School of Archeology at Jerusalem, and to Mr. Joseph Saad, Secretary of the Palestine Archeological Museum at Jerusalem. Assistance in obtaining and selecting these photographs was kindly given by Mr. and Mrs. Philip C. Hammond, Jr.; Mr. Hammond also prepared the drawings for Figures 1 and 2. For photographs of the caves and the Taamireh Bedouins and for the map of the Qumran Caves Expedition (published previously in the Bulletin of the American Schools of Oriental Research for October 1954) I am indebted to Professor William L. Reed, Director of the American School of Oriental Research at Jerusalem in 1951–52. Permission to use the photograph of a column of the Habakkuk Commentary was graciously given by Mrs. G. R. Walton, Business Manager of the American Schools of Oriental Research.

Others have rendered very important assistance by reading portions of my manuscript and making suggestions for its improvement. Professors William H. Brownlee and John C. Trever have helped to revive and correct my memories of the events connected with the first discovery of manuscripts and our connection with these events. They have also cleared up some technical points for me. My wife has very greatly helped me to clarify some of the most abstruse parts of my exposition. Much of it still makes heavy reading, for what is essentially complex cannot be made simple without misrepresenting it; but it is much plainer now than it would have been without her criticism and suggestions. I owe much to the skill and patience of my secretary, Mrs. C. E. Schweitzer. Miss Eudosia F. Adzima deserves credit also for her faithful work as Mrs. Schweitzer's substitute during the hot days of summer.

Without the invitation of Mr. Robert O. Ballou of the Viking

Press this book would not have been undertaken at all. For his considerate, helpful cooperation and encouragement throughout its preparation I am indeed grateful.

MILLAR BURROWS

Yale University
May 9, 1955

A Word to the Wise

~~~~~~

This book is not intended for the scholar. I have tried to write with a man's pen, so that he who runs may read. Even so, I fear, an attempt to read these chapters on the run will prove to be quite an obstacle race. I could not level the hills and valleys and make all the rough places plain without giving up my main purpose in writing, which was to give a fairly definite idea of what the Dead Sea Scrolls are, why there has been so much excitement over them, and how they are important.

I hope he who starts to read will not run away. In this kind of race, after all, there is no rule against cutting across the course and skipping the rugged places. If the reader chooses to turn at once to the last chapter to see how the story comes out, there is nothing to prevent him. It might be a good idea.

PLATE I. Two of the Taamireh Bedouins. Muhammad adh-Dhib, who discovered the first cave in 1947, is the young man on the right

PLATE II. Cave 1Q, where the first discoveries were made

PLATE III. Jars of the type in which the Dead Sea Scrolls were kept

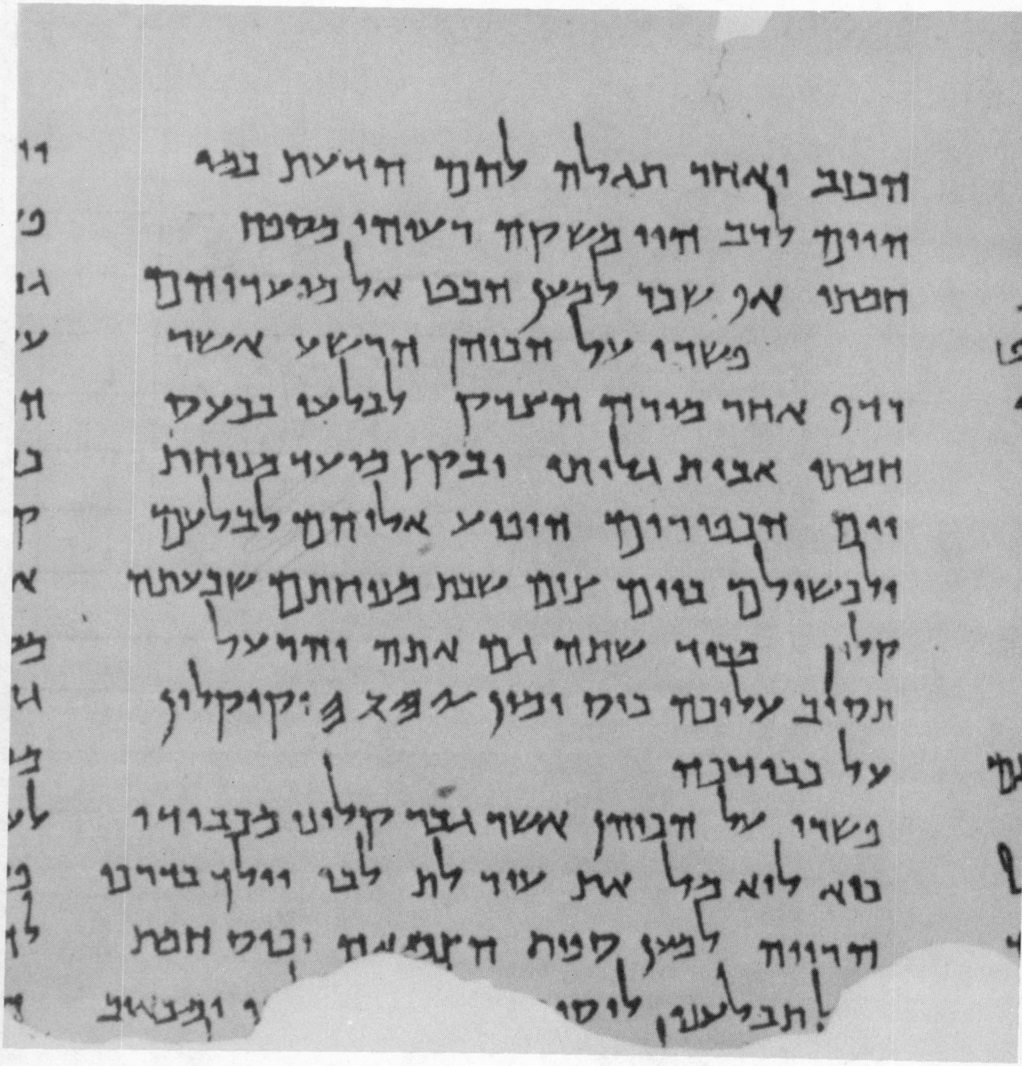

הכוב ואחר תגלה להמ חיעת נבה
חיינך לרב חוו משקה רעיהו מספח
חמתו אף שכר למעץ הבט אל מגעיוחתמ
פשרו על הכוהן הרשע אשר
רדף אחר מורה הצדיק לבלעו בכעס
חמתו אבית גלותו ובקץ מיעד מנוחת
יום הכפורים הופיע אליהמ לבלעמ
ולכשילמ ביום צומ שבת מנוחתמ שבעתה
קלוץ בצדי שתה גמ אתה והרעל
תחיוב עליכה כוס ומין יא תסבב עליכ הקיקלוץ
על כבודכה
פשרו על הכוהן אשר גבר קלונו מכבודו
כיא לוא מל את עור לת לבו וילך בדרך הרויה
למען ספות הצמאה וכוס חמת
אל תבלענו לוסי ... וקלוץ ...

PLATE IV. Column XI of the Habakkuk Commentary, showing the Divine Name in the archaic script

PLATE V. The excavation of Khirbet Qumran, seen from the hills, with the Dead Sea in the background. PLATE VI. The cisterns of Khirbet Qumran

PLATE VII. The bronze scrolls found in cave 3Q. PLATE VIII. Scholars working on the manuscript fragments at the Palestine Museum

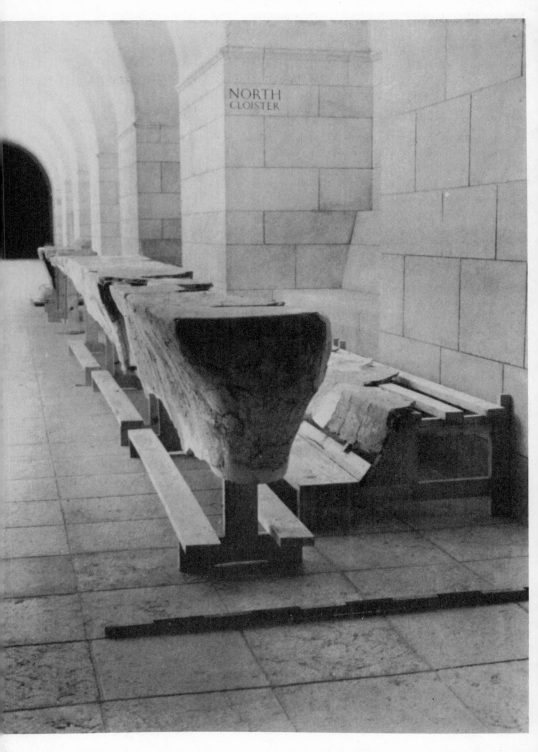

PLATE IX. Remains of writing tables and benches from the scriptorium of Khirbet Qumran, set up in the Palestine Museum at Jerusalem

PART ONE

DISCOVERIES AND DISCUSSIONS

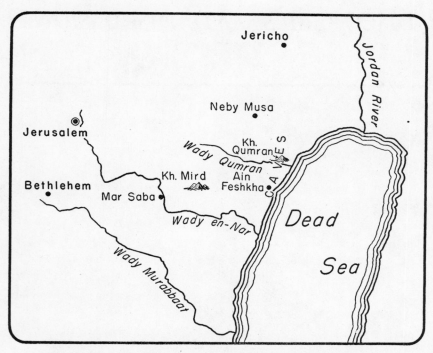

MAP SHOWING WHERE THE DISCOVERIES WERE MADE

I

The First Discoveries

⎍⎍⎍⎍⎍⎍⎍⎍⎍⎍⎍⎍⎍⎍⎍⎍⎍⎍⎍⎍⎍⎍⎍⎍⎍⎍⎍⎍

If we had only known it when we went down to the shore of the Dead Sea on October 25, 1947, we could have walked to the cave where an extraordinary discovery of manuscripts had been made some seven or eight months earlier. Conducting field trips to study the archeology and historical geography of Palestine was one of my duties as Director of the American School of Oriental Research at Jerusalem that year. This particular excursion, however, was not so much a scientific expedition as a pleasure trip and pilgrimage combined. At Kallia, near the northwestern corner of the Dead Sea, some of our party took a swim in the thick brine before we proceeded to the traditional site of the baptism of Jesus and then back to Jerusalem by way of Jericho. In the party were two young scholars who will have a prominent part in this narrative, Dr. John C. Trever and Dr. William H. Brownlee, who were both students at our school that year on fellowships. At the time of our excursion the manuscripts, which were later to become famous, were already at Jerusalem in the possession of the Syrian Monastery of St. Mark and of the Hebrew University, but we at the American School of Oriental Research did not learn of their existence for another four months.

Because these manuscripts were found in a cave near the Dead Sea, they are commonly called the Dead Sea Scrolls. Father de Vaux of Jerusalem, whose name will appear often in our story, protests that the scrolls did not come out of the Dead Sea. The

3

name is convenient, however, and will be used here. A more exact designation is the Wady Qumran Manuscripts, but this does not cover the manuscript fragments found later at other places in the region.

Exactly when and how the first cave and its contents were discovered can hardly be determined now, though the discoverer, a fifteen-year-old boy of the Taamirah tribe of Bedouins, was identified and questioned about two years later. His name was Muhammad adh-Dhib (more exactly *al-ḍi 'b,* i.e., "the wolf," pronounced *adh-dheeb,* the *dh* representing the sound of a soft *th* in English, as in *the*). It was probably in February or March 1947 that he found the scrolls. The Syrian Orthodox archbishop who bought some of them says that he first heard of them in the month of Nisan, which corresponds roughly to our month of April; and Father van der Ploeg of Nijmegen saw them at the Syrian Orthodox monastery late in July. According to one form of the story, Muhammad adh-Dhib was herding goats or looking for a lost sheep when he found the cave; according to another, he and one or two companions were taking goods, perhaps smuggled across the Jordan, to Bethlehem. One story has it that they took refuge from a thunderstorm in the cave. Another story is that a runaway goat jumped into the cave, Muhammad adh-Dhib threw a stone after it, and the sound of breaking pottery aroused his curiosity, whereupon he called another lad, and the two crawled into the cave and so found the manuscripts.

The cave is in a cliff about five miles south of the place where we went swimming at the northwest corner of the Dead Sea, and about a mile and a quarter back from the shore, in the foothills of the Judean plateau. It is within a mile of an old ruin named Khirbet Qumran. The name Qumran, as pronounced by the Bedouins, sounds a little like Gomorrah, and some of the early European explorers of Palestine thought that Khirbet Qumran might be the site of that ill-fated city. That is quite impossible. Gomorrah was not in this vicinity at all. Another association with the Old Testament is more pertinent. The track from the Jordan Valley to Bethlehem passes near this spot. When Elimelech and his family went from Bethlehem to Moab, and when Naomi and Ruth went back to Bethlehem, they must have followed approximately this same route.

Whenever and however the discovery came about, the cave, when first entered, contained several jars, most of them broken, with pieces of many others. Protruding from the broken jars were scrolls of leather wrapped in linen cloth. They were very brittle and rather badly decomposed, especially at the ends, but it was possible to see that they were inscribed in a strange writing. Muhammad Adh-Dhib and his friends, the story goes, took these scrolls to a Muslim sheikh at their market town, Bethlehem. Seeing that the script was not in Arabic and supposing that it was Syriac, the sheikh sent them to a merchant who was a member of the Syrian Orthodox (Jacobite) community at Bethlehem, Khalil Eskander, who informed another merchant belonging to their church at Jerusalem, George Isaiah; and he in turn informed their Metropolitan-Archbishop, Athanasius Yeshue Samuel. In the meantime, if the late Professor Sukenik of the Hebrew University at Jerusalem was correctly informed, the great manuscript of the book of Isaiah, the largest and oldest of all the scrolls, had been offered to a Muslim antiquities dealer at Bethlehem for twenty pounds, but he, not believing that it was ancient, had refused to pay that much for it.

In the heart of the Old City of Jerusalem, just south of what the British and Americans call David Street, there is an interesting little monastery with a fine library of old Syriac manuscripts. This is the Syrian Orthodox Monastery of St. Mark. There is a tradition that it stands on the site of the house of Mark's mother, where the disciples were gathered for prayer when Peter came to them after his miraculous deliverance from prison (Acts 12:12–17). A few years ago a Syriac inscription recording this tradition was found in the monastery. Here Khalil Eskander and George Isaiah brought one of the scrolls and showed it to Archbishop Samuel.

The archbishop recognized that the writing was not Syriac but Hebrew. After breaking off a little piece and burning it, he perceived by the odor that the material was leather or parchment.

He told the merchants that he would buy the scrolls. Several weeks went by, however, before they could again get in touch with the Bedouins, who came to Bethlehem only for the weekly market on Saturday. It was not until the first Saturday of the month of Tammuz, which corresponds to July, that the Metropolitan received a telephone call from Khalil Eskander, the merchant in Bethlehem, saying that three Bedouins were there with the scrolls.

Even then the archbishop did not see the Bedouins. Instead of coming with them, Eskander apparently sent them to George Isaiah, the Jerusalem merchant. He took them to the monastery but was refused admission, because the priest who met them at the door thought that their dirty, dilapidated manuscripts were of no interest. When the archbishop learned what had happened he telephoned in considerable perturbation to Eskander, who said that two of the Bedouins had returned and consented to leave their scrolls with him, but the third had decided to look elsewhere for a buyer and had taken his share of the scrolls to the Muslim sheikh at Bethlehem. It was presumably this portion that Professor Sukenik acquired in November for the Hebrew University.

Khalil Eskander told Archbishop Samuel further that when George Isaiah and the Bedouins were sent away from the monastery they proceeded to the square just inside the Jaffa Gate. Here they encountered a Jewish merchant who offered to buy the scrolls for a good price and asked the Bedouins to come to his office for the money. George Isaiah, however, persuaded them to refuse this offer.

Two weeks later the two Bedouins who had left their scrolls with Eskander at Bethlehem came back to his shop, and both he and George Isaiah went with them to St. Mark's Monastery. This time they succeeded in seeing the archbishop, and he bought the manuscripts still in their possession—five scrolls. Two of the five scrolls turned out to be successive portions of one manuscript, which had come apart. This was what I named later the "Manual of Discipline." The other three scrolls were the great manuscript of Isaiah already mentioned, a commentary on the book of Habakkuk, and a badly decomposed Aramaic scroll which at this writing has still not been unrolled. For some time we called this simply "the fourth scroll" (counting the two parts of the Manual of Discipline as one). After our return to America, Dr. Trever detached one column, and on the basis of its text identified the document tentatively as the lost book of Lamech; from then on we called it the Lamech Scroll.

At the suggestion of the archbishop, George Isaiah persuaded the Bedouins to take him to the cave, where he saw one whole jar and fragments of others, a mysterious piece of wood lying on a stone, and many fragments of manuscripts, as well as bits of cloth in which the scrolls had been wrapped. In August the archbishop sent one of his priests, Father Yusef, to examine the cave again. The idea of removing the whole jar still in the cave was considered but abandoned, because the jar was too heavy to carry in the intense summer heat of that region, more than a thousand feet below sea level.

During the course of the summer Archbishop Samuel consulted several scholars and showed his scrolls to a number of visitors at the monastery, hoping to gain accurate information concerning the contents, age, and value of the manuscripts. The first person consulted seems to have been a member of the Syrian Orthodox Church, the late Stephan Hannah Stephan, a well-known Orientalist, who was then working with the Department of Antiquities of Palestine. He confidently pronounced the scrolls worthless. Since his special competence was in the field of Arab history rather than in Hebrew archeology or paleography, his judgment in this case can only be attributed to general skepticism.

Archbishop Samuel also mentioned the scrolls to one of the scholars of the French Dominican School of Archeology, Father A. S. Marmadji, another Arabist. It happened that an eminent biblical scholar from Holland, Father J. P. M. van der Ploeg, was then staying at the Dominican Monastery of St. Stephen, with which the School of Archeology is connected. Father Marmadji therefore brought him to see the scrolls and the other manuscripts at the Syrian monastery. Father van der Ploeg at once identified the largest scroll as the book of Isaiah, being perhaps the first to make this identification.

Early in September, Archbishop Samuel took his scrolls to Syria and showed them to the Patriarch of his church at Homs. He tried also to consult the professor of Hebrew at the American University of Beirut, but found that he had not yet returned from his vacation. After returning to Jerusalem, the archbishop tried again to get information from Stephan Hannah Stephan, who at his request brought him some books about the Hebrew alphabet, but these did not give him much help. Still skeptical, Stephan offered to bring a Jewish scholar of his acquaintance, who, he said, was a specialist in such matters. Apparently this was Toviah Wechsler, who later took a prominent part in the public controversy concerning the scrolls.

Wechsler agreed with Stephan that the scrolls were not ancient. Archbishop Samuel quotes him as pointing to a table and saying, "If that table were a box and you filled it full of pound notes, you couldn't even then measure the value of these scrolls if they are two thousand years old as you say!" Later Wechsler decided that he had been misled by some marginal corrections in one of the manuscripts, which were written in ink still so black that he thought it could not be ancient.

Early in October, Archbishop Samuel showed his scrolls to Dr. Maurice Brown, a Jewish physician who had called at the monastery in connection with the use of a building owned by the Syrian Orthodox community. Dr. Brown informed President Judah L. Magnes of the Hebrew University, at whose request two men were sent to the monastery from the university library. After seeing the manuscripts, however, they suggested that someone from the university more competent than they were should be invited to examine the scrolls. Meanwhile Dr. Brown spoke to a Jewish dealer in antiquities named Sassun, who came and looked at the scrolls and suggested that pieces of them be sent to antiquities dealers in Europe and America, but this the Metropolitan was unwilling to do.

The late Dr. E. L. Sukenik, Professor of Archeology at the Hebrew University, had been in America while all this was going on and did not hear of the manuscripts immediately when he returned to Palestine. On November 25 he was shown a fragment of a scroll by an antiquities dealer, who told him about the discovery of the cave and asked whether he would like to buy the scrolls. Although he naturally suspected forgery, Sukenik answered in the affirmative. Four days later he met the dealer again and bought from him some bundles of leather, together with two pottery jars in which the Bedouins claimed to have found the manuscripts.

On the very day that this purchase took place the General Assembly of the United Nations passed the fateful resolution recommending the partition of Palestine. Welcomed by the Jews but bitterly resented by the Arabs, this led to a rapid deterioration in the relations between Jews and Arabs, so that peaceful communication between them soon became impossible. Before this point was reached, however, Sukenik managed to bring his two jars from Bethlehem to the Jewish part of Jerusalem and to buy a few more portions of manuscripts. In this he was encouraged and assisted by President Magnes, who provided money for the purpose.

Up to this time Sukenik had not been informed of the scrolls acquired by Archbishop Samuel. Early in December he learned about them from one of the men in the university library who had visited the monastery during the summer. Rightly supposing that these manuscripts probably belonged to the same collection as those he had purchased, Sukenik endeavored to visit the monastery, but found that this was no longer possible. There the matter rested until the latter half of January, when he received a letter from a member of the Syrian Orthodox Church named Anton Kiraz, in whose property south of Jerusalem he had previously excavated an ancient tomb. Kiraz wrote that he had some old manuscripts which he would like to show to Sukenik.

Since by this time there was no going back and forth between the Arab and Jewish quarters, the meeting took place at the YMCA, located in what was then Military Zone B, to which passes could be secured for entry from other parts of the city. On seeing the scrolls, Sukenik recognized at once that they and the portions of manuscripts in his possession were indeed parts of the same collection. Kiraz admitted that they had been found in a cave near the Dead Sea, and said he had been to the cave. He offered to sell the scrolls to the Hebrew University and proposed a conference with the archbishop to discuss terms. Archbishop Samuel, however, says that all this was done without his consent or knowledge.

Kiraz allowed Sukenik to borrow three scrolls for two days, and Sukenik took this opportunity to copy several columns, which he later published, from the Isaiah manuscript. On February 6, according to his account, he returned the scrolls to Kiraz and was shown two others, one or both of which belonged to the Manual of Discipline. It was agreed that there should be another meeting, and that President Magnes and Archbishop Samuel should be present, in order that negotiations for the purchase of the scrolls might be concluded. This meeting never took place.

Meanwhile Archbishop Samuel was making his own arrangements. One of the monks at St. Mark's Monastery, the late Butrus Sowmy, suggested that a trustworthy judgment concerning the scrolls might be obtained from the American School of Oriental Research. To this end he telephoned on February 17 to Bishop Stewart at the Collegiate Church of St. George and asked for the name of some person at the American School whom he might consult. I was absent from Jerusalem at the time, having left on the preceding Sunday for a visit to Iraq. It happened, however, that one of my students, Dr. William H. Brownlee, who was taking Arabic lessons at the Newman School of Missions, had found it necessary to obtain from a resident clergyman a statement certifying that he was a Christian, so that the Arab guards at the roadblocks would allow him to pass back and forth between our school and the Newman School of Missions. He had obtained this certificate from Bishop Stewart, who therefore thought of him at once and gave Sowmy his name, mentioning the fact that I had just left for Baghdad.

Accordingly on Wednesday, February 18, 1948, Butrus Sowmy telephoned to the American School of Oriental Research and asked for Brownlee. Shortly before the call came Brownlee had gone out to buy some wrapping paper for shipping his personal effects to America. The servant who answered the telephone told Sowmy, therefore, that Dr. Brownlee was not in the building, and that I was out of the city, but that Dr. John C. Trever was the Acting Director of the school in my absence. Trever was therefore called to the telephone and invited Sowmy to bring the manuscripts to the school the next day.

At two-thirty Thursday afternoon, as agreed, Butrus Sowmy and his brother Ibrahim came to the school with the scrolls. This time Brownlee had gone to the post office and had again been delayed in passing through roadblocks, so that he missed this opportunity to meet the Syrians. Trever received them and looked at the scrolls, and with Sowmy's permission copied two lines from the largest scroll. Puzzled by the form of the Hebrew alphabet used in the manuscript, he compared it with the script of several old Hebrew manuscripts, as illustrated in a collection of Kodachrome slides which he had prepared. The manuscript whose writing seemed most like that of the scrolls was the Nash Papyrus, a fragment variously dated by different scholars from the second century B.C. to the third century A.D.

When Brownlee returned, Trever showed him the passage he had copied, which he had soon found to be the first verse of the sixty-fifth chapter of Isaiah. Others, as we have seen, had already identified this scroll as the book of Isaiah; one of the Syrians, indeed, said that he thought one of the scrolls was Isaiah, but Trever did not take the statement seriously because the Syrians could not read Hebrew, and he did not know then that other scholars had seen the manuscript.

The following morning Trever managed to get into the Old City and visit St. Mark's Monastery, where Butrus Sowmy introduced him to Archbishop Samuel. He was given permission to photograph the scrolls, and the archbishop and Sowmy agreed to bring them to the American School for that purpose. They also brought out the Isaiah manuscript, in order that Trever might see how much of the book of Isaiah it contained. Unrolling it with difficulty, he copied what seemed to be the beginning of the first column, which turned out to be the first verse of the first chapter of Isaiah.

The scrolls were brought to the school on Saturday, February 21, and the two young scholars began the difficult task of photographing them. The following Tuesday afternoon, having completed the first stage of their task, Brownlee and Trever took the scrolls back to the monastery in the Old City. During the rest of the week the development of the negatives was completed, and prints were made from them. A few of the first prints made were sent to Professor William F. Albright of Johns Hopkins University, to get his judgment on the nature and age of the manuscripts. Prints of the Isaiah scroll and the two scrolls later identified as parts of the Manual of Discipline were made first. On Friday, February 27, prints of another scroll were completed, which Brownlee discovered to be a commentary on the first two chapters of the book of Habakkuk. The contents of the other two scrolls were not determined until after I returned from Baghdad.

A complete set of the photographs was given to Archbishop Samuel. According to his account, it was after he received these that Kiraz asked his permission to show the scrolls to Sukenik at the YMCA. The Archbishop suggested, he tells us, that Kiraz take the photographs, but Kiraz protested that they were not large enough. This does not agree with Sukenik's statement that, after copying some of the Isaiah manuscript, he returned the scrolls to Kiraz on the sixth of February, three weeks before Trever's photographs were finished. How the discrepancy is to be resolved I do not know. In any case, Archbishop Samuel decided to retain possession of the scrolls and entrust their publication to the American School of Oriental Research, while Kiraz assured Sukenik that the Hebrew University would be given priority whenever the scrolls should be offered for sale.

Late Saturday afternoon, February 28, our party returned to Jerusalem. To my relief I learned that there had been no trouble at the school during our absence, though there had been a frightful bomb explosion in the city, causing more than fifty deaths. My diary says: "Everything OK at the school, but John and Bill all excited over manuscripts at the Syrian Convent in script John thinks older than the Nash Papyrus, including the whole book of Isaiah, a text of Habakkuk with midrashic material in verse (so Bill says), and an unidentified composition resembling Wisdom Literature." The unidentified composition was, of course, the Manual of Discipline.

Monday morning, March 1, I went with Trever to the monastery, after securing fom the Arab Higher Committee a pass into the Old City, now carefully guarded at every entrance. At the monastery I met Archbishop Samuel and saw the scrolls. In a small fragment of the badly damaged fourth scroll which had come loose, my eye caught the word *'ar'ā,* and I remember exclaiming in surprise, "This is Aramaic!"

That afternoon we had our first class session on the Habakkuk Commentary. One of the courses I was giving was in epigraphy, and we agreed to devote the rest of our time in this course to the study of the scrolls.

The first photographs of the Isaiah scroll proved unsatisfactory because the limited amount of film at hand compelled Trever to photograph two columns on each sheet, and so the photographs were too small for adequate enlargement. It was therefore necessary to photograph the scroll again, but finding suitable film of the right size proved very difficult. The best that could be found was some outdated portrait film.

Under such circumstances it was remarkable that the photographs came out as well as they did. The plates in our subsequent publication of the Dead Sea Scrolls were made from these photographs. Critics of the publication who do not consider the reproductions satisfactory have not seen the manuscript itself. Some have said that the manuscripts should have been rephotographed after they were brought to the United States, but they were not then in our possession, and Archbishop Samuel was unwilling to have them photographed again.

Still the Aramaic scroll had not been unrolled. On Wednesday, March 3, the archbishop gave Trever permission to attempt to open it; Butrus Sowmy, however, with some justification, was opposed to the undertaking, and it was postponed in the hope that it might be carried out later with better facilities in Europe or the United States.

On the morning of Thursday, March 4, Mr. R. W. Hamilton, the Director of the Department of Antiquities, came to see me at the school. As I looked back on our conversation later, it seemed strange that the subject of the scrolls had not come up at all. Both Mr. Hamilton and I were just then much more concerned about other matters. The purpose of his call was to discuss plans for the administration of the Palestine Museum after the impending termination of the British Mandate.

The department, however, was not uninformed about the scrolls. It will be remembered that one of the first persons to see the manuscripts at St. Mark's Monastery was a member of the Department of Antiquities, Stephan H. Stephan. Mistakenly regarding them as useless, he apparently did not think it worth while to make any report to the department concerning them. Two years later Hamilton wrote to me that Stephan had never even mentioned the scrolls to him.

He was told about them by Trever, but at the time of their first conversation Trever did not yet know that the scrolls had been discovered within the past year. Archbishop Samuel and Sowmy, with characteristic caution, had talked vaguely at first about the manuscripts as being in the library of their monastery, leaving the impression that they had been there for about forty years, and Trever was still under this impression when he first discussed the scrolls with Hamilton. Not until March 5 was he told that the scrolls had been found in a cave only about a year earlier.

Soon thereafter this information was passed on to Mr. Hamilton. On March 20 Trever wrote to his wife: "I have already talked with Hamilton at the Museum about the proper procedure. He has given me permission to visit the place to gather up any loose materials left." On February 27, the day before my return from Baghdad, Trever had spoken about the antiquities laws with the archbishop, who consequently relinquished a plan to visit the cave and assured Trever that he "would cooperate in every way possible with the American School of Oriental Research and the Department of Antiquities in carrying out the excavation of the cave."

My diary mentions a visit of Archbishop Samuel and Butrus Sowmy at the school on Monday, March 8, after which I drove them back to Allenby Square in the school's station wagon. My note continues, "Three or four cars, especially station wagons, have been stolen lately in broad daylight at the point of guns, though most politely, so we aren't eager to take ours out." Three days later the building of the Jewish Agency was damaged by explosives believed to have been brought in by an Arab using a car that belonged to the American Consulate.

Most of the entries in my diary during these weeks record shootings, explosions, and casualties in Jerusalem and in other parts of the country, with many rumors, like the one we heard on March 15 that our water supply had been poisoned. That same day, however, Trever received a reply from Professor Albright, confirming his judgment as to the age of the manuscripts and pronouncing the find "the greatest manuscript discovery of modern times."

On March 18 the archbishop called on me at the school, and Trever and I discussed with him several matters concerning the manuscripts. I expressed to him my conviction that the Isaiah scroll was the oldest known manuscript of any book of the Bible, and he was duly impressed. I also submitted for his approval a news release I had prepared. Having learned by this time that the manuscripts had been discovered in a cave near the Dead Sea, I felt that it would materially help us in establishing their age if we could visit the cave and find any remains of the jars in which they had been found. We therefore discussed with the archbishop the possibility of a trip to the cave. We talked also about plans for the publication of the manuscripts by the American Schools of Oriental Research.

My diary for March 19 says: "John saw the bishop again today and learned that Dr. Magnes was taking an interest in the manuscripts!" This was our first intimation of the negotiations between the Hebrew University and St. Mark's Monastery. We still knew nothing of the scrolls and fragments Professor Sukenik had acquired.

During the morning of the twentieth we went with guards sent by a good friend to the Haram, the sacred enclosure containing the Dome of the Rock. Here we met a man from the shrine of Nebi Musa, near the Jericho road, who said he could arrange for us a trip to the cave. We were to drive to Nebi Musa and proceed on foot to the cave, with a local Bedouin as guide. To our great disappointment, when the appointed day came the man who was to come for us did not put in an appearance. We were later told that the trip was considered too dangerous because Jewish troops were in training on the plain north and west of the Dead Sea. Who was really responsible for the frustration of our plan we shall probably never know, though we have our suspicions. We could not go by ourselves, and could not have found the cave if we had attempted it.

On March 25, Archbishop Samuel told Trever that Sowmy was on his way with the manuscripts to a place outside of Palestine. I myself had suggested that they were not safe in the monastery in the Old City, and Trever had mentioned the possibility of removing them to another Syrian Orthodox monastery down by the Jordan River. The soundness of these suggestions was demonstrated when St. Mark's Monastery was damaged by shellfire and Butrus Sowmy himself was killed not many weeks later. The removal of the scrolls from the country, however, without an export license from the Department of Antiquities, was illegal. How fully the archbishop realized this I cannot say; I know only that we tried to tell him. He had already, of course, taken the scrolls to Syria and back.

In all fairness it should be remembered that for many centuries Palestine had not had an independent government of its own, but had been ruled by one foreign power after another. Under such circumstances it was not unnatural that there was sometimes, even in high places, an attitude toward law which is not entirely unknown in the Western democracies. It should be said also, not as extenuating but as partly explaining what happened, that in March 1947 there was no longer any effective government in the country, and no perceptible prospect of any. The Department of Antiquities was still carrying on as best it could, but its major anxiety was to protect its treasures in the face of impending chaos. What the future would bring, both to Jerusalem and to the Dead Sea Scrolls, could not then be foreseen.

During the rest of the month of March we spent many hours in making arrangements for our trip home. Conditions were growing steadily worse. Facilities for transportation, communication, banking, and other needed services had reached a point where the word "facility" was no longer appropriate. On March 27 we held our last class, completing the first reading of the Habakkuk Commentary.

The next day, Easter Sunday, was one of the saddest days I can remember. An effort had been made to obtain a truce for the day, but it broke down completely. On Tuesday, March 30, Brownlee departed for America. My wife and I left Jerusalem on April 2 but could not get away from Haifa for another two weeks. Trever, after a final conference with Archbishop Samuel and Butrus Sowmy on April 3, went down to Lydda on the fifth and took a plane to Beirut.

On April 11, while my wife and I were still in Haifa waiting impatiently for our ship to come into the harbor, the statement I had sent from Jerusalem was released to the newspapers in America. Unfortunately a mistake had somehow been introduced into the version given to the press. I had written, "The scrolls were acquired by the Syrian Orthodox Monastery of St. Mark." As released to the press in America the statement said that the scrolls had been "preserved for many centuries in the library of the Syrian Orthodox Monastery of St. Mark in Jerusalem." Who inserted this I do not know. Professor Sukenik, on reading the published account, issued a statement to set the matter right, pointing out that the scrolls had been found in a cave near the Dead Sea within the previous year. From this statement, which I read in the *Rome Daily American* of April 28, 1948, when our ship stopped at Genoa, I first learned that the discovery included manuscripts other than those bought by Archbishop Samuel.

During the leisurely, restful voyage home in a small Norwegian freighter I had time to "collate" the whole text of the Isaiah manuscript with the Masoretic or traditional Hebrew text, having brought with me a set of Trever's photographs as well as a standard edition of the Hebrew Old Testament. This collation was the basis of articles published during the ensuing year.

The first trickle of published statements concerning the scrolls soon swelled into a veritable flood. The American Friends of the Hebrew University issued a special news bulletin on July 16. A further statement appeared in their November bulletin. The September number of the *Biblical Archaeologist* carried an article by Trever on the discovery of the scrolls and one by me on their contents and significance.

The same month saw the publication of Sukenik's first volume on the manuscripts, entitled *Megilloth Genuzoth* (Hidden Scrolls). In this he gave an account of his acquisition of the manuscripts in his possession, with a summary of their contents as far as they had been ascertained at that time, and the text of selected passages, together with notes and some excellent photographs. The text of Chapters 42 and 43 of the book of Isaiah, as copied by him when he had Archbishop Samuel's scrolls in his possession, was included in this volume, side by side with the Masoretic text.

The October number of the *Bulletin of the American Schools of Oriental Research* carried an article by Trever entitled "Preliminary Observations on the Jerusalem Scrolls," and the first part of an article by me on variant readings in the Isaiah manuscript. The December and February numbers contained a translation of the Habakkuk Commentary by Brownlee, an article by H. L. Ginsberg on Sukenik's scrolls, the remainder of my article on the variant readings in Isaiah, an article on the paleography of the scrolls by Trever, and one on the date of the Isaiah scroll by Solomon A. Birnbaum. Interested scholars were therefore fairly well informed on the general nature and contents of the scrolls within a year

after we first learned of their existence. At the meetings of the
Society of Biblical Literature and Exegesis and the American
Schools of Oriental Research at New York in December 1948,
Brownlee presented two papers on the Habakkuk Commentary,
anticipating some ideas that were later published independently by
other scholars.

Further discoveries were to follow, but already the first gun in
what soon came to be called "the battle of the scrolls" had been
fired. Suspicions and charges—with few, if any, retreats—followed
thick and fast. The smoke of battle has not even yet been quite
cleared away by the wholesome breezes of unimpassioned investigation and discussion. Before we take up this rather fantastic
tale, however, something more should be said about the contents
and character of the scrolls.

Six distinct compositions are represented by the eleven scrolls,
or parts of scrolls, first discovered and removed from the cave by
the Bedouins in 1947. These are: (1) the Old Testament book of
the prophet *Isaiah,* contained in its entirety in the largest and
oldest of the scrolls, and also in part in one of those acquired by
the Hebrew University; (2) the *Commentary on Habakkuk;* (3)
the *Manual of Discipline,* which had come apart, so that when
discovered it was in two separate scrolls; (4) the Aramaic manuscript, now tentatively called the *Lamech Scroll,* which has not
been unrolled;(5) the *War of the Sons of Light with the Sons of
Darkness;* and (6) the *Thanksgiving Psalms* contained in four
of the pieces bought by Professor Sukenik. Many fragments of
other books were found later when the cave and other caves in
the vicinity were explored. Others were bought from Bedouins
who had found them. No text discovered since 1947, however, is
comparable in extent to the first scrolls found then by the
Bedouins.

(1) The *St. Mark's manuscript of Isaiah* is a scroll of leather
made of strips sewed end to end. When unrolled it is about 1 foot
wide and 24 feet long. It is remarkably well preserved, though
considerably worn by much use. In several places where the skin

was torn it was repaired in antiquity, sometimes by careful sewing and sometimes by attaching strips of skin to the back of the scroll. The Hebrew text, written in fifty-four columns, is for the most part still clearly legible. It does not, of course, have our familiar division into chapters and verses, but it is divided into sections and paragraphs, indicated by beginning a new line in the margin when the preceding line has not been filled out, and by indentation when the preceding line is full. Occasionally extra space is left between the lines. Sometimes the larger divisions correspond to our chapters; sometimes they do not. Within the paragraphs there are often spaces between sentences, indicating subdivisions which again may or may not correspond to the much later division into verses.

There is a curious system of marks in the margins. Sometimes a short horizontal line, with or without a small hook at one end, marks the beginning or end of a passage. Sometimes there are very elaborate figures, the meaning of which has not yet been determined. The purpose of all these marks, in fact, can only be guessed. Possibly they have something to do with a selection or Scripture lesson for use in meetings or services of worship, though the passages between two consecutive marks often seem too short for such a purpose. Possibly they indicate portions of the text considered especially important by those who used the manuscript.

The Hebrew text is written in the square or Aramaic alphabet, the same alphabet from which the one still used for printing Hebrew was developed in later times. The forms of the letters in the Isaiah manuscript and the other Dead Sea Scrolls resemble those found in Palestinian inscriptions from about the last century before the birth of Christ. Usually the different letters are quite distinct in form, so that such confusion between one letter and another as often occurs in other ancient manuscripts is hardly possible. Unlike brief inscriptions, this manuscript is so extensive that it gives a great many examples of each letter of the alphabet, making possible a comparison that shows many interesting variations and sometimes enables us to see just how the scribe wrote the letters. Some of the details and their significance must be discussed when we come to the question of the age of the manuscripts.

The text itself is by and large the same as that of our familiar book of Isaiah, with many more or less important differences in details. Both the differences from the traditional text and the agreements with it are important, and we must consider them later in attempting to assess the importance of the manuscript for textual criticism. The text has evidently been examined and corrected, for at many points words written by mistake have been erased or crossed out, and corrections have been inserted. Minor corrections of a single letter or word appear in the scribe's own hand; more extensive corrections have been made in another hand. Letters and words omitted by the copyist are frequently inserted above the line. Where there is not room between the lines for all that has been omitted, the inserted material runs on down the left-hand margin. There are clear indications also at many points that the copyist left a space for something that was missing or not clear in the manuscript he was copying. The omitted portions of the text were usually copied in later from another manuscript.

The *Hebrew University manuscript of Isaiah,* one of the scrolls bought by Professor Sukenik, is not, like the first, a complete copy of the book. Its contents were not identified for some time after the discovery and purchase of the scrolls, because it was so tightly compressed that the attempt to unroll it was postponed until the other scrolls had been opened and some skill for the delicate task had been developed. When this was undertaken, the scroll was found to consist of one large piece and several smaller pieces. The material had deteriorated to such a degree, however, that the writing was in many places illegible except by means of infra-red photography. Finally it was ascertained that the large piece contained the last third of the book of Isaiah, from Chapter 38 to the end, with some gaps. The smaller pieces contained parts of Chapters 10, 13, 19–30, and 35–40. Apparently the scroll had been already in a fragmentary condition when it was deposited in the cave. The text of this manuscript, unlike that of the St. Mark's Isaiah scroll, agrees closely with the Masoretic text of later manuscripts. This fact is important for assessing the value of both manuscripts and their significance for the history of the text of the Old Testament (see pp. 303–15).

(2) The scroll containing the *Commentary on Habakkuk* is relatively small. The beginning has been lost, but apparently only one column is missing. The rest is fairly complete, except that the bottoms of the columns have been eaten away, and there are a few holes in some of the columns. Unrolled, the scroll is 5 feet long; originally it must have been 6 or 7 inches longer. At present it is only 5½ inches wide at the widest points. The original width can be fairly estimated at about 7 inches. The text is even more clearly and beautifully written and much better preserved than that of the first Isaiah scroll. The form of the script indicates a somewhat later date, and the scroll was not handled as much as the Isaiah manuscript before it was left in the cave.

In some respects this curious little document is the most interesting and important of all those found for the identification and history of the group that produced it. Reference is made to specific persons and events in a mysterious way that is tantalizing. These allusions require some discussion later, in connection with the authenticity and dates of the scrolls and the history and beliefs of the sect that possessed them. At this point a general description and a few brief excerpts will suffice to convey an idea of the nature and contents of the work.

The first column of which any part is preserved begins with words from the second verse of the first chapter of Habakkuk. Only a few words at the ends of the lines remain in this column; those at the bottom are from the fourth verse of the same chapter. The next column is better preserved, but with a wide gap from top to bottom in the middle of the lines. Its first words are from the fifth verse of Habakkuk 1.

The method followed throughout the work is to quote the text of Habakkuk, a few words at a time, and follow each quotation with an explanation in terms of the history of the sect, in which the fulfillment of the prophecy is seen. For example, the sixth verse of the first chapter of Habakkuk, "For lo, I am rousing the Chaldeans, that bitter and hasty nation," is quoted with this comment: "This means the Kittim, who are swift and men of valor in battle." But who are the Kittim? The answer to this question is important for determining when the commentary was written, and we shall have to look into it in that connection. More is said about the Kittim in the comments on subsequent verses, but there is nothing sufficiently definite to make their identity entirely certain. For the first readers, who knew the historical background and could recognize allusions obscure to us, the author's meaning was no doubt unmistakable.

There are other and even more mysterious references, not only to nations and groups but to individuals. The second half of the thirteenth verse of Habakkuk 1 is quoted, for instance, with slight variations from the standard text: "Why do ye look on faithless men, but thou art silent at the swallowing by the wicked man of one more righteous than he?" Then comes the comment: "This means the house of Absalom and the men of their party, who kept silence at the chastisement of the teacher of righteousness, and did not help him against the man of the lie, who rejected the law in the midst of their whole congregation." If we can tell who the house of Absalom, the teacher of righteousness, and the man of the lie were, and what was the event referred to here, we shall know something definite about the history of the religious community in which this commentary was written. Many ingenious theories have been proposed, but we cannot adopt any one of them without examining them all and comparing them carefully.

The teacher of righteousness was clearly, in any case, the leader and perhaps the founder of this community. He was evidently believed by his followers to be endowed with the gift of interpreting prophecies; in fact, he could explain what was dark even to the prophets themselves. He was violently opposed and persecuted by a man called in the commentary "the wicked priest." The persecution reached its climax in a vaguely described event on the Day of Atonement. No passage in any of the Dead Sea Scrolls has aroused more discussion and even controversy than this.

These and other exasperatingly vague references to persons and events tell us almost all that we know about the origin and early history of the sect. All must be considered later, but what has been said may suffice to give a general preliminary conception of the character of the document.

(3) The *Manual of Discipline,* as has been said, was in two pieces, rolled up separately, when it was brought to the American School of Oriental Research. Many cracks in the very brittle leather showed that it had already been unrolled, perhaps several times, so that it is uncertain whether the two pieces were already separated when they were found by the Bedouins. In any case, they are consecutive portions of what was originally a single scroll made of five strips of leather or parchment sewn together. The two pieces together would make a scroll a little more than 6 feet long. The beginning is missing, but the original length of the complete scroll must have been about 7 feet at least. The width is about 9½ inches.

The skin of which this scroll is made is of coarse texture, much lighter in color than that of the other scrolls bought by Archbishop Samuel. It shows little evidence of hard wear and has not suffered as badly as have some of the other scrolls from the ravages of time. White ants have eaten into the upper and lower edges, but not deeply enough at the top to destroy any of the text except in the first column, which has lost parts of the first two lines. At the bottoms of the columns parts of from one to three lines have been eaten away, except in the last column, only two-thirds of which were needed to complete the document.

The title "Manual of Discipline" is not given in the text itself, but came to my mind when I first read the text in Jerusalem in March 1948. Noting the combination of liturgical directions with rules concerning procedure in the meetings of the group and the personal conduct of the members, I was reminded of the manual of discipline of the Methodist Church. I am not a member of that church and cannot be sure I have ever seen its manual of discipline, but I have the impression that it contains a somewhat similar combination of liturgical and disciplinary directions.

Since the scroll clearly did not represent the beliefs and practices of rabbinic or "normative" Judaism, but came from some sect or group within Judaism, we at first spoke of it as "The Sectarian Document," but this was obviously not a satisfactory designation. In our initial news release of April 11, 1948, the composition was called "a manual of discipline of some comparatively little-known sect or monastic order, possibly the Essenes." In the *Biblical Archaeologist* for September 1948, I spoke of it as "a curious work which I will call for the present the Sectarian Document" (p. 57), but I added (p. 58): "The text which I have called the Sectarian Document may be described as the manual of discipline of some group within Judaism." After a summary of its contents I concluded (p. 60): "This again appears to confirm the idea that our text is the manual of discipline of a group organized like the later monastic orders in Christianity."

Sukenik, at the suggestion of Henoch Yalon, proposed later the Hebrew title *Serek ha-Yahad* ("The Order of the Community"), a title which is not only descriptive but also appropriate, because it uses two of the most characteristic terms in the vocabulary of this document. For scholarly discussions in various languages this title may well displace mine, but for the purpose of a more general account "Manual of Discipline" is convenient, and it has the advantage of having been adopted already by many of the scholars who have written about the scrolls.

The original title, if there was one, has been lost, because the beginning of the scroll, like that of the Habakkuk Commentary, had been damaged and detached before the manuscript came into the possession of Archbishop Samuel. Unfortunately there is nothing to indicate how many columns are lost. Among the fragments later purchased by the Palestine Museum from antiquities dealers there were two almost complete columns that apparently belonged to this manuscript. There was also a tiny fragment bearing a few letters in larger writing, which may have been part of the original title of the composition, but they are not sufficient to show what that title was.

The first of the two columns recovered by the Palestine Museum begins with an expression that introduces several sections of the Manual, but it clearly does not mark the beginning of the whole compositon. The bottom of the second column is unfortunately too much damaged to allow us to determine whether or not it immediately preceded what is now the first column of the scroll. Father Barthélemy believes that these two columns are not really part of the Manual of Discipline, but contain a distinct document that was merely copied at the beginning of the scroll. There must have been at least one more column, and probably more than that, preceding the present beginning of the scroll. As a matter of fact, parts of as many as five columns belonging to this document are believed to have been identified at the Palestine Museum.

If Barthélemy is right in supposing that the two relatively complete columns, though from the same manuscript as the Manual of Discipline, did not originally form part of the same composition, both of the two documents copied together in the scroll must have been accepted by the group at the time when the manuscript was made. In fact, the lack of unity or logical order in the contents of the Manual of Discipline itself suggests that it was compiled gradually in scrapbook fashion from various sources.

A brief summary must suffice for the present to indicate the general contents of this document. The first column of the scroll begins in the midst of a passage that states what is expected of those who "enter into the covenant," and so become members of the community. Then follow directions for the ceremony of entering into the covenant, an annual observance in which not only the new members but the whole community must participate. At the middle of the third column a new section begins, dealing with the origin and future destruction of sin. At the top of the fifth column we come to rules of organization and discipline, which occupy five columns. The document is concluded with a devotional poem or psalm.

(4) The *Lamech Scroll* is compressed and coagulated. It is brittle and hard and tends to crumble. In places the leather has solidified into a kind of natural glue. A few little scraps and one whole column have become detached since the scroll was discovered, but only very careful, expert treatment can ever unroll enough to recover any considerable part of the text, if indeed this

is possible at all. The unsuccessful efforts made by the American Schools of Oriental Research to arrange for such treatment are related in another chapter.

(5) The scroll of the *War of the Sons of Light with the Sons of Darkness* seems to be unique in being almost entirely preserved, except that its lower edge is badly eaten away. It is more than 9 feet long when unrolled, and a little more than 6 inches wide. It consists of three strips of leather, with pieces of another strip. When bought by Sukenik, it was still wrapped in a piece of parchment. That some of the other scrolls originally had covers sewn to the outermost columns is shown by a row of needle holes at the end that was outermost when the scroll was rolled up. The scroll of the War of the Sons of Light with the Sons of Darkness is the only one that still has its outer wrapping.

There are nineteen columns of text. The document contains directions for the conduct of a war between the tribes of Levi, Judah, and Benjamin, who are called the sons of light, and the Edomites, Moabites, Ammonites, Philistines, and Greeks, who are called the sons of darkness. Whether the war contemplated is an actual conflict that was being waged or was impending at the time when the document was written, or whether it is an eschatological war, like that predicted in the book of Ezekiel and the Revelation of John, is a question to which no final answer can yet be given.

(6) The *Thanksgiving Psalms* (*Hodayot*), when Sukenik bought them, were in four pieces. Three of these were crushed together in a bundle; the fourth was one of the two scrolls which Sukenik was for some time unable to open. The four pieces contain altogether twelve columns, each about 13 inches high, with as many as thirty-nine lines of writing in a column. The columns are thus a little higher and contain more lines than those of the St. Mark's Isaiah manuscript, none of which has more than thirty-two lines. The columns are of about the same width and the writing of about the same size as in the Isaiah manuscript.

The psalms, of which there are about twenty altogether, resemble somewhat those of the Old Testament and often echo the language of the Bible. They are of interest as showing that the practice of composing hymns of praise was by no means extinct. While they may not have the same degree of poetic power and originality as the old Testament Psalms, they are at least the equal of most of the hymns we sing in our churches, and the difference between them and the biblical psalms is a relative matter, concerning which our judgment may not be entirely objective. A fairer comparison may be made with other post-biblical psalms, such as the Psalms of Solomon and the canticles in the first two chapters of the Gospel of Luke. Because of our ignorance concerning events and circumstances to which allusion is occasionally made, some portions of the text are now obscure.

In addition to these complete or relatively complete scrolls, there are the small fragments of other manuscripts sold to Archbishop Samuel and Professor Sukenik, others which turned up later in the hands of Bedouins and antiquities dealers, and enormous quantities discovered since in the caves. The extent and variety of their contents must be indicated very briefly.

Among the fragments acquired by the Syrian archbishop, apparently from an illegal excavation of which more will be said later, there are three bits of the book of Daniel. Two of them, containing part of the Aramaic text of Daniel 3:23–30, are from a single manuscript, written in a script like that of the St. Mark's Isaiah scroll. The other, which includes parts of two adjacent columns, is from a later manuscript whose writing resembles that of the Habakkuk Commentary. The extant portion of the right-hand column contains portions of Daniel 1:10–17; the one to the left contains part of Daniel 2:2–6. The first two pieces measure respectively 4 by 4½ inches and 2½ by 2½ inches. The third is 5 inches high and 3 inches wide. Students of biblical language and text are interested to observe that the point in Daniel 2:4 where the language shifts from Hebrew to Aramaic is included in the left-hand column of the third fragment, and the change of language appears there just as in later manuscripts. This is especially significant, because these scraps may be closer in date to the original composition of the book of Daniel than is the case with any other extant manuscript of a book of the Bible.

II

Alarms and Excursions

ᒍᒐᒍᒐᒍᒐᒍᒐᒍᒐᒍᒐᒍᒐᒍᒐᒍᒐᒍᒐᒍᒐᒍᒐᒐ

The first question that occurs to one who hears for the first time of such an extraordinary discovery as that of the Dead Sea Scrolls is, "Can they be genuine?" The forgery of antiquities is a prosperous occupation in countries where archeologists have been at work for many years and have found statues, coins, inscriptions, and other objects for which museums and collectors pay good prices. Skillful craftsmen can make imitations of such antiquities which the best experts are hardly able to detect. Forgeries of inscriptions and manuscripts have not been unknown in Palestine also, though they have not hitherto been very common, because Palestinian excavations do not yield many objects that lend themselves to this nefarious purpose.

When I first saw Trever's photographs of Archbishop Samuel's manuscripts, I naturally asked myself, "Are these not forgeries?" I confess, however, that I could never really bring myself to take this question seriously, especially after I had seen the manuscripts themselves. The fact that they looked old, of course, proved nothing, and the writing was amazingly clear. What impressed me most from the beginning, however, was the fact that the forms of the letters represented a period in the history of the alphabet for which we had relatively few specimens, and most of these had become known fairly recently.

For somewhat earlier and somewhat later periods we have many more inscriptions, and also papyri. As I have already related, Dr.

Trever noted immediately the resemblance between the scrolls and the Nash Papyrus. He saw also, however, that the two types of script were not quite contemporary, and he judged that the Nash Papyrus was somewhat later than the scrolls. I agreed with him, and our judgment was supported by the letter which Trever soon received from Professor Albright.

Paleography, the comparative study of the script, was at first our only means of dating the scrolls. It remains one of the most important criteria. Scientific analyses of the leather, the ink, and the linen wrappings of the scrolls would later contribute somewhat to the solution of the problem, but such techniques were not available to us in Jerusalem in the troubled circumstances of that time.

All these criteria, of course, apply to the age of the manuscripts themselves and the time when they were made. Archeological evidence later served to fix the time they were left in the cave, but that too was beyond our reach in the spring of 1948 because of our inability to visit the cave. Since the scrolls were presumably copies, not original manuscripts, the time when the books they contained were composed could not be determined by paleography, by analysis of the leather and ink, or by the archeological context. Only the internal evidence of the texts themselves could help us here.

There were surprising peculiarities of spelling and grammar in the texts. These might have been attributed to the individual eccentricities or mere ignorance of the scribes but for the fact that the same peculiarities occurred in different manuscripts, obviously not copied by the same scribe. The possibility that these features reflected a local dialect had to be considered, but it was possible also that they might point to a particular period in the history of the Hebrew language. Only careful and prolonged investigation could show whether or how far geographical or chronological differences might explain the grammar and spelling of the scrolls. There were also distinctive words and ideas that might be found especially characteristic of a particular historical period. These too called for protracted study and discussion by many scholars. It is a satisfaction to be able to say now that all the subsequent investigations, debates, and further discoveries have only confirmed the substantial accuracy of Trever's first estimate of the age of the scrolls.

In our news release of April 11, 1948, we risked the statement that the Isaiah manuscript came from "about the first century B.C." Sukenik's release later in the same month also said that some of the manuscripts were "more than two thousand years old." This judgment did not stand long without challenge. As early as October 1948, Professor Solomon Zeitlin of the Dropsie College, without having seen any of the texts, included in an article on another subject an expression of doubt concerning the authenticity of the Habakkuk Commentary. In January 1949 he published an article declaring on the basis of a portion of the first two columns, of which a photograph had then appeared, that the commentary was not ancient but medieval in origin. The Manual of Discipline was assigned to the same period on the basis of one column which had been published. Sukenik's first volume, which had come out meanwhile, received equally cavalier treatment, with the conclusion, "It seems that the entire find is not an important discovery but possibly a hoax." The arguments marshaled then and later by Zeitlin against the antiquity of the scrolls are examined in Chapters IV and V of this book. They dealt chiefly with words and ideas which he maintained did not occur in Jewish writings before the Middle Ages. He denied categorically that commentaries on books of the Bible existed in earlier times.

Other scholars on the whole accepted the genuineness and antiquity of the scrolls with only mild expression of quite laudable caution, reserving final judgment until the texts could be published. Professor Zeitlin, however, stood by his guns and continued to bombard all and sundry who came to the defense of the scrolls. To follow here in detail the warm debate which ensued in learned journals and in the public press would be unprofitable. The essential points receive attention when we take up the question of dating the manuscripts.

The discussion entered a new phase when the cave where the

manuscripts had been found was rediscovered and excavated. Much of the controversy and doubt might have been obviated if the cave could have been immediately excavated or even inspected by competent archeologists when the first scrolls were found. Not only was that impossible; the cave was visited several times by unauthorized and incompetent persons before any archeologist knew of the discovery. In November or early December 1948, before order had been established in the country after the fighting of that year, unscrupulous individuals interested in nothing but plunder and gain cut a second opening into the cave, lower than the natural opening. They dug up the floor of the cave and threw some of the rubbish outside. An accurate description of the cave's condition and contents as first found by the Bedouins was thus rendered forever impossible.

The man whose efforts finally led to the rediscovery and excavation of the cave was an observer for the United Nations, the Belgian Captain Philippe Lippens, who had studied at the University of Louvain. Shortly before taking up his work in Palestine he had read an account of the first discovery which aroused his keen interest. Early in December 1948, while staying at the King David Hotel, he discussed the matter with the head of the Pontifical Biblical Institute in Jerusalem; and on December 15, when he first had an opportunity to cross the armistice line, he visited St. Mark's Monastery and talked with two of the monks, whom he found "very polite but suspicious." Thence he betook himself to the American School of Oriental Research and learned that Professor O. R. Sellers, my successor as Director of the School, was equally interested in locating the cave.

On January 11, 1949, Captain Lippens, after a brief leave of absence, returned to Jerusalem and talked with Professor Sellers. He also called on Father de Vaux of the French School of Archeology, who showed him several articles about the Dead Sea Scrolls. A reference in an article by Trever to our unsuccessful project of visiting the cave fanned the spark of Captain Lippens' interest into a flame of passionate determination. On the seventeenth of January he visited Father de Vaux again and agreed that if he succeeded in finding the cave he would proceed to excavate it with Father de Vaux as technical director.

Through the mediation of another Belgian officer attached to the United Nations, Major Simon, Captain Lippens was able on January 24 to talk with General Lash, the British Commander of the 3rd Brigade of the Arab Legion at Ramallah, who summoned his archeological adviser, Colonel Ashton. General Lash also telephoned to Mr. G. L. Harding, Chief Inspector of Antiquities for the government of Jordan at Amman, and learned that he too was interested in finding the cave. As a result of these conversations General Lash decided to send two Bedouins serving in the Arab Legion to look for the cave under the command of Colonel Ashton, with the understanding that Captain Lippens would serve as technical consultant and the enterprise would be conducted in full cooperation with Mr. Harding.

Five days after his conversations with General Lash and Colonel Ashton, Captain Lippens was transferred from Jerusalem to Amman. He immediately consulted Mr. Harding, who informed him that the project of General Lash had already been carried out and the cave had been found. Later Captain Lippens learned that the two Bedouins had been unable to secure the desired information, but Colonel Ashton himself and Captain Akkash el-Zebn of the Arab Legion had searched for the cave and discovered it on the twenty-eighth of January. The keen eye of Captain Akkash el-Zebn had detected in front of the cave the fresh earth and potsherds thrown out by the clandestine treasure-hunters in November or December. Colonel Ashton had then entered the cave and found in it many pieces of linen wrappings and a large quantity of potsherds.

Whether this was actually the same cave as that in which the discovery of 1947 had been made could not be determined without excavation. Harding visited the place early in February. A few days later he went again, taking with him, at Captain Lippens' suggestion, Father de Vaux. Professor Sellers, on his way to Beirut on February 3, saw at Amman some manuscript fragments and potsherds that Harding had found in the cave.

A systematic excavation was then carried out by Harding and de Vaux, with the help of two men from the Palestine Museum, one from Amman, and a guard from the Arab Legion. They worked fifteen days, during a period of almost three weeks, until March 5. Lippens visited the excavation on February 11 and on two later occasions. Sellers, whose return from Beirut had been delayed by rain and snow, visited the site on February 18 and February 26 with D. C. Baramki of the Palestine Museum.

Working with difficulty in the narrow space, so restricted that only small implements could be used and not more than two men could work in the cave at the same time, the excavators carefully gathered every little potsherd, every bit of linen, and every tiny fragment of parchment, whether or not it bore any writing. The results removed all doubts on the part of the archeologists themselves that this was the cave in which the Bedouins had originally found the scrolls bought by Professor Sukenik and Archbishop Samuel.

At first, indeed, they believed that some of the fragments they found belonged to the same scrolls. This impression was not substantiated by the more thorough investigation made subsequently. What seemed to be pieces of the Habakkuk Commentary turned out to be bits of similar commentaries on other books of the Old Testament. One fragment has been found to belong to a commentary on the book of Micah and another to a commentary on Psalm 110. Further examination, however, only made it more and more evident that the fragments found in the excavation and the scrolls sold by the Bedouins were alike in material, writing, state of preservation, and contents. They had indubitably belonged to the same collection of documents.

Much recent evidence of depredation was found also. Mixed up with the ancient débris were found exasperating remains of the disastrous efforts of the treasure-hunters the previous winter. There were bits of modern cloth, scraps of newspapers, cigarette stubs, and even a cigarette roller bearing the name of one of the illegal excavators, which Mr. Harding returned to its owner.

The pottery found in the cave confirmed the Bedouins' story

of finding the scrolls in jars and also established the antiquity of the manuscripts, though the date first assigned to it by de Vaux and Harding, about 100 B.C., proved later to be somewhat too early. A few bits—the spout of a lamp and some pieces of a cooking pot—seemed to be later, coming from the late second or early third century A.D. The excavators concluded that this handful of later Roman potsherds, comprising not more than 5 per cent of the total quantity, must have been left by intruders who had broken into the cave and perhaps removed some of the manuscripts during the Roman period. It was recalled that the great theologian and biblical scholar of the third century, Origen, had written of a discovery of biblical manuscripts in a jar near Jericho in his time. While the conclusions from this first excavation were to be corrected and modified somewhat by later discoveries, some questions were answered. The first important step had been taken in the scientific investigation of the problems raised by the discovery of the scrolls.

The manuscript fragments found in the 1949 excavation included bits of several of the canonical books of the Old Testament and some fragments of apocryphal writings, as well as several works hitherto unknown. By 1952 about twenty different works had been identified. Most of the fragments were in a script like that of the scrolls found in 1947, but there were some in the archaic Hebrew script, sometimes called Phoenician, and in a form of it closely resembling that of the Lachish Letters from the early sixth century B.C. Whether the scrolls of which these fragments were the only surviving remnants were really as old as the Lachish Letters, or whether they represented a later archaistic use of the ancient script, has been much discussed. We shall have to come back to this question in considering the age of the manuscripts. Several different documents were represented, but a number of the fragments contained bits of Chapters 19 and 20 of the book of Leviticus.

If anyone supposed that all the questions would be answered and all doubts allayed by the excavation, he was doomed to speedy disillusionment. Not a few scholars, especially those whose competence was in fields other than archeology, received the new evidence with considerable skepticism. What, after all, they asked, does the finding of jars from the Hellenistic period prove? What exactly was the relation between the jars and the manuscripts? Had the jars been made for the express purpose of containing the manuscripts, or had jars much older than the manuscripts been used for this purpose when the scrolls were hidden in the cave? Might not the latter supposition explain the fact that a few Roman potsherds were found with them? Might not the manuscripts, for that matter, have been put in the jars by the Bedouins, who claimed to have found them but perhaps had smuggled them into Palestine from Egypt?

Meanwhile the argument from paleography was being developed, but it was also being subjected to attack. I have mentioned two articles that appeared in February 1949. One was by Trever; the other, which dealt with the St. Mark's Isaiah Scroll only, was the first of a series of articles by an eminent British authority on Hebrew paleography, Solomon A. Birnbaum, of the University of London. He concluded that the forms of the letters indicated the first half of the second century B.C. as the time when the Isaiah manuscript was made. Trever's date for this scroll was a little later, about 125–100 B.C.; he proposed a date about 75 B.C. for the Manual of Discipline, and one between 25 B.C. and 25 A.D. for the Habakkuk Commentary and the Lamech Scroll. In June appeared an article by Birnbaum in which he dated the Habakkuk scroll between 100 and 50 B.C., again considerably earlier than Trever's date. In a subsequent article Birnbaum dated the Manual of Discipline at 150–100 B.C.; in another he narrowed his date for the Habakkuk Commentary down to about 50 B.C., and put the Manual of Discipline at 125–100 B.C.

The methods used in reaching these conclusions were vigorously attacked by Professor E. R. Lacheman of Wellesley College in an article published in July 1949. Beginning with a re-examination of the script of the Nash Papyrus, he criticized at length the method which Albright had employed in assigning this papyrus to a pre-Christian date, and which Trever had adopted in his treatment of the Dead Sea Scrolls. Birnbaum's arguments were mentioned only incidentally. At the same time brief replies by Albright and me to Zeitlin's previous articles were published, with a rebuttal by Zeitlin. In October Albright issued a reply to Lacheman's article. This was followed by a brief rejoinder from Lacheman with comments by Albright.

Meanwhile Archbishop Samuel had come to the United States, having been appointed by his Patriarch as an Apostolic Delegate to the Syrian Orthodox congregations in this country and Canada. With him came his manuscripts, but in spite of widespread interest in them efforts to find a buyer met with no success. Newspaper reports putting the value of the manuscripts at the fabulous amount of a million dollars probably discouraged some potential purchasers; there were also ugly rumors in circulation concerning the ownership of the scrolls, and these may have caused some to hesitate. The matter was not simplified by the manner in which the scrolls had been removed from Palestine. The former government was gone, and a new one did not take shape at once in the part of the country still held by the Arabs. When this territory, including the area in which the manuscripts had been found, was incorporated with Transjordan in the Hashemite Kingdom of Jordan, that government felt that the scrolls belonged to it as the successor of the British mandatory government.

Public exhibitions of the scrolls were held at several places, beginning with one at the Library of Congress at Washington in October and November 1949. During the next few years there were exhibitions at Duke University, at the Walters Art Gallery in Baltimore, at the Oriental Institute of the University of Chicago, and at the Art Museum of Worchester, Massachusetts. Still there were no buyers. At last, early in 1954, the scrolls were purchased for the government of Israel by Sukenik's son, the former Israeli Army Chief of Staff, Yigael Yadin. The acquisition was officially announced about a year later, on February 13, 1955.

The fragments found in the excavation of the cave in February 1949 were taken to London for processing and study. Dr. Harold J. Plenderleith, a chemist in charge of the research laboratory at the British Museum, worked patiently with them for three months, gently trying to separate the brittle, partly decomposed leaves of parchment or leather. By subjecting them to a controlled humidity under glass until they were softened enough to come apart, and then putting them into a refrigerator to harden the decomposed matter, he was able gradually to separate about a hundred pieces and fit them together. He ascertained also that the writing had been done with carbon ink. Another result of Dr. Plenderleith's work was the discovery that what had at first been supposed to be pitch, used presumably to seal up the scrolls, was actually decomposed leather.

An article about the manuscripts by Mr. Harding appeared in the London *Times* of August 9. Two days later the fragments were placed on exhibition in London, and Dr. Plenderleith held a news conference. Both the excavated fragments and the scrolls found in 1947 now became a "front-page sensation" in the popular press, which rediscovers the discovery every once in a while. A dash of the spice of controversy was provided to whet the appetite of the public by an interview with Professor G. R. Driver of Oxford University in the *Daily Mail* of London. Speaking of the scrolls bought by Archbishop Samuel, Driver was reported to have said, "These things should have been submitted to the British Museum laboratory, the only place qualified to handle them. The idea of taking the scrolls to America seems to have been: 'How much money can we make out of it?'" Asked to comment on this statement, I pointed out that the scrolls were not in the possession of the American Schools of Oriental Research, that the photographs were to be published soon, and that meanwhile these photographs were available on request to responsible scholars.

Professor Driver of course did not know that since April I had been corresponding with Sir Alan Gardiner concerning the best place and person for opening the Aramaic scroll. He had kindly written to T. C. Skeat of the British Museum; and Skeat had discussed the problem with Plenderleith, who said that he would like to see the scroll but could make no suggestions without seeing it. This correspondence only convinced us that there was no one in

England better qualified for the delicate task of unrolling the scroll than one or two men here in the United States. In Sir Alan Gardiner's last letter to me, written just a week after Professor Driver's interview, he expressed regret at not having been able to help us and concluded, "But now my old friend Ibscher is gone, I should really not know where to turn in the case of very fragile MSS."

Driver not only criticized the manner in which the discovery had been treated; he denied the pre-Christian date which Sukenik and we had assigned to the scrolls. In a series of letters to the London *Times* he presented his views, and other scholars joined in the debate. The editor of the *Palestine Exploration Quarterly* wrote in the issue for July–October 1949, "During the summer months of this year the columns of the *Times* have served as the arena of a pretty gladiatorial combat in which the *retiarius* with his net and trident, in the person of Professor Godfrey Driver, seeks to entangle the *mirmillo*, in the person of Mr. Leveen of the British Museum, and to puncture the bubble of a pre-Christian date for the scrolls. Dr. Birnbaum also has entered the fray and from the expert epigraphist's point of view has pronounced in favour of the early date, as readers of this issue will see." The reference here is to Birnbaum's article on the date of the Manual of Discipline.

The debate was not restricted to the columns of the newspapers. A lecture by Driver, which illness prevented him from delivering, was read by Professor S. H. Hooke at a meeting of the Palestine Exploration Fund in London. Dismissing the external archeological evidence as inconclusive, Driver argued that only the internal evidence of script, spelling, and language could determine the date of the manuscripts, and on this basis he judged them to be possibly as late as the sixth or seventh century A.D. In the discussion following the lecture Birnbaum insisted that the script was definitely pre-Christian, and no arguments drawn from internal evidence could outweigh this fact. Driver's arguments were presented more fully in an article that appeared in October, followed later by several other articles in various journals and by a lecture that was published in 1951 as a monograph. While he eventually modified his conclusions somewhat, he adhered to his main line of argument, discounting the significance of archeological evidence and maintaining a late date on the basis of paleography and language.

Meanwhile the efforts to arrange for unrolling Archbishop Samuel's Aramaic scroll were proceeding. The archbishop sent the scroll to the Fogg Museum of Harvard University, where thoroughly competent treatment could have been given it. The American Schools of Oriental Research took every step possible to make sure that the work would be successful, but before it could be begun the archbishop changed his mind and withdrew the scroll.

During the previous spring Trever had detached a piece containing the major portion of one column of the text. It was on the basis of what he could decipher in this column with the aid of photography that he concluded, in consultation with Professor Albright and Professor Charles C. Torrey, that the scroll contained the lost "Apocalypse of Lamech," known hitherto only by name from an ancient Greek list of apocalyptic writings. Trever now tells me that I first called his attention to the name Lamech in the text, and I remember suggesting that he look up the references to lost apocalyptic works. His conclusion was announced in October 1949. During the summer of that year it was announced also that Sukenik, working on his manuscripts at Jerusalem, had succeeded in unrolling another scroll and had found it to be a second manuscript of Isaiah. This, of course, was the one that has already been briefly described.

It must not be supposed that only British and American scholars were interested in the scrolls. Within a year after the first announcement of the discovery articles about the manuscripts had appeared in Danish, Dutch, French, German, Hebrew, Latin, Norwegian, Spanish, and Swedish, to mention only those of which I have a record. There must have been many others, and many more followed as the months went by. Not everything written was important, of course, but significant contributions to the understanding of the texts were made by scholars of many nationalities.

The most important of them are considered when we come to examine the points in question.

Beginning in February 1949, an important series of articles on the scrolls appeared in Germany in the *Theologische Literaturzeitung*. One of the first articles was by Professor Paul Kahle, who discussed the discovery of the scrolls, the significance of the Isaiah manuscript for textual criticism, and the occasion and cause of the hiding of the scrolls in the cave. An interesting new note was injected into the discussion by Professor Otto Eissfeldt in the October number. He compared the discovery of the manuscripts with an earlier incident in the same region, related in a Syriac letter written about 800 A.D. by Timotheus, the Nestorian patriarch of Seleucia, to Sergius, the Metropolitan of Elam. Among other matters, Timotheus told Sergius of information he had received from some trustworthy Jews who had been instructed in the Christian faith. They said that books had been found ten years earlier in a cave near Jericho. An Arab hunter, whose dog had pursued an animal into the cave, followed it and found in the cave a little building containing many books. He informed the Jews of Jerusalem, who came in great numbers and found the books of the Old Testament and others in Hebrew writing, including more than two hundred psalms of David. This story, we shall see, has played a considerable part in subsequent discussions.

One of the first serious attempts to determine the historical setting of the Dead Sea Scrolls was made by a Swedish scholar, Bo Reicke, then of Uppsala and now of Basel. In a previous publication he had discussed the Damascus Document, a curious work that will demand a good deal of our attention because it is closely related to the Manual of Discipline and the Habakkuk Commentary. In 1949 he published a study of the Dead Sea Scrolls and the Damascus Document, propounding a theory that is still important, in spite of the fact that its author himself later abandoned it.

Both the "teacher of righteousness," who appears in the Damascus Document as well as in the Habakkuk Commentary, and his adversary, the "wicked priest," were regarded by Reicke as "super-individual" figures, representing respectively the true and the false priests. In part, however, they were taken also to represent individual high priests of the early second century B.C. The teacher of righteousness was identified in particular with Onias III, whom the Syrian king Antiochus Epiphanes deposed in 175 or 174 B.C.

The wicked priest was identified with Jason, the brother of Onias and his successor as high priest, and also with Menelaus, who succeeded Jason. That Jason or Menelaus might be the wicked priest was suggested also in 1949 by I. L. Seeligmann in an important review of Sukenik's volume.

The "house of Absalom," which according to the Habakkuk Commentary failed to support the teacher of righteousness when he was persecuted by the wicked priest, was thought by Reicke to be a prominent family known as the Tobiads. They espoused the adoption of Greek culture and customs, whereas the party of Onias stood for the strict observance of the old Jewish traditions. In spite of certain difficulties, this theory seemed to me for some time very probable.

In December 1949 there appeared in a Hebrew periodical in Israel an article that not only added new fuel to the fire of controversy but also injected an element of mystery and suspicion. I have already told of the visit of Mr. Toviah Wechsler to the Monastery of St. Mark with Mr. Stephan of the Antiquities Department in the summer or early autumn of 1947. The newspaper article, which appeared two years later, stated, without mentioning his name, that when Wechsler saw the scrolls in 1947 he recognized that they were forgeries. Having in the meantime been convinced that the scrolls were both genuine and ancient, Wechsler now wrote an article, which was published on December 1, 1949, explaining why he had at first doubted the authenticity and antiquity of the Isaiah manuscript.

Chief among his reasons was the fact that with the manuscript of Isaiah he was shown also another scroll, similar in appearance, which he found to be a scroll of the Haftarot—i.e., the selections from the books of the prophets assigned for reading in the synagogue after the reading from the Pentateuch. Between the successive Haftarot, he said, there were blank lines, and the last column of the scroll was in part blank. At the end, he recalled dimly, were the blessings to accompany the reading of the Haftarot. The writing was like that of the Isaiah manuscript, but in the margins were corrections of the texts in much blacker ink which appeared quite new, suggesting that the scrolls must have been in use fairly recently.

Wechsler concluded that both scrolls had been taken from a synagogue *genizah,* or repository for discarded scrolls. Since there had been no further mention of the Haftarot scroll in the meantime, Wechsler suggested that the Syrians, on hearing his adverse judgment, had decided not to make known the existence of this scroll until they could sell the others. Later, when Sukenik's manuscripts became known, Wechsler decided that the Isaiah scroll and the cave deposit as a whole were authentic and ancient, but that the Haftarot scroll was of other and later origin.

This of course was grist for Zeitlin's mill, and he lost no time in using it. In January 1950 he printed an article with the challenging title, "Where Is the Scroll of the Haftarot?" Other scholars were naturally puzzled and concerned, and there were many demands that the mystery be cleared up. Not the least of Zeitlin's contributions to the debate was his cordial readiness, as editor of the *Jewish Quarterly Review,* to publish articles criticizing his own arguments. In the number following that which carried his article on the Haftarot scroll he printed a reply by Trever, which proposed what I believe to be the true explanation of the mystery.

Trever pointed out that Wechsler's article, which acknowledged frankly that his memory of the affair was vague at some points, gave an inaccurate description of the Isaiah manuscript. Speaking of the corrections which he remembered seeing in the margin of the Haftarot scroll, Wechsler said, "Such corrections were not found in the Isaiah scroll." He said also that while the Haftarot scroll was soiled and worn, the Isaiah manuscript showed little evidence of having been used. The fact is that the Isaiah scroll has many corrections, both in the margins and between the lines, and it is of all the scrolls perhaps the one which shows most evidence of much handling.

On the other hand, what Wechsler mistakenly said of the Isaiah scroll on these points is true of the Manual of Discipline, and his observation that there are blank lines between successive sections is equally applicable to that document. A hasty perusal of one or two pages in which the language of the prophetic books was used may have suggested a collection of Haftarot, and the end of the concluding psalm in the partly blank last column of the Manual of Discipline may have looked, at a quick glance, like a blessing. Trever's presentation of these facts did not convince either Wechsler or Zeitlin. The controversy blazed up again a year later, but meanwhile other and more important things were happening.

Early in 1950 the first volume of *The Dead Sea Scrolls of St. Mark's Monastery* was published by the American Schools of Oriental Research. Brownlee and Trever assisted me in editing it. It contained photographic facsimiles of the text of the Isaiah manuscript and the Habakkuk Commentary, with a transcription in the familiar printed form of the Hebrew alphabet, chapters and verses being marked, to facilitate the use of the photographs. Scholars the world over were thus enabled to study these two documents in their entirety. Our purpose in issuing the texts in this form was to allow time for scholarly discussion before we attempted to publish a volume of critical studies. None of us anticipated the enormous volume of discussion that actually ensued, and of course no man could have foreseen the vast quantity of new manuscript material that was still to be discovered.

In March 1950 Professor Sukenik issued his second volume of the Hebrew University's manuscripts. This included a few more excerpts from texts that had not been published in the first volume and gave a fuller account of Sukenik's purchase of the scrolls and his work on them.

The cloud of controversy was not at all dispelled by the publication of the texts; in fact it grew larger and spread farther. In the spring of 1950 France became the center of very lively debate in response to the stimulating ideas of Professor André Dupont-

Sommer of the Sorbonne. On the twenty-sixth of May he presented to the Académie des Inscriptions et Belles Lettres a communication in which for the first time he propounded an interpretation of the Habakkuk Commentary that was destined both to gain many adherents and to arouse strong opposition. Within the same year he published several articles and a small book, later translated into English, further expounding and defending his views.

Dupont-Sommer maintained that the commentary was composed shortly before 40 B.C., after the annexation of Palestine by the Romans in 63 B.C., but before the end of the reign of Hyrcanus II, the last ruler of the Hasmonean Jewish dynasty. The "Kittim" of the commentary, he argued, were the Romans. The mysterious "wicked priest" he regarded as representing both Aristobulus II, the brother and predecessor of Hyrcanus II, and also Hyrcanus himself. It was Aristobulus who persecuted the "teacher of righteousness" and put him to death only a few months before the capture of Jerusalem by Pompey, but the members of the community founded by the teacher of righteousness believed that he would soon return and take part in the last judgment. Dupont-Sommer confidently identified this community with the Essenes and held that the manuscripts had been hidden in the cave at the time of the first Jewish revolt against Rome in 66–70 A.D. A recent modification of this theory at one point is noted later.

On the same day that Dupont-Sommer's communication was presented in Paris, the *Jerusalem Post* carried the first part of an article by M. H. Segal, Professor Emeritus of the Hebrew University, maintaining a very different view of the date and historical background of the manuscripts. The rest of the article appeared on June 2. As far back as 1912 Segal had advanced the theory that the Damascus Document, which had been found in the Old Cairo genizah and had then only recently been published, reflected the conditions of the reign of Alexander Janneus, 103–76 B.C. Between this monarch and the Pharisees there was a bitter struggle. According to Segal, the members of the sect that produced the Damascus Document, though violently opposed to some of the teachings of the Pharisees, had been united with them in opposition to

Alexander Janneus, and with them had been compelled to take refuge in Syria. The Dead Sea Scrolls now seemed to him to afford a striking confirmation of his theory. The sect founded by the teacher of righteousness, Segal suggested, probably arose among the pietistic Hasidim of the Maccabean period. These and other arguments and theories we must consider more fully later.

In July 1950 Zeitlin attempted to dispose of the whole subject of the Dead Sea Scrolls by an article entitled, "The Hebrew Scrolls, Once More and Finally." It did not prove to be his last utterance on the subject. In October a new ally came to his support in the person of Dr. P. R. Weis of the University of Manchester, whose article, "The Date of the Habakkuk Scroll," undertook by a very learned discussion of the vocabulary and ideas of the commentary to show that it betrayed Arabic influence. He concluded that it referred to the crusaders and the Seljuk Turks, and was written about 1096 A.D. by a member of a medieval Jewish sect. The Hebrew University scroll of the War of the Sons of Light with the Sons of Darkness was interpreted as a work of Messianic speculation, referring not to any historical war but to the final struggle of the Messiah with Gog. Weis suggested that the "Kittim of Egypt" and the "Kittim of Assyria" in this document might represent "the Fatimids and the Seljuks who in 1071 fought each other for the possession of Palestine."

In October 1950 appeared another article by G. R. Driver, who on the tenth of the same month also delivered the fourth Dr. Williams Lecture for the Friends of Dr. Williams's Library of London, taking the Dead Sea Scrolls as his subject. This lecture was published the following year by the Oxford University Press as a monograph. Still dismissing all the external evidence and even the paleography as "useless," Driver accepted as significant only the "orthography and linguistic peculiarities," and on the basis of these proposed a date between 200 A.D. and 500 A.D., "towards the end rather than the beginning of this period."

The rising interest in the Dead Sea Scrolls among biblical scholars was attested by the fact that when the First International Congress of Old Testament Scholars was held at Leiden from

August 30 to September 2, 1950, I was invited to speak about the scrolls at the opening session. My paper, together with the others delivered at the congress, was published in the eighth volume of *Oudtestamentische Studien,* which was printed and bound in time to be delivered to the delegates at the closing session of the congress.

The following week there was an International Congress on the History of Religions at Amsterdam, and I gave a brief paper there on an interesting section of the Manual of Discipline which presents theological conceptions recalling characteristic Iranian ideas. I had hoped that there would be in my audience some specialists in Iranian religion, and that in the discussion following my paper they might elucidate the beliefs and possibly the derivation of the sect. Unfortunately for me, at the same hour another of the eleven sections into which the congress was divided had a paper by Professor Baumgartner of Zürich on some recently discovered Manichean documents, and the experts in things Iranian naturally went to hear that paper instead of mine. I should have liked to hear it myself; but the little group of distinguished Old Testament scholars who heard my presentation made the time pass pleasantly, and I dare say I learned at least as much from them as they learned from me.

In an article published in September 1950, Paul Kahle took up the question of the time when the scrolls were deposited in the cave. Rejecting as inconclusive the archeological evidence of the pottery for an early date, he approached the problem from the point of view of paleography and related considerations and concluded that the manuscripts could hardly have been left in the cave before the third century A.D.

The Old Testament text of the biblical manuscripts was considered also. Here for the first time Kahle made public an important observation: the St. Mark's Isaiah manuscript, he said, exhibited not one but two forms of the Hebrew text, that of the second half of the scroll being of a different type from that of the first. In the second half, moreover, the scribe had left out portions of the text, which had been filled in later, and in one case the text of the later insertion agreed exactly with that of our traditional text. It could not, therefore, have been inserted in the manuscript, Kahle declared, before the third century A.D. Sukenik's Isaiah manuscript, he said, was not written before the second century. In the Old Testament text of the Habakkuk Commentary he found nothing to prevent ascribing it to the beginning of the Christian era. Some of these arguments, as we shall see, involve fallacies, but Kahle's article raised important questions.

It also expressed a feeling shared by many scholars, which soon led to unexpected and important results. Harding had remarked in an article in the *Illustrated London News* that the small quantity of Roman pottery found in the cave seemed to come from the time when the nearby site now known as Khirbet Qumran was occupied. A preliminary sounding there by Harding and de Vaux in 1949 had not revealed any connection with the cave, but Kahle now called for an adequate excavation of the ruin, suggesting that it might prove to be not merely a small Roman fortress but something directly associated with the use of the cave.

At the annual meeting of the Society for Old Testament Study at London in the first week of January 1951, Kahle expounded again his views concerning the Dead Sea Scrolls. His paper appeared the same month in the first number of *Vetus Testamentum,* the organ of the International Society of Old Testament Scholars, which had been founded at Leiden the previous summer. A little later Kahle published a book containing some lectures on the scrolls which he had delivered at German universities in 1950.

In these publications Kahle aligned himself with the view of Dupont-Sommer that the scrolls were the work of Essenes. He accepted also Dupont-Sommer's view that the Habakkuk Commentary was composed about 40 B.C. and argued that the copy of it found in the cave was probably made before 70 A.D. He still, however, maintained that the manuscripts had not been deposited in the cave before the third century A.D., and again he called for the excavation of Khirbet Qumran.

Kahle also called attention to the importance of the Dead Sea Scrolls for the study of the medieval Jewish sect of the Karaites, not because the scrolls were produced by Karaites, as Zeitlin argued, but because the Karaites had been influenced by this earlier Essene literature. He expressed the opinion that the cave in which the manuscripts were found was the same one that had been previously discovered about 800 A.D., as related in the letter of Timotheus; indeed, he suggested that some of the texts found in the Cairo genizah were medieval copies of manuscripts that had been taken from the cave at the time of that discovery.

In order to pursue a more thorough investigation of the paleography of the scrolls, Trever secured a leave of absence from his work with the International Council of Religious Education. With the aid of grants from the American Schools of Oriental Research and the American Philosophical Society he spent about two months early in 1951 visiting the principal museums and libraries in England and France. While there he photographed and studied many of their manuscripts and discussed them with the leading British and French scholars in the field, who afforded him every courtesy and assisted him most generously. The results of his study were summarized in a report to the American Philosophical Society presented on April 25, 1952, and published in the *Proceedings* of the Society. In a revised form it was also issued later by the Smithsonian Institution.

Meanwhile, as a little interlude in the more serious scholarly debate, the mystery of the "Haftarot Scroll" was revived. In January 1951, a year after his first article on this subject, Zeitlin published one by Wechsler and another by himself. Wechsler, who felt that his moral integrity had been impugned, now claimed that Trever himself had actually seen the Haftarot scroll "and had examined it and recognized it as such!" He had also recognized, Wechsler said, that it was of late date, but had been "told that it did not come from the finds in the cave." This startling charge was based on a letter from Carl H. Kraeling, my successor as President of the American Schools of Oriental Research, which, Wechsler said, "stated explicitly" that Professor Kraeling had learned of Trever's having seen the Haftarot scroll "from conversations with Professor Burrows."

Being thus dragged into a dispute on a matter of which I had no first-hand knowledge, I felt compelled to look into the question. At the meeting of the American Oriental Society at Philadelphia in the spring of 1951 I presented the results of my inquiry, with a reply to some of Zeitlin's arguments; and he, with characteristic good sportsmanship, published my paper in the October number of his journal. Among other things, I pointed out that what I had told Professor Kraeling was not that Trever had seen a Haftarot Scroll, but that Archbishop Samuel, after coming to America, had shown him a late Torah Scroll that had nothing to do with the Dead Sea Scrolls. The statement cited by Wechsler was the result of a misunderstanding on the part of Professor Kraeling.

I quoted also a letter from Archbishop Samuel, assuring me emphatically that he had no scrolls or pieces of scrolls from the caves, either in his own possession or in the monastery at Jerusalem, except those Trever had photographed. He added that there was another modern Torah scroll in the monastery in addition to the one he had shown Trever after coming to this country.

In the meantime, at my request and with the approval of Archbishop Samuel, Professor F. W. Winnett, then serving as Director of the American School of Oriental Research at Jerusalem, had gone to St. Mark's Monastery with Professor R. B. Y. Scott to find what Hebrew scrolls were in the library there. He was assured, as I learned just in time to report it to the meeting at Philadelphia, that the only Hebrew manuscript in the monastery in 1947, aside from the Dead Sea Scrolls, was a late Torah scroll that had been acquired in 1929—presumably the one mentioned in Archbishop Samuel's letter.

Since it seemed to me incredible that Wechsler could have supposed such a late scroll to be from one and the same collection as the manuscript of Isaiah, I could only conclude from all these facts, and still believe, that Trever was right in thinking that Wechsler must have mistaken the Manual of Discipline for a scroll of Haftarot. The physical characteristics of this scroll and those of the Isaiah scroll must have become confused later in his memory.

If anyone still has doubts or misgivings about this, I can say only that no more probable explanation of the facts has been suggested.

While all this was going on, the discussion of Dupont-Sommer's views on the scrolls was becoming very warm in France. As a journalist put it in *Le Figaro littéraire* for February 24, 1951, "From the learned world the thunder rolls to the general public." What especially provoked no little excitement was the distinguished scholar's suggestion that in the person and career of the teacher of righteousness many points in the belief of the Christian religion concerning its Founder were anticipated. According to Dupont-Sommer, the teacher of righteousness was believed to be an incarnate divine being, who was put to death by his enemies and was expected by his followers to rise from the dead.

Alarmed by what seemed a threat to the uniqueness of Jesus, a number of Catholic scholars promptly attacked the interpretation advanced by Dupont-Sommer. In the Jesuit journal *Études* for February 1951, J. Bonsirven, an eminent authority on post-biblical Judaism, accused the Sorbonne professor of sowing Christianity all through the Dead Sea Scrolls and then being amazed to find it there. Dupont-Sommer stoutly defended his position in a series of publications. The points at issue will have to be considered on their merits when we are ready to examine the meaning and implications of the texts.

Another theory made its appearance in England early in 1951. An article on the Dead Sea Scrolls by J. L. Teicher appeared in February, and a few months later a series of articles by the same scholar began to be published. In these he proposed and defended the view that the sect represented by the manuscripts was not Jewish at all, but the primitive Christian sect known as the Ebionites. This theory must of course be as fully and fairly considered as any other. All that can be said of it at this point is that it shows at least how complicated the problem is.

Throughout the year 1951 the stream of publications concerning the scrolls continued to swell. It was naturally not abated by the fact that we were able to issue in February a fascicle of the second volume of *The Dead Sea Scrolls of St. Mark's Monastery*, containing the photographic facsimiles and a transcription of the Manual of Discipline. At about the same time an English translation of the same document by Brownlee was published. We had hoped to include with this text in our second volume the Aramaic Lamech Scroll and the fragments bought by Archbishop Samuel, but since the arrangements for unrolling the Lamech Scroll were not proceeding satisfactorily, and we were unwilling to keep the world of scholarship waiting longer for the Manual of Discipline, we decided to bring this out separately. Of course it not only provided very important material for solid research but also added new fuel to the fires of debate. Translations of the scroll and articles about it in several languages were published during the ensuing months.

New evidence bearing on the dating of the manuscripts appeared also early in 1951. A piece of linen cloth found in the cave when it was excavated was sent by Harding to America and subjected to the carbon-14 process by Professor W. F. Libby of the Institute for Nuclear Studies of the University of Chicago. The result of the test was reported by Professor Libby to President Kraeling of the American Schools of Oriental Research on the ninth of January, and was published by Professor O. R. Sellers in February. The date thus established for the piece of cloth was 33 A.D., plus or minus 200 years; i.e., some time between 167 B.C. and 233 A.D.

While this did not establish the age of the manuscripts themselves, or provide as exact a date for their deposit in the cave as might have been desired, it clearly indicated the general period of history to which the scrolls belonged, confirming what had already been inferred from other considerations. Any idea that the Dead Sea Scrolls were of medieval origin thus became less defensible than ever. It would have been helpful to apply the carbon-14 test to the manuscripts themselves, but this would have involved the destruction of a large piece of one of them.

When the International Congress of Orientalists met in September at Istanbul, one morning's session of the Old Testament section was devoted to papers on the Dead Sea Scrolls. One of the participants was Professor Sukenik from Jerusalem, who showed some of the photographs made for the publication of his texts which he was preparing, but which he was not destined to see issued before his death. It was brought out posthumously in 1954.

III

Later Discoveries

While excavating the first cave in 1949, Harding and de Vaux, as I have said, inspected briefly the nearby ruin, Khirbet Qumran. They also excavated two nearby tombs. Since they found nothing to indicate any connection with the cave and its manuscripts, the common belief that the ruined building had been a small Roman fortress still seemed as probable as any other explanation. Such merely negative conclusions, however, did not satisfy scholars. Kahle's insistence that the site should be thoroughly excavated has been mentioned. The debate raging over the nature and date of the deposit of scrolls in the cave made this clearly imperative.

Consequently, almost two years after their excavation of the cave, Harding and de Vaux, with fifteen men, worked at the ruin from November 24 to December 12, 1951. The main building, about 118 feet long and about 94 feet wide, was uncovered at the southwestern and northeastern corners. Two soundings were made on the outside of it, and several more tombs in the adjoining cemetery were excavated. In the southwestern corner of the building three rooms with walls preserved to a height of about 9 feet were cleared. Extending along the base of the walls in the largest of these rooms was found a carefully plastered bench, about 8 inches high. There was also a small plastered area forming a kind of basin just outside this corner of the building. Two other rooms were excavated at the northeastern corner, one of them being the corner room and the other an outside room built against the north wall of the main building. Parts of a wall were found in digging a trench to the west of the building.

The evidence provided by the plan and masonry was by no means clear. New and specific information was afforded, however, by bronze coins found in almost all the rooms, usually on the floor. Their dates ranged from the beginning of the Christian era to the first Jewish revolt (66–70 A.D.). It was thus evident that the building had been in use during the first two-thirds of the first century A.D., and its occupation had come to an end at about the year 70, probably during the Jewish revolt. There were also indications of a previous but, as it then seemed, less important period of occupation, and what seemed to be traces of an Arab occupation in the Middle Ages. Further excavation later necessitated some reinterpretation of this evidence.

A large amount of pottery was found also, some of it conforming in type to forms found elsewhere in tombs from the time of Herod the Great and the first century A.D., and some of it to pottery found, together with coins of the same period, in excavations along the north wall of Jerusalem. Among the potsherds at Khirbet Qumran were some representing the same types as those found in the excavation of the cave, indicating that these were not so early as had then been supposed.

Even more surprising and significant was the appearance of a complete jar of the same type as those in which the manuscripts had been deposited in the cave. It was sunk in the ground in a corner of one of the rooms, its mouth covered by a square piece of limestone set level with the pavement. Although it was empty when found, it must have been used for the storage of water, wine, oil, or food. From this find de Vaux and Harding concluded that they had been mistaken in regarding the jars that had contained the manuscripts as of earlier manufacture than the Roman period. It was therefore no longer necessary to suppose that the Roman lamp and cooking pot whose fragments were found in the cave had been brought in by intruders of a later century.

Another result of the excavation was to refute the supposition that the building was a Roman fort. This was excluded by its plan and the type of its construction. On the other hand, it did not seem to have been a private dwelling and certainly could not have housed all the people buried in the adjoining cemetery. The natural inference seemed to be that the people who had used it had lived in caves or tents in the vicinity. For what purpose they had used the building was still not made clear, but it seemed likely that it had served as a meeting place for the community, especially if this was such a religious order as we find reflected in the Manual of Discipline. In short, the excavation reversed the previous impression that the cave and the ruin were unconnected.

Meanwhile other evidence had been coming in unsought. Toward the end of the summer Bedouins brought to Jerusalem two fragments of leather inscribed with a few words in Hebrew and a few words in Greek. The secretary of the Palestine Museum and the Inspector of Antiquities visited the cave in which these fragments were believed to have been found, but it seemed unpromising, and they could not be sure that this was actually the place from which the fragments had come. It was evidently imperative, however, that the region should be thoroughly explored. Awni Bey Dajani, Inspector of the Department of Antiquities, invited the American School of Oriental Research to join him in looking for one of the caves that had been found by the Bedouins, and on the third day of November, three weeks before the beginning of the excavation of Khirbet Qumran, some of the members of the school went with him and by strenuous walking and climbing located the cave. They gathered a few samples of pottery but decided that excavation would be necessary to accomplish anything further.

At the end of November some leather and papyrus fragments were offered to de Vaux by an antiquities dealer in Bethlehem. He claimed that they had been found in the first cave discovered in 1947, but this was obviously false. Being strictly questioned, he admitted that the fragments had come from another place, but quite near to the cave. He was evidently anxious to avoid an investigation. De Vaux informed Harding, who purchased the fragments from the merchant for the Palestine Museum.

More pieces of manuscripts continued to be brought in by the

Bedouins to the Department of Antiquities and the French School of Archeology. Some of them were written on leather and some on papyrus. Some were in Hebrew, some in Aramaic, and some in Greek. Father de Vaux, with consummate tact and patience, negotiated with the Bedouins in the hope of finding the source of all this material. When he suggested working with them they said that this would be impossible because the presence of a stranger in the desert would attract the attention of the police and spoil everything.

Later, in the course of bargaining over the high price they asked for one fragment, they protested that the place was very far away and the work very difficult, and when de Vaux indicated some skepticism on this point they told him that if he came with them he could see for himself. They assured him that this could be managed; they had sentries on the nearby heights who would inform them if the police appeared, so that they could hide in the caves. He suggested that he could get permission from the Department of Antiquities, and they need then have no fear of being arrested. They heartily approved. He then suggested that the Director of Antiquities might come with them, and they agreed to this also. Finally he proposed a police escort, not to protect him from them—was he not their brother?—but to protect them from jealous tribesmen. This seemed to them an excellent idea.

All this, of course, took time, but on January 21, 1952, de Vaux and Harding, with an experienced Arab foreman, a police officer from Bethlehem, two soldiers, and two Bedouin guides, went to the place where the Bedouins had been at work. This proved to be a group of caves in the Wady Murabbaat, about ten or eleven miles south of Khirbet Qumran. Accordingly the Department of Antiquities and the French School of Archeology undertook another expedition together and worked for a total of six weeks during the first six months of 1952. This enterprise was rewarded by a rich find of manuscript fragments and coins.

The most important new fact that emerged from the exploration and excavation in the Wady Murabbaat was that caves in the slope of the Judean plateau had been used and inhabited not only

at the time represented by the cave found in 1947 and the settlement at Khirbet Qumran, but also in later periods. Evidence of
occupation at various times was found, but most of the coins and
manuscript fragments were from the time just before and during
the second Jewish revolt against Rome (132–135 A.D.). One of the
contracts written in Greek, of which there were several, was dated
in the seventh year of the Emperor Hadrian, corresponding to
124 A.D. Among the fragments there were only a few brief bits of
books of the Bible, including some from Genesis and Exodus, one
from Deuteronomy, and one from Isaiah. Interesting for the history
of Jewish religious practices was a complete phylactery.

Some of these texts afford new and important, though scanty,
source material for the history of the second revolt. Among them
are several that mention by name the leader of the revolt, commonly known as Bar Kokhba (or Cocheba), that is "Son of the
Star," who was believed by some of his contemporaries to be the
"Star out of Jacob" predicted in Numbers 24:17. His enemies
sometimes called him Bar Kozebah, "Son of the Lie." In the Wady
Murabbaat texts he is called Simon ben Kosebah, and this has
revived discussion among scholars concerning the original form
and meaning of his name.

One text, of which several incomplete copies were found, was
dated by "the deliverance of Israel by the hand of Simon ben
Kosebah." There are even two letters bearing his name and believed by the excavators to be original letters from him in person.
The officer to whom they were addressed was named Yeshua (that
is, Jesus) ben Galgola. There was also a letter to the same man
from two officials of a Jewish community. Two contracts and a few
other documents in Greek bearing definite dates in the second
century A.D., together with a few small fragments in Latin, suggest
that after the suppression of the Jewish revolt a Roman garrison
held the place for some time.

Exciting as these discoveries were, the archeologists were given
little time to study the new material before another expedition
proved necessary. The Taamirah Bedouins had by now become
such ardent seekers of manuscripts that reports of new finds in

other caves kept coming in. To forestall such unauthorized operations, and also to get as much work done as possible before the season of intolerable heat and malaria, a joint expedition of the French
School of Archeology, the Palestine Museum, and the American
School of Oriental Research was undertaken in March. The
Bedouins had found manuscript fragments in a cave only about
a hundred yards from the one in which the first manuscripts had
been discovered, and in another somewhat farther to the south
they had found a complete jar and lid like those in which the manuscripts discovered in 1947 had been kept. Two lots of the newly
found manuscript fragments were bought by the French School
and the Palestine Museum from an antiquities dealer in Bethlehem.

The new expedition, which was entitled the Qumran Caves
Expedition, engaged therefore in a thorough search of the area
surrounding the Wady Qumran. Father de Vaux and Professor
William L. Reed of Texas Christian University, who was serving
that year as Director of the American School of Oriental Research
at Jerusalem, directed the enterprise. Their staff consisted of
Fathers Barthélemy and Milik and M. Henri de Contenson of the
French School of Archeology. There were also two foremen from
the Palestine Museum and one from Amman, who supervised the
work of a number of Taamirah Bedouins.

After a preliminary visit on March 6, the systematic exploration
was begun on March 10 and continued until the twenty-ninth. The
whole region within a radius of about five miles in each direction
from Khirbet Qumran was carefully examined. The area was
divided into sectors, each of which was assigned to a small crew of
workmen under the direction of a member of the expedition. With
their Arab workers, the directors and staff scrambled over the
valleys and cliffs, using rope ladders where necessary.

Something like forty caves or crevices in the rock, most of them
too small to serve for anything but storage, were found to contain
pottery and other objects. In twenty-five of them there was pottery
of the same type as that from the cave found in 1947. All of these
twenty-five caves were in the lower of two stages of a limestone
cliff, which rises to the west of the marly terrace just back of the

coastal plain. The most dense occupation was found to have been near the mouth of the Wady Qumran, where the water supply was relatively good and access to the headquarters of the community was most convenient. Traces of two roads, at some points crudely paved and supported by walls, were discovered.

In two caves, one of them found by the Bedouins and the other newly discovered by the expedition, manuscript fragments were found. These included another bit of the book of Leviticus written in the archaic "Phoenician" script, and pieces of two manuscripts of Exodus, two of Ruth, and one each of Isaiah, Jeremiah, and Psalms. There were also non-biblical texts in Hebrew and Aramaic.

Quite unique were two scrolls of copper, one of them consisting of two sheets rolled up together. The length of each rolled-up scroll, which would be the width of the unrolled strips, was about a foot. By counting the convolutions at the ends it was possible to tell that each strip was about 32 inches long. The three strips had originally been riveted end to end; the complete scroll, there-fore, had been approximately 8 feet long. The material was much too oxidized and brittle to permit the unrolling of the scrolls without protracted treatment by some chemical process not yet fully worked out.

The text was inscribed so deeply that it stood out in relief on the back. A few characters could therefore be read in reverse on the outside of the scrolls. They belonged to the "square" Hebrew alphabet employed in most of the manuscripts, but not enough letters were legible to indicate the nature of the contents. Father de Vaux was convinced that the text was not from the Bible. He suggested that it was probably a rule or ordinance posted in the central building at Khirbet Qumran. One is reminded of the ref-erences in I Maccabees to proclamations and notices inscribed on bronze tablets and posted in public places. The historians Josephus and Polybius also speak of this practice.

About a year after the discovery of these scrolls K. G. Kuhn ex-amined them at the Palestine Museum, deciphered what he could of the writing visible in reverse on the back, and conceived the hypothesis that the scrolls were a record of the community's

treasures and the places where they were buried when the settlement was abandoned. Whether this will be verified when the
scrolls can be unrolled remains to be seen. If so, an exciting
treasure-hunt will no doubt ensue, and careful measures for
security will be necessary. No doubt the scrolls themselves will
be carefully guarded in the meantime.

Still the eager Taamirah tribesmen continued to scour the dis-
trict, and still with amazing success. New fragments of manuscripts kept coming in and were bought by the Palestine Museum
and the Jordan government. A large quantity of relatively late
manuscript material was found in a cave in the Wady en-Nar, the
southwestern continuation of the Kedron Valley, in which the
famous monastery of Mar Saba is located. Among the manuscripts
found in this cave or its vicinity were Arabic papyri from the early
centuries of Islam. There were also Greek manuscripts of the
Gospels of Mark and John, the Acts of the Apostles, and the
apocryphal Wisdom of Solomon. These came from the same
general period or slightly earlier (fifth to eighth centuries A.D.).
Manuscripts of non-biblical writings in Greek and biblical manuscripts in Syriac were represented among the fragments, which
included also a letter written in the Syriac language on papyrus.

From a group of caves whose location was not definitely identified came another lot of manuscript material related in contents
and date to those found previously in the Wady Murabbaat. It
included a few fragments from the books of Genesis, Numbers, and
Psalms. There was also another phylactery. There was a letter
addressed to the leader of the second Jewish revolt, Simon ben
Kosebah. Two Aramaic contracts were dated in the third year of
the "liberation of Israel" by the same leader. Two other Aramaic
documents and two in Greek were dated according to the era of the
Roman province of Arabia. A group of papyri in the Nabatean
dialect affords important matter for the study of Semitic languages, Aramaic in particular, because these papyri provide more
extensive and continuous texts than the inscriptions on which our
knowledge of this dialect has depended hitherto. Especially in-

teresting to biblical scholars was a fragmentary column from a Greek manuscript of the book of Habakkuk, affording what Father Barthélemy has called a missing link in the history of the Septuagint.

Our major concern here, however, is the manuscripts of the Wady Qumran. In a cave hardly large enough to deserve the name, not far from the Khirbet Qumran, more fragments were found by the Bedouins. Among these was one containing a passage of the Damascus Document. As I have already remarked, this work is closely related to the Dead Sea Scrolls. The presence of even a small bit of it among the other Qumran texts proves that the Damascus Document is not, as some have maintained, a medieval composition. Other fragments, as a matter of fact, were found later.

The climax of the whole extraordinary series of discoveries was reached at an out-of-the-way spot in the plateau on which Khirbet Qumran stands. This plateau is cut by a ravine, and at the point where the ravine joins the Wady Qumran the Bedouins found a chamber, hollowed out of the soft marl, containing many fragments of manuscripts. This is the cave now known as 4Q—i.e., Cave No. 4 of the Wady Qumran. Immediately on receiving the news of its discovery the Department of Antiquities stopped the Bedouins, and a fourth expedition was dispatched to excavate this cave, again in cooperation with the French School of Archeology and the Palestine Museum.

A week's work, beginning September 22, 1952, sufficed to complete the work begun by the Bedouins. The combined results of the unauthorized and the authorized excavations yielded a large quantity of manuscript material, surpassing in interest, according to the judgment of the excavators, even the initial discovery of 1947. In addition to the chamber that had been found by the Bedouins, the expedition found also another containing manuscript fragments, but these were not as well preserved as the others.

The preliminary task of identifying and cataloguing the contents of all these texts is being industriously pursued by the Department of Antiquities and the Dominicans with the assistance of the American School of Oriental Research. Not all of the fragments by any means have yet been identified, but it has already been determined that at least sixty different manuscripts are represented in the fragments from Cave 4Q alone. Perhaps as many as a hundred different biblical manuscripts may be counted when the scrolls and fragments from all the caves are included.

Almost all, if not all, of the books of the Old Testament are among the writings thus far identified. The Pentateuch and Isaiah are most largely represented, but there are also many fragments of Psalms, Daniel, and Jeremiah. There are also commentaries on the Psalms, Isaiah, and some of the minor prophets. There are sectarian hymns like Sukenik's Thanksgiving Psalms, bits of the Manual of Discipline, both in the same text as that of Archbishop Samuel's scroll and also in another text of an earlier type. There is something belonging or related to the War of the Sons of Light with the Sons of Darkness. The apocryphal book of Tobit appears in both Hebrew and Aramaic fragments. The Damascus Document, several apocalyptic writings, and other works previously unknown are represented also. All of these writings, used, if not composed, by members of the group that occupied the region, demonstrate the amazing intensity and scope of their interest in religious literature.

On October 4, a few days after the conclusion of this excavation, the American School of Oriental Research gave a large tea party, and Father de Vaux was among the guests. Dr. A. D. Tushingham, who had meanwhile succeeded Professor Reed as Director of the school, had just returned with other members of the school from a trip of two weeks in Syria. Father de Vaux took the opportunity to tell him of the new discoveries and urged upon him the need of further exploration before it should be too late. In spite of weariness from their long trip and the demands of other duties, Dr. Tushingham and the two Fellows of the school, Neil Richardson and Gus Van Beek, rose to the occasion and set out the next morning with Father Milik of the French School and Yusif Saad of the Palestine Museum. Unfortunately their zeal was not rewarded.

The experience of making one discovery after another was not repeated this time.

Meanwhile the government of Jordan was having the area patrolled to check further unauthorized and unsupervised digging. A liberal amount of money was appropriated also for the purchase of everything brought in by Bedouins, so that no important material might be lost. There was no telling what valuable manuscripts might still be in the hands of the Bedouins or what might still be found, in spite of every precaution.

And now another group joined in the quest. The Belgian Colonel (formerly Captain) Philippe Lippens, who in the winter of 1948–49 had taken a leading part in the search for the first cave, had not in the meantime lost his interest. Now a professor at the University of Louvain, he joined his colleague, Professor R. de Langhe, in organizing and conducting a Belgian expedition for a campaign of excavation, which lasted from February to May of the year 1953. The site chosen was one named Khirbet Mird, the ruins of a Byzantine monastery about two and a half miles northeast of the monastery of Mar Saba in the Wady en-Nar. On the top of a mountain shaped like a truncated cone are the remains of hermits' cells, reservoirs, and an aqueduct, the tumbled walls and mosaic pavement of a church, and a number of tombs. Manuscript fragments were found here, both by Bedouins and by the Belgian scholars, including bits of Greek and Syriac manuscripts of Old and New Testament books and Christian ritual texts, all from the fifth to eighth centuries A.D., as well as Arabic fragments and a few bits of Aramaic. In fact, the excavators were convinced that the fragments found by Bedouins the previous summer in the Wady en-Nar had come not from a cave but from Khirbet Mird.

Harding and de Vaux also directed another season's work at Khirbet Qumran from February 9 to April 24, 1953, obtaining further information concerning the history of the site and the people who occupied it, and correcting some of their own previous conclusions. The greater part of the ruin was uncovered, and it was found to have had three periods of occupation. The first of these had been ended by an earthquake.

Coins of John Hyrcanus (135–104 B.C.) and Alexander Janneus (103–76 B.C.), with three of the Seleucid King Antiochus VII (138–129 B.C.), showed that the occupation had begun much earlier than the 1951 excavation indicated, and the first period of occupation had been much more important than was then supposed. The pottery in this level and in a deposit about 30 meters north of the building (apparently left when the building was cleared out before being restored in the next period) was all of a type found in levels belonging to the late Hellenistic period at Beth-zur and in the citadel at Jerusalem.

Other coins indicated that the first period of occupation had continued to about the end of the Hasmonean period (39 B.C.) or the reign of Herod the Great (37–4 B.C.). Josephus tells us of a severe earthquake in the seventh year of Herod, just before the naval battle of Actium in which Antony and Cleopatra were decisively defeated by Octavius. On the very plausible assumption that this was the earthquake that destroyed the building at Qumran, de Vaux believes that the end of the first period can be definitely dated in the spring of 31 B.C. Other recorded earthquakes in the same general period were either too early or too late to fit the evidence of the coins.

The building, which had two stories, was erected certainly not later than the reign of Alexander Janneus (103–76 B.C.), and perhaps in the reign of his brother Aristobulus (104–103 B.C.) or his father John Hyrcanus (135–104 B.C.). At the northwest corner it had a strong tower with thick walls, evidently intended for defense. In its basement were rooms for storage. In the southwest corner of the building were large rooms for meetings or meals, and in the northwest corner what seemed to be a large kitchen.

Only one coin of Herod was found, and one of the city of Tyre from the year 29 B.C. From the time of Herod's son Archelaus (4 B.C.–6 A.D.) the coins again became more numerous and continued so to the time of the first Jewish revolt (68–70 A.D.), after which there was another and longer gap. These facts indicate that the building was not rebuilt immediately after being destroyed by the earthquake of 31 B.C., but was probably restored in the time of

Archelaus and continued in use until it was violently destroyed during the first revolt. It must have been restored by the same group, however, that had occupied it before, because the same general plan and manner of use were continued.

The pottery of the second period of occupation corresponded to what had been found in the excavation of 1951. It was related to the pottery of the first level but showed some further development, resembling most closely what had been found elsewhere in tombs of the time of Herod. The fact that the first two levels could not be distinguished in the 1951 excavation had led to an unduly late dating of the earliest pottery, in accordance with the later forms and the coins of the first century A.D., which actually belonged to the second period. It is the pottery of this second period that corresponds with what was found in the first cave, which therefore, as de Vaux informs me, "is certainly homogeneous and dates from the first half of the first century A.D."

As has been said, the general plan of the building was not changed in the second period, though there were minor modifications in the interest of greater isolation and security. The room in the southwest corner with a bench along the walls still seemed to have been intended for common meals or general meetings. A still larger room adjoining it on the east might have served for meetings or worship, but there were no objects to indicate how these rooms on the ground floor were used.

From the upper story, however, came portions of what proved, when carefully assembled at the Palestine Museum, to have been a brick table about 16 feet long and about 20 inches high, with parts of two shorter tables also. The room seemed rather too far from the kitchen to have been a dining room. Moreover, a bronze inkstand and one of clay, one of them still having some dried ink in it, were found in the same room. Another inkstand was found in another room. All this pointed to the conclusion that this had been the scriptorium of the order, where the manuscripts were written.

The manuscripts of the whole Wady Qumran area, with the exception of any the first settlers may have brought with them, came from these first two periods of occupation at Khirbet Qumran. Two fragments found in caves at some distance from each other were found to have been written by the same scribe. A few of the potsherds found in the excavation of the building bear Hebrew writing in the same form of the alphabet as that of the manuscripts, a form clearly earlier than the script of the Wady Murabbaat and the Wady en-Nar manuscripts. One potsherd from the first level at Khirbet Qumran had the Hebrew alphabet rather crudely written on it. Presumably it shows the efforts of a student practicing to become one of the scribes who copied the manuscripts.

Ashes and iron arrowheads show that the second period of occupation came to a violent end. Josephus again helps us to fix the date when this happened. He says that Vespasian was at Jericho in June of 69 A.D. and left a garrison there. Perhaps, as de Vaux infers, a part of this garrison, which belonged to the famous 10th Legion, attacked and destroyed the building at Qumran at that time and occupied the ruin as a post for watching and guarding the shore of the Dead Sea. A coin of Vespasian from the year 70, two of the city of Ascalon from the years 72–73, three of *Judaea capta* from the reign of Titus (79–81), and one of Agrippa II from about the year 86 were found in the excavation and had probably been left by the Roman garrison.

From the third period of occupation there was very little pottery, and what there was came from the beginning of the period, close to the time when the building had been destroyed. In this period the building was no longer such as to serve the needs of an organized community, but only those of a small military guard. Some time after the Roman soldiers left, the ruin was apparently occupied for a while by Jewish rebels, who no doubt left the thirteen coins of the second revolt (132–135 A.D.) that were found. Five later coins and the bits of Arab pottery that in 1951 were thought to indicate a later reoccupation proved to be too few to indicate anything more than the presence of a few shepherds camping there overnight.

A third campaign of excavation was carried out from February

15 to April 15, 1954. Only a brief summary of the results has been published thus far, but in general the conclusions indicated by the previous year's work were confirmed. The large building was found to extend farther to the south than had been supposed. The remains of an industrial quarter, with elaborate arrangements for assuring an adequate supply of water, were uncovered.

A large hall more than 70 feet long was cleared. It had undoubtedly been used for meetings and perhaps for sacred meals. In a small adjoining room there was a large collection of pottery, neatly arranged according to the various kinds of vessels, like the dishes in a china-closet.

Evidence that these vessels were of local manufacture was afforded by what de Vaux describes as the most complete and best preserved potter's establishment ever excavated in Palestine. At the opposite end of the excavation was found a mill, with its millstones nearby.

The evidence of the coins for the dates of occupation in the three successive periods remained the same as before. Further indications of the earthquake that terminated the first period were found, and also further evidence of the Roman occupation in the third period.

One quite new discovery was made. Potsherds of the eighth and seventh centuries B.C. showed that there had been a pre-exilic Israelite settlement at this place. One sherd had written on it a few letters in the "Phoenician" alphabet. No remains of buildings from this early occupation had survived. There was of course no connection between it and the occupation by the covenanters; a lapse of several centuries, in fact, intervened between the two occupations.

On February 1, 1955, Father de Vaux wrote to me: "We leave tomorrow for a new campaign at the Khirbeh. We must clear the surroundings of the main building to the west and a little building half carried away by the erosion of the wady. I do not expect any sensational discoveries in this area of secondary importance. We shall stop about the first of April (I do not know whether we shall be able to finish the whole exploration or whether we shall have to come back again the next year)." On March 29 he wrote: "Our excavation at Khirbet Qumran will be finished in a dozen days. It has been very interesting and will add much to the history and the knowledge of the life of the community."

Meanwhile the fragments assembled at the Palestine Museum are being diligently examined. Frank M. Cross, Jr., has written a vivid account of this work. The fragments must first be softened and placed between glass plates to flatten them. They must then be cleaned very carefully, because the ink may come away with the clay. Some fragments are so brittle that they crumble even when touched with a soft camel's-hair brush. In some cases a light application of castor oil helps to bring out the writing, but this too must be done with great care lest the material itself be discolored. Infra-red photography helps in many cases to bring out writing otherwise illegible. When flattened and cleaned, the fragments must be sorted out and, if possible, pieced together. If they belong to books of the Bible or other known works, the identification is relatively easy with the aid of concordances. Occasional surprising discoveries keep up the interest of this trying task.

The acquisition of Archbishop Samuel's manuscripts by Israel has already been mentioned. It is to be hoped that the Israeli scholars will be able to open the Lamech Scroll and publish the text, so far as it can still be deciphered, in the near future.

On May 22, 1954, it was announced that a substantial part of the manuscript fragments from Cave 4 had been purchased by McGill University of Montreal for $15,000. A condition of the purchase is that they are to remain at the Palestine Museum for study and to be published in the same series with the other fragments. It is expected that this will take about two years. It is reported that other material has been purchased on the same basis by the University of Manchester in England.

Thus far the work has continued to the time of this writing. It is certainly not finished. The only fit conclusion for this chapter seems to be the words "to be continued."

PART TWO

THE AGE OF THE MANUSCRIPTS

IV

The Evidence of Archeology and Paleography

⊔⊓

The most important question about an ancient document is not when it was written but what it means, and what historical or other significance it has. A book is not necessarily important because it is old, or unimportant because it is more recent. In our day, indeed, it is more commonly assumed that the latest book is the most important, but that too is a precarious assumption. Age and value are quite different matters, and neither necessarily depends upon the other. This should be obvious, but it has not always been remembered. There is some justice in the complaint that thus far the debate about the Dead Sea Scrolls has been too much preoccupied with the question of their age.

At the same time the interpretation of the texts cannot be completely separated from the question of their date. Particularly when we deal with the historical significance of a text, we cannot evade the question for what time in history it is significant. To use medieval documents as primary sources for pre-Christian Judaism would be like using one of President Eisenhower's messages to Congress as evidence of conditions in the time of George Washington.

When we are dealing with an ancient work preserved in one or more manuscripts, the question of the time when the book was composed depends in part on the age of the oldest surviving copy.

The manuscript may have been written much later than the original composition of the text it contains; it may be only the last of a long series of copies. But it cannot be older than its contents. If we can date the manuscript, we have at least the latest possible date to which the author and his work can be assigned. If it can be definitely proved, for instance, that the scroll containing the Habakkuk Commentary was made in the first century A.D. or earlier, we can be sure that the Habakkuk Commentary itself is not a medieval composition. Before discussing the question of the time when each work was originally written, we shall therefore consider the age of the manuscripts found in the caves of Qumran.

Anyone who has read the foregoing chapters knows already that even specialists do not agree as to the antiquity of the Dead Sea Scrolls. Some of the arguments for their divergent views have appeared incidentally in the course of our narrative. Clearly somebody must be wrong. All the evidence, if complete and interpreted rightly, would converge upon the one and only true conclusion, making it so clear and certain that there could be no disagreement. The evidence is actually not complete, and its interpretation is at many points not at all certain. The fact that many different kinds of evidence are involved makes the situation all the more confusing. There is still, therefore, room for considerable variety of opinion.

Some of the ideas that have been put forward, however, have been definitely disproved and should by this time be discarded. The range of possibilities has been narrowed, and the range of probabilities is narrower still. To see clearly how the matter now stands we must review all the kinds of evidence and lines of argument appealed to by scholars who have seriously studied the problem.

Not only must the time when the manuscripts were made be distinguished from the time when the books contained in them were composed; we must also distinguish the time when the manuscripts were made from the time when they were left in the caves. Some of them are obviously much older than others. Some were probably quite new when the caves were abandoned;

others were already old. In other words, the time when each manuscript was left in one of the caves may have been much later but was certainly not earlier than the time when it was written. If the abandonment of the caves can be dated, we shall therefore have the latest possible date for the most recent of the manuscripts.

Our first question, then, is when the manuscripts were left in the caves. This is tied up to some degree with the question of why they were put there in the first place. For some time after the discovery of the first cave there was a good deal of disagreement. Sukenik contended from the beginning that the scrolls had been placed in jars and hidden in the caves, not because they were highly valued, but because they were considered unfit to be used. The St. Mark's Isaiah manuscript, in particular, differed to such a degree from the standard text that, according to this view, it had to be abandoned. Such scrolls could not lawfully be destroyed. The common custom was to set them aside in a place called a genizah (from the Hebrew verb *ganaz,* to hide). From time to time the scrolls accumulated in the genizah were taken out and ceremonially buried. Sukenik held that the cave was such a genizah.

Supporting this theory, Henri Del Medico observed that the scrolls had been wrapped up in linen like mummies—"they were dead books." According to rabbinic regulations, not only defective copies of the sacred books but also works pronounced apocryphal by the religious authorities were relegated to the genizah. Both kinds of manuscripts were included among the Dead Sea Scrolls. Del Medico called attention to two particular efforts during the Roman period to gather up and dispose of unorthodox books. In the years just preceding the first Jewish revolt against Rome, in the first century A.D., false prophets were inciting the people to reckless violence by proclaiming that the divine deliverance of Israel was at hand. To allay the excitement and disorder Rabbi Simon ben Gamliel, son and successor of Gamliel I (the Gamaliel of Acts 5:34), sent men throughout the country to gather up all the writings of the false prophets and hide them in a secret place. This,

Del Medico suggested, might have been the occasion of the first deposit of manuscripts in the cave near Khirbet Qumran. The capture of Jerusalem and the destruction of the temple by the Romans in 70 A.D. was followed by the appearance of a new body of apocryphal literature, and Rabbi Gamliel II (about 92–100 A.D.) endeavored to confiscate these dangerous books. Most of the apocryphal texts found in the cave, said Del Medico, must have been put there at this time.

Against the idea of a genizah it was argued that manuscripts were ordinarily put in a genizah one or two at a time and later solemnly buried, but the manuscripts in the cave, carefully wrapped and packed in jars with covers to protect the contents from dampness, must have formed an extensive library, which was hidden in an hour of danger—not to dispose of it but to preserve it. Del Medico's idea that the scrolls were put in the cave on one or two particular occasions implies something rather different from an ordinary genizah; and the great care taken for the preservation of the manuscripts is hardly explained by his allusion to mummies.

Sukenik too, while insisting that the collection of manuscripts was a genizah, assumed that it was put in the cave on a particular occasion. He identified this with the migration to "the land of Damascus" mentioned in the Damascus Document, which is so called because of its references to this migration and to the new covenant which it says was made in the land of Damascus. Sukenik's view was that before leaving Judea the group discarded all of its manuscripts that were worn out, damaged, or in any way defective.

Sukenik and Del Medico were almost alone in considering the deposit of manuscripts a genizah. Most of the other writers who discussed the matter agreed with the excavators of the cave that the scrolls had been hidden to preserve them in a time of danger, when the group that used them was scattered by war or persecution, or perhaps compelled to emigrate in a body under circumstances that prevented them from taking their library with them. This hypothesis also, however, made use of the migration to the land of Damascus, which Sukenik supposed to be the occasion for using the cave as a genizah. Unfortunately we do not know when that migration occurred, if it occurred at all. Even scholars who believe that there was such a migration do not all agree that the scrolls were hidden at that time.

The whole question was placed in a new light by the discovery of the other caves and the excavation of the building at Khirbet Qumran. The large quantity of manuscripts represented by the fragments found in a number of caves showed that there must have been a library containing hundreds of manuscripts, with several copies of some of the books. Apparently the collection was broken up and placed in different caves for safekeeping when the community was forced to abandon the settlement of which the building at Khirbet Qumran was the center. The copper scrolls found in one of the caves testified even more forcibly than the manuscripts to the hasty abandonment of the place. Containing a long continuous inscription, which had presumably been affixed to a wall of the central building, they had been taken down, separately rolled up in two portions, and hidden in a cave about a mile and a quarter away.

The time when the caves and the manuscripts in them were abandoned can be determined only by archeological evidence. What, then, is the archeological evidence concerning the occupation and abandonment of the caves, and how conclusive is it? This may seem to be a somewhat embarrassing question for the archeologists, because their first conclusions were later found to be mistaken. What proved them wrong, however, was more archeological evidence, and it was the archeologists themselves who recognized and corrected the mistake.

Archeological evidence, as far as it goes, is the most solid and certain of all kinds of evidence for the reconstruction of past history. It consists of objective and undeniable facts. It may be and often is incomplete. Solid facts must then be supplemented by conjectures to provide even a hypothetical interpretation. The archeologist, however, knows what is fact and what is conjecture and recognizes the tentative nature of his interpretation.

The archeological evidence from the excavation of the first cave in 1949 consisted almost entirely of pottery. When coins and dated documents or inscriptions are lacking, pottery is the archeologist's chief criterion for determining when the site he is excavating was occupied. Vessels made of pottery, whole or more often smashed to bits, are found in abundance at all ancient sites except those from the very earliest ages. Systematic comparison of the results of many excavations enables archeologists to work out the succession of fashions in the forms, decoration, and material of pottery in each part of the ancient world.

Relying on this comparative "ceramic index" of chronology, the most competent experts in ancient Palestinian pottery were at first unanimous in pronouncing the jars found with the Dead Sea Scrolls "Hellenistic" or at least "pre-Herodian"—in other words, from the second century or the early first century B.C. Jars very much like them, though not exactly the same, had been found elsewhere, particularly at Beth-zur, together with coins of the Hellenistic period. The museum at Turin possesses two jars of similar form from Egypt, which contained papyri of the second century B.C.

The jars in the cave were all of the same general type. There was no indication of transition from one type to another or of the introduction of new types. Everything pointed to the same period, with the exception of the small quantity of Roman pottery, which the excavators then supposed to have been left by later intruders.

Just what was the relation between the jars and the manuscripts, of course, was not certain. There was much discussion on this point. Most of the debate took place before the excavation of Khirbet Qumran and the finding of other caves containing manuscripts, and consequently many arguments that seemed logical enough at the time were refuted by the later discoveries. Very few scholars seriously doubted that the manuscripts had actually been found in the jars, but there was much diversity of opinion concerning the relative antiquity of the jars and the scrolls. Because of the unusual shape and size of the jars—nearly 2 feet high and about 10 inches in diameter—some scholars supposed that they had been made for the express purpose of containing the scrolls. It was suggested that in a time of peril, when the manuscripts had to be hidden, the jars may have been made within a few days, as containers for them. Against this it was argued that in such an emergency men would not have lingered to design special containers and wait to have them made. But, said others, the emergency might have been foreseen before it became urgent.

Not all agreed that the jars and manuscripts came from the same period. Some said that even if the jars were made in the Hellenistic period, the manuscripts might have been written much later. Bandits in the days of Herod, or even warriors of the Maccabean period, might have used the jars for food and drink or to hold some of their booty, and then left them in the cave, where they were later found useful for storing the manuscripts. Some of the manuscript fragments in the cave, it was suggested, might have been the remains of older scrolls previously kept in the jars but later discarded and replaced by new manuscripts.

Even if the jars were made to contain scrolls, said one scholar, they might have served this purpose for centuries in a school or synagogue library. Worn-out manuscripts would then have been replaced from time to time by new ones. It was equally possible, of course, as many recognized, that some if not all of the manuscripts might have been much older than the jars. If the jars belonged to a library, some of its books might have been very old.

A few writers were never convinced that the jars were made in the Hellenistic period. Changes of style, it was pointed out, might have proceeded more slowly in remote areas, and the period of transition from Hellenistic to Roman types might have been of considerable duration. In that case the small amount of Roman pottery found with the jars might not be, as was supposed, a later intrusion. It might show merely that the Hellenistic culture had not yet been wholly superseded by the Roman culture in this region. Even if the jars were much older, indeed, the presence of Roman pottery with them might indicate only that the jars and manuscripts, after being long kept elsewhere, were moved to the cave in the Roman period.

At this point there was some confusion. The preliminary report of the excavation of the first cave, mentioning the handful of Roman sherds, dated them in the late second or early third century A.D. The first sounding at Khirbet Qumran in 1949 indicated an occupation of that site in the third or fourth century. It seemed reasonable to infer that the cave had been in use and the manuscripts had been placed in it during the third or fourth century, even though the manuscripts themselves and the jars containing them may have been much older.

When Khirbet Qumran was more fully excavated in 1951, Roman pottery of the same type and jars like those from the cave were found associated with coins attesting an occupation from the reign of Augustus (31 B.C.–14 A.D.) to the first Jewish revolt (66–70 A.D.). Other jars of the same type were later found, together with Roman pottery, in some of the other caves. When one of the jars was acquired by the Walters Art Gallery of Baltimore, Albright examined it and wrote to de Vaux that the "paste" or composition of the clay was "definitely Roman." By all these facts de Vaux was convinced that the jars themselves were not Hellenistic but Roman.

But if the jars were of later origin than had been supposed, the Roman pottery in the cave was earlier, not from the third or fourth century but from the first. The assumption of a later intrusion was thus rendered unnecessary, and the archeological evidence, reinterpreted in the light of more archeological evidence, was found to support the conclusion that the manuscripts had been deposited in the cave during the first two-thirds of the first century A.D. Father de Vaux so reported to the Académie des Inscriptions et Belles Lettres on April 4, 1952, adding, however, that the manuscripts were older than the pottery, and the texts copied in them were still older.

Archeological material of a different kind affords another means of dating the deposit of the manuscripts in the caves, though only within a range of time even wider than that indicated by the pottery. The first manuscripts discovered were wrapped in badly decomposed cloth, and innumerable scraps of the same material were found in the cave when it was excavated. Like the jars, the cloth wrappings may have been younger or older than the manuscripts, though it would seem more natural to wrap an old manuscript in new cloth than to wrap a new one in a very old piece of cloth. When Harding took the manuscript fragments from the first cave to England, in the summer of 1949, he took also some of the cloth and asked Mrs. G. M. Crowfoot to examine it. Another box full of pieces was later sent to her from Jordan. A microscopic examination of the fiber was undertaken by Major G. O. Searle of H. M. Norfolk Flax Establishment, who ascertained definitely that the cloth was linen.

According to Sukenik, the Bedouins who found the first scrolls threw out the linen wrappings because of the bad smell. Mrs. Crowfoot reported that when her first box of pieces was opened it emitted an odor "like that of an ancient Egyptian tomb." As far as the rottenness of the pieces permitted, she cleaned them carefully, mounted many of them, and studied the weaving technique and decorations. She concluded that the linen was of Palestinian manufacture, and that the wrappings of the scrolls were made especially for this use. Her examination, however, led to no definite conclusions concerning the age of the linen. Another piece from the cave was brought to the United States by Professor O. R. Sellers and examined by Miss Louisa Bellinger of Dumbarton Oaks and the Textile Museum at Washington. Her report also indicated that the linen was a native Palestinian product, and ancient, but that nothing more specific could be said concerning its date.

On this point more definite evidence was secured through the carbon-14 process, mentioned earlier, which, by measuring the rate of carbon-14 disintegration of a piece of organic material, can determine its age within a margin of error of about 5 to 10 per cent. Since this involves the destruction of the material, the process cannot be directly applied to the Dead Sea Scrolls themselves. The cloth in which they were wrapped, however, is not so precious as to preclude the sacrifice of some of it in such a good cause.

Professor J. L. Kelso, Director of the American School of Oriental Research at Jerusalem for the year 1949–50, brought back to America on his return a piece of the linen Harding had provided for the purpose of the test. As I have said, this was subjected to the carbon-14 process by W. F. Libby of the Institute of Nuclear Studies of the University of Chicago, one of the pioneers in the development of the process. His measurement showed that the piece of linen submitted to him late in the year 1950 was then 1917 years old, plus or minus 200 years; that is, it was made within 200 years of 33 A.D., or between 167 B.C. and 233 A.D. While this does not afford a precise date, it supports the other evidence to the extent of establishing a general period within which the linen wrappings of the scrolls were made.

Our first question is now answered. The scrolls found in the caves of the Wady Qumran were undoubtedly left there when the central building was destroyed and the neighborhood was abandoned. As our account of the excavations has shown, this was during the war of 66–70 A.D., quite possibly in the spring of 68. How long the manuscripts had been in the caves at that time is less certain, but de Vaux may well be right in believing that they were hidden at the time when the necessity of abandoning the settlement was imminent.

If the latest of the manuscripts must have been written before 70 A.D., our next question is how long before that they were written. The answer to this must of course be in terms of a somewhat protracted period, because the manuscripts were not all made at the same time. The fact that one of the rooms in the main building at Khirbet Qumran was evidently a scriptorium indicates that many of the manuscripts were written there during the two major periods of the occupation of the site. This would carry some of them back as far as the reign of Alexander Janneus at the beginning of the last century before Christ, or possibly twenty or thirty years earlier, to the reign of John Hyrcanus. The adjacent cemetery, with its more than a thousand graves, was evidently used during the same time. The first occupation of the site, however, does not fix the earliest possible date for the oldest manuscripts. They were not all necessarily written in this scriptorium. Some of them may have been brought to this place when the community was first established there, and they may have been already old at that time.

We are thus thrown back to the examination of the manuscripts themselves for the answer to our second question. Here our principal criterion must be paleography, the study of the form of script employed by the scribes. On this basis, the first announcements from the American School of Oriental Research and the Hebrew University agreed in dating the manuscripts not far from the beginning of the Christian era.

The controversy that ensued, it will be remembered, centered largely about the scientific status and reliability of paleography. The number of competent specialists in this field is not large, and not all who have made pronouncements on the subject belong to that number. The subject is too technical to be presented adequately here, but the most essential points may be stated in such a way that one who does not know the Hebrew alphabet can understand the nature of the problems and the major issues.

The essence of the method of paleography is the careful, exact comparison of the different forms of each letter of the alphabet found in documents of different periods, and their arrangement in tables showing the gradual modifications. This procedure is like that by which a paleontologist arranges fossil skeletons in order and shows how the prehistoric Eohippus evolved into the horse. No inherent process of evolution, of course, was at work in the history of the alphabet. We are dealing here simply with the fact that forms and styles of writing have actually changed as time went on, like styles of clothing, architecture, or pottery. The changes did not follow any inevitable or predictable course, but systematic observation enables us to determine the order in which they occurred and to arrange the successive forms of the letters in historical sequence.

Sometimes, instead of being gradually modified, a script has been abandoned and a different one adopted. Naturally we do not often find a sudden and complete replacement of one script by another, like the adoption of the Roman alphabet for the Turkish language in our own day. Even in that case, with a strong government endeavoring to enforce the change, it was not actually as complete as it was intended to be. A much less drastic change from one script to another took place in the history of ancient Hebrew writing.

The older script is often called Phoenician because it was used in Phoenician inscriptions, but it was also used in early times for writing Hebrew and other languages. It is perhaps most appropriately called Canaanite. Still another designation sometimes used is old or archaic Hebrew. Inscriptions found in Palestine and Transjordan from the period before the Babylonian exile are written with this alphabet. The other and later form of writing is the square or Aramaic script. This is found in documents from the fifth century B.C. and has been used in modified forms for writing Hebrew down to the present day.

The substitution of the Aramaic for the Canaanite script was not sudden, complete, or final. The old script appears again on Hebrew coins of the Maccabean period. The Samaritans still use a form of it. Some of the fragments found in the Judean caves employ this old script. In the Habakkuk Commentary it is used for the divine name, Yahweh, and one of the excavated fragments has the Hebrew word *El*, meaning God, written with the ancient alphabet in the midst of a text in the later square script. One fragment from Cave 4 even uses a mixture of the two scripts.

For the most part, however, we are concerned with a gradual process of modification within the square script. Even here there are complicating factors. Changes in the writing of different letters do not all proceed together like a line of well-drilled soldiers. Apart from individual peculiarities of handwriting, two manuscripts written not far apart in time will sometimes exhibit differences in the forms of some letters of the alphabet, while using the same forms for others. Some letters prove more significant than others because they show more clearly and consistently the evolution of the alphabet. Local, national, or sectarian variations may appear too, of course. Different writing materials also affect the script. When inscriptions are carved in stone the letters are not formed in exactly the same way as when documents are written on parchment with pen and ink.

Paleography by itself cannot fix specific dates. It can arrange manuscripts in a chronological series; but it cannot tell how far apart any two items of the series are in time except in a relative way by observing the number and degree of the differences. If the ends of the series or any of the items in it can be dated by other means, then the relative chronology determined by paleographical data can be pegged down at one or more points to a more exact date. In this respect paleography has much the same possibilities and limitations as the use of pottery for the same purpose.

Scholars who have questioned the dates assigned to the Dead Sea Scrolls on the basis of paleography have made much of these obvious limitations to justify their preference for other criteria. Some of these criteria are important, but it is a mistake to suppose that they are more exact or objective than paleography. The successive modifications of the letters of the alphabet are facts that can be observed, recorded, and studied; and their significance can be assessed by dispassionate discussion. If paleography is not an exact science, it is a scientific discipline in the sense that it deals with specific facts that can be recorded and studied objectively. It is becoming more and more nearly exact as the material accumulates.

Several scholars have said that for dating the Dead Sea Scrolls in particular paleography is of little use, because the material available for comparison is not sufficiently abundant, and what there is cannot be exactly dated. If what is meant is that we cannot assign a manuscript to a specific year or decade, this is true; we have quite adequate material, however, for determining the period to which a manuscript belongs within, say, a half or a quarter of a century.

Let us take a brief look at some of this material. Adopting the procedure of S. A. Birnbaum, and following in general his treatment of the material, we may begin with medieval manuscripts and work back to earlier texts. Birnbaum presents first a bill of

sale from the eleventh century A.D. A real similarity between such
a late text and the Dead Sea Scrolls would be significant. Actually
there is no such similarity, though Zeitlin had actually adduced
this very manuscript in support of his argument for a medieval
dating of the Dead Sea Scrolls. The bill of sale, in fact, is written
in a cursive script, related to the formal "book hand" of biblical
manuscripts somewhat as our handwriting is related to our printed
alphabet, though the difference is not so great. The same thing is
true of "Fragment B" of the Damascus Document from the tenth
century A.D., which Zeitlin cited in the same connection. This looks
a little more like the Dead Sea Scrolls, but it could hardly be mistaken for any of them.

Moving backward in time, Birnbaum gives charts showing some
of the most characteristic letters in the Dead Sea Scrolls side by
side with the same letters as they appear in a tenth-century codex
in Leningrad, a ninth-century codex in the British Museum, and a
fragment from the seventh century in the Cambridge University
Library. In another publication he shows also letters from a liturgical papyrus fragment of the eighth century A.D., whose script
has been supposed to resemble that of the Habakkuk Commentary.
Comparison of the forms in the tables reveals marked differences
among the Dead Sea Scrolls themselves, but the differences between any one of them and any one of the medieval documents
are much more notable. This is equally true of a fifth-century Hebrew letter that has been compared with the Habakkuk Commentary.

Birnbaum next presents a Hebrew papyrus fragment from Egypt,
which he dates in the fourth century A.D. Here some points of
similarity with the script of the Dead Sea Scrolls may be detected,
but the forms of the letters have developed much farther in the
direction of the medieval and modern scripts. From the early third
century comes a papyrus fragment of a liturgical text excavated at
Dura Europas on the Euphrates. Here again the script shows no
such resemblance to that of the Dead Sea Scrolls as to indicate
that they were contemporary.

Hebrew inscriptions of the third and second centuries exist in sufficient number to supplement the scanty manuscript material. They include mosaic pavements of synagogues, such as the famous mosaic of Beth Alpha, near Beisan, which shows the signs of the Zodiac with their Hebrew names. Two inscriptions from about 200 A.D., found at Beth Shearim in 1953, have been published. The forms of the letters in them contain nothing that requires any qualification of what has just been said.

Hebrew papyri and manuscripts from the second century A.D. have not been known until the last few years. Some of the manuscript fragments found in the caves of the Wady Murabbaat in 1952, however, are specifically dated in the first half of the second century A.D. Only preliminary accounts and a few photographs of them have been published, but these indicate that the forms of the script found in the fragments show a development well beyond that of the Qumran documents.

For the first century A.D. and the first century B.C. we have no definitely dated manuscript material for comparison. We are therefore largely dependent upon inscriptions. These include a few of the formal type usually indicated by the term "inscription"; there are also many of the more casual kind, known as graffiti, consisting chiefly of names scratched in stone. Most of the latter are found on ossuaries, small stone chests used as containers for human bones during the period from the beginning of Herod's reign (40 B.C.) to the destruction of the temple (70 A.D.). Such roughly scratched letters represent the ordinary writing of the time better than the more artistic and more artificial lettering of carefully carved inscriptions.

With the ossuary inscriptions may be mentioned a graffito found in the tomb of Queen Helen of Adiabene at Jerusalem, popularly known as the Tombs of the Kings. It is dated in the decade between 50 and 60 A.D. There is also, carved on the architrave of a tomb in the Kedron Valley at Jerusalem, a memorial inscription of eight priests of the family of the sons of Hezir. Its script is like that of the ossuaries, and, like them, it is generally recognized as belonging to the period preceding the destruction of the temple.

The closest affinities with the writing in the Dead Sea Scrolls that have been found anywhere appear in the graffiti on ossuaries and in a few other inscriptions of the same period. It is the script of the later scrolls, moreover, that the script of the ossuaries resembles most closely. Among the latest forms of writing in the scrolls found in 1947 is the script used in the Habakkuk Commentary and the Lamech Scroll. Trever and Albright find the closest resemblance to this in an Aramaic *dipinto*, or painted inscription, found in a Jewish tomb and published by Sukenik in 1934. Sukenik dated it shortly before the destruction of the temple; Albright puts it a little earlier, near the beginning of the Christian era.

More artistically carved, a really beautiful piece of work, is the Uzziah inscription, so called because it states that the bones of King Uzziah of Judah were moved from their previous resting place to the place where this inscription was originally set up. Like the ossuaries, it cannot be dated exactly, but it has long been recognized as contemporary with them. Albright dates it after the outbreak of the revolt of 66–70 A.D. It therefore affords a further basis for comparison with the Dead Sea Scrolls, and the results of the comparison are the same as in the case of the ossuaries.

For anything like the script of the older Dead Sea Scrolls we must go back still further. About a century older than the inscriptions just mentioned are some quite different in nature, but still significant, with proper and obvious qualification. These are the brief inscriptions carved on boundary stones found long ago at Gezer. No exact date can be given for them, but epigraphists are agreed in assigning them to the first half or third of the last century B.C. The letters in these inscriptions, though quite roughly cut in the stone, are notably like those of the St. Mark's Isaiah Manuscript.

Another very brief inscription, but more neatly carved than the Gezer boundary inscriptions, appears beside the doorway of a rock-cut tomb at Araq el-Emir, east of the Jordan. There is also another inscription like it nearby. This is the place where the Tobiads, a Jewish family prominent in the third and second centuries B.C., built a famous castle, the ruins of which can still be seen there. We shall hear of the Tobiads again. The inscription, which consists merely of the name Tobiah, is dated by Birnbaum between 183 and 175 B.C., though Vincent considers it still earlier by more than a century. The forms of three of the five Hebrew letters in it resemble those in the St. Mark's Isaiah scroll, while the other two are earlier. Even allowing for the possibility that the script of an inscription carved in stone might be more conservative than that of a manuscript written with pen and ink, we may fairly suppose that with this inscription we have reached a point not far from the time when the Isaiah manuscript was written—if, indeed, we have not gone back a little beyond it.

From here on we again have papyri to compare with our scrolls. First of all there is the much-discussed Nash Papyrus, which was first noted by Trever as having a script resembling that of the Dead Sea Scrolls. Trever places it, paleographically, between the earliest and the latest Dead Sea Scrolls, later than the St. Mark's Isaiah manuscript and the Manual of Discipline, but earlier than the Habakkuk Commentary, the Lamech Scroll, and the latest corrections in the Isaiah manuscript. Unfortunately the date of the papyrus itself is still disputed. The earliest date claimed for it is that of Birnbaum, who assigns it to the early second century B.C. He puts the Isaiah scroll slightly later, in "about the second quarter" of the century. He thus disagrees with Trever as to the relative age of these two manuscripts, but agrees with him that they cannot be dated far apart. For myself I can only say here that, on the basis of Birnbaum's own tables, the Nash Papyrus still seems to me slightly later than the Isaiah scroll and very close to the Manual of Discipline. The resemblances are so close, and the differences so slight, that it is hardly safe to say more than that all three manuscripts probably belong to the same half or three-quarters of a century.

The comparison must be carried back, of course, not merely to the point where we find a script so close to that of the Dead Sea Scrolls as to indicate the same period; it must be pursued to a point where documents appear in a script clearly earlier than that of the scrolls. With the Nash Papyrus we have almost reached that point.

Two Aramaic papyri and a few ostraca from the third century B.C., found at Edfu on the upper Nile River, have been published. Driver objects to their use for our purpose on the ground that they "come from a different country, and their bulk is insufficient to afford a proper standard of comparison." This would have some force if it were claimed that the comparison conclusively demonstrated a specific date, but no such claim is made. As a part of the total picture, together with all the other material, comparison with these texts is valid and significant.

The Edfu papyri and ostraca exhibit a form of the alphabet definitely more archaic than that which appears in the Dead Sea Scrolls or the Nash Papyrus. Whether this means that they were actually written at an earlier time—and, if so, how much earlier—may be open to argument; but until some reason to believe the contrary is shown it is fair to suppose that the documents with the more archaic script are earlier in date. Birnbaum adduces also a legal papyrus of the third century B.C., now in the Bodleian Library at Oxford, and by comparison with the Isaiah scroll concludes that here "we have gone too far back." The forms of the letters in the Isaiah scroll fall between those of the papyrus and those of the ossuaries.

That the period of the Dead Sea Scrolls has been passed becomes still more evident when we move back two more centuries, and farther up the Nile, and consider the Aramaic papyri found at Assuan, the ancient Elephantine. These documents come from a Jewish military colony that lived in Egypt in the fifth century B.C. In these documents, which use a very early form of the square script, there are still some interesting similarities with the script of the Dead Sea Scrolls, but there can be no question that the papyri were written long before the Dead Sea Scrolls. An even earlier papyrus from the sixth century B.C. has been compared with the Isaiah scroll by Birnbaum.

This survey, while by no means exhaustive, will give a fairly adequate idea of the amount and nature of the material at the disposal of the paleographer. Its use, to be convincing, obviously demands much closer attention to innumerable details than can be given here. One great advantage of the Dead Sea Scrolls, as compared with brief inscriptions or papyrus fragments, is that we have not one or a few examples of each letter but a great many. In order that the uninitiated reader may see more clearly how the forms of the letters changed in the course of the centuries, typical forms of the letter *m* are shown here in Figures 1 and 2.

Literary records have been adduced in an effort to control or refute the findings of paleography. Zeitlin "has studied all passages in the Talmud and Midrash wherein the forms of the Hebrew letters are described." Examining the forms of *h* and *m* in the Dead Sea Scrolls in the light of this literary evidence, he reaches the conclusion that they are the forms used in the second and third centuries A.D. If we had no actual documents for comparison that could be even approximately dated, this line of argument might be impressive; but even if the date and authenticity of the rabbinic statements could be safely assumed, verbal descriptions of letters of the alphabet would have to be very exact indeed to be as reliable as actual examples in manuscripts and inscriptions. The descriptions quoted by Zeitlin do not inspire much confidence in this respect.

Five of the letters of the Hebrew alphabet (*k, m, n, p,* and *ṣ*) have two forms in the developed square script. One is used at the beginning or in the middle of a word and is called the "medial" form; the other is used at the end of a word and is called the "final" form. The use of the two forms of these letters and the distinction between the medial (or initial) and final positions developed gradually and unevenly. In the St. Mark's Isaiah manuscript the two forms of *m* and *n* are used, but the "medial" form of the *m* often appears at the end of a word, and the "final" form is sometimes found in the middle of a word. The other three letters in this group do not yet have special final forms, though the *k* and *ṣ* are somewhat longer when written at the end of a word. The Manual of Discipline exhibits much the same phenomena.

In the Habakkuk Commentary and the Hebrew University's Isaiah manuscript, at the other end of the series of Dead Sea Scrolls, all five letters have their final forms, and these are regularly

	(a)	(b)	(c)	(d)
1				
2				
3				
4				
5				

Line 1—Forms in the St. Mark's Isaiah scroll
2—Forms in the Manual of Discipline
3—Forms in the Habakkuk Commentary
4—(a) Manuscript A of the Damascus Document
(b) Manuscript B of the Damascus Document
(c) A Dura parchment
(d) A Wady Murabbaat fragment
5—(a) The Uzziah Inscription
(b) The Nash Papyrus
(c) An Edfu papyrus
(d) An Elephantine papyrus

FIGURE 1. EVOLUTION OF THE LETTER M: MEDIAL FORMS

used in the final position. The Dead Sea Scrolls themselves, therefore, provide important evidence for the development of the final forms of these letters. Within the St. Mark's Isaiah scroll, as a matter of fact, there is an interesting bit of such evidence, for a passage omitted by the first scribe and later inserted has a final *p*, which occurs nowhere else in the manuscript.

Can these facts be used to establish the age of the scrolls? Here again statements in the rabbinic literature have been adduced to establish the time when the final forms of the letters were adopted, and hence the dates of the Dead Sea Scrolls. H. Tur-Sinai (Torczyner) argues that the partial and irregular use of the final letters in the St. Mark's Isaiah manuscript corresponds to a rabbinic deci-

Line 1—Forms in the St. Mark's Isaiah scroll
  2—Forms in the Manual of Discipline
  3—Forms in the Habakkuk Commentary
  4—(a) Manuscript A of the Damascus Document
      (b) Manuscript B of the Damascus Document
      (c) A Dura parchment
      (d) A Wady Murabbaat fragment
  5—(a) The Uzziah Inscription
      (b) The Nash Papyrus
      (c) An Edfu papyrus
      (d) An Elephantine papyrus

FIGURE 2. EVOLUTION OF THE LETTER M: FINAL FORMS

sion at the beginning of the second century A.D., whereas the regular use of all the final forms in the later Dead Sea Scrolls represents the practice at the middle or end of that century. Zeitlin contents himself with the claim, likewise based on rabbinic pronouncements, that the final forms of the five letters were introduced after the destruction of the temple and "came into vogue" after the time of Akiba, but were still not well established in the second century.

This conclusion is made untenable by the archeological demonstration that the manuscripts were already in the caves before the end of the first century. It is refuted by other considerations also. Birnbaum has shown that the Talmudic passages on which it is based do not really imply what Tur-Sinai and Zeitlin infer from them. Even if they did, their testimony could not outweigh the plain fact that the final forms are actually found in papyri and inscriptions before the second century A.D.

Forms resembling the final or "closed" form of $\dot{m}$ begin to appear as early as the fifth century B.C. Final forms of n and p also are found in the Edfu papyri and the ossuaries. The use of the "final" form in the medial position and the "medial" form in the final position, as in the St. Mark's Isaiah manuscript, is characteristic of the ossuaries also.

Aside from the way in which the separate letters are formed, an important characteristic of the writing of the scrolls is the use of ligatures connecting two successive letters. In the centuries with which we are concerned ligatures occur more frequently in earlier than in later documents. In the papyri of the fourth and third centuries B.C., and in the Nash Papyrus, they appear often, but from the early half of the first century they become more and more rare. By the third century A.D. they have practically been abandoned. They appear frequently in the Dead Sea Scrolls, especially in the St. Mark's Isaiah scroll.

The letters of the Hebrew alphabet are all consonants, though a few of them came to be used also for vowels. Systems of signs for the vowels began to be used by about the fifth century A.D. The presence or absence of such "vowel points" is therefore significant for dating manuscripts. In the manuscripts found in the Cairo genizah, vowel signs are occasionally used. None appear in the Dead Sea Scrolls. Some excitement was aroused for a while by a scholar's announcement that he had detected what he thought might be vowel signs in the Habakkuk Commentary, but these proved to be only accidental specks such as occur often in the manuscripts, without any relation to the writing. While the absence of signs for the vowels is not positive evidence of an early date, their presence would have been an important indication of a relatively late date.

Thus far we have considered only the forms of the square or Aramaic script used in the Dead Sea Scrolls. The picture is complicated and made more interesting, however, by the fact, already mentioned, that the archaic script also appears in some of the manuscripts. Here two problems must be distinguished: the occasional use of the archaic script for the divine name, and for the word for God—*El*—in the midst of texts otherwise written in the square script; and the use of the archaic script for entire manuscripts. The occasional use may be considered first.

The material available for comparison in this case is less plentiful and satisfactory than what we have found for the study of the square script. For the period before the Babylonian exile there is an abundance of material, including the Lachish Letters of the sixth century B.C., written on potsherds. For the centuries after the Babylonian exile, when the Aramaic script was coming into general use, we have much less comparative material for the old Hebrew script. There are many Phoenician, Punic, and neo-Punic inscriptions. There are also Jewish coins using the old alphabet from the Maccabean-Hasmonean period (second and first centuries B.C.) and from the two Jewish revolts against Rome (66–70 and 132–135 A.D.). The highly developed and ornamental form of the archaic script used by the Samaritans is found in many inscriptions from the early Christian centuries.

On the basis of this varied and yet not very plentiful material David Diringer considers the writing of the divine name in the Habakkuk Commentary "stylized and rather unusual" and thinks it was done "by a scribe who had no experience of early Hebrew script." The writing of the word *El* in a fragment from the first cave, on the other hand, he regards as "non-stylized" and "probably in the same literary hand as the Leviticus fragments." Birnbaum finds the form of the archaic script used for the divine name in the Habakkuk Commentary intermediate between the Lachish Letters and the Jewish coins. Baruch Kanael concludes from a comparison with the coins that the manuscripts of the Habakkuk Commentary and the Thanksgiving Psalms (in one of which the word *eli* appears in the archaic script) were written between the reign of Herod and the destruction of the temple, that is between 40 B.C. and 70 A.D.

A somewhat different kind of evidence has been adduced to

support a later date. Copies of Greek translations of the Old Testament written during the early Christian centuries sometimes used Hebrew characters for the divine name. Some of them used the square characters, or Greek letters more or less resembling them, but two fragments, one of the third century and one of the fifth century A.D., have the divine name in the old Hebrew script. Another example has now appeared in one of the Greek fragments from Khirbet Mird. The third-century theologian Origen wrote that in the best biblical manuscripts of his day the divine name was written in the ancient Hebrew characters. Jerome also, about a century later, remarked that in some Greek manuscripts the divine name was still found in archaic letters.

While there may be some connection between this practice in Greek translations and the use of archaic characters for the divine name or the word *El* in Hebrew texts, we cannot take the one as proving anything about the other. The indirect literary evidence of Origen and Jerome could not at best have equal weight with the paleographic evidence of the texts themselves; its implications in any case are not at all clear. The usage of the Greek manuscripts, in short, has no significance for our purpose.

We thus come to the other problem, the use of the old Hebrew script for entire texts, as exemplified by the fragments of Leviticus found in the first cave in 1949 and the other fragments in the archaic script that have been found since in other caves. For comparison here we have not only the relatively late material already mentioned but also the whole mass of ancient inscriptions in the old Hebrew script. None of this, it is true, is quite like the Qumran fragments. We have no other texts in the archaic script written on leather or parchment. The fragments are also the only known specimens of a formal "book hand" in that script. In comparing them with the inscriptions we must remind ourselves again that different kinds of writing may be used contemporaneously. Characters carved in stone, the formal book hand of literary manuscripts, and the cursive script of such documents as the Lachish Letters, written with ink on potsherds, may differ considerably.

The differences are not so great, however, as to make the inscriptions and letters useless for comparison.

The Leviticus fragments from the first cave have been carefully compared by paleographers with the ninth-century B.C. Mesha inscription, the ostraca of Samaria, and the Siloam inscription of the eighth century B.C., seals and seal-impressions and the stamped impressions on jar-handles of the seventh and sixth centuries B.C., the Lachish Letters of the sixth century B.C., later jar-handle stamps of the fifth and fourth centuries B.C., Jewish coins of the first century B.C. and the first and second centuries A.D., and Samaritan inscriptions ranging in date from the second century A.D., or earlier, to the eighth or ninth century. The conclusions reached vary quite widely, placing the fragments at dates ranging from about 450 B.C. to about 50 B.C.

This discrepancy of about three centuries in the conclusions of competent scholars is somewhat disturbing. Those who put no trust in paleography cannot be blamed for contemplating it with satisfaction. The explanation may be found in the nature of the evidence. The material for comparison is all somewhat different in character from the Leviticus fragments, being carved in stone, stamped in clay, or written on potsherds instead of skin, while the script is either monumental or cursive rather than literary. This fact may be enough to explain why the interpretation of the same data by competent scholars can differ so widely. Diringer points out also that a professional literary script like that of the Leviticus fragments might become standardized and continue in use for several centuries without much change.

Yet while the evidence is unsatisfactory, it is not negligible. We can be quite sure that the fragments are not earlier than the fifth century B.C. or later than the first century B.C. The earlier rather than the later half of this period of five centuries seems more likely, unless the script was deliberately archaistic.

As was the case in the other matters previously discussed, the argument concerning the date of the Leviticus fragments was not allowed to rest on paleographic comparisons alone. Literary evidence was adduced to show that the use of the old Hebrew alphabet by Jews continued down into the present era. Without denying that the square script was commonly used for biblical manuscripts in the first century A.D., scholars have found reason to believe that the old Hebrew script also continued in use, and that biblical manuscripts in that script were still in existence as late as the second century. A rabbinic statement that only texts written in the square script were holy has been used as evidence both for and against this contention. It seems most reasonable to infer from it that the old script would no longer be used for new manuscripts of the law, even if old manuscripts written with the ancient alphabet still survived. In any case, conjectures based on literary sources have no force as against the concrete data of paleography. These point, as we have seen, to a pre-Christian date, probably not later than the third or second century B.C. What is most significant, after all, is not the mere fact that the old script is used, but the particular form of it used in each manuscript.

It must be remembered that all this discussion is concerned with the five Leviticus fragments found in 1949. Very few of the numerous fragments in the archaic script found later and now being studied at the Palestine Museum have yet been published. F. M. Cross, who has been working on them, has mentioned the third century B.C. as a possible date, but he considers it more likely that the script is an archaizing revival of the second century, the Maccabean period.

The science of paleography involves more than the forms of the letters. Other characteristics of the manner of writing must be considered also. One of the most conspicuous features of the Dead Sea Scrolls is the fact that lines were carefully ruled to guide the writing. The antiquity of this practice is well attested. The Palestinian Talmud attributes it to a regulation of Moses from Sinai. Zeitlin dismisses this as merely a fictitious justification of what was really a new procedure only recently adopted from the Greeks and Romans. Birnbaum considers it rather an indication that the process was known to be very ancient. He cites another statement by a famous second-century rabbi, which carries the origin of the ruling of manuscripts back to Adam. In fact, he points out, even the Leviticus fragments in the old Hebrew script are ruled.

Still another feature of the scrolls that comes under the heading of paleography is the use of marks in the margins of the columns. The Habakkuk Commentary frequently has a simple cross like a capital X at the end of a line. Similar crosses appear occasionally in the St. Mark's Isaiah scroll, but in the margin. Teicher has interpreted these as the Greek letter *chi*, which he thinks stood for *Christos* and was used to mark Christological passages. This is a corollary to his theory that the covenanters were Jewish Christians. I. Sonne has shown that it involves several improbable assumptions. He takes the X to be a Hebrew *taw*, meaning simply "mark," and believes that it was used to mark passages considered for any reason helpful or useful. In the St. Mark's Isaiah scroll and in the Manual of Discipline there is often a short horizontal line in the margin, or a line having a hook at one end. Most striking, however, are several very elaborate and mysterious signs in the margins of these two manuscripts.

The meaning of all these signs has not yet been satisfactorily explained. Some of them may mark passages selected for public reading or regarded as especially significant for doctrine. Some may possibly call attention to errors in copying that require correction. Some are so elaborate as to tempt one to regard them as mere idle "doodling" by an absent-minded scribe or student, but of course such an explanation can be entertained only as a last resort. For a convincing solution of the problem we may have to wait until comparable examples of the same kind of marking have been found in other manuscripts.

When the fragments found in the excavation of the first cave in 1949 were exhibited in London, Kahle announced that he had found writing on both sides of some of them, showing that they had been parts of books in codex form—i.e., volumes of bound pages. On the ground that manuscripts are not known to have been made in this form in the East before the second century A.D., Kahle concluded that the latest of the manuscripts in the cave could not be earlier than that century. To this Birnbaum replied that none of the fragments written on skin had writing on both sides. Six out of about thirty fragments of papyrus bore writing on both front and back, but in no case was the writing clearly the same on both sides; in fact, in three fragments it was plainly different, and in one the writing on the two sides ran in different directions. It seems more likely, therefore, that these pieces of papyrus had been used twice than that they were parts of pages from codices.

Still other considerations have helped to complicate the plot. It was supposed at first that one of the fragments found in the first cave bore two Greek letters. Later it was seen that these characters more probably belonged to a cursive Hebrew script found on some of the other fragments. Kahle thought he could identify on one fragment two letters of the Estrangelo Syriac script, which was probably unknown in Palestine before the first or second century A.D. Other scholars, however, who have looked for these letters could not find them.

The net result of all the investigation and debate concerning the paleographical evidence is that the initial impressions of those who first examined the scrolls from this point of view have been substantially confirmed. The arguments of those who maintained a date later than the first century A.D.—to say nothing of the Middle Ages—have been refuted both by the archeological evidence from the excavations and by the paleographical evidence of the manuscripts themselves. There are still differences of opinion as to the quarter or half of a century to which this or that scroll should be assigned. There is less agreement regarding the fragments in the archaic script. Among scholars qualified to judge the paleographic data, however, no great divergence concerning the major scrolls remains. There is even some justification for the complaint of Birnbaum that the whole debate was not a controversy among paleographers but an attack on paleography by specialists in other fields.

Unexpected confirmation of the general result has been afforded by the later material found in the caves of Wady Murabbaat. Some of these texts contain exact dates. Their script is plainly much later than that of the Qumran scrolls and fragments. The reliability of the paleographical method of dating manuscripts has thus been brilliantly vindicated.

While paleography remains our principal means of determining how old the manuscripts are, there are some other criteria to supplement and check its results. One of these is the nature of the material of which the scrolls are made. The use of leather and papyrus instead of parchment for the scrolls has been adduced as evidence for a date before the fourth century A.D. The significance of this fact, however, is only relative at best. As far as it goes, it supports the rest of the evidence, but it is less precise and less conclusive than the other criteria afforded by archeology and paleography.

Not only the skin but the ink has been considered as a means of dating the manuscripts, but it has not proved helpful. From statements in the Talmud, scholars have inferred that metallic ink was not used by the Jews before the second or third century A.D. Birnbaum has pointed out, to be sure, that the ink of the Lachish Letters in the sixth century B.C. already contained iron. But when the ink on the manuscript fragments from the first cave was analyzed in 1949 by Dr. Plenderleith of the British Museum, it was found to be non-metallic. Later this proved true also of the dried ink in one of the inkwells unearthed at Khirbet Qumran. The composition of the ink, therefore, provides no evidence concerning the age of the Dead Sea Scrolls.

All the lines of investigation converge fairly well on a historical period within which all the manuscripts were written, extending from about 300 B.C. to 68 or 70 A.D. The relative age of the different manuscripts is fairly clear also, and the approximate place of each within the period is reasonably assured. Two more lines of investigation, however, have been pursued, and we must still consider the results of these inquiries. They are concerned not with the leather and ink or the forms of the letters, but with the language and text of what is written in the manuscripts.

V

The Evidence of Text and Language

⊔⊔⊔⊔⊔⊔⊔⊔⊔⊔⊔⊔⊔⊔⊔⊔⊔⊔⊔⊔⊔⊔⊔⊔⊔⊔⊔⊔⊔⊔⊔⊔⊔⊔

If it could be assumed that the original compositions had been copied without change or error, the form of the text and the language of the documents would have no immediate bearing on the age of the particular copies found in the caves. Actually manuscripts are never copied with complete accuracy. The ancient scribes were not always as careful as they might have been, and the best of them were only human. It is interesting to observe how often they made the same kinds of mistakes that typists and printers make now.

When many copies of various ages are available for comparison, as in the study of the Greek text of the New Testament, it is possible to group the manuscripts by types and families in a kind of pedigree, and so to determine more or less completely the history of the text with its successive modifications. For the Dead Sea Scrolls this line of investigation is open only in the case of the biblical manuscripts, because they are the only ones of which we have other copies. Even for these, unfortunately, we do not have other manuscripts of an age approaching that of the Dead Sea Scrolls. Between the two Qumran manuscripts of the book of Isaiah and the next oldest Hebrew manuscripts of that book there is a gap of several centuries, to put it very conservatively. Consequently we cannot compare the scrolls with any older copies of the Hebrew text.

Aside from the scrolls and fragments from the Wady Qumran

and a few scraps of papyrus from Egypt, all our manuscripts of the Hebrew Old Testament contain the text as it was edited and standardized during the first few centuries of the Christian era. This was done by Jewish scholars called Masoretes (from the Hebrew word *masora,* meaning tradition), and the text they established is called the Masoretic text. The question at issue as regards the age of the Dead Sea biblical manuscripts is their relation to this Masoretic text.

The large extent of agreement with the Masoretic text in some of the scrolls has been cited as evidence against an early date. Since the Masoretic text was not fixed before the Christian era, it is assumed that any text that agrees with it cannot be pre-Christian. Stated thus baldly, the argument involves obvious fallacies. It is never actually put quite so crudely, but the fallacies are only obscured by the refinements of the argument. Before considering how these considerations affect the dating of the Dead Sea Scrolls, we must examine the presuppositions a little more closely.

First of all, the time when the Masoretic text was established is not a fixed point, before or after which any form of the text can be dated. The standardization of the text was not an event but a process. In the second place, the Masoretes did not create an entirely new text; they did not compose a new Bible out of nothing. They tried to discover and restore the correct text. An absolutely correct text, if it could be recovered, would be the original text as it came from the author of each book. The best attainable text is that which goes back most nearly to that original form. The Masoretes, in other words, were editing ancient writings. If they were at all successful in achieving their purpose, a manuscript written long before their time might and should agree closely with the text which they adopted. This would show only that they had good manuscripts at their disposal and did their work well.

If a long manuscript agreed exactly with the Masoretic text at every point, or with only rare exceptions, then we might reasonably infer that it was a copy of the standard text established by the

Masoretes, and consequently that it was made after they did their work. In a brief passage, however, even complete agreement proves nothing except that the text adopted by the Masoretes agreed at this particular point with the one followed by the scribe who made the manuscript. No scholar would seriously maintain that every copy made before the time of the Masoretes would necessarily differ from their text in every verse, yet this seems to have been tacitly assumed in much of the discussion of the Dead Sea Scrolls.

Differences from the Masoretic text, on the other hand, do not necessarily indicate that a manuscript was written before the time of the Masoretes. The official adoption of a standard form of the text and the elimination of all other forms are two different matters. Unofficial texts varying considerably from the standard may have remained in existence for some time.

Three stages in the formation of the Masoretic text must be distinguished. First, there was the gradual development of various forms of the text, including that which was later to be accepted as normative. No one manuscript, perhaps, contained the whole text of any book exactly as the Masoretes adopted it. Their work was presumably eclectic, and perhaps even to some extent creative, though not intended to be so. On the whole, however, the text they approved must have had ancient traditions behind it.

The second stage was therefore the choice among variant traditions, involving a decision as to what reading was to be accepted for each verse and word. Third and last came the elimination of all manuscripts that did not conform to the approved text. Not until after this had been accomplished would the production of new manuscripts containing variant readings cease altogether. Only when all new copies were carefully corrected, and all old or new copies that differed from the official norm were destroyed, was the process of standardization complete. That point may not have been reached before the eighth century A.D.

The importance of these distinctions becomes apparent when one reads what has been written about the text of the St. Mark's Isaiah scroll. This manuscript is full of minor deviations from the

Masoretic text in details of spelling and grammar. There are also many variant readings of greater importance. In Isaiah 34:17–35:1, thirty-one words which the scribe had omitted were later inserted between the lines in a hand which we have already seen to be different from that of the rest of the scroll. Unlike the rest of the manuscript, this inserted matter agrees throughout with the Masoretic text. On the ground that this text would not have been available before the second century A.D., it has been argued that the completed manuscript, with this correction in it, could not have been left in the cave before the second century. Here one sees clearly the strange and quite unwarranted assumption that agreement with the standard text, even in a brief passage, is inconsistent with a pre-Masoretic date.

The difference between the inserted words and the rest of the manuscript is more significant than their agreement with the Masoretic text. It indicates, or at least suggests, that the scroll may have been already quite old when these words were copied into it. Another insertion at the end of Chapter 38 agrees likewise with the Masoretic text, whereas the main text to which it has been added differs from that of the Masoretes at many points. This fact has been taken as evidence of the early origin of the scroll itself and of a considerable interval between the time when it was first written and the time when this addition was made. During this interval the Masoretic text is supposed to have become generally known and accepted. This does not necessarily follow, however. All that we can safely say is that during the interval the same readings in these verses that were adopted by the Masoretes had been accepted by the corrector who made the insertions.

Before drawing conclusions from the differences between the St. Mark's Isaiah scroll and the Masoretic text, we must ask how far they are merely mistakes made in the writing of this manuscript. Certainly there are many obvious mistakes, including the omission or addition of one or more words, the confusion of words and letters, the substitution of one word for another, the transposition of words or of letters within a word, and various errors of other kinds. A few of these may be mentioned here by way of illustration.

There are a good many omissions, sometimes of considerable extent. In Isaiah 2:9–10, where there is clearly something wrong with the Masoretic text, the scroll omits twelve Hebrew words. The omission does not improve matters. Probably the text followed by the scribe was already corrupt, and he could make nothing of it. The scroll contains three good examples of a familiar error called *homoioteleuton,* the omission of a passage between two occurrences of the same word or two words that end with the same letters. In Isaiah 4:5f. the phrase "by day"—in Hebrew an adverb —occurs in the middle of verse 5 and again in the middle of verse 6. Our scribe has skipped from the former occurrence to the latter, omitting what comes between. In Chapter 16 the town of Sibmah is mentioned in verse 8 and again in verse 9. Again the scribe has jumped from the one to the other, leaving out in this instance twenty words. The city of Tyre is named twice in verse 15 of Chapter 23, and again the same thing has happened.

These are errors of the eye rather than of the ear. If our manuscript was written from dictation, as there is some reason to believe, it must have been the reader's eye that jumped from one word to another, unless the error had already been made in the copy from which he was reading. As we have already observed, words omitted have been inserted later in a number of places, sometimes in the hand of the scribe himself and sometimes in a later hand.

The scroll has also some additions to the traditional text. To the words "your hands are full of blood" in Isaiah 1:15 our text adds "and your fingers of iniquity." These words occur later in 59:3 and may have been inserted here through a slip of memory. In 34:4 the clause "and all the host of heaven shall be dissolved" becomes "and the valleys shall be cleft asunder and all the hosts of heaven shall fade." The mention of valleys goes well with the references to mountains in the preceding verses, but the repetition introduced into the latter part of the verse arouses suspicion. At the end of 52:12, after the words "the God of Israel," the scroll adds, "the God of all the earth shall he be called." Here again these words, which appear later in 54:5, may have been inserted by an error of the scribe or reader, or by one of their predecessors.

Diametrically opposite inferences have been drawn from the abundance of such mistakes in this manuscript. If a manuscript is made soon after the composition of the book it contains, it should be relatively free from errors. The mistakes naturally accumulate as one copy after another is made. For this reason it has been argued that the St. Mark's Isaiah scroll is too full of mistakes to be very ancient. On the other hand, the very fact that such liberties are taken with the biblical text has been cited as proof that the manuscript must be pre-Masoretic. Certainly the degree of accuracy in a manuscript is no sure indication of its age. The Masoretic text undoubtedly rests on manuscripts both older and better than the St. Mark's manuscript of Isaiah. At the same time this manuscript is certainly older than the work of the Masoretes. The archeological and paleographical evidence we have already discussed is sufficient proof of that.

Aside from obvious or probable mistakes in copying, there are many variations that cannot be explained in this way. Even so, by and large the wording of the text is substantially the same as that of the Masoretes. This very fact, indeed, has been used against it. Zeitlin argues that if the scroll were pre-Christian it would have some of the variant readings found in early rabbinic sources. He gives a list of fifty such variants and finds that in all cases the scroll agrees with the Masoretic text instead of the rabbinic sources. Here again is the curious assumption that a pre-Masoretic text would necessarily be different from the Masoretic text. It is even assumed that the differences would necessarily be the same as those in the rabbinic literature. Neither assumption, or course, is justified. To suppose that before the official text was fixed there was one and only one set of variant readings is purely gratuitous. The fact that two quite different manuscripts of Isaiah were found in the same cave shows that more than one type of text was known at the same time in the same place. This was what made the work of the Masoretes necessary. Zeitlin's argument has been subjected to searching analysis by I. Sonne, who not only exposes the unwarranted assumptions it involves but also shows that the list of variants is itself open to criticism. Some of these readings do not appear in the best manuscripts of the same rabbinic sources. Sometimes other quotations of the same biblical text elsewhere in the same source actually agree with the Masoretic reading.

The manuscript of Isaiah acquired by Sukenik in 1947 agrees very closely with the Masoretic text. This may well mean that it is considerably later than the St. Mark's manuscript, as the paleography indicates. It is surely unnecessary to say again that the agreement with the Masoretic text does not demonstrate a date after the fixation of the text. The archeological evidence shows that this is impossible. The agreement shows simply that this scroll represents the same textual tradition as the manuscripts followed by the Masoretes.

The Habakkuk Commentary quotes the text of all but the third chapter of Habakkuk, except that the beginning of the first chapter is lost. Kahle holds that this manuscript was copied before the destruction of the temple, because it has not been influenced by the Masoretic text. It is not quite clear just what is meant by the influence of the Masoretic text, or how such influence could be detected. To do this with certainty would require a knowledge of the earlier text that is supposed to have been altered under the influence of the Masoretic text. It seems precarious also to assume that any manuscript copied after the destruction of the temple would necessarily betray influence of the standard text. Delcor, in fact, denies Kahle's claim that the text of Habakkuk in the Commentary shows no such influence. Even where a different reading is given in quoting the text, the commentary on it sometimes seems to imply the Masoretic reading. We can only conclude that the text of Habakkuk in this document gives no significant evidence of the date of the manuscript. Certainly it contains nothing to cast doubt on the results reached in other ways.

Birnbaum remarks that even the text of the Leviticus fragments in the old Hebrew script agrees with the Masoretic text. He rightly observes, however, that this affords no basis for dating the fragments, since the material is very scanty, and the date of the Masoretic text itself is disputed. Other fragments found in the caves show marked deviation from the readings of the Masoretes. The fragments of the books of Samuel consistently agree with the Septuagint as against the Masoretic text. They have also some readings not attested elsewhere, which seem to be superior both to the Masoretic text and to the Septuagint.

By and large it appears that the form of the biblical text in the Dead Sea Scrolls cannot be used as evidence for dating them. Arguments based on it involve too many questionable assumptions to be convincing. The dates of the manuscripts must be established on other grounds; then conclusions can be drawn from them concerning the history of the text. What these conclusions may be we must consider when we are ready to discuss the importance of the manuscripts.

For at least one of the scrolls, if not more, some indication as to the time when the manuscript was made is afforded by its language. In general the language of a document indicates the date of the original composition rather than that of a particular copy. Since no text is ever copied exactly, however, the language may be altered more or less consciously by the copyists under the influence of their own language or dialect. Even in printed books the spelling and to some extent the language is often modernized in new editions of such works as Shakespeare's plays, not to mention the King James Version of the Bible.

A conspicuous example of such alteration is the St. Mark's Isaiah scroll. The book of Isaiah certainly comes from a time several centuries before the earliest date to which this manuscript can be assigned on any grounds. Most of the differences between the scroll and the Masoretic text consist of changes in spelling and in the grammatical forms of words. In these respects, with some notable exceptions, the Masoretic text has preserved a form of the Hebrew language closer to the dialect of Jerusalem as it was spoken in the time of Isaiah than the language of the scroll is. In other words, the text of the scroll has more changes in grammar and spelling from the original language of Isaiah than the Masoretic text has. The manuscript thus represents a particular dialect of Hebrew, or a particular stage in the history of the language. Our question now is whether this affords any clue for dating the manuscript.

Some of the peculiarities in spelling may be attributed to the ignorance or carelessness of the scribe. The fact that he is not consistent in his idiosyncrasies shows that he was not adhering to any particular system of orthography. His peculiar spelling may betray merely a lack of education. It may reflect also a stage of transition in Hebrew orthography.

The most conspicuous feature of the orthography of this manuscript is its lavish use of what is known as *scriptio plena*—that is, the use of letters of the alphabet to indicate vowels. Since the Hebrew alphabet consists only of consonants, there were many possibilities of ambiguity in written texts until ways of indicating the vowels were devised. As in English the consonants *bd* might represent *bad, bed, bead, bid, bud, bide, bode, abide, abode,* or even *body,* so a group of Hebrew consonants may often represent any one of several words. There are many places in the Old Testament where reading the same consonants with different vowels makes a material difference in the meaning of the text. In our printed Hebrew Bibles the vowels are indicated by a system of "pointing" devised in the Middle Ages.

Before this or any similar system had been invented, the only means of indicating the vowels was the use of *w* to indicate *o* or *u,* of *y* to indicate *i* or *e,* and of *h* to indicate *a* or sometimes *o* or *e.* Another letter used in this way was *aleph,* the first letter of the alphabet (represented in transliteration by '), which did not originally represent the vowel *a,* as in our alphabet, but a light consonantal sound, the so-called glottal stop.

The practice of using these "vowel letters," technically called *matres lectionis,* began very early; but it was not highly developed until after the Old Testament period. In the St. Mark's Isaiah scroll it is followed to an extraordinary degree. The result is that many words appear longer than they do in the Masoretic text, and this effect is enhanced by the use of longer forms of some pronominal suffixes. The difference is sometimes almost grotesque. For instance, *bhltw* becomes *bhwlywtyw; r̄šm* becomes *rw'šyhmh.*

The prevalence of *scriptio plena* in this scroll has been discussed by scholars at considerable length in the effort to establish the date of the manuscript. Such a lavish and unsystematic use of *matres lectionis* would hardly be found in a biblical manuscript written after the text had been standardized. Kahle has called attention to the fact that the use of vowel letters is not uniform throughout the manuscript. The *scriptio plena* is used more freely in Chapters 34–66 than in Chapters 1–33. The paleography does not change, but the same scribe may have followed two different manuscripts for the two halves of the book. Kahle therefore sees here an indication of two different types of text. He does not infer that either type was earlier than the other, but merely that the two manuscripts used by our scribe exemplified different habits of spelling.

The difference between the two halves of the scroll in this respect is real. Kahle's explanation of it, however, is not necessarily correct. The change at the end of Chapter 33 is not quite so sharp or complete as he implies. Monsignor Patrick Skehan, who is preparing a collation of this manuscript for the American Schools of Oriental Research, feels that the scribe merely slipped into a less exact manner of copying and indulged more freely in the use of vowel letters as he went on.

When did the *scriptio plena* begin to be used? Some scholars, attempting to use the orthography of the scroll as an aid in dating it, have made much of the idea that vowel letters were unnecessary so long as Hebrew was a living language. This is not quite true: there is always a large degree of ambiguity in a merely consonantal text even for a people brought up in the living use of the language. Vowel letters, or some other indications of the vowels, were unnecessary only when and where the correct pronunciation of the text was preserved by oral tradition. The written text was then only an aid to memory. The introduction of vowel letters in biblical manuscripts may have been motivated by a fear that the correct oral tradition was dying out, or by the fact that divergent oral traditions had developed. Against the view that *scriptio plena* came into use when Hebrew ceased to be a living language, Birnbaum argues that Hebrew was no longer the spoken language of the Jews in the third century B.C., when the Greek version known as the Septuagint was made; yet the Septuagint often presupposes different vowels from those of the pointed Masoretic text, thus showing that there were possibilities of misunderstanding that would not have existed if vowel letters had been used.

An interesting variation on the theme that *scriptio plena* was introduced because Hebrew was no longer a living language has been put forward by Kahle. The vowel letters must have come into general use, he says, at a time when many Jews were beginning again to study Hebrew. This points to the nationalistic revival of the Maccabean period. From that time on until the destruction of the temple the use of vowel letters was customary. Kahle therefore takes the abundant use of them in the St. Mark's Isaiah scroll, especially its second part, to indicate that the scroll was written between the Maccabean period and 70 A.D. This conclusion is more convincing than the argument. A more probable view is that *scriptio plena* was introduced gradually during the centuries before the Masoretes established the standard text, and the Masoretes eliminated most of the vowel letters on the basis of their oldest manuscripts.

According to Driver the introduction of *scriptio plena* did not precede but followed the Masoretic standardization of the text. It was just coming into use in the third century A.D., he argues, because Origen makes very few mistakes that can be explained by a lack of vowels in his manuscripts, and Jerome in the fourth century makes hardly any such mistakes. The earliest attempts at vowel-pointing were made in the fifth century. After that the *scriptio plena* was unnecessary and began to die out. The free use of vowel letters in the Dead Sea Scrolls leads Driver therefore to the conclusion that they cannot be dated before the time of Origen or Jerome. This argument is extremely precarious. The absence of mistakes in reading vowels in Origen and Jerome may indicate only that they were still acquainted with an accurate oral tradition of the pronunciation.

There is abundant evidence of *scriptio plena* long before the time of Origen. Vowel letters begin to appear in inscriptions as early as the eighth century B.C., though their use was not fully developed until later. They occur much more frequently in the latest books of the Old Testament than in the earlier books. A study of Hebrew orthography by Cross and Freedman points to the Maccabean period as the time when *scriptio plena* reached its highest development.

The peculiarites of orthography in the St. Mark's Isaiah manuscript and other Dead Sea Scrolls are not necessarily to be explained in terms of time only. They may, at least in part, represent local differences. It is possible also, as Kahle points out, that the free use of vowel letters was characteristic of unofficial or "vulgar" texts. A group like that which produced the Qumran manuscripts may not have felt bound by the rules governing scribes who made "official" copies for the temple and the synagogues.

It is a curious fact that mutually contradictory arguments have been based on the presence or absence of *scriptio plena*. Sukenik's manuscript of Isaiah agrees very closely with the Masoretic orthography. Kahle holds, therefore, that it could not have been written before the second century A.D. But the spelling of the Masoretes was not a new creation of the second or third century. It is more reasonable to suppose that this manuscript follows an older text, not influenced by the newer type of spelling used in the St. Mark's manuscript.

Sukenik himself stated the matter accurately. During the last century before the destruction of the temple, he said, the full writing with vowel letters was already being used to facilitate reading, both in new compositions and in the ancient text of the Bible. During the same period, however, biblical manuscripts using the older orthography were in circulation also. Sukenik's manuscript preserves the old spelling; the St. Mark's manuscript uses vowel letters to indicate the pronunciation of the words; but both scrolls were probably read with the same pronunciation.

Other distinctive features of the spelling in the St. Mark's manuscript are of purely technical interest and need not be mentioned here. Frequently the spelling is so peculiar as to suggest that the scribe was writing by ear rather than copying another manuscript directly. He may have been writing from dictation or even from memory. In any case, he was unquestionably rather careless and often used a kind of rough-and-ready phonetic spelling of his own.

There is one rather important indication, however, that in some respects he was following a very ancient tradition. His spelling of proper names and titles, as Dewey Beegle has shown, is sometimes more in accord with their original meaning than the spelling of the Masoretes. For example, the Assyrian title that is spelled *Tartan* in the Masoretic text appears in the scroll as *Turtan*. The original Assyrian form is *turtannu*. The name given by the Masoretes as *Sharezer* is *Sharuzer* in the scroll, corresponding again more closely to the Assyrian spelling. The Masoretic text spells *Rabshakeh* as one word; this was originally an Assyrian title consisting of two words, and in the St. Mark's manuscript there is a space between them—*Rab Shakeh*. The preservation of forms closer to the original Assyrian names or titles does not necessarily prove that this manuscript is very ancient, but it indicates dependence at these points on a tradition older than the Masoretic text.

From all this it can be seen that for the purpose of dating the St. Mark's Isaiah scroll its distinctive orthography gives little help. It neither confirms nor refutes the conclusions of archeology and paleography. At most we may say that it is not inconsistent with those conclusions.

But the language of the scroll has other distinctive features. There are peculiarities not only of spelling but also of grammatical forms in the Dead Sea Scrolls, and especially in the St. Mark's Isaiah scroll. Since many of the readers for whom the present book is intended cannot be expected to know Hebrew, only a general indication of a few of these grammatical peculiarities can be given here. For example, in some places where the Masoretic text has unaccented short vowels, there are vowel letters in the scroll suggesting that in the dialect of its scribe these vowels were long and presumably accented. Certain pronouns and suffixes that end with consonants in the Masoretic text have an additional long *a* at the end in the manuscript. This is rather striking, because such a final *a* is believed to have been used in the earliest form of the language; it then dropped out of use in Hebrew, but it reappears in medieval compositions, probably under the influence of classical Arabic. Occasionally it appears in the Masoretic text of the Old Testament, where it can be explained either as an archaic survival or as a medieval innovation. Apparently the Qumran community still used the old pronunciation. It is worth noting in this connection that the Samaritan dialect still preserves these final vowels.

Other grammatical features of the St. Mark's Isaiah scroll suggest Aramaic influence. Some have supposed, therefore, that the manuscript must have been written after Aramaic had become the language of Jewish scholars. Others have argued, however, that these forms support an early date for the manuscript, because they do not appear in the transcription of the Hebrew text in Greek letters given by Origen in his Hexapla. Aside from affinities with the Aramaic language in general, points of contact with the Palestinian Christian dialect of Aramaic have been noted.

To make a long story short, it seems that while the spelling of this scroll is relatively late, the grammatical forms indicated by that spelling are older than those preserved in the Masoretic text. The syntax as well as the forms of the words sometimes differs from that of the Masoretes, but these differences cannot be described without using technical language. As in the spelling and the forms of words, there is no consistency in the peculiarities of syntax. The scribe who wrote the manuscript followed his copy on the whole, but now and then he slipped into forms of speech more familiar to him in his own dialect. All these facts are important for the historical grammar of the Hebrew language, but in the present state of our knowledge they afford no clear evidence as to the age of the scroll. In fact, the linguistic peculiarities need not have originated in this particular manuscript; many of them may conceivably have crept into the text in earlier copies.

These matters of spelling and grammar must be investigated in all the biblical texts found in the caves, with the Masoretic text as a basis of comparison. For the non-biblical texts we have no other manuscripts to serve this purpose. It is impossible to tell

how far the language in these documents is that of the original
compositions, and how far it has undergone such changes in the
course of the transmission as we find in the St. Mark's Isaiah scroll.
We have therefore no means of knowing how far the linguistic
evidence reflects the time of the author of each book and how
far it reflects the time when the manuscript was made. It is fairly
safe to assume that the difference in time between the original
composition of the non-biblical documents and the making of the
Qumran manuscripts containing them was considerably less than
in the case of the biblical texts. Even this rule, however, may have
exceptions. The fragments of the book of Daniel, for example, may
be as near in time to the composition of the book as the scroll of
the Manual of Discipline is to the time when that work was
composed. Only in a very general and tentative way, therefore, can
any conclusions as to the age of these manuscripts be drawn from
their language. In fact, the criterion of language has proved to
to be of much less use for dating the manuscripts than was at first
supposed.

Before we leave the subject of the age of the manuscripts, one
more line of evidence remains to be mentioned. Soon after the
first discovery of the scrolls in 1947 became known, scholars began
to recall references to similiar discoveries in early Christian times.
The Masoretes, de Vaux reminds us, sometimes cite variant readings from a text they call the Jericho Pentateuch. The great third-
century theologian Origen compiled an edition of various Greek
versions of the Old Testament called the Hexapla. He mentions
as the source of one of his texts a discovery of manuscripts at or
near Jericho. The discovery is mentioned also by the fourth-century
church historian Eusebius and by Jerome. Eusebius says that it
occurred during the reign of the emperor Caracalla (211–217 A.D.).
Origen was in Palestine in 217, and it was probably then that he
secured his manuscript. It was, of course, in Greek and was
found among other Greek manuscripts, but Hebrew manuscripts
also are said to have been found with them.

It is not impossible that Origen's manuscript came from one of
the caves that have recently been explored, but the discoveries in

the Wady Qumran do not indicate that the Judean covenanters possessed Greek manuscripts. In any case, we do not know how old the manuscripts that were discovered in Origen's time were.

The letter of Timotheus concerning a discovery of manuscripts at about 800 A.D. is mentioned in Chapter III. Naturally there has been much discussion about the authenticity of the story told by Timotheus and its possible relation to the Dead Sea Scrolls. Before the discovery of other caves it was natural to suppose that the first cave might have been the one mentioned by Timotheus. Now, however, even assuming a substantial degree of authenticity for the story of Timotheus, we have no reason to identify the cave involved in that incident with the one found in 1947 or with any of the caves discovered later. The story merely underlines the fact that manuscripts were often hidden in caves in ancient times.

Perhaps no more than this can be inferred from another reference to a discovery of manuscripts in a cave, which is given by the tenth-century Karaite Al-Qirqisani. In the second chapter of his history of Jewish sects, just after speaking of the Sadducees, he says, "Thereupon appeared the teaching of a sect called Magharians; they were called so because their books were found in a cave" (the Arabic word for cave being *maghara*). What relation, if any, these Magharians may have had to the covenanters of the Wady Qumran we must inquire in Chapter XIII.

Stanislav Segert has called attention to still another medieval report of a discovery of ancient Hebrew manuscripts in a cave. This is found in a letter written by a diplomat at the court of the caliph of Cordova to the king of the Khazars in the tenth century A.D. Speaking of the Chaldean conquest of Judah in 586 B.C., the writer says that at that time the Jews "buried in a cave the books of the law and the holy writings, and on this account they prayed in the cave." The letter continues:

And because of the books, they taught their sons to pray in the cave evening and morning until the times were prolonged, and in the multitude of days they forgot and did not know concerning the cave why they were accustomed to pray within it, but carried on the custom of their fathers without knowing why. But at the end of many days there arose a certain Jew, and he sought to know why; and he came to the cave and found it full of books and brought them out from there. And from that day until now they set their faces to learn the law. Thus our fathers have told us as the men of old heard, hearing from the mouth of one who heard, and these matters are ancient.

Here, as Segert points out, the circumstances and manner of the discovery are entirely different from those related in the letter of Timotheus. The story implies that the cave to which it refers was much larger than any of the Wady Qumran caves. While the incident has obviously no connection with the one of which Timotheus tells, Segert suggests that this cave may be the one in which the books of the Magharians were found, as related by Al-Qirqisani. We have then at least two if not three independent medieval accounts of discoveries of manuscripts in caves. Such discoveries, Segert concludes, were probably frequent. Saul Liebermann recalls a statement of the thirteenth-century Rabbi Moses Taku that the Karaites of the eighth century used to hide their heretical writings in the ground and then take them out and claim that they had discovered ancient books. Such a charge by their enemies might grow out of actual discoveries of old manuscripts.

None of these literary references to manuscript discoveries has any direct connection with the caves in which the Dead Sea Scrolls were found. These accounts have therefore no real bearing upon the time when the scrolls were left in the caves, to say nothing of the age of the manuscripts before they were put there. They are of interest merely as illustrations of an ancient custom.

The net result of all the investigation into the age of the manuscripts found in the caves may be summarized very briefly. They were all made before 70 A.D. Between the earliest and the latest of them a considerable period intervened. The earliest of the biblical fragments may possibly go back as far as the third century B.C. but are probably a century or more later. The oldest of the more or less complete scrolls, the St. Mark's Isaiah scroll, probably comes from a little before 100 B.C., or possibly a little later. The Manual of Discipline cannot be dated much later than 100 B.C.

From perhaps the last quarter of the first century B.C. comes the manuscript of the Habakkuk Commentary. The Lamech Scroll, the War scroll, the scroll of the Thanksgiving Psalms, and the Hebrew University Isaiah scroll were all probably made during the first half of the first century A.D. The innumerable fragments of other manuscripts from the Wady Qumran lie scattered along the way between 100 B.C., or earlier, and 70 A.D. The Wady Murabbaat fragments and other texts, of course, are later.

PART THREE

THE DATES OF COMPOSITION

VI

Historical Allusions in the Habakkuk Commentary: The Kittim

Unless a manuscript comes from the author of the book himself, its age does not indicate the time when the work it contains was first written. When the date of the earliest extant copy is known, we know that the book was in existence at that date, but we cannot tell how long it had been in existence or how many copies had been made in the meantime. The time when a book was first composed must be determined by internal evidence.

The most important and specific internal evidence is that of historical allusions. Before coming to this, however, one other kind of internal evidence must be mentioned briefly. As a possible indication of the age of the Dead Sea Scrolls we have considered their language. To the degree that the author's language has not been altered by later copyists, the language of a book is also a criterion of the original date of its composition. The biblical texts in the Dead Sea Scrolls have had in general a longer time than the non-biblical works to undergo alteration by copyists. Even in the non-biblical manuscripts some allowance must be made for the possibility of changes in language, but on the whole it may be assumed that there has been less change here than in the biblical manuscripts. We may regard the language of the non-biblical documents as approximately that of the authors themselves.

The Habakkuk Commentary exhibits many of the same linguistic features as the St. Mark's Isaiah scroll. Here too there are peculiarities of spelling and grammar for which parallels have been found in Aramaic, in the Samaritan and rabbinic dialects of Hebrew, and in early medieval Hebrew poems. Aside from these particular points, the language is quite simple; it is drawn almost entirely from the Old Testament, giving the impression, as van der Ploeg says, that the author was not a highly educated man, but knew the Hebrew language chiefly from reading the Bible. Much the same features of language appear also in the Manual of Discipline. Some words that seem to be late are used; at any rate they have been known hitherto only in rabbinic or medieval literature, simply because we have almost no other post-biblical literature in Hebrew with which to compare them. Driver characterizes the Thanksgiving Psalms as "the work of a scholar playing in his study at composition in a dead language." The fairness of this description is open to question; but in any case it gives no indication of date, because Hebrew was already a dead language for the Jewish people in general long before the Christian era.

The fact is that the language of these texts does not enable us to tell when they were written. If we had no evidence of other kinds, the apparently late expressions and forms might seem, as they have seemed to some scholars, to indicate a date well down in the Christian era. In broad terms we may describe the type of Hebrew represented by the scrolls as intermediate between the Hebrew of the latest Old Testament books and the rabbinic dialect. Nothing in the language of the scrolls, in any case, is necessarily inconsistent with composition in the early post-biblical period down to 70 A.D., the latest possible date for the latest of the manuscripts.

Far more exact and certain internal evidence of the time when a book was written may be found in its historical allusions, if there are such and if they are sufficiently specific. References to reigning monarchs, to contemporary world powers, and to particular persons and events often provide conclusive evidence for dating ancient documents. In considering the Dead Sea Scrolls from this point of view, we must of course examine each composition separately, just as each manuscript has been examined separately from the point of view of paleography.

It must be emphasized also that the arrangement of the manuscripts in a chronological series indicates nothing as to the order in which the books were originally composed. Early manuscripts cannot contain late books, but late manuscripts may be simply new copies of much older writings. An important example of this fact is the relation of the Dead Sea Scrolls to the Damascus Document. Because the manuscripts of this work found in the Old Cairo genizah can be dated in the tenth century A.D., many centuries later than the Dead Sea Scrolls, it is all too easy to assume that the book itself was written later than the works contained in the scrolls; but the fact that the manuscript of the Manual of Discipline, for instance, is centuries older than the manuscripts of the Damascus Document does not prove that the Manual of Discipline is a more ancient composition than the Damascus Document. The possibility that the Damascus Document may be as early as any of the non-biblical Dead Sea Scrolls is now demonstrated by the fact that fragments of it were found in the Qumran caves.

Of all the Dead Sea Scrolls, the one that is richest in historical allusions is the Habakkuk Commentary. Particular groups, persons, and events appear in this text, though unfortunately in such a vague and ambiguous way that they have suggested several plausible arguments for quite different theories. Before accepting any such theory we must ask whether it fits the references in the text and fits them better than other theories do, and also whether the persons and events referred to are mentioned as being in the distant past, as recent, as contemporary, or as future. Sound historical procedure requires further that we try to interpret the historical references in this work on their own merits, without any presupposition as to the relation between it and other documents. Parallels in other texts will have to be considered later, but it must not be taken for granted that the same term necessarily means the same thing in two different documents.

As has been said, the allusions in the Habakkuk Commentary are not too specific. With one barely possible exception, no proper names are given. In their place we have vague, mysterious designations. They are not like the weird symbolic beasts and horns of some of Daniel's visions, but resemble rather the references to "the king of the south" and "the king of the north" in Daniel 11. Perhaps the persons and groups referred to are deliberately disguised in order to avoid censorship and persecution. To the members of the community the references would be obvious.

Elliger explains the absence of proper names on the supposition that the writer is speaking of his contemporaries. So today, he says, we do not say "George VI" but "the king;" we do not say "Pius XII" but "the pope." The analogy is not wholly convincing. In the United States, at least, we often speak of our President by name (or nickname!) instead of saying simply "the President." Incidentally Elliger's illustration affords an instance of the possibility of dating a text by historical allusions—he evidently wrote it before the accession of Queen Elizabeth.

Before we examine the references in the Habakkuk Commentary it may be well to sketch the background by reviewing briefly the history of the times with which we are concerned. A fairly detailed account is provided for us by the Jewish historian Josephus, who lived in the first century A.D. We cannot, of course, expect the author of our commentary to express the same attitudes toward persons and events that we find in Josephus. On controversial matters the two writers may represent opposite sides. It cannot be assumed, moreover, that either account is entirely accurate. Ignorance of the exact facts or prejudice may have distorted the record. With Josephus we can sometimes compare material in the apocryphal and rabbinic literature. A succinct summary of much of the history appears in fairly transparent symbols in the eleventh chapter of Daniel.

For our purpose three major periods may be distinguished: the pre-Maccabean, the Maccabean or Hasmonean, and the Roman. Following the death of Alexander the Great and the division of his empire, Palestine lay between two of the resulting kingdoms.

the kingdom of the Ptolemies in Egypt and the kingdom of the Seleucids in Syria. For about a hundred years, coinciding almost exactly with the third century B.C., Palestine was under the dominion of the Ptolemies. During the first third of the second century (198–168 B.C.), the Seleucids held Palestine. This brings us to the end of the pre-Maccabean period.

The Maccabean period begins with the revolt of Judas Maccabeus in 168 B.C. This achieved first religious and then political independence. The Jewish kingdom that then emerged was ruled by the descendants of Judas's brother Simon, who are called Hasmoneans. The terms Maccabean and Hasmonean are not used uniformly by historians. For convenience we may here consider them practically synonymous and so call the period beginning with 168 B.C. the Maccabean or Hasmonean period. This lasted until 63 B.C., when the Roman general Pompey annexed Palestine to the Roman province of Syria, thus inaugurating the Roman period of Palestinian history.

The first quarter-century of Roman domination was followed by the reign of Herod the Great (37–4 B.C.), the pseudo-independent reigns of his sons, and the successive but hardly successful administrations of several Roman procurators. The suffering and resentment of the Jews led to the armed revolt of 66 A.D., the bitter war with the Romans, and finally the capture of Jerusalem and destruction of the temple by Titus in 70 A.D. The three periods within which we must try to place the historical allusions of the Habakkuk Commentary are therefore the pre-Maccabean (to 168 B.C.), the Maccabean or Hasmonean (168–63), and the Roman (63 B.C.–70 A.D.).

The archeological evidence, as we have seen, makes any date later than 70 A.D. impossible for the composition of any of the Dead Sea Scrolls. Since the manuscript of the Habakkuk Commentary, however, is one of the relatively late scrolls, a considerable range of possibility is left open for the original composition of the book. The author may have lived and written this commentary, so far as archeology and paleography can determine, at any time before 70 A.D.

Many of the references in the commentary have to do with the internal affairs of the community. One term, however, clearly refers to foreign invaders and conquerors. They are called the Kittim. Who are the invaders designated by this term? Within the chronological limits we have in view there are two possibilities. The Kittim might be the Macedonians (Alexander or his successors, the Ptolemies and Seleucids), or they might be the Romans. Can we tell whether the Macedonians or the Romans are referred to in what is said about the Kittim?

The word Kittim (a plural form) occurs several times in the Old Testament. In Genesis 10:4 the sons of Javan are said to have been Elishah, Tarshish, Kittim, and Dodanim. The parallel text of I Chronicles 1:7 is the same, except that it has Rodanim instead of Dodanim (a good example of the way *d* and *r* are often confused in Hebrew manuscripts). In Isaiah 23:1 the name Kittim occurs at the beginning of an oracle against Tyre. While the King James Version here reads Kittim (spelled Chittim), the Revised Standard Version reads Cyprus, and this is clearly what is meant (so also in verse 12 of the same chapter, in Jeremiah 2:10, and in Ezekiel 27:6). In Numbers 24:24, however, the meaning seems less specific; accordingly the Revised Standard Version reads, "but ships shall come from Kittim." This verse is quoted in Daniel 11:30, "for ships of Kittim shall come." Here the context shows that the reference is to the Romans, and the Septuagint reads "ships of the Romans." The Aramaic Targum, in fact, reads "Romans" in Numbers 24:24, but that can hardly be the meaning there. The opening verse of I Maccabees says that Alexander the Great came from the land of Kittim, and in 8:5 King Perseus of Macedon is called king of Kittim. The Book of Jubilees also refers to the Macedonians as Kittim (24:28f).

In view of all these facts it is reasonable to ask first whether the Macedonians are not the foreign invaders called Kittim in the Habakkuk Commentary. Several scholars hold that they are; others, however, believe that the name here refers to the Romans, as in Daniel 11:30. The theory that the Kittim are the Macedonians, or more specifically the Seleucids of Syria, implies or at least admits an earlier date of composition than the theory that they are the Romans. The decision must rest on the interpretation of details in the text. We must therefore consider what the commentator says about the Kittim and examine the interpretations put on what he says by the advocates of the Macedonian and Roman theories respectively. It will be sufficient here to quote or summarize very briefly the passages referring to the Kittim. For greater detail the translation of the Habakkuk Commentary at the end of this volume may be consulted.

The Kittim are "swift and men of valor in battle." They "do not believe in the statutes" of Israel's God. "Over smooth ground they go, smiting and plundering the cities of the earth." They plan evil and carry out their plans "with cunning and deceit." They "trample the earth with their horses and with their animals; and from afar they come, from the coasts of the sea, to devour all the peoples like a vulture without being satisfied. And with wrath and indignation, with hot ire and furious anger they deal with all the peoples." They "mock at great ones and despise honored men; of kings and princes they make sport, and scoff at a multitude of people." They "despise the fortresses of the peoples and with mockery laugh at them, and with a multitude of people they surround them to seize them, and in terror and dread they are delivered into their hands; and they overthrow them because of the iniquity of those who dwell in them." Once the commentator speaks of "the rulers of the Kittim, who by the counsel of a guilty house pass on, each before his fellow: their rulers come, one after another, to destroy the earth." At another point the commentator says, apparently referring to the Kittim, that "they gather their wealth with all their booty like the fish of the sea." The reference is clearly to the Kittim when he adds that "they sacrifice to their standards, and their weapons of war are the object of their worship." Again, they "parcel out their yoke and their tribute, their food, upon all the peoples year by year, laying waste many lands." In their ruthless advance they "cause many to perish by the sword—youths, men, and old men; women and little children—and on the fruit of the womb they have no mercy."

And finally, speaking of "the last priests of Jerusalem," the commentator says that they "assembled wealth and booty from the spoil of the peoples, but at the end of days their wealth with their spoil will be delivered into the hand of the army of the Kittim, for they are the remainder of the peoples."

Most of this might be said of any invading army, but there are a few points that are more specific, and they have been seized upon as evidence for one theory or the other. Much of the debate has dealt with ambiguous expressions that may as plausibly be connected with one nation as with another. Only a very few points can really be accepted as unequivocal evidence; in fact—we may as well admit it at the outset—not one of them is definitely conclusive. Otherwise, of course, there would have been no debate. The most we can hope for is a preponderance of probability on either side.

Let us hear first the exponents of the Macedonian theory. In the clause, "over smooth ground they go," the expression I have translated "smooth ground" means literally something straight or level. Talmon translates the clause, "by level road they will come." Others render the word "plain." Delcor suggests that what is meant is the high plateau east of the Dead Sea, between the Arnon River and the city of Heshbon. This is mentioned, he believes, because it was a part of the territory conquered by the Hasmonean king, Alexander Janneus (103–76 B.C.), the particular reference here being to a campaign of the Seleucid king Antiochus XII (87–84 B.C.) against the Nabateans. There is nothing in the text to substantiate such a specific allusion. The phrase "over smooth ground" may, in fact, mean only "smoothly" or "unopposed."

The mention of the "cunning and deceit" of the Kittim has been taken as pointing to the Seleucids because these qualities are often attributed to them by I Maccabees and Josephus, whereas the Romans are given credit for wise counsel and patience. Against this, it is recalled that cunning and deceit were equally characteristic of the Roman general Pompey.

Another argument for the Macedonians as the power referred to is drawn from the commentator's statement that the Kittim "trample the earth with their horses and with their animals." E. Stauffer and others take the "animals" to be the war elephants of which the Seleucid kings were so proud that they had them pictured on some of their coins. Dupont-Sommer replies with dry irony that the elephants are indeed a weighty argument, but the Hebrew language has a word for "elephant." Our commentator says "horses" when he means horses; why should he not say "elephants" if that is what he means? The noun translated "animals" is actually used here in the singular; it is intended, says Dupont-Sommer, in a collective sense to include all kinds of animals used by the armies. Of course the singular could also be used in a collective sense for elephants.

Elliger agrees that Stauffer's elephants cannot carry the load he puts on them. Michel, on the other hand, still insists that some kind of animals used in battle must be meant, and these could only be elephants; but it is quite possible that the word refers to beasts of burden accompanying the army. Only if other and more conclusive evidence shows that the Seleucids are contemplated have we any reason to think of elephants at all in this connection. There is nothing to show that the "animals" were any more characteristic of the Kittim in particular than were the horses. These too, as a matter of fact, are taken by Michel to indicate the Seleucids. Citing the frequent references in I Maccabees to the formidable numbers of the Seleucid cavalry, he observes that cavalry are not mentioned in connection with the Roman campaign of 63 B.C. against Judah. Perhaps the horses are stronger evidence for the Seleucid hypothesis than the elephants.

The statement "from afar they come, from the coasts [or isles] of the sea," is applied to the Seleucids also. Josephus says that two of the Seleucid kings had mercenaries from "the islands." In I Maccabees, Antiochus Epiphanes is said to have sent letters from "the isles of the sea." This is not very impressive evidence. As a matter of fact, the noun used in the commentary does not necessarily mean "isles." It is often used for coastal regions. In Daniel and I Maccabees it may be that the islands, not the coasts, of the Mediterranean are meant. The reference in the commentary is much too vague and general, in any case, to be restricted to any particular people or event.

Other allusions are equally indefinite. The description of the ruthlessness of the Kittim would be appropriate for the Macedonians or the Romans. The wrath and fury with which the Kittim are said to deal with their victims, and even more their insolence and mockery, are stressed by Michel as fitting the Seleucids much better than the Romans. The boastful, derisive words of Antiochus Epiphanes and his generals are often mentioned in I Maccabees and Daniel. The haughty pride of the Romans is well known, but it does not seem to have been particularly evident in their treatment of Judah in 63 B.C. Michel suggests that the "great ones" and "honored men" whom the Kittim despised may have been the Jewish priests and elders who were insolently mocked by the Macedonian general Nicanor in 161 B.C.; the "kings and princes" of whom the Kittim "made sport" may have been the kings of Egypt and the lesser rulers of the East who were treated with scorn by Antiochus Epiphanes. All this may be true if the Kittim are the Seleucids, but it gives us no positive evidence to that effect.

A rather curious argument is derived by Michel from an apparent contradiction which he sees between the statement of the commentary that the Kittim "scoff at a multitude of people" and the statement a few lines later that they surround and seize fortresses "with a multitude of people." In the former reference he finds an implication that the Kittim routed forces more numerous than their own, whereas the latter seems to him to indicate that they outnumbered those who opposed them. In the one case he sees an allusion to the victory of Antiochus Epiphanes over Egyptian armies much larger than his own; in the other he sees a reference to the crushing numerical superiority of the Seleucid armies in the Macedonian wars. The assumption that the "multitude" implies in either place a significant numerical superiority or inferiority is quite gratuitous.

The commentator says that the rulers of the Kittim "pass on, each before his fellow: their rulers come, one after another, to destroy the earth." Delcor applies this to the Seleucid kings at about the end of the second century B.C., quoting the statement of Bouché-Leclercq that the history of that period is nothing but "a monot-onous series of vicissitudes." It is possible, as a few scholars do, to take the verb in this passage as a causative form, meaning not "pass on" but "cause to pass on." With this interpretation, which seems to me quite unlikely, it has been supposed that the reference is to the deposition and replacement of one high priest after another by the Seleucid kings. Other at least equally plausible interpretations have been proposed, as we shall see.

It would help to identify the Kittim if we could tell what was meant by the "guilty house" by whose counsel their rulers "pass on." It has been taken to mean the pro-Hellenistic family of the Tobiads, in response to whose appeal Antiochus Epiphanes in 175 B.C. came to Jerusalem and took it by storm, slaughtered many of the Oniads, the pro-Egyptian adversaries of the Tobiads, plundered the temple, and stopped for three and a half years the daily sacrifice. This crisis and the parties concerned engage our attention further in Chapter VIII; meanwhile we can say only that there is nothing here which points specifically to the Tobiads as the "guilty house."

A bit of "anti-Syrian polemic" is seen by Stauffer in the state-ment that the Kittim "gather their wealth like the fish of the sea." He compares this with a passage in the Testaments of the Twelve Patriarchs, which speaks of kings who will "swallow men like fishes." It is by no means certain, however, that this passage refers to the Seleucid kings of Syria. In any case, there is no necessary connection between the reference to fishes in the Testaments and the expression used in the commentary, which has to do not with swallowing fishes but with gathering them in nets, and is obviously suggested by the text of Habakkuk.

Few passages in the whole composition have aroused as much debate as the statement that the Kittim "sacrifice to their standards, and their weapons of war are the object of their worship." This immediately calls to mind the veneration of the military standards by the Roman armies; Stauffer argues, however, that the worship of the standards was practiced by the Seleucid armies. He cites the use of the same Hebrew word for "signs" or "standards" in Psalm 74:4, 9, where he thinks there is a reference to the policies of Antiochus Epiphanes.

Rowley also accepts this interpretation. He admits that the worship of standards is not recorded either for the time of Antiochus or for the republican period of Roman history, but he considers it more probable in the former than in the latter period. Since Antiochus Epiphanes claimed to be an incarnation of Zeus, Rowley thinks that the banners of his armies may have borne a likeness of the king as Zeus. Delcor argues that the Assyrians, Persians, and Egyptians as well as the Hellenistic armies practiced the cult of the standards. There is actually no evidence sufficiently clear and specific to demonstrate the practice of sacrificing to the standards before 70 A.D. The weight of probability, however, seems greater for the early Roman period than for the pre-Maccabean or the Maccabean period, the time of the Seleucid kingdom.

Michel even doubts that there is any reference here to a real cult of the standards: the word translated "standards" means literally "signs" and does not necessarily refer to the military standards at all; if it does, the "sacrifice" may not be meant more literally than the fisherman's sacrificing to his net and burning incense to his seine, of which Habakkuk speaks in the passage the commentator is here expounding. A reference to the Roman practice of sacrificing to the standards, one must admit, is not certain here; none the less, it seems so inherently probable as to be almost certain.

An "exactor of tribute," mentioned in Daniel 11:20, was sent to Palestine in 166 B.C. by Seleucus IV, the successor of Antiochus Epiphanes. The payment of tribute to the Seleucid rulers ceased in 141. The reference to annual tribute in the Habakkuk Commentary seems to Stauffer to indicate a date between these two events. On the assumption that the Kittim are the Seleucids, this seems probable enough; those who hold that the Kittim are the

Romans, however, naturally see here a reference to the "yoke" and "tribute" imposed by the Romans on conquered peoples. The reference is too general to prove anything one way or the other.

In the statement "and on the fruit of the womb they have no mercy" Delcor sees a specific reference to a campaign of Ptolemy VIII and his mother in Palestine in 100 B.C. A statement of Josephus about this campaign is thought by Delcor to refer to atrocities committed by Ptolemy against pregnant women, and he thinks that the Habakkuk Commentary alludes to the same atrocities by distinguishing between children and the fruit of the womb. Elliger rightly rejects these extraordinary interpretations of both Josephus and the commentary. Michel sees in this passage a specific reference to the earlier frightful massacre of Jews by Antiochus Epiphanes when he returned from Egypt in 168 B.C. Here again, however, the reference is too general to be used as evidence. Neither the Seleucids nor the Romans had any monopoly on massacres and atrocities.

The mention of "the last priests of Jerusalem," whose "wealth with their spoil will be delivered into the hand of the army of the Kittim," is a challenge to interpreters. Vermès maintains that only the warrior-priests of the Hasmonean dynasty can be meant by the "last priests of Jerusalem." The Hellenizing priests of the pre-Maccabean period, he says, would not have attacked their Macedonian allies and patrons. On the other hand, the later priests of the time of Herod and the time of the Roman procurators were not warriors, and the high priests of 66-70 A.D. are excluded by archeological evidence. All the Hasmonean high priests, however, attacked neighboring peoples and amassed wealth by despoiling them. At the same time, as we see presently, Vermès believes that the Kittim are the Romans.

The last statement of the commentary about the Kittim—"for they are the remainder of the peoples"—is compared by Michel with the representation of the Seleucid kingdom under Antiochus Epiphanes in the book of Daniel, where it appears as the last and most extraordinary human kingdom before the final catastrophe and the resurrection. Once more the possibility of such an application shows that the reference is not necessarily to the Romans, but it gives no positive ground for supposing that the Seleucids are meant.

As a final argument for identifying the Kittim with the Seleucids, Michel adduces the condemnation of idolatry by the commentary. In the Roman period, he says, this was not a serious danger for the Jews, but it was in the time of Antiochus Epiphanes. The Kittim, he adds, were themselves idolaters and promoters of idolatry. The Romans were pagans but allowed the Jews religious freedom; Antiochus Epiphanes proscribed and tried to extirpate the Jewish religion. Unfortunately for this argument the commentator does not mention the Kittim in connection with idolatry. His very general denunciation of idolaters is only what the text of Habakkuk seems to require.

The whole case for the identification of the Kittim with the Seleucid armies of the pre-Maccabean or the Maccabean period boils down to little or nothing. Perhaps all the allusions to the Kittim may, with a little stretching at a few points, fit the Seleucids; but there is nothing in any of them that clearly points to the Seleucids rather than to the Romans. The most that can be maintained is that the Kittim *may* be the Seleucids if other evidence clearly indicates that the commentary was written before the Romans could have been in the picture.

Are there any stronger reasons for believing that the Kittim of the Habakkuk Commentary are the Romans? The commentator's statement, "over smooth ground they go," Dupont-Sommer thinks, is a reference to coming by sea. The word I have translated "smooth ground" he renders "(liquid?) plain." Even if it were certain that Romans were meant here and that they actually came by sea to Palestine, this interpretation of the Hebrew word would be decidedly questionable.

The statement "from afar they come, from the coasts [or isles] of the sea," which Stauffer applies to the Seleucids, may equally well or better be applied to the Romans. Dupont-Sommer goes somewhat too far, however, in claiming that the Romans came from the isles of the sea but the Seleucids did not. If the reference is to the Macedonians in general, from Alexander on, they may be said to have come from the region of the Aegean. Furthermore, as we have seen, the noun commonly taken to mean "isles" can just as well mean "coasts" or "coastal regions." If it refers here to the coasts of Phoenicia and Philistia, as it sometimes does in the Old Testament, Dupont-Sommer's argument that the Macedonians came by land and not by sea has no force. The language of the commentary applies no more definitely to the Romans than to the Seleucids.

The statement of Habakkuk 1:8 that the horsemen of the enemy "fly like a vulture" is applied by the commentary to the Kittim. Since the word for "vulture" is often translated "eagle," Dupont-Sommer reminds us that the eagle was the emblem of the Roman legions. This fact may have been in the commentator's mind if he was thinking of the Romans, but the connection is not close enough to make the reference certain. What the commentator especially stresses, as a matter of fact, is the insatiable rapacity of the Kittim, and this, as Michel says, is characteristic of the vulture rather than of the eagle.

Where the commentator mentions "the rulers of the Kittim," Dupont-Sommer argues that the word for rulers is equivalent to the Roman *imperator*, whereas the Seleucid rulers were called kings. In Psalm 105:20, however, the same word is applied to the Egyptian pharaoh, and elsewhere it is used in a very general sense.

The commentator's account of the contemptuous, mocking attitude of the Kittim as they surround and seize "the fortresses of the peoples" is taken by Elliger as an allusion to the capture of Jerusalem by Pompey in 63 B.C. Michel protests, as we have seen, that the Romans at this time displayed no such attitude toward the Jews. Dupont-Sommer, while finding elsewhere in the commentary a reference to Pompey's conquest, thinks that here the treatment of several Palestinian cities by Gabinius in 57 B.C. is meant. Once more the reference is not sufficiently specific to afford evidence of one date or period rather than another.

We have found unconvincing an attempt to place in the Maccabean or Hasmonean period the statement that the rulers of the Kittim "by the counsel of a guilty house pass on, each before his fellows" and "come, one after another, to destroy the earth." Not one but several interpretations of this passage as referring to the Romans have been put forward. Dupont-Sommer sees here a clear allusion to the Roman civil wars that began in 49 B.C. and ended in 29 B.C. One after another, the contenders in these wars passed on and disappeared. The year 41 B.C., Dupont-Sommer believes, is the time referred to especially in the Habakkuk Commentary. The whole Roman world was then anxious about the political situation, and the Parthian invasion from the east was imminent.

Another interpretation is proposed by van der Ploeg. He believes that the reference is to the military campaigns of the Roman generals who were sent out by the Senate, one after another, to conquer the world. Barthélemy similarly sees here an allusion to the Roman proconsuls in Asia. The procurators who governed Judea in the first century A.D. are thought by Ben-Zion Katz to be the rulers of the Kittim. Vermès in 1951 thought of the rapid succession of Roman emperors between 68 and 70 A.D.; he has since abandoned this identification, however, having been constrained by both archeological and literary evidence to adopt an earlier date for the composition of the commentary. The very multiplicity of theories shows that none of them can be regarded as conclusive.

A suggestion that the "guilty house" by whose counsel their rulers "pass on" was the pre-Maccabean Tobiad family has been noted. Several scholars see here a reference to the Roman Senate. It might be easier to choose between these interpretations if we knew what was meant by the "counsel" of the guilty house, but this is not clear.

It is not surprising that the commentator's reference to "their wealth with all their booty" is understood by more than one scholar as an allusion to the enormous booty amassed by the Romans. But again, other invading armies in other periods of history have acquired abundant spoils of war.

Our attention has already been drawn to the statement of the commentary that the Kittim "sacrifice to their standards, and their weapons of war are the object of their worship." When I first read the commentary at Jerusalem in 1948, this was one of the points that made me feel that the Kittim were the Romans. When the text was published Dupont-Sommer promptly seized on this point as supporting his identification of the Kittim with the Romans. We have considered the efforts of a few scholars to prove that the Seleucids also practiced the worship of the standards. Segal, who formerly identified the Kittim with the Seleucids, has since been convinced by the reference to the cult of the standards that the Kittim are the Romans.

The principal question of fact in this connection is whether the Roman soldiers not only venerated their standards but actually offered sacrifices to them before the time of the empire. The only explicit attestation of this practice is given by Josephus in connection with the conquest of Jerusalem by Titus in 70 A.D. An excellent survey of the evidence on this question is given by G. R. Driver, who concludes that the incident related by Josephus is the earliest occasion to which the commentator on Habakkuk may be supposed to refer. Even though the archeological evidence conclusively rules out a reference to this incident in the Habakkuk Commentary, Driver's argument is very impressive. He has shown at least that the practice of sacrificing to the standards before the time of the empire cannot be demonstrated. It may well be, therefore, that the reference in the Habakkuk Commentary is the earliest extant attestation of this practice. That Roman soldiers may have sacrificed to their standards during the time of the republic (i.e., before 31 B.C.), or during the century between 30 B.C. and 70 A.D., is not to be thought impossible merely because it is not demonstrable. At any rate, while not as definite as we might wish, this is the most specific point yet encountered in support of the contention that the Kittim in the Habakkuk Commentary are the Romans.

Dupont-Sommer argues that "the last priests of Jerusalem" were the two brothers, Aristobulus II (67–63 B.C.) and Hyrcanus II (63–40), with whom the Hasmonean dynasty came to an end.

Others also, including Brownlee, have adopted this view. Elliger, however, sees no reason to single out these two priests in particular. He believes that the reference is to the whole priesthood. After saying that the wealth of "the last priests of Jerusalem" will be delivered to the Kittim, the commentator adds, "for they are the remainder of the peoples." Both Dupont-Sommer and Elliger explain this statement as meaning that the Kittim are the last people who are to play a part on the stage of history—namely, the Romans. This may be correct, but the commentator, when-ever he lived, might well have regarded the dominant world power of his day as the last in the series of empires before the end of history. This has always been characteristic of the apocalyptic point of view, and while the Habakkuk Commentary is not an apocalyptic work, its point of view has much in common with that of the apocalyptic literature.

It thus becomes plain that the references to the Kittim are too general to point clearly and unmistakably to any one nation. Any interpretation required by other evidence concerning the historical setting of the commentary is possible. The one allusion that most definitely favors one nation more than another is the reference to the cult of the standards. Other things being equal, this seems to indicate the Romans rather than the Seleucids.

If we may then at least tentatively accept the identification of the Kittim with the Romans, it does not necessarily follow that the commentary was written after the conquest of Palestine by the Romans. We must still ask whether the commentator thinks of the Roman invasion as in the distant past, as recent, as con-temporary, or as still future. Segal holds that there is no reference in the commentary to the conquest of Judah, but only to the sub-jugation of other nations by the Romans. The plunder of the last priests of Jerusalem has not yet been delivered to the Kittim. Segal even believes that the descriptions of the Kittim in the commentary are not based on first-hand acquaintance with the Romans, but on hearsay and on what is said in Habakkuk about the Chaldeans. Elliger vehemently rejects this judgment. The commentator, he feels, speaks with the vividness and passion of one who has experienced the terrible things of which he tells. Other scholars believe that for the commentator the Roman invasion of Judah is still in the future, but not necessarily as distant as Segal supposes.

The use of the Hebrew tenses is stressed by van der Ploeg. Past events, he says are indicated in the commentary by Hebrew verbs in the "perfect" tense, which indicates completed action. The acts of the Kittim, however, are indicated either by the "imperfect" tense, which usually (though not necessarily) refers to the future, or else by the active participle. The most natural inference is that the Romans were not yet in Judea when the commentary was written, but that they were expected to come soon. Vermès accepts van der Ploeg's interpretation of the verbs and agrees with him that the commentary was written shortly before Pompey's coming to Jerusalem in 63 B.C. The plundering of Israel's neighbors by the Hasmonean warrior-priests has been going on for generations, but their spoil will soon be taken from them by the Romans.

Dupont-Sommer, however, rejects van der Ploeg's argument. The imperfect tense, he points out, is regularly used for repeated or continuous action in the present or even in the past. This is quite true, and verbs in the imperfect tense in the Habakkuk Commentary often clearly refer to the present. The use of the participle too, says Dupont-Sommer, refers not to the future but to the present. Again one must agree that this is sometimes clearly the case. The use of the Hebrew tenses may but does not necessarily imply that the Kittim have not yet arrived.

The impression of vividness and immediacy in the descriptions, which Elliger emphasizes as against Segal, is cited also by Dupont-Sommer to confirm his interpretation. He stresses also the severe, violent tone of denunciation in the allusions to the Kittim, as contrasted with the favorable attitude toward the Romans expressed in I Maccabees. The inference is that when the commentary was written Judea had already suffered severely at the hands of the Romans.

On the other hand, not everything that is said of the Kittim seems to fit what happened at the time of Pompey's conquest of

Judea. Michel observes that nothing indicates a particularly swift advance of the Roman armies; that Pompey's coming was not the execution of a deliberate military plan but a response to an invitation, whereas the commentary says of the Kittim that "with deliberation all their planning is to work evil, and with cunning and deceit they proceed with all the peoples"; and finally, that the Romans treated the Jews with severity but not with insolence or signal cruelty during the first decades of their rule in Palestine. All these facts are easily understood if we suppose that when the commentary was written the Romans were known and feared but had not yet intervened in Palestine.

Reviewing all the evidence, Elliger comes to the conclusion that the commentary was written after 65 B.C., when a Roman legate first came to Judea to settle the quarrel between Hyrcanus and Aristobulus, but before the reign of Herod. I see no good reason for putting it quite that late. So far as the references to the Kittim are concerned, it seems to me most probable that the Romans are meant, but that the commentary was written some time before 63 B.C. A final decision, however, cannot be reached apart from the other historical allusions in the commentary.

VII

Historical Allusions in the Habakkuk Commentary: Dramatis Personae

⎍⎍⎍⎍⎍⎍⎍⎍⎍⎍⎍⎍⎍⎍⎍⎍⎍⎍⎍⎍⎍⎍⎍⎍⎍⎍⎍⎍⎍⎍⎍⎍⎍

In addition to the references to the international situation, much is said in the Habakkuk Commentary about parties and individuals within the Jewish nation. There is practically no point of attachment between these references and the others. They allude to individuals and groups not mentioned in the passages about the Kittim, and in turn they do not mention the Kittim. The only exception is the statement, already considered, that the spoil of the last priests of Jerusalem will be given up to the Kittim, and this has no clear connection with the parties and persons mentioned elsewhere.

The identification of these individuals and groups is something like the solution of a picture puzzle. The problem is to fit what the commentary says about the characters into what is known of Jewish history from other sources. The fact that with only one or two barely possible exceptions no personal names are given makes the choice all the more difficult.

The various characters interact in such a way that they cannot be separately identified and placed in different historical periods or situations. If possible, we must find one set of circumstances and one group of persons that will correspond to everything said about all of them. If this cannot be done we may have to consider the possibility that not one but several situations and sets of characters are referred to, but this should be contemplated only as a last resort. The best procedure, therefore, seems to be to get all the *dramatis personae* on the stage at once, look at all of them together, and see whether we can recognize them and the scene they are playing. Our picture puzzle thus takes on something of the nature of a charade.

The hero of the drama is a man called "the teacher of righteousness." The title "teacher of righteousness"—or, as it may equally well be translated, "righteous teacher"—is probably derived from several passages in the Old Testament. The exact term does not occur in any of them, but there are two references to a teacher of falsehood (or false teacher), with whom the teacher of righteousness in the commentary may be consciously contrasted. One of these is Isaiah 9:14–15:

> So the Lord cut off from Israel head and tail,
> palm branch and reed in one day—
> The elder and honored man is the head,
> and the prophet who teaches falsehood is the tail.

The other reference to a "teacher of falsehood" is in the book of Habakkuk itself (2:18):

> What profit is an idol
> when its maker has shaped it,
> a metal image, a teacher of falsehood?

The earliest approach to the title "teacher of righteousness" in the Old Testament is Joel 2:23:

> "Be glad, O sons of Zion,
> and rejoice in YHWH your God;
> for he has given the early rain for your vindication,
> he has poured down for you abundant rain,
> the early and the latter rain, as before."

The phrase here rendered (following the Revised Standard Version) "for your vindication" is translated in the King James Version "moderately," and in the American Standard Version "in just measure," with a marginal note, "Or, *in* (or, *for*) *righteous-ness*." The Hebrew word for "early rain" in the third and last lines of the verse is exactly the same as the word for "teacher," both in spelling and in pronunciation. The whole expression, "the early rain for your vindication," could therefore be translated literally (though it would make nonsense of the passage), "the teacher for righteousness." This makes possible a play on words, and indeed some confusion in the interpretation of the text. Such interpreters as the author of the Habakkuk Commentary do not mind giving words and phrases meanings that have nothing to do with the context, provided they suit the interpreter's immediate interest.

The same possibility of confusion appears also in Hosea 10:12:

> "For it is the time to seek the Lord,
>   that he may come and rain righteousness upon you."

It might seem that the context here, with its references to sowing, reaping, and plowing, would prevent any interpreter from misunderstanding the words "rain righteousness." It is possible, however, to translate "teach righteousness," and in this case the Latin Vulgate of Jerome, which is the official version of the Catholic Church, actually translates, "when he comes who will teach you justice" (*cum venerit qui docebit vos justitiam*). The Syriac versian similarly reads, "until he comes who will show you his righteousness." This should be sufficient to acquit the writer of the Habakkuk Commentary of any charge of mere ignorance of Hebrew. Both he and his predecessors, including the teacher of righteousness himself, probably connected the title with these passages in the Old Testament. Weis has observed that the ninth-century Karaite Daniel al-Qumusi identified the "former rain for righteousness" in Joel 2:23 with the prophet Elijah, and in this connection cited also Hosea 10:12 as well as Malachi 3:24.

Other persons are mentioned in connection with the teacher of righteousness. The commentator speaks of "those who acted treacherously with the man of the lie, for they did not heed the words of the teacher of righteousness from the mouth of God." Nothing is said here to show who the "man of the lie" may be, but there is more about him later.

The commentator goes on to speak of treacherous men "who do not believe when they hear all the things that are coming upon the last generation from the mouth of the priest into whose heart God put wisdom to explain all the words of his servants the prophets." The similarity of the language used with reference to the teacher of righteousness and the priest strongly suggests that they are the same man. Their identity, in fact, seems to be established by another passage, which says of the teacher of righteousness what is here said of the priest. Habakkuk's words, "that he may run who reads it," are applied to "the teacher of righteousness, to whom God made known all the mysteries of the words of his servants the prophets."

The teacher of righteousness, then, was a priest who was believed by his disciples to be endowed with power to interpret the words of the prophets. We are not told, as Elliger observes, that he was inspired also to interpret the law, but since there are many indications that his followers considered themselves the only true observers of the law, it is fairly safe to infer that his authority was recognized in this area also.

The commentary says, "Into the hand of his elect God will deliver the judgment of all the nations, and by their chastisement all the wicked among his people will be punished." Dupont-Sommer takes "his elect" here to mean the teacher of righteousness, and therefore holds that the teacher of righteousness was expected to be the agent of the last judgment, first upon the nations and then upon Israel. While the form of the Hebrew word would normally be taken as singular, one of the peculiarities of spelling in the Dead Sea Scrolls is that the singular and plural forms of nouns cannot be distinguished when they have the possessive suffix of the third person masculine. Here the noun "elect" is probably plural, agreeing with "his people" in the preceding clause, and refers not to the teacher of righteousness but to his followers. If so, "their chastisement" probably means "the chastisement [of the wicked] by them." Not the teacher of righteousness but his followers will execute God's judgment on "the wicked among his people." This passage must therefore be left out of account in our attempt to get a clear picture of the teacher of righteousness.

Our list of *dramatis personae* is enlarged by a group cryptically designated as "the house of Absalom," which is mentioned in connection with a conflict of some kind between the teacher of righteousness and the man of the lie. Explaining the expression in Habakkuk 1:13, "the swallowing by the wicked of a man more righteous than he," the commentator says, "This means the house of Absalom and the men of their party, who kept silence at the chastisement of the teacher of righteousness and did not help him against the man of the lie, who rejected the law in the midst of their whole congregation."

What is meant by the "house of Absalom" is one of the most warmly debated points in the discussions of the historical allusions in the Habakkuk Commentary. Several questions are involved. One is the meaning of the expression, "the chastisement of the teacher of righteousness." The word I have translated as "chastisement" may mean reproof, rebuke, refutation, proof, condemnation, or punishment. Only the context can indicate what it means in any particular place. Elliger argues that the phrase "by their chastisement," which occurs a few lines before this, led the commentator to speak here of "the chastisement of the teacher of righteousness."

The fact that the former phrase is associated with the word "judgment" seems to Elliger to imply that there was a legal trial, in which a charge was made against the teacher of righteousness and sustained by the court. He therefore interprets the expressions used here to mean that the teacher of righteousness was condemned in court because the house of Absalom abandoned him and the man of the lie made an improper use of the law. If true, this affords a specific item in the biography of the teacher of righteousness that should help us to identify him. Unfortunately there is not much to support Elliger's inference.

Assuming the meaning "chastisement" or the like, we cannot

be entirely sure whether the teacher of righteousness was the chastiser or the chastised. In other words (speaking academically, and imposing upon Hebrew the categories of Indo-European grammar), is this a subjective or an objective genitive? I have said that in the previous passage "their chastisement" probably means "chastisement by them"; in other words, I take the possessive suffix there as a subjective genitive. Here the fact that the teacher of righteousness needed help suggests that perhaps he was the one who was chastised, yet the meaning may be that he was administering chastisement when he was not supported by the "house of Absalom." Brownlee originally interpreted the genitive as objective; more recently, however, he has adopted the view that the teacher of righteousness was active rather than passive in the matter. But, as Reicke points out, the teacher of righteousness appears all through the document as one who is persecuted, and this fits the expression of Habakkuk that is here expounded, "the swallowing by the wicked of a man more righteous than he." Probably, therefore, the man of the lie was the chastiser, and the teacher of righteousness was the one chastised.

What is meant by the word I have translated as "party" is another debated point. Elliger argues that it means either a deliberative assembly or the result of deliberation, a decision, sentence, or plan. For the meaning "council" or "deliberative assembly" he cites three other passages where the same word is used. In one of them the meaning "party" fits the context better, and I so translate it. In another what is meant is probably the council or assembly of the community, as in the Manual of Discipline. In the other passage adduced by Elliger the occurrence of the word itself depends upon his own conjectural reconstruction of the text; my translation presupposes a different Hebrew word that seems to me more probable.

For the meaning "decision" or "plan," Elliger refers to a passage about the Kittim, which I translate, "and with deliberation all their planning is to work evil." The word under discussion here is the one there translated "deliberation"; it does not mean, however, the decision of a deliberative assembly but the deliberate inten-

tion or conscious plan of the conquering Kittim. In the passage
with which we are now concerned the word "plan" would not be
appropriate, yet what is meant may be something not very different. The expression I render "the men of their party" may mean
"the men of their persuasion" or "the men of their way of thinking."
Altogether, the argument for an allusion to a legal trial in this
passage is not convincing.

What then is implied by the expression "house of Absalom"?
Are we to suppose that a man actually named Absalom is in view,
or is the name used in a symbolic fashion? It has frequently been
pointed out that no other person in this document is indicated by
his real name. The nearest analogy to the use of the name Absalom
is the use of the name Kittim, and this would suggest that Absalom
here is not the real name of a man. Several interpretations of the
passage that have been offered, however, presuppose that a historical person named Absalom is meant, and several men of that
name have been suggested as the person referred to by the commentator. To me it seems altogether unlikely that a particular
group would here be named explicitly, while the identity of all the
other characters in the drama is veiled and obscure.

The commentator implies that the house of Absalom should have
helped the teacher of righteousness in his conflict with the man
of the lie. It may therefore be true that some of the followers of
the teacher of righteousness are called the house of Absalom because they deserted him. If so, not all of his followers can be
meant. He had at least a sufficient number of faithful disciples left
to carry on his movement and preserve its literature. Later the
commentary speaks of "all the doers of the law in the house of
Judah, whom God will rescue from the house of judgment because
of their labor and their faith in the teacher of righteousness."

Both Del Medico and Brownlee take the designation "doers of
the law in the house of Judah" to mean that Judah was the name
of the teacher of righteousness. It is much more probable that the
house of Judah means the Jewish nation, and "the doers of the law
in the house of Judah" are a group within the nation distinguished
from those who do not keep the law. The "house of judgment" is

supposed by Del Medico to mean the Roman courts. This expression occurs again, however, in a passage where it clearly does not mean a group that pronounces judgment but one that is to be judged and severely punished.

The reference to "their faith in the teacher of righteousness" is believed by some to mean "their fidelity to the teacher of righteousness." As Barthélemy points out, however, the teacher of righteousness is an inspired interpreter of the Scriptures, and it is therefore necessary to believe what he teaches. The use of the preposition "in" with the noun further establishes this meaning, in Hebrew as in English idiom. One may recall also the condemnation of those who "do not believe when they hear all the things that are coming upon the last generation from the mouth of the priest into whose heart God put wisdom to explain all the words of his servants the prophets."

And now, enter the villain!—unless, indeed, he has already entered as "the man of the lie." Here he appears under his usual designation, "the wicked priest." The person of whom Habakkuk says, "Woe to him who heaps up, but it is not his own," is said by the commentary to be "the wicked priest, who was named according to the truth when he first took office; but when he had begun to rule in Israel, his heart was lifted up, and he forsook God and betrayed the statutes for the sake of wealth. He plundered and assembled the wealth of men of violence who rebelled against God. He took the wealth of peoples, adding to himself iniquity and guilt; and ways of abominations he wrought, in all impurity of uncleanness."

Elliger makes the appealing suggestion that the term "the wicked priest" (*hak-kohen ha-raša'*) may be a deliberate caricature of the official title, "the chief priest (*hak-kohen ha-ro'š*). This may very well be true; if so, it indicates that the man so designated is to be sought among the high priests.

The passage just quoted is the first explicit reference to "the wicked priest" in the extant portions of the commentary, but he was probably mentioned earlier in a part of the first column that has been lost, just before the first reference to the teacher of righteousness. This is assumed in the reconstruction of the text underlying my translation. It is suggested by the fact that the commentator at that point is interpreting Habakkuk's complaint that "the wicked man encompasses the righteous man."

The expression "named according to the truth" in the passage quoted is obscure. It plays a considerable part in the proposed identifications of the wicked priest, but its meaning is not so clear that it can be used as evidence for one identification as against another. Some scholars interpret the Hebrew as meaning "called by his true name"; others take it to mean "called by the true Name." The translation I have given is suggested by a Hebrew expression closely resembling this, "he was named according to his end," meaning that he was given a name indicating his fate.

At the bottom of the eighth column the last words left are "the priest who rebelled." What followed this we do not know. The ninth column begins in the middle of a sentence: ". . . his scourge with judgments of wickedness; and horrors of sore diseases they wrought in him, and vengeance in his body of flesh." Presumably "the priest who rebelled" is the same as the wicked priest of the previous quotation. The gap in the text makes any interpretation of the first lines of the ninth column very precarious. The worms or ants that ate away the last lines of all the columns made the task of exegesis difficult. It is hard to be sure of the meaning of words that are not there. To suppose with Elliger, for example, that the teacher of righteousness fell ill in the course of his trial or while his sentence was being executed, and that his followers held his adversaries responsible for his illness, is hardly justifiable.

Dupont-Sommer conjectures for the missing last line of the eighth column, referring to "the priest who rebelled," something like this: "and he persecuted the teacher of righteousness, who was . . ."; he then interprets the opening words of the ninth column as meaning "smitten by him by virtue of wicked judgments." The teacher of righteousness is thus supposed to be the one who suffered the dire fate here described. That is not impossible, but the fact that "the priest who rebelled" is the last person mentioned makes it at least equally probable that it was he who suffered these afflictions; and this is supported by the fact that the passage in Habakkuk that is here expounded is a threat of punishment. Elliger objects that the commentary speaks of unjust judgments, but the expression "judgments of wickedness" probably means "judgments on wickedness," not "wicked judgments."

Dupont-Sommer infers from this passage, as he interprets it, that the teacher of righteousness who suffered "vengeance in his body of flesh" was a divine being, who had become incarnate in order to live and die as a man. This is one of the points at which Dupont-Sommer sees in the Habakkuk commentary an anticipation of Christianity. Part of his argument, as he first stated it, was based on the expression "his body of flesh," but this point he later abandoned. Surely no convincing argument can be built on such a passage as this, where even the person referred to is in doubt.

Already it is clear that the identification of the hero and villain of the piece, not to mention the minor characters, is complicated by the frequent uncertainty both as to what is really said and as to the person of whom it is said. What do we know thus far about the characters in the drama?

We know that the teacher of righteousness, a priest believed to have a gift for interpreting prophecy, had difficulties with men who did not believe him and dealt treacherously with him in concert with a man called the man of the lie. There was also a group called the house of Absalom and their party—perhaps the same group or perhaps another—who, instead of helping the teacher of righteousness when he either suffered or administered chastisement, remained silent. As for the wicked priest, we know that he was a man who ruled in Israel and who became proud, forsook God and the law, amassed wealth by violent measures, and wrought all manner of unclean abominations.

Either the wicked priest or the teacher of righteousness suffered some kind of horrible bodily affliction. Who it was that suffered this mysterious visitation is debatable, but it becomes fairly clear a few lines later. After the statement about the last priests of Jerusalem, which we discussed in connection with the Kittim, and which may or may not have anything to do with the wicked priest, there is a reference to "the wicked priest, whom, for the wrong done to the teacher of righteousness and the men of his party, God delivered into the hand of his enemies, afflicting him with a destroying scourge, in bitterness of soul, because he acted wickedly against his elect." Here, quite clearly, it is the wicked priest who is punished by his enemies because of a wrong committed against the teacher of righteousness and his followers. Any identification we may adopt for the wicked priest will have to include this element of a punishment already inflicted.

At the top of the tenth column, after another gap in the text, there are obscure references to stones and beams in connection with oppression and robbery and to "the house of judgment," but no particular person is mentioned. The following lines, however, speak of "the preacher of the lie, who enticed many to build a city of delusion in blood and to establish a congregation in falsehood for the sake of its honor, making many grow weary of the service of delusion and making them pregnant with works of falsehood, that their toil may be in vain, to the end that they may come into judgments of fire, because they reviled and insulted God's elect." Here building operations of some kind are attributed to "the preacher of the lie." Whether he is the same as the man of the lie or the wicked priest there is nothing in the passage to show. It is not even clear whether the building is literal or figurative.

The eleventh column begins with the words, "the lie." Whether they belong to the title "the preacher of the lie" or "the man of the lie" can only be conjectured. Presumably one or the other of these expressions was used, and perhaps the same person was meant in either case. Habakkuk's denunciation of "him who makes his neighbors drink" is quoted next, and the commentator says, "This means the wicked priest, who persecuted the teacher of righteousness in order to confound him in the indignation of his wrath, wishing to banish him; and at the time of their festival of rest, the Day of Atonement, he appeared to them to confound them and to make them stumble on the day of fasting, their sabbath of rest."

This passage affords the principal basis for Dupont-Sommer's theory of the occasion and date of the Habakkuk Commentary. Several questions of interpretation will have to be considered when we come to the discussion of his theory. There are a few points concerning the meanings of words, however, that can be disposed of here. The verb which I have translated "confound" may mean literally "swallow," and so figuratively "destroy"; or it may mean "cause to stumble" or "confuse." In this context the second meaning is more probable. The same verb is used in Isaiah 28:7 and Psalm 107:27 to express the effect of drinking wine. This meaning fits the text just quoted from Habakkuk. It is also supported by the words "to confound them and to make them stumble" in the next clause, though the object of the verb there is in the plural, meaning presumably the followers of the teacher of righteousness, whereas here it is in the singular, doubtless meaning the teacher himself.

The words I have translated "wishing to banish him" are obscure, and their meaning is much debated. Each of the two Hebrew words constituting the expression raises difficult questions. In the script of the commentary, *w* and *y* are written alike; it is therefore possible to read the first word with either of these letters. Several forms of a verb meaning "to be willing" or "to wish" have been suggested, yielding various shades of meaning. An entirely different interpretation rests on the supposition that this is not one word but a contraction of a preposition and a noun, making a phrase that means "to the house." Emendations of the text to produce the same meaning have been proposed also. It is even possible that the scribe of this manuscript intended to write the phrase in full and merely omitted a letter by mistake.

Whatever form or explanation is assumed, the phrase "to the house" would have to be connected with the verb "persecuted" or "pursued" rather than with the verb "confound." In that case, however, it seems strange that the phrase does not more closely follow the verb with which it belongs. We might conceivably suppose that the phrase I have translated "in order to confound him" is parenthetical; we could then translate: "who pursued the teacher of righteousness, making him stumble in his wrathful indignation, to the house of"—but now comes the equally puzzling question of what the next word means.

The word I have translated "banish" may mean "uncover." It may, in fact, be a noun instead of a verb. Dupont-Sommer, assuming the meaning "uncover," formerly supposed that here it referred to the removal of a condemned criminal's clothing before his execution. Elliger objects that this interpretation would never have been conceived apart from the notion that the commentator, whose preceding quotation of Habakkuk 2:15 reads "to gaze on their festivals," knew and had in mind also the reading of the Masoretic text, "to gaze on their nakedness."

Elliger himself suggests several interpretations of the verb "uncover" that seem to him possible. Perhaps the wicked priest wished to "expose" the teacher of righteousness as a heretic or an impostor; or perhaps by his treatment of the teacher of righteousness the wicked priest unwittingly revealed his own character and intentions. Elliger even finds it conceivable that "uncover" or "unclothe" is a technical term meaning, as we should say, "unfrock." These suggestions are too far-fetched to be taken seriously, but Elliger is surely right in insisting that what the wicked priest wanted was not to kill the teacher of righteousness but to silence him.

Over against all these suggestions stands the possibility that the verb here does not mean "uncover" at all but "banish" or "exile." Dupont-Sommer urges against this interpretation the fact that a different form of the verb is commonly used in biblical Hebrew for this meaning. A noun meaning "his exile," however, would be spelled exactly the same as the infinitive "to exile him," and it may be that the scribe intended to write this noun here. Whatever form we assume, it seems clear that if the preceding word is taken as a phrase, "to the house of," the reference is more probably to exile than to uncovering. The expression "to the house of his exposure," meaning the place where he was exposed, is not impossible; but the meaning "to the place of his exile" seems more natural. The idea of exile or banishment does not require such forced explanations of grammar and context as the idea of uncovering or exposure.

Be all that as it may, something important undoubtedly happened on the Day of Atonement. What was it? Here again different scholars take widely divergent ways in their interpretations. Elliger supposes that the conflict between the teacher of righteousness and the wicked priest remained latent until it came to an open breach on the Day of Atonement, when the high priest revealed his real intentions. Either then or soon afterward the teacher of righteousness was arrested and brought to trial.

Much depends upon the implications of the verb "appear." Since it is used in the Old Testament for appearances of God, Dupont-Sommer takes it here to mean that the teacher of righteousness, who had been put to death, reappeared supernaturally to execute judgment on his foes. Many scholars have pointed out that the verb does not necessarily imply a divine manifestation, especially in late Hebrew. Dupont-Sommer admits that it went through some evolution in meaning after biblical times, but he protests that its original biblical meaning was not thereby eliminated. Without definite confirmation in the context, however, the verb by itself cannot be taken to imply anything supernatural.

There is another and more serious objection to Dupont-Sommer's interpretation. In the preceding clause the subject is the wicked priest; it is natural to suppose therefore that he is also the subject of the verb "appeared." Dupont-Sommer reminds us that in ancient Hebrew there is often a change of subject with no explicit indication. That is true, but the question is whether the context requires a change of subject here. If such a change is intended, a new sentence begins after "banish him," or "his exile," and the conjunction means not "and" but a strong "but." The whole statement then reads, "This means the wicked priest, who persecuted the teacher of righteousness in order to confound him in the indignation of his wrath, wishing to banish him. But at the time of their festival of rest, the day of atonement, he (the teacher of righteousness) appeared to them to confound them and to make them stumble on the day of fasting, their sabbath of rest." This is not impossible, but if it was the teacher of righteousness who appeared, who were the people whom he confounded and caused to stumble?

What the stumbling means is not indicated. Talmon interprets it in terms of a difference between the official priesthood and the teacher of righteousness concerning the calendar of festivals. This would explain why the sacred day is called *their* festival of rest. The teacher of righteousness and his followers were observing the festival according to their own calendar, when the wicked priest appeared before them and endeavored to make them violate their own convictions. In view of the frequent stress on the proper observance of times in the Dead Sea Scrolls, this interpretation is plausible and attractive.

What has this obscure but crucial passage added to our knowledge of the characters and plot of our drama? We have learned that the wicked priest persecuted the teacher of righteousness. The purpose of this persecution was either uncovering of some kind or banishment, probably the latter. One of the parties, probably the wicked priest, appeared on the day of atonement to some group, probably the followers of the teacher of righteousness, with the intent to make them do something which the commentator calls stumbling. What happened then we are not told.

A little more is said about the crimes of the wicked priest. The expression in Habakkuk 2:16, "You are sated with ignominy instead of glory," is applied to "the priest whose ignominy was greater than his glory, because he did not circumcise the foreskin of his heart, but walked in the ways of drunkenness, that his thirst might be removed." A few lines later it is said that the wicked priest "plotted to destroy the poor," and the mention of "violence to a land" in Habakkuk 2:17 is applied to "the cities of Judah, because he plundered the wealth of the poor." The "blood of a city" in the same verse is said to mean "Jerusalem, in which the wicked priest wrought abominable works and defiled God's sanctuary." How far the language of this passage is symbolic one cannot tell, but there is a strong suggestion that the wicked priest was a man of evil life, addicted in particular to drunkenness. He was also evidently guilty of violence and oppression, and even of desecrating the temple.

All this wickedness will not go unpunished. "The cup of the wrath of God will confound him, increasing his confusion. And the pain—" Here the text breaks off again, at the bottom of the eleventh column, but in the next column the language of Habakkuk 2:17 is said to mean "the wicked priest, that to him may be paid his recompense, as he recompensed the poor. . . . God will execute judgment upon him and destroy him." With the reference to the cup of God's wrath the tense of the verb changes suddenly to the "imperfect," indicating that while the priest has already suffered humiliation he has a greater punishment still to suffer in the future. This is perhaps the only clear indication in the commentary that its writer was speaking of events in his own lifetime. When the commentary was written the wicked priest had not yet received his full punishment; presumably, therefore, he was still alive, unless we are to suppose that the final judgment was to be executed in the world to come.

Interpreting the prophecy in Habakkuk 2:17—"For the violence done to Lebanon will overwhelm you; the destruction of the beasts will terrify you"—the commentator says that the wicked priest will "be paid his recompense as he recompensed the poor"; then he explains, "for Lebanon is the council of the community, and the beasts are the simple ones of Judah, the doers of the law." This recalls the earlier mention of "all the doers of the law in the house of Judah, whom God will rescue from the house of judgment because of their labor and their faith in the teacher of righteousness." All these expressions evidently refer to the disciples of the teacher of righteousness, and they are identified with the poor whom the wicked priest plundered and persecuted.

Our *dramatis personae* are now all before us. The hero is the inspired and persecuted teacher of righteousness. The villain is the rapacious, violent persecutor, the apostate, impious, drunken, defeated, apparently tortured, perhaps diseased, and certainly doomed wicked priest. The man of the lie is probably a third character; the preacher of the lie may be the same man or a fourth member of the cast. The house of Absalom is a group of people who for some unexplained reason should have helped the teacher of righteousness but instead kept silence. God's elect, the men of truth, the poor, the simple ones of Judah, the doers of the law, are those who have persisted in their faith in the teacher of righteousness. All these, together with the Kittim, the guilty house, the house of judgment, and the last priests of Jerusalem, constitute our cast, both principals and chorus.

VIII

Identifications of Persons and Events

ⅢⅢⅢⅢⅢⅢⅢⅢⅢⅢⅢⅢⅢⅢⅢⅢⅢⅢⅢⅢⅢ

With all the characters on the stage, can we recognize them and the historical events in which they take part? The plot is by no means clear; even the separate episodes in it are obscure. In trying to connect it with historical movements and events, we must keep one point in mind, although it does not simplify the problem. We cannot assume that the incidents occurred in the order in which we read of them. The exposition is governed by the order of the text of Habakkuk; each sentence or phrase brings to the commentator's mind events and persons in the history of his nation and his own religous community, and he mentions them as they occur to him. No chronological sequence, therefore, can be inferred from the commentary.

It may seem that all this leaves very little ground for any specific identification of our characters and the events in which they were involved. Actually, perhaps just because of the obscurity and ambiguity of the data, scholars have managed to produce an abundance of theories. Most of these, it is true, are not based exclusively upon the Habakkuk Commentary. Much use is made, especially, of the Damascus Document, where the teacher of righteousness and others mentioned in the commentary appear again. Since we are now concerned solely with the time when the Habakkuk Commentary was written, as indicated by the historical references in it, all interpretations and arguments based on the Damascus Document or other texts must for the present be ignored. The relation between the Damascus Document and the Dead Sea Scrolls is a problem that must be considered by itself in the proper place.

Both logic and convenience favor a review of the theories in the historical order of the situations and events to which they attach our document. We have found it probable that the Kittim are the Romans rather than the Macedonians. This tentative judgment, however, must not be allowed to prejudice us against arguments for placing the teacher of righteousness and the wicked priest in an earlier period. If it should turn out to be probable that they were men who lived long before the Roman conquest of Palestine, our conclusion concerning the Kittim may have to be revised, or we may conceivably conclude that these persons and the Kittim were not contemporaries.

In connection with the Kittim we have considered the conflict between the Hellenists and the conservative Jews in the pre-Maccabean period and mentioned the prominent family known to historians as the Tobiads. Late in the third century B.C., when Palestine was under the dominion of the Ptolemies of Egypt, a member of this family named Joseph secured from the king by guile and impudence a concession for farming the taxes of cities in Syria and Palestine. His maneuvers to secure this opportunity for gaining power and wealth involved a decidedly unethical treatment of his uncle, the high priest Onias II, whose family is called by historians the Oniads. No less than four high priests by the name of Onias came from this family. Joseph's treacherous dealing with his uncle, it has been suggested, may have led the Oniad party to compare him with David's disloyal son Absalom, and so the Tobiads may have come to be called "the house of Absalom."

Another suggestion is that it was a son of Joseph, named Hyrcanus, whose disloyalty caused the Tobiads to be called the house of Absalom. With methods much like his father's, Hyrcanus too won the favor of the Egyptian king, but by so doing he aroused the wrath of his father and the jealousy of his brothers. As a result he was attacked by his brothers and forced to withdraw to Transjordan. There he lived until the accession of Antiochus Epiphanes, when he committed suicide. The disloyalty of Hyrcanus toward his own father, his underhanded procedure, and the fact that he was forced to take refuge in Transjordan all seem to constitute an impressive parallel with the story of Absalom and David. For a while this theory seemed to me the most probable view of the historical background of the commentary. I now feel that the explanation of the name "house of Absalom" should be sought in the disloyalty of some group to the teacher of righteousness himself. The obligation to which this group was unfaithful need not have been that of discipleship; it may have been the obligation of family or any other relationship.

Those scholars who hold that the situation reflected in the commentary is pre-Maccabean put it a little later than the time of Joseph and Hyrcanus. Early in the second century B.C. the control of Palestine finally passed from the Ptolemies of Egypt to the Seleucids of Syria. When Antiochus Epiphanes came to the throne of Syria in 175 B.C. the Jewish high priest was Onias III, a grandson of Onias II. The Tobiads, who had recently been driven out of Jerusalem by the Oniads, now appealed to Antiochus, who took Jerusalem by force and wrought great havoc in the city. Onias was deposed from the high priesthood and driven from the country. His brother Jeshua was appointed in his place and proceeded to show his devotion to his royal patron by taking the Greek name Jason and ardently promoting the adoption of Greek practices by Jewish priests and aristocrats.

This abandonment of the ways of the fathers did much to stiffen the reaction of devout Jews against all Hellenistic innovations. Jason was soon replaced by a man named Menelaus, who had promised the king a bigger bribe than Jason's. A few years later, at about the same time that Antiochus was compelled by the Romans to relinquish his newly won advantage in Egypt (168 B.C.), Jason was restored to office by a revolt of the pro-Egyptian Oniads at Jerusalem. The revolt was quickly put down, however, and Antiochus gave the high priesthood back again to Menelaus.

It has been argued that both the teacher of righteousness and the wicked priest in the Habakkuk Commentary were "super-individual" figures, representing not one person but two or more persons of the same type. According to this view, the teacher of righteousness was both the legitimate high priesthood in general and also Onias III in particular; the wicked priest was both Jason and Menelaus, and perhaps also Alcimus, the successor of Menelaus, not to mention others. Some scholars, without accepting a collective interpretation, have espoused what may be called multiple interpretations, applying the title "teacher of righteousness" or "wicked priest" not to an office in general but to several individual incumbents of the office. A conflict may have raged for generations, it is said, between teachers of righteousness and wicked priests. Usually, however, the teacher of righteousness is believed to have been an individual.

It must be admitted that there is nothing impossible in this idea of multiple identifications. The commentator might see in Habakkuk references to several wicked priests, and therefore say in one place, "*This* means the priest that did such and such," and in another, "*This* means the one that did so and so." We should then translate the passage in question, not "This means the wicked priest, who . . . ," but "This means the wicked priest that . . ." and so forth. This is all the more plausible if the term "wicked priest" is a parody of the official title "chief priest," as we have seen to be quite probable.

On the other hand, to apply a designation in one passage to one person and the same designation in another passage to another person means in effect that no one individual has been found to whom all the allusions are applicable. A multiple interpretation is quite possible if the text compels us to adopt it, but it should surely be adopted only as a last resort. Our inabilty to identify the persons in question may mean simply that their lives are not recorded in the historical sources that have come down to us. The supposition that there was only one teacher of righteousness but more than one wicked priest especially arouses misgivings. Surely in that case there would have been some clearer indication of the plurality of the wicked priest.

Not all who find the historical background of the commentary in the pre-Maccabean period consider it necessary to adopt any multiple interpretation of the titles in question. Several scholars identify the teacher of righteousness with Onias III and the wicked priest with Menelaus. What our sources tell us about Onias III can be summarized very briefly. He is said to have been a man of such godliness that during his high priesthood the temple was honored even by gentile rulers. One of them, however, attempted to despoil the treasures deposited there, but a divine apparition frustrated the impious design. A king of Sparta sent a letter to Onias declaring that Jews and Spartans alike were descendants of Abraham. When Onias was deposed at the accession of Antiochus Epiphanes, he took refuge in Egypt. There, some years later, according to one story, he built a temple like the one at Jerusalem; elsewhere Josephus attributes this to Onias IV, while the Talmud gives the credit for it to Onias II. According to II Maccabees, Onias III sought refuge in Syria but was murdered at the instigation of Menelaus in the sacred grove of Daphne on the outskirts of Antioch.

There is really very little in all this that can be connected with the inspired teacher of righteousness of the Habakkuk Commentary. The supposition that he was exiled and pursued to the house of his exile, as Onias was, depends on a particular interpretation of the difficult expression which I translate as "wishing to banish him." Like Onias, the teacher of righteousness was a champion of the covenant; both he and Onias had trouble with treacherous men and wicked priests. That is about all. The case for the identification of the teacher of righteousness with Onias III really depends upon the degree to which other characters in the commentary can be identified with his contemporaries.

For the role of the wicked priest, Menelaus is the favorite candidate of those who consider the situation reflected by the commentary to have been in the pre-Maccabean period. He was conspicuously guilty of plundering and persecuting devout Jews in collaboration with his royal patron, Antiochus Epiphanes. It was while he was high priest that "the abomination of desolation" was set up in the temple, unclean animals were sacrificed, and the sacred courts were defiled by pagan debauchery. His death corresponds, at least in part, to what is said in the commentary about the humiliation and horrible agony of the wicked priest: according to II Maccabees he was dropped from a high tower into hot ashes.

Not every point in what is said about the wicked priest, however, can be connected with anything known about Menelaus. The statement that the wicked priest "was named according to the truth when he first took office" hardly refers to Menelaus, and the "horrors of sore diseases" said to have been suffered by the wicked priest are not recorded of him.

The man of the lie is commonly believed by advocates of the pre-Maccabean hypothesis to be Antiochus Epiphanes himself. This view has been criticized on the ground that it draws a distinction between the man of the lie and the wicked priest. There is no basis in the text, it is claimed, for distinguishing them. One may ask whether there is any basis in the text for identifying them. It is true, however, that much the same charges are brought against them, and both were adversaries of the teacher of righteousness.

On the other hand it is argued that no Jewish priest of that time could be said to have "rejected the law among all peoples," whereas that statement fits Antiochus admirably. This argument depends upon a conjectural restoration of the text different from the one underlying my translation. There is a gap in the manuscript between the first and last letters of the last word in the passage just cited. By supplying the two missing letters in different ways we can get the meaning "peoples" or "their council" or "their congregation." No sound argument can be based on any such purely hypothetical reconstruction of a word. Whether the man of the lie and the wicked priest are to be regarded as the same person remains uncertain.

That the man of the lie and the preacher of the lie are the same man is hardly more certain, though most interpreters have assumed this to be the case. The preacher of the lie, says the commentator, "enticed many to build a city of delusion in blood and to establish a congregation in falsehood." How does this apply to

Antiochus Epiphanes? It has been suggested that the city was the Akra or citadel at Jerusalem, of which I Maccabees 1:33 says that the Syrian army "fortified the city of David . . . and it became their citadel."

But did Antiochus establish a congregation? An answer to this question has been found in I Maccabees 1:34, which speaks of "a sinful people, lawless men," whom the Syrians stationed in the Akra. This was not a mere mob but an organized body with a definite mission; therefore, it is claimed, the Hebrew word translated "congregation" could be appropriately used of it. That this word would ever have been used in such a sense is decidedly doubtful.

The theory that the house of Absalom, who did not help the teacher of righteousness against the man of the lie, was the Tobiad family or party has been weighed and found wanting. Another suggestion remains to be considered in connection with the pre-Maccabean hypothesis. In I Maccabees 11:70 a Mattathias, son of Absalom, is mentioned, and II Maccabees 13:11 refers to a Jonathan, son of Absalom. Possibly the same Absalom was the father of both these men; he may also have been the Absalom named in II Maccabees 11:17 as an envoy of Judas Maccabeus. A few scholars believe that his family was the house of Absalom of the Habakkuk Commentary. There is nothing in what we are told about this Absalom, or any of these Absaloms, to explain such a connection between him and the group mentioned in the commentary. He may have been at first an ally of Onias III, it is said, and later may have turned against him or remained neutral in one of the several conflicts which Onias had with his rivals. But this is pure conjecture. Only the fact that he was a contemporary of Onias III and the fact that his name was Absalom afford any ground at all for the suggestion. The latter point does not impress those of us who find it hard to believe that the commentator had in mind a man named Absalom.

Let us try to put together the whole picture according to the pre-Maccabean hypothesis. If we substitute names for the cryptic designations used in the commentary, the theory implies that God made known to the high priest Onias III the meaning of the words of the prophets, and through him declared what was coming upon the last generations. His enemies, who betrayed the covenant, did not believe Onias. He was persecuted by his rival, Menelaus, and had some trouble also with the king, Antiochus Epiphanes. The Tobiads, or the family of Absalom, kept silence at his chastisement and did not help him against Antiochus, who rejected the law of God in the midst of their whole congregation. Many were enticed by Antiochus to build a city of delusion in blood and to establish a congregation in falsehood. They reviled and insulted God's elect, but the doers of the law believed in Onias and persevered in the service of the truth when they were in distress. Menelaus was named according to the truth when he first took office, but when he had begun to rule in Israel he became proud, forsook God, and betrayed the statutes for the sake of wealth. He plundered and assembled the wealth of the men of violence who rebelled against God; he also took the wealth of peoples, and plundered the wealth of the poor in the cities of Judah, plotting to destroy them. He walked in the ways of drunkenness and wrought unclean abominations. He did abominable things in Jerusalem and defiled God's sanctuary. He persecuted Onias, wishing to banish him (or pursued him to the place of exile). On the Day of Atonement he appeared to the followers of Onias to confound them and make them stumble on their sabbath of rest; but for the wrong done to Onias and his party God delivered Menelaus to his enemies, afflicting him with a destroying scourge in bitterness of soul. Horrors of sore diseases were wrought in him, and vengeance in the body of his flesh.

Much, if not all, of this may have happened, but very little of it is recorded in any of the sources for the history of the period. Conceivably some of the allusions might be clearer if we knew more about Onias and Menelaus. The weakest part of the theory is the idea that Onias III was the teacher of righteousness. No doubt he was a good man and was persecuted. He certainly had difficulties with Antiochus Epiphanes. But nothing indicates that he was in any special way a teacher of righteousness beyond the statement of II Maccabees 3:1 that because of his godliness and his hatred of wickedness the laws were strictly observed while he was high priest. Actually there is nothing in the commentary to suggest that the teacher of righteousness was a high priest. If what he suffered at the hands of the man of the lie and the wicked priest included expulsion from the high priesthood, the lack of any hint of this in the commentary is very strange.

For the Maccabean or Hasmonean period several situations and combinations of persons have been proposed as solutions of our problem. In 168 B.C. the rebellion provoked by the repressive measures of Antiochus Epiphanes broke out openly. By a series of brilliant campaigns Judas Maccabeus in four years achieved religious liberty, and then went on toward the attainment of political independence.

A dual identification of the teacher of righteousness has been suggested for the very beginning of this period. The term "teacher of righteousness" can be translated "guide of righteousness." So understood, according to this theory, it was applied to Mattathias, the father of Judas, and also to Judas himself. It is hard to see any connection between either Mattathias or Judas and the teacher of righteousness of the Habakkuk Commentary. During the first years of the Maccabean revolt Menelaus was still high priest, but nothing in his recorded relations with Judas corresponds to the persecution, the appearance on the Day of Atonement, or any of the other incidents referred to by the commentator.

In 164 B.C. Antiochus Epiphanes died. His son, Antiochus V, reigned only two short years but in that time defeated Judas in an important battle, regained control of Jerusalem, deposed Menelaus and had him put to death. The supplanter and successor of Antiochus V, Demetrius I, gave the high priesthood to Alcimus, who is the next candidate for the post of wicked priest. The devout Jews, known as Hasidim, who had at first supported the Maccabean revolt, welcomed Alcimus, but, after swearing not to harm them, he had sixty of them murdered. In rabbinic traditions he appears as a persecutor of the righteous and a pillager of the temple treasures.

In his attainment of the high priesthood and his struggle with the Maccabees, Alcimus was strongly supported and aided by the Syrian general Bacchides, who has therefore been nominated for the double role of the man of the lie and the preacher of the lie. Josephus attributes to him the faithless murder of sixty of the Hasidim, as well as a fruitless effort to entrap Judas Maccabeus by treachery.

The same family of Absalom suggested under the pre-Maccabean hypothesis serves here too as the house of Absalom of our commentary. The references in I and II Maccabees to a man (or men) named Absalom indicate that he was (or they were) allied with the Maccabees; for that reason the family of Absalom might well have refused to support the Hasidim, who had withdrawn from the Maccabean movement. How they could have been expected to support these Hasidim under the circumstances is not so easy to see.

The teacher of righteousness may have been, it is suggested, an unknown member of the group of murdered Hasidim. There is also a specific individual, however, who has been seriously considered in this connection. An uncle of the high priest Alcimus named Jose ben Joezer was, according to rabbinic tradition, both a priest and an eminent master of the law. It is related of him that he was condemned to be hanged and was taunted by Alcimus, but replied with such wisdom that his cruel nephew was moved to repent.

After about four years in office Alcimus ordered the wall of the inner temple court torn down, but before his impious command could be carried out he was struck dumb and paralyzed. Some days later he died in agony. It is not surprising that scholars have seen a reference to his dire end in what is said of the "horrors of sore diseases" and "vengeance in the body of his flesh" suffered by the wicked priest. The similarity is impressive, but it should not be forgotten that a reference here to the wicked priest, though probable, is not certain; moreover, there is at least a faint suggestion that his suffering was inflicted by his enemies.

This theory deserves at least a résumé such as I have given for the pre-Maccabean hypothesis. Using the name of Jose ben Joezer rather than an unknown and unnamable Hasid, we may say that God made known to Jose the meaning of prophecy and through him declared what was coming upon the last generations. His enemies, who betrayed the covenant, did not believe him. He was persecuted by the high priest Alcimus and had some trouble also with Bacchides. The family of Absalom kept silence at his chastisement and did not help him against Bacchides, who rejected the law of God in the midst of a whole congregation. Many were enticed by Bacchides to build a city of delusion in blood and to establish a congregation in falsehood. They reviled and insulted God's elect, but the Hasidim believed in Jose and persevered in the service of the truth when they were in distress. Alcimus was named according to the truth when he first took office, but when he had begun to rule in Israel he became proud, forsook God, and betrayed the statutes for the sake of wealth. He plundered and assembled the wealth of the men of violence who rebelled against God; he also took the wealth of peoples and plundered the wealth of the poor in the cities of Judah, plotting to destroy them. He walked in the ways of drunkenness and wrought unclean abominations. He did abominable things in Jerusalem and defiled God's sanctuary. He persecuted Jose ben Joezer, wishing to banish him (or pursued him to the place of his exile). On the Day of Atonement he appeared to the Hasidim to confound them and make them stumble on their sabbath of rest; but for the wrong done to Jose and his party God delivered Alcimus to his enemies, afflicting him with a destroying scourge in bitterness of soul, because he acted treacherously against the elect. Horrors of sore diseases were wrought in him and vengeance in the body of his flesh.

This makes a total picture at least as impressive as the one presented by the pre-Maccabean theory, though again not every point fits what we find in our sources about the persons involved. The weakest point here too is the identification of the teacher of righteousness. Strictly speaking, Jose ben Joezer and Bacchides should not be combined in the same theory. If Jose is supposed to be the teacher of righteousness it is better to make Alcimus play the part of the man of the lie as well as that of the wicked priest; whereas if Bacchides is regarded as the man of the lie, an unknown victim in the slaughter of the sixty Hasidim will serve better than Jose as the teacher of righteousness.

Before the death of Alcimus, Judas Maccabeus was defeated and killed in the battle of Elasa in 160 B.C. His brother Jonathan then assumed the leadership of the Jews. Bacchides, who had defeated Judas, found himself helpless against Jonathan's guerrilla tactics. Finally, in 157 B.C., he made peace with Jonathan. The anxious two years between the death of Alcimus in 159 and the final withdrawal of Bacchides in 157 have been suggested as the time when the Habakkuk Commentary was written.

A slightly later date is contemplated by a very different theory, which sees in Jonathan himself the wicked priest of some passages in the commentary. Jonathan's assumption of the high priesthood, it is thought, was resented by the teacher of righteousness and his followers, who believed that only the descendants of Zadok could legitimately be high priests. After maintaining and improving his position, both by astute political relations with the contenders for the throne of Syria and by military victories, Jonathan fell a victim of treachery and was captured, thrown into a dungeon, and finally assassinated. These events are believed to be reflected in what is said of the "destroying scourge" inflicted on the wicked priest by his enemies.

This interpretation, however, is only one part of a dual identification of the wicked priest. The priest who was a drunkard, plundered the poor, and defiled the temple is thought to be not Jonathan but his brother Simon, who succeeded him as high priest in 142 B.C. and was assassinated while drunk in 135 B.C. He is supposed to be also the preacher of the lie who built a city in blood. Impressive as this theory is at certain points, it not only suffers from the weakness of being unable to find one priest to whom all that is said about the wicked priest can be applied, but also fails to provide a satisfactory identification for other characters in the story.

Simon's son, John Hyrcanus, was high priest from 135 to 104 B.C.

At this time the major groupings within Judaism, which we find well established in New Testament times, were taking definite shape. The most influential of these, which ultimately prevailed and set the pattern for orthodox Judaism in succeeding centuries, was the party known as the Pharisees. They were devout and strict in their obedience to the law, though capable of some elasticity in its interpretation. They opposed the assumption of both priestly and royal offices by the Hasmoneans. For this reason John Hyrcanus, after having aligned himself with them at first, withdrew his support near the end of his reign and persecuted their leaders so aggressively that some were forced into exile.

According to Josephus, the Pharisees in general had approved the conduct of Hyrcanus, but the break with them came when one of them, named Eleazar, told the king that he ought to give up the high priesthood and be satisfied with governing the people. The same story appears, with some differences, in the Talmud. Brownlee suggests that Hyrcanus was the man of the lie, that Eleazar was the teacher of righteousness, and that the house of Absalom means the Pharisees, who did not support Eleazar when he rebuked Hyrcanus. The chastisement or reproof of the teacher of righteousness is thus taken to mean the teacher's reproof of the man of the lie.

From the Dead Sea Scrolls in general, and from the Habakkuk Commentary in particular, it would not seem that the teacher of righteousness and his followers were Pharisees. This difficulty is met by the suggestion that Eleazar was an extremist, whose followers would not go all the way with him; but the point is that the doctrines and practices reflected by the Dead Sea Scrolls are not at all those of Pharisaism as it is known to us from other sources. We shall have to come back to this question again.

Some support for the view that Eleazar the Pharisee was the teacher of righteousness has been found in the fact that the Talmud's account of the same incident gives his name not as Eleazar but as Judah ben Jedediah. Brownlee suggests also that Judah ben Jedediah and Judah the Essene, of whom we shall hear more presently, were the same man. This involves a conception of the

Essenes as an extreme branch of the Pharisees, another idea we must discuss later.

That the teacher of righteousness was named Judah is thought to be indicated, as we noted in the last chapter, by the references to "the house of Judah," "the simple ones of Judah," and "the cities of Judah" in the commentary. Even the use of the expression "I will praise thee" at the beginning of some of the Thanksgiving Psalms is adduced as evidence for this theory, because the same verb is used in Genesis 29:35, where Leah, in naming her son Judah, says, "I will praise the Lord."

With full appreciation of the ingenuity and originality of these ideas, one finds it difficult to take them quite seriously. A complicated structure built out of clever guesses is no more solid than the materials of which it is made. It has been pointed out that whereas the wicked priest in the commentary is accused of pride and greed, the objection against Hyrcanus raised by Eleazar, according to Josephus, was that he was believed to be the son of a captive woman, and therefore ineligible for the high priesthood.

The theory that Eleazar was the teacher of righteousness and John Hyrcanus was the man of the lie is part of a rather elaborate multiple interpretation of the historical allusions in the commentary. Hyrcanus is thought to be also one of several wicked priests, the one in particular who was at first named according to the truth but forsook God and betrayed the statutes after he began to rule in Israel. This is more impressive than the interpretation of the man of the lie and the teacher of righteousness with which it is combined. The chief point in its favor is the fact that Hyrcanus was on good terms with the Pharisees when he first took office but broke with them later. This could possibly be what is meant by his being called at first by the name of truth, though the connection is hardly obvious.

It is perhaps both an advantage and a weakness of such multiple interpretations that they do not have to find one person to whom all the statements about the wicked priest apply. Since it is not claimed that all these passages refer to Hyrcanus, it would be pointless to try to reconstruct a unified picture for all of them.

This deprives us, however, of a helpful test to which the more comprehensive theories can be subjected.

The successor of John Hyrcanus was his son, Aristobulus I. Although he ruled only one year (104–103 B.C.), he retained and perhaps even extended the realm that had been won by his predecessors. He was also apparently the first member of the Hasmonean dynasty to assume openly the title of king. On his accession he imprisoned all his brothers with the exception of one named Antigonus. Later, aroused to jealousy against Antigonus, he brought about his death by treachery, for which the pangs of remorse were added to the agony of the lingering intestinal disorder of which he died.

The manner of his death makes Aristobulus a promising contender for the role of the wicked priest who suffered "horrors of sore diseases" and "vengeance in the body of his flesh." Because of the loss of one or two lines at the bottom of the eighth column, however, we cannot now say whether the whole passage could be applied to Aristobulus. No scholar, so far as I know, has claimed that what we know of Aristobulus fits all the statements about the wicked priest.

A curious incident in the reign of Aristobulus affords a tempting identification of the teacher of righteousness. It is especially attractive to those who believe that the Qumran covenanters were Essenes. According to Josephus, a member of the Essenes named Judah was noted for his accurate predictions of the future. Having predicted the death of Aristobulus's brother Antigonus on a certain day and at a certain place, he was dismayed at seeing Antigonus alive late that day and far from the place where he was expected to die. The prophecy was exactly fulfilled, however, for Antigonus was waylaid and murdered at a nearby place of the same name. What makes this incident especially interesting for our purpose is that Judah is said to have had disciples whom he instructed in the art of foretelling the future.

Aristobulus was followed by the eldest of his surviving brothers, Alexander Janneus (103–76 B.C.). An ambitious and able warrior, he both conquered new territory and suppressed rebellion within his kingdom, but only at the cost of great bitterness. Like others of his family, he was not only a hard fighter but a hard drinker, and in his last years he suffered much from an affliction caused by his intemperance. He died, however, in battle.

Several scholars have seen in Alexander Janneus the wicked priest of the Habakkuk Commentary. He is qualified for the role on several points, including drunkenness, luxury, immorality, love of riches, sickness, and final punishment by his enemies. An interesting explanation has been offered also for the statement that the wicked priest "was named according to the truth when he first took office." The name according to the truth (literally, "name of the truth"), it is suggested, was Alexander's Jewish name, Jonathan (i.e., "The Lord gave"), from which the late Hebrew form Yannai and the Greek form Janneus are thought by some to have been derived. His forsaking God when he began to rule is explained as an allusion to his assumption of the royal title, which meant forsaking the fidelity to the house of David symbolized by the name Jonathan. For the same reason the dynasty of Alexander Janneus is thought to be meant by the term "house of Absalom." The glory of Janneus consisted in winning a kingdom as large as that of David and Solomon; his ignominy, which surpassed his glory, consisted in the blood, cruelty, and hatred that marked his reign.

The commentator's statement that the wicked priest was delivered to his enemies is regarded by some scholars as an allusion to a disastrous defeat of Alexander Janneus by the Nabateans, from which he barely escaped alive. Before this there had been a riot in the temple when Alexander officiated at the Feast of Tabernacles; after his defeat the people rose against him again, and for several years there was a civil war which is said to have caused the death of fifty thousand Jews. Although Alexander tried to make peace with the people, he was unable to achieve a reconciliation.

The mysterious appearance on the Day of Atonement, inevitably central in all the theories, has been connected by a number of scholars with the rising of the people against Alexander Janneus at the Feast of Tabernacles. This, it is thought, may have been a popular reaction to the provocation on the Day of Atonement. The Feast of Tabernacles comes five days after the Day of Atonement, when the incident in question took place. It is possible, however, as we have already seen, that this event hinged upon a difference concerning the religious calendar. If so, we cannot tell what was the chronological relation between the official Feast of Tabernacles and the Day of Atonement observed by the disciples of the teacher of righteousness.

The discussion of Alexander's candidacy for the role of the wicked priest has unfortunately been confused by being combined with the discussion of the Kittim. Those who regard Alexander as the wicked priest are not agreed as to whether the Kittim are the Seleucids or the Romans. Thirteen years intervened between his death in 76 B.C. and the occupation of Judah by Pompey. For the advocates of multiple identifications, of course, there is no problem here at all: some allusions may refer to the time of the Seleucid domination, and others to the Roman period. But the power of the Romans was known in Palestine long before the time of Pompey. The commentator may have expected them to come sooner than they did.

If Alexander Janneus was the wicked priest, who was the teacher of righteousness? No answer to this question has been offered on the supposition that Alexander was the only wicked priest envisaged by the commentator; but if there were two or more wicked priests in close succession, the same teacher of righteousness can be postulated for episodes involving both or all of them. Thus Eleazar or Judah, who rebuked John Hyrcanus, is believed also to have been the teacher of righteousness who was persecuted by Alexander Janneus. As a matter of fact, the story Josephus tells in connection with the break between the Pharisees and Hyrcanus appears in the Talmud under the reign of Alexander Janneus. Moreover, if Judah ben Jedediah was Judah the Essene, he was involved also with Aristobulus I, who reigned between John Hyrcanus and Alexander Janneus. All this is, to say the least, very confusing. The confusion is in part inherent in our sources themselves. One is tempted to feel also, however, that the theories which resort to a multiple identification of the wicked priest have an unfair advantage in being free to distribute what is said of him among several different men.

Not all who regard Alexander Janneus as the wicked priest make him share that doubtful honor with others. In one form of the hypothesis, indeed, Alexander not only keeps to himself the role of the wicked priest but also plays the part of the man of the lie and even, paradoxically, that of Absalom, whose house did not support the teacher of righteousness against the man of the lie. According to another view, Absalom was a brother of Alexander Janneus who refrained from intervening in the conflict between the latter and the teacher of righteousness. Still another theory distinguishes the man of the lie from the wicked priest and identifies him with a famous leader of the Pharisees, Simon ben Shetah, who was a brother of Salome Alexandra, the wife of Alexander Janneus.

From all these variations of the thesis that Alexander was the wicked priest, or one of the wicked priests, we cannot expect a clear picture to emerge. Perhaps the very existence of so many different theories connected with Alexander Janneus should arouse suspicion as to the validity of any association between him and the Habakkuk Commentary. Serious objections to him as the wicked priest have been raised. With all his drunkenness and rapacity, and all the bloody conflicts during his reign, he did not, Michel argues, abandon the statutes or the covenant. His enemies within the Jewish nation were the Pharisees, with whom the disciples of the teacher of righteousness cannot be identified, and the struggle was more political than religious. Another difficulty is that none of the proposed identifications of other characters in his reign seems more than remotely possible. At the same time, the contacts between his career and what the commentary says of the wicked priest are still impressive. If any dual or multiple identification must be adopted, Alexander Janneus was probably one of the wicked priests.

It may be well to remind ourselves at this point that we have reached the time when the community of Qumran was certainly in existence. Coins of John Hyrcanus, Aristobulus I, and Alexander Janneus were found in the remains of the first building at Khirbet Qumran. If the career of the teacher of righteousness must be dated later than the reign of Alexander Janneus, the teacher was not the founder of the sect but a leader who arose in the course of its history. In that case, however, any convincing identification must take account of the fact that the sect was already leading a separate life of its own in the desert.

The successor of Alexander was his widow, Salome Alexandra, who reigned from 76 to 67 B.C. No scholar has yet proposed her for any role in our drama, but this cannot be said of her sons, Hyrcanus and Aristobulus. During her life Hyrcanus served as high priest, and after her death he would normally have succeeded her. Aristobulus, however, attacked and defeated him and compelled him to give up both throne and high priesthood, reigning in his stead as Aristobulus II (67–63 B.C.).

If Hyrcanus had been left to himself, Aristobulus might have had things his own way; but now an able and ambitious man saw an opportunity to advance his own interests by promoting the strife between the two brothers. This man was Antipater, son of a governor of Idumea, and perhaps his father's successor as governor. At his instigation Hyrcanus sought help from the king of the Nabateans across the Jordan, who, nothing loath, attacked and defeated Aristobulus.

Not only the Idumean Antipater but also the Roman general Pompey, who at this time represented the power of Rome in Syria, was quick to take advantage of this situation. In 65 B.C. his legate intervened on behalf of Aristobulus, and in 63 Pompey himself received at Damascus appeals from the two contending brothers and also from the people of Judah, who were tired of both of them. Finding Aristobulus unreliable, the Romans arrested him. At Jerusalem they were allowed by the party of Hyrcanus to enter the city, but the adherents of Aristobulus took refuge in the temple. Only after a siege of three months did Pompey capture this stronghold. The high priesthood was restored to Hyrcanus, who held it until 40 B.C. as a vassal of Rome. Although commonly known as Hyrcanus II, he was not allowed to call himself king.

So began the Roman period of Jewish history, to which not a few scholars assign the events referred to by the Habakkuk Commentary. The most widely and warmly discussed theory is that of Dupont-Sommer, who sees the historical setting of the commentary in the circumstances and events just related. In this theory, as it was first propounded, the statement that the wicked priest was delivered to his enemies and cruelly afflicted was taken to refer to the tragic end of Aristobulus II, who was led in chains in Pompey's triumphal procession at Rome after the capture of Jerusalem, and died by poison in prison in 49 B.C. In his reign Dupont-Sommer finds also an Absalom, whom he takes to be the head of the house of Absalom mentioned in the commentary. He was the father-in-law of Aristobulus and also his uncle; he may therefore have been a brother of Alexandra, and in that case he was probably a Pharisee. The commentator's statement about the house of Absalom means therefore, according to this theory, that the Pharisees remained neutral when the teacher of righteousness was persecuted by Aristobulus, who is assumed to be the man of the lie as well as the wicked priest. The implication that the house of Absalom should have helped the teacher of righteousness is not explained by this hypothesis, and the parallel is not close enough to justify the improbable assumption that a man actually named Absalom was referred to by the commentator.

The most distinctive and controversial point in Dupont-Sommer's theory is his interpretation of the passage about the Day of Atonement. His insistence that the verb "appeared" implies a divine manifestation has already been discussed, together with his contention that it was the teacher of righteousness who appeared. With these unacceptable premises, Dupont-Sommer argues that on the Day of Atonement the teacher of righteousness, who had previously suffered martyrdom, appeared as a divine being to confound and punish the wicked priest. Such a divine manifestation, overwhelming the people of Jerusalem, can only have been, he thinks, the capture of Jerusalem by Pompey on the Day of Atonement in 63 B.C.

If the teacher of righteousness had been put to death before the coming of Pompey, when was this crime committed? According to Josephus, Aristobulus spent some time at Jerusalem in the spring of 63, making preparations for war. Under such circumstances he would naturally attempt to get rid of his enemies, and it may have been then that he liquidated the teacher of righteousness. Another possible occasion, somewhat earlier, would have been the time when Aristobulus was besieged by his brother Hyrcanus and the Nabatean king in 65 B.C.

Who then was the teacher of righteousness? The original theory did not answer this question, but an answer was soon proposed by one of its advocates. Both Josephus and the Talmud record the stoning of a man called Onias the Righteous in 65 B.C. He was a saintly man and was believed to have brought rain by his prayers. He was probably, it is thought, an Essene. He was stoned by the followers of Hyrcanus for refusing to curse Aristobulus. If Aristobulus was the wicked priest, one would suppose that he was the one that put Onias to death, but it is suggested that perhaps each party accused the other of the crime. Another difficulty is that the wicked priest is supposed to have been punished by the fall of Jerusalem, but according to Josephus the stoning of Onias was punished by violent winds that destroyed the crops and caused a famine. On the other hand, the Talmud regards this famine as judgment for a different offense by the followers of Hyrcanus. The conclusion is therefore drawn that there were two stories about the death of Onias; indeed, he may actually have been persecuted by both parties. Several weaknesses in this argument have been pointed out. There is no evidence that Onias was an Essene, or that he was the founder or reformer of a sect. There is no real reason to believe that he was in any sense a Messianic figure or that, even if he was, he would be the teacher of righteousness.

Quite apart from the identification of the teacher of righteousness, it is surprising that the interpretation of the incident on the

Day of Atonement as the conquest of Jerusalem by Pompey has
been accepted as widely as it has been. Even if the interpretations
of particular words we have found questionable could be accepted,
there would still be nothing in the passage to suggest the capture
of a city by a foreign army. If such an allusion was intended, it
is strange that no occasion for it was found in the passages concerning the Kittim. Why and how the capture of Jerusalem by
Pompey should be regarded as brought about by the teacher of
righteousness is not apparent, except as any national calamity
can be considered a divine punishment for any sin. As a matter of
fact, historians seriously question the statement of Josephus that
Jerusalem fell on the Day of Atonement.

This theory suffers further from the weakness already found in
several of the others, the necessity of postulating two wicked
priests. Passages in the commentary which imply that the wicked
priest's punishment is still in the future are taken to refer not to
Aristobulus II but to Hyrcanus II, who was high priest from the
fall of Jerusalem to the Parthian invasion of Palestine in 40 B.C.
Since the commentary does not refer to this event, Dupont-
Sommer believes that it was written shortly before 40 B.C.

The statement that the wicked priest "was named according to
the truth when he first took office, but when he had begun to rule
in Israel his heart was lifted up," is taken to mean that while
Hyrcanus was high priest during the reign of Alexandra, he forsook God by becoming also ruler after the fall of Aristobulus in
63. Since Hyrcanus was only a figurehead under the Roman
dominion, this interpretation of the passage is not very impressive.
The building of a city in blood by the prophet of the lie is interpreted as an allusion to the permission given to Hyrcanus II in
47 B.C. to rebuild the walls of Jerusalem. It has been pointed out,
however, that permission to repair breaches in the temple enclosure did not make Hyrcanus a city-builder.

The theory maintains also that "the last priests of Jerusalem,"
whose wealth is to be delivered to the Kittim, are Aristobulus II
and Hyrcanus II. This is more plausible than the idea that the
wicked priest is a dual figure; at least we have here "priests"

instead of "the wicked priest." If Aristobulus and Hyrcanus are the "last priests of Jerusalem," it does not follow that any passage that mentions the wicked priest refers to either of them.

Altogether the theory that the wicked priest means both Aristobulus II and Hyrcanus II raises more questions than it answers. It seems strange that after speaking first of Aristobulus II the commentator should turn to Hyrcanus in the eighth column, then return to Aristobulus in the ninth column, again to Hyrcanus in the tenth column, back to Aristobulus in the eleventh column, and to Hyrcanus again at the bottom of column eleven and the top of column twelve. This is not in itself, of course, a conclusive objection. As I have said before, the commentator was not bound by our conceptions of logical procedure. In referring to one priest or the other he would have been guided by what the particular text he was interpreting suggested to him. Still, such an extreme oscillation back and forth arouses some misgiving. The chief difficulty, however, with this as with other similar theories, is that nothing in the text suggests a double or multiple application except the fact that it is difficult to find one historical character to whom all the passages can be applied. Dupont-Sommer himself, in fact, now declares himself ready to recognize Hyrcanus II alone as the wicked priest, provided the whole ministry of the teacher of righteousness is dated before 63 B.C.

Elliger also places the events of the commentary in the Roman period, but avoids the weakness of a plural identification of the wicked priest. Aristobulus and also Antigonus, who succeeded Hyrcanus in 40 B.C., are eliminated for several reasons, including the fact that the enemies to whom they were delivered were the Romans, whereas the enemies to whom the wicked priest was delivered seem to be distinguished from the Kittim in the commentary. Hyrcanus II is thus left as the most likely candidate. His enemies were the Parthians, who took him captive and, by cutting off his ears, made him ineligible to serve again as high priest. Since nothing in the Commentary shows any knowledge of the ransom of Hyrcanus by Herod in 37/36 B.C., the date of the commentary, Elliger concludes, must fall between 40 and 37/36.

A few theories have been proposed which place the characters of our story in the Christian era. While the archeological evidence now excludes a date after the fall of Jerusalem in 70 A.D., this fact should not prevent us from giving any consideration to theories that place the date of the Habakkuk Commentary after that date. Later "intrusions" are not unknown to archeologists. If we discovered a document clearly reflecting events of the twentieth century A.D., any archeological evidence that pointed to an earlier date would have to be re-examined. Plausible arguments for impossible theories may at least expose the danger of relying too much upon obscure and ambiguous historical allusions.

A date in the first century A.D., of course, would not be archeologically impossible, though the paleography of the scroll would make it rather hard to accept. The reference to building a city in blood has been supposed by Ben Zion Katz to indicate that the commentary was written during the reign of the emperor Tiberius (14–37 A.D.), the city in question being Tiberias, which was built by Herod Antipas (4 B.C.–39 A.D.) and named in honor of the emperor. The preacher of the lie who enticed many to build the city is thought to be a follower of the famous Rabbi Hillel, who advised Jews to settle in Tiberias in spite of reports that the city was built over a cemetery.

In other passages references to events of the first century A.D. are found. In 6 A.D., when the Roman prefect of Syria took a census of Judea for purposes of taxation, the high priest Joazer ben Boethus induced the people of Jerusalem to submit to the census, but in Galilee a violent revolt broke out under the leadership of Judas the Galilean. With him was associated a Pharisee named Sadduk or Zadok. Josephus names Judah and Zadok as the founders of what he calls the "fourth philosophy" in Judaism. It has been suggested that the wicked priest who persecuted the teacher of righteousness was Joazer ben Boethus, and the teacher of righteousness was Zadok the Pharisee. The "counsel of the community" (instead of "council"—the Hebrew word may mean either) is taken to mean the advice of Judas the Galilean and Zadok the Pharisee not to submit to enrollment or taxation; the "simple ones of Judah" are supposed to be those who allowed themselves to be counted. This is clearly impossible, because the "simple ones of Judah" are the "doers of the law," evidently the followers of the teacher of righteousness.

The crucial passage concerning the events on the Day of Atonement is connected also with Zadok the Pharisee. He advocated a calendar in which every month had thirty days; this made the Day of Atonement fall on a day which for the followers of Hillel, who determined the festivals by observation of the moon, would be a profane day. Joazer ben Boethus, it is supposed, made the followers of Zadok stumble by prescribing work on the day which for them was the Day of Atonement. We have seen a similar suggestion applied to an earlier period. Other details of this theory are less important. The situation contemplated by it lies within a period when the commentary may possibly have been written. On the whole, however, it seems no more appropriate or convincing than any of the others.

The most startling of all theories concerning the identification of the characters in our document is that of Teicher. According to him the teacher of righteousness was Jesus, who was venerated as the true prophet by the Jewish Christian sect called Ebionites. The name Ebionite is derived from a Hebrew word meaning "poor." This word occurs in the commentary, and Teicher takes it to be an explicit reference to the Ebionites. The preacher of the lie is supposed to be the Apostle Paul, whom the Ebionites regarded as a false apostle and a traitor to the Gospel. Most readers will find little in the commentary that recalls either Jesus or Paul. It must be recognized, however, that what the theory contemplates is not the Jesus and Paul of the New Testament but the ideas of them held by the Ebionites. This theory too lies within the limits of chronological possibility. It is less plausible than several other theories, but more must be said about it when we consider the problem of identifying the Qumran community.

For one who considers all these theories without prejudice, and with no sense of obligation to propose a new theory to end all theories, it will hardly seem that the result of the debate can be stated with a confident Q. E. D. Perhaps not even one individual, group, or event has been identified with certainty. The Kittim are probably the Romans, but not certainly. Whether they had already conquered Palestine when the Habakkuk Commentary was written is still less certain. The scholars who have discussed these problems have all been more successful in refuting one another's theories than in establishing their own.

It is easier to find identifications for the wicked priest than for the teacher of righteousness, and identifications of the house of Absalom are all too plentiful, yet no priest recorded in history quite corresponds at every point to the wicked priest described in the commentary. If even one passage clearly and certainly referred to a particular individual, that fact could be accepted, even though other passages still remained obscure. Unfortunately we cannot get beyond a debatable degree of probability with regard to any passage.

After all, our sources for the history of the Jews in Hellenistic and Roman times are not so exhaustive or so completely reliable in detail that we can expect to find in them accounts of individuals and movements capable of being equated at every point with the data of the Dead Sea Scrolls. Every document reflects a particular point of view, and the point of view reported by the Dead Sea Scrolls was rejected and condemned by those from whom our other sources have come. Just as we find almost no reference to Jesus in Roman history, it should not be altogether surprising if the rise of a dissenting group and the career of its leader have left no trace in the extant sources for the history of the period.

If the identifications of individuals and groups must remain uncertain, our inquiry has not been entirely fruitless from the point of view of our major purpose in undertaking it. What concerns us here is the time when the Commentary of Habukkuk was written, as indicated by its historical allusions. The variety and range of possible applications is perhaps disappointingly wide, but it is not entirely unlimited. At least we can see that within the limits indicated by archeology and paleography there is abundant room for the events to which the book refers and the composition of the book itself.

We can be a little more definite than that. If the Kittim are the Romans, the Romans were at least in sight at the time when the commentary was written. If their occupation of Palestine had not yet taken place, it was at least contemplated as imminent. On the other hand, the Jewish revolt against Rome and the destruction of the temple were not within the author's range of view. There is nothing to suggest that he knew of the reign of Herod, and the one passage that might be taken to refer to the Roman procurators can with equal or greater appropriateness be interpreted otherwise.

In brief, the Commentary on Habakkuk was in all probability written, at the earliest, not very long before 63 B.C., and at the latest not long after that date. In other words, its composition falls roughly in the last century B.C., between 150 and 100 years before the final abandonment of the caves in the Wady Qumran. This agrees with the indications of paleography that our manuscript of the commentary is one of the younger members of the family of the Dead Sea Scrolls.

IX

Historical Allusions in the Other Documents

None of the other Dead Sea Scrolls compares with the Habakkuk Commentary in the abundance of its historical allusions. There are many such allusions, however, in the Damascus Document, two incomplete manuscripts of which were discovered in a genizah in Old Cairo near the end of the nineteenth century and published by Solomon Schechter in 1910. In March 1948, when we were reading the Habakkuk Commentary for the first time in Jerusalem, I said to Brownlee and Trever, I remember, "This reminds me of the Damascus Document." They immediately went to our library and looked up Schechter's publication. The facsimile of one column Schechter had printed showed them at once that the manuscripts of the Damascus Document were much later than the Dead Sea Scrolls, but the similarity of contents was unmistakable. I remember Brownlee's enthusiasm when he found the teacher of righteousness and other characters of the Habakkuk Commentary in the Damascus Document. In our preliminary description of the scrolls in the *Biblical Archaeologist* for September 1948, I mentioned this connection (p. 58). Every writer who has discussed the Habakkuk Commentary and the Manual of Discipline has had something to say about it.

Because of this obvious and extraordinary affinity, it will be convenient to consider the historical allusions in the Damascus Document before we proceed to those of the other Dead Sea Scrolls. First, however, something must be said concerning the nature and significance of the relationship between the scrolls and the Damascus Document. Many characteristic and unusual expressions are shared by the Damascus Document and the Dead Sea Scrolls. Not only the teacher of righteousness but the man of the lie and the preacher of the lie appear in the Damascus Document as well as in the Habakkuk Commentary. The expression "the new covenant" occurs also in both of these documents, though at present it is found in the commentary only by a restoration of the text which is practically certain. Even the Hebrew word *pishro,* which I translate "this means," is used once in the Damascus Document. There are also several distinctive terms that appear both in the Damascus Document and in the Manual of Discipline. The characteristic words for "rank," "order," and "purity" (applied to "sacred food") may be mentioned as examples. The second of these terms occurs frequently in both documents in a formula introducing new sections, "And this is the order for . . ." The expression "enter the covenant" occurs once in the Manual of Discipline in the same form used in the Damascus Document, though elsewhere the Manual uses a different verb. The "lot of Belial" and the "dominion of Belial" are characteristic of both the Damascus Document and the Manual of Discipline. An unusual word meaning "tribulation" occurs once in each of these two documents. A mysterious book called "the book of *HGW*" (or perhaps *HGY*), which is referred to in the Damascus Document, is not mentioned in the scrolls published by the American Schools of Oriental Research or those published by Sukenik, but it is named in one of the "two columns" related to the Manual of Discipline that were acquired by the Palestine Museum.

Not only do we have these and other instances of a common terminology; there are also rather extended passages that appear in almost identical form in the Damascus Document and the Manual of Discipline. Some of the most striking of these may be quoted to show how close the relationship is. The passages from the Manual will be indicated by the letter M, those from the Damascus Document by the letter D.

(M) . . . and to love all that he has chosen and hate all that he has rejected, to be far from all evil and cleave to all good works, and to do truth and righteousness and justice in the land; to walk no longer in the stubbornness of a guilty heart and eyes of fornication.

(D) And now, my sons, listen to me, and I will uncover your eyes to see and understand the works of God, and to choose what he likes and reject what he hates; to walk perfectly in all his ways, and not to go about with thoughts of a guilty impulse and eyes of fornication.

(M) Those who are passing into the covenant shall confess after them, saying, "We have committed iniquity, we have transgressed, we have sinned, we have done evil, we and our fathers before us, in walking contrary to the statutes of truth."

(D) . . . and confess before God, "We have sinned, we have done wickedly, both we and our fathers, in walking contrary to the statutes of the covenant."

(M) So they shall do year by year all the days of the dominion of Belial. The priests shall pass over first in order, according to their spirits, one after another; and the Levites shall pass over after them, and all the people shall pass over third in order, one after another.

(D) They shall all be enrolled by their names: the priests first, the Levites second, the sons of Israel third, and the proselyte fourth.

(M) . . . that each may not walk in the stubbornness of his heart or go astray after his heart and his eyes and the thought of his guilty impulse.

(D) . . . and not to go about with thoughts of a guilty impulse and eyes of fornication; for many went astray in them, and mighty men of valor stumbled in them, formerly and until now. In their walking in the stubbornness of their hearts the watchers of heaven fell.

(M) . . . he shall reprove him and shall not bring upon him iniquity; and also a man shall not bring against his neighbor a word before the masters without having rebuked him before witnesses.

(D) You shall reprove your neighbor, lest you bear sin because of him . . . any man of those who enter the covenant who brings a charge against his neighbor without having rebuked him before witnesses.

(M) And in every place where there shall be ten men of the council of the community there shall not be absent from them a priest.

(D) And in a place having ten there shall not be absent a priest learned in the book of *HGW*.

(M) . . . but they shall judge by the first judgments by which the men of the community began to be disciplined, until there shall come a prophet and the Messiahs of Aaron and Israel. These are the statutes for the wise man, that he may walk in them with every living being.

(D) And this is the order of the session of the camps. Those who walk in these during the period of wickedness until arises the Messiah of Aaron and Israel. . . . And these are the statutes for the wise man, that he may walk in them with every living being.

So close is the relationship that at some points the text of one or the other document can be corrected by comparision with the other. For example, there is an expression in the Damascus Document that seems to mean "unique teacher" or "teacher of the only (or favored) one." In another passage we find the expression "men of the only (or favored) one." The Manual of Discipline now shows that these expressions should be very slightly emended to read respectively "teacher of the community" and "men of the community." There is a Hebrew word in the Damascus Document which Schechter copied as *rwy*. This made no sense, and various emendations were proposed. L. Rost, in his edition of the text, read *rzy* ("mysteries of"), and this is now confirmed by the frequent occurrence of the same expression in the Dead Sea Scrolls. In one instance a correction of what seems to me to be a scribe's mistake in the Manual of Discipline is suggested by a similar passage in the Damascus Document: the meaningless word *w''m* should probably read *w'šm* ("and guilt").

Apart from such close contacts in language, there are many more general similarities in ideas and points of view, such as the interest of both documents in Aaron and the sons of Zadok, the idea of a Messiah from the priestly family of Aaron instead of from the royal tribe of Judah, and the manner of citing and interpreting the Old Testament.

On the other hand, there are some differences worth noting. For example, while the Damascus Document regularly speaks of coming into the covenant, the Manual of Discipline usually speaks of passing into the covenant. The Damascus Document speaks of the congregation or the association, while the Manual speaks of the community. The Hebrew word *mwšb* is used in different ways in the two documents: in the Manual of Discipline it means a session of the group; in the Damascus Document it sometimes seems to mean a settlement. The Damascus Document uses a word for property (*m'd*) that does not appear in the Manual. A rather interesting detail is the fact that to the list of priests, Levites, and people (or sons of Israel) the Damascus Document adds the proselyte, who is never mentioned in the Manual of Discipline. There is also much in the Damascus Document about camps and a little about cities, whereas the Manual of Discipline has nothing concerning either. These differences suggest that the two documents come from the same general religious movement but do not represent exactly the same group within the movement, or perhaps the same stage in its history.

The conclusions to be drawn from these comparisons will depend upon the answers to two questions: first, is the Damascus Document earlier or later than the Dead Sea Scrolls? and second, when was the Damascus Document itself written? The discovery of ancient fragments of the Damascus Document in the caves of the Wady Qumran has already been mentioned. Even without this discovery the references to the temple in the Damascus Document show that the book must have been written when worship was still going on in the temple—i.e., before 70 A.D.

It has been generally supposed that the Dead Sea Scrolls were of earlier origin than the Damascus Document. One reason for this belief is the fact that a flight into the wilderness and a settlement in the land of Damascus seem to be presupposed in the Damascus Document, while there is no clear indication that such a flight and a return to Judea had taken place when the Dead Sea Scrolls were written. It seemed natural, therefore, to suppose that the flight referred to in the Damascus Document was probably the occasion for abandoning the scrolls in the caves, and many scholars still proceed on this assumption. Further study and discussion have raised questions about the references in the Damascus Document itself, and indications that this composition may be older than the scrolls have been detected.

Arguments pointing in the opposite direction have been advanced also. M. H. Gottstein finds in the Damascus Document a relaxation of the strict discipline and close organization reflected by the Manual of Discipline. On the ground that the normal development in such a group is "from a strictly disciplined organization to a more and more loosely knit community," he concludes that the Damascus Document is later than the Manual of Discipline. At least, he says, the burden of proof is on him who maintains the contrary. While this seems fair enough if definite evidence is found to support it, a sociological generalization cannot take the place of historical evidence.

It is conceivable that the Damascus Document was written during the same period in which the Dead Sea Scrolls were produced, so that it is later than some of them but earlier than others. Thus Rost argues that the Damascus Document is later than the Manual of Discipline, but he maintains that it does not represent merely a later stage of the same movement. The group represented by the Damascus Document, he suggests, tried to win over the older group represented by the Manual of Discipline. The Thanksgiving Psalms also, Rost believes, are older than the Damascus Document, because they do not yet mention the teacher of righteousness, and the word for "community," which is characteristic of the Manual of Discipline and occurs at least once in the Thanksgiving Psalms has been practically replaced by other words in the Damascus Document. There is also a very close relation between the ending of one of these psalms and the closing psalm of the Manual of Discipline. But while the Damascus Document is considered later than the Manual of Discipline, Rost maintains that the Habakkuk Commentary is later than the Damascus Document, because the latter refers to the teacher of righteousness as still living and says nothing about his suffering, of which much is made in the Habakkuk Commentary.

Another possibility to be taken into account is that the Damascus Document itself is not a single composition written at one time, but a compilation of material of different dates. The portions found in the Old Cairo genizah were parts of two, if not three, different manuscripts. Two pieces (A1 and A2) seem to be written in the same script and were probably parts of one manuscript, but the script of another piece (B) is very different and apparently some-what later. To a large extent the two major manuscripts run parallel, but there are many differences in parallel passages, including sometimes the insertion in one manuscript of material that is entirely lacking in the other.

Isaac Rabinowitz distinguishes three literary strata in the Damascus Document: one is a "discourse of admonition," of which parallel versions are given in manuscripts A1 and B; the second consists of later "glosses" and comments in these same manuscripts; the third stratum is the legal material contained only in fragment A2. A more elaborate analysis has been worked out by A. Rubinstein, who also finds three major portions of somewhat different date. The earliest is the "historical-admonitory" part; the second, which appears in two separate sections, consists of "camp rules" developed in the time when the members of the community were living in camps; the third portion, which has been inserted between the two sections of the second part, consists of "urban laws," which reflect a time when the members had settled in cities. There are also some passages that were probably added at a still later time. The closest parallels with the Manual of Discipline, Rubinstein finds, are in the second section of the "camp rules."

The Manual of Discipline itself may be a compilation from several sources. The arrangement of subjects does not follow any clear logical order, and there is sometimes no connection in thought between the successive sections. The work seems to consist of material from several different compositions put together in scrapbook fashion. Most of the sections contain rules by which the life of the community was governed, but in the midst of these there is the little theological statement about the two spirits in man, which is quite different from anything else in the document, and at the end there is a devotional poem like the Thanksgiving Psalms.

Our discussion of the relationship between the scrolls and the Damascus Document has touched upon some questions we are not quite ready to take up, but it seems necessary as a preparation for examining the historical allusions in the Damascus Document. Before returning to that problem, we may summarize the major results of our hasty survey. The Damascus Document is evidently a product of the same general period as the Dead Sea Scrolls. It is probably later than the earliest scrolls, but may very well be earlier than the latest ones. The exact relationship can be determined, if at all, only by a closer examination of the Damascus Document itself, and in particular of its historical allusions.

One passage that enters prominently into the discussion refers to the teacher of righteousness and to the man of the lie: "And from the day of the gathering in of the unique teacher until the annihilation of all the men of war who returned with the man of the lie will be [or was] about forty years." (Charles's translation is somewhat different. He reads: ". . . who walked with the man of the lie about forty years," but this leaves the sentence incomplete.) Here we learn of an interval of forty years after the death ("gathering in") of the "unique teacher," extending to some event either in the past or still in the future. If a future event is referred to, it may be the expected coming of "a Messiah from Aaron and Israel." An unspecified interval "from the day of the gathering in of the unique teacher until a Messiah arises from Aaron and from Israel" is mentioned in another passage.

If the statement about the forty years is interpreted as referring to the past, not only has the death of the unique teacher already taken place; it occurred forty years before another event that is already past, whatever may be meant by "the annihilation of all the men of war," et cetera. The death of the unique teacher must then have occurred more than forty years before the composition of the Damascus Document. Another passage, however, speaks of those "who give heed to the voice of a teacher of righteousness," implying that the teacher is still alive. For this reason L. Rost, as we have seen, distinguishes the teacher of righteousness from the unique teacher, whom he takes to be the founder of the sect.

We have seen that Rost considers the Damascus Document older than the Habakkuk Commentary, because the persecution and suffering of the teacher of righteousness are apparently not yet known to the writer of the Damascus Document. Believing, with Dupont-Sommer, that the Habakkuk Commentary was written at about 50 B.C., Rost consequently dates the Damascus Document at some time before that. If the unique teacher had been dead for more than forty years, his death must then have occurred at about 100 B.C. His career therefore falls in the Hasmonean period, in the second half of the second century B.C. The teacher of righteousness, however, according to this interpretation of the evidence, lived about half a century later, at about the beginning of the Roman period.

A still more crucial passage in the Damascus Document reads as follows:

> For when those who forsook him trespassed, he hid his face from Israel and from his sanctuary; but when he remembered the covenant of the ancients, he left a remnant to Israel and did not give them up to destruction. And in the period of wrath—three hundred and ninety years, when he gave them into the hand of Nebuchadnezzar, king of Babylon—he visited them and caused to sprout from Israel and from Aaron a root of planting to inherit the land and to grow fat on the goodness of his soil. Then they perceived their iniquity and knew that they were guilty men; yet they were like men blind and groping for the way for twenty years. And God observed their works, that they sought him with perfect heart; and he raised up for them a teacher of righteousness to lead them in the way of his heart.

In the next to the last sentence of this passage R. H. Charles translates, "they knew that they were guilty men and had like the blind been groping," implying that the twenty years of blindness preceded the sprouting of the root from Aaron and Israel. It seems more natural to take the verb, as most interpreters have done, to indicate an additional period of 20 years after the end of the 390 years. The number 390 is obviously taken from Ezekiel

4:5, which says that this will be the number of the years of Israel's punishment. Where the number 20 comes from is not apparent. If the "root of planting" means the community of covenanters, as is generally supposed, then the teacher of righteousness would seem to have appeared after the community had been established and had been blindly groping for twenty years.

On the assumption that the 390 years were reckoned as beginning with the conquest of Judah by Nebuchadnezzar in 586 B.C., this passage has commonly been interpreted as meaning that the visitation and the sprouting of the root occurred in 196 and the teacher of righteousness appeared in 176 B.C. This was the prevailing interpretation before the discovery of the Dead Sea Scrolls. One of the first to apply it to the interpretation of the scrolls was Bo Reicke, whose identifications of the teacher of righteousness and the wicked priest we have already noted in connection with the Habakkuk Commentary. It will be remembered that Reicke's theory—which he has since modified—identified the teacher of righteousness at least partially with the high priest Onias III. Onias was deposed in 175 B.C. How long had he been high priest before he was deposed? Josephus puts his accession in the reign of Seleucus IV (187–175 B.C.); it must therefore have occurred not many years before 176 B.C., the date inferred from the references to 390 years and 20 years in the Damascus Document.

Other more or less plausible computations have been based on the 390 years and 20 years. Zeitlin adduces a late Talmudic tradition to the effect that the temple stood for 420 years. Adding this to the 70 years of the Babylonian exile, he gets a total of 490 years. The great Rabbi Hillel is said to have become the head of the Sanhedrin 100 years before the destruction of the temple. Subtracting 100 from 490, Zeitlin gets 390 as the number of years from the beginning of the Babylonian exile to the appointment of Hillel. This implies that the author of the Damascus Document was acquainted with a late rabbinic tradition, which is quite in accord with Zeitlin's belief that the Damascus Document is a medieval composition. But Zeitlin identifies Hillel with the "man of the lie," whereas it is the unique teacher whose coming is dated

20 years after the end of the 390 years. The 20 years, in fact, seem to be ignored in Zeitlin's chronology. He speaks of 20 years as the time when Hillel and Menahem were together at the head of the Sanhedrin, but this is derived from a combination of the 20 years of this passage with a questionable interpretation of the entirely different passage about the 40 years from the death of the unique teacher to the destruction of the men of violence.

Weis accepts Zeitlin's interpretation of the 390 years as extending from the beginning of the Babylonian exile to the appointment of Hillel, but he adds that if Hillel was appointed 100 years before the destruction of the temple, his appointment must be dated in 30 B.C. The 20 years will then bring us to 10 B.C. According to Tertullian, the birth of Jesus occurred in 9–6 B.C. Weis therefore infers that Jesus may have been the unique teacher of the Damascus Document and one of the series of teachers of righteousness honored by the medieval Karaites.

A searching critique of all these theories has been presented recently by Isaac Rabinowitz. They all rest, he points out, on the assumption that the phrase "when he gave them [or, more literally, 'to his giving them'] into the hand of Nebuchadnezzar," means "*after* he gave them into the hand of Nebuchadnezzar." This is contrary to normal Hebrew usage. The phrase would ordinarily mean either "at his giving" (i.e., "when he gave") or "to his giving" (i.e., "until he gave"). Rabinowitz takes it in the latter sense. In other words, the period of 390 years did not follow but preceded the fall of Jerusalem in 586 B.C.

The author of the Damascus Document, Rabinowitz argues, found the figure 390 in Ezekiel 4:5 and interpreted it as referring to the time preceding the Babylonian exile. The years of the reigns of all the kings of Judah, from the accession of Rehoboam to the eleventh year of Zedekiah, when Jerusalem was taken by Nebuchadnezzar, add up to 393. In II Chronicles 11:16–17 three years of good conduct at the beginning of Rehoboam's reign are mentioned; subtracting these three years, we get 390 years, or the duration of the "period of wrath." The "visitation" was therefore the destruction of Jerusalem. It is interesting to recall that Louis

Ginzberg long ago interpreted this passage as referring to the period before the Babylonian exile. He began farther back, however, and supposed that the figures indicated the reigns of all the kings from Saul to Josiah. He therefore held that the teacher of righteousness was probably the high priest Hilkiah, who rediscovered the book of the law in the temple during the reign of Josiah.

The explanation of the 390 years is bound up with the interpretation of several references to a departure from Judah and a sojourn in the land of Damascus. It is these references that have caused the name "Damascus Document" or "Damascus Fragments" to be given to this composition, which Schechter, when he published it, called "Fragments of a Zadokite Document." Following a quotation from Ezekiel 44:15 concerning the Levites and the sons of Zadok, the text continues, "The priests are the captivity of Israel who went out from the land of Judah, and [the Levites are] those who joined them." In another place a quotation of Numbers 21:18 introduces this statement: "The well is the law, and those who dug it are the captivity of Israel, who went out from the land of Judah and sojourned in the land of Damascus." The star of both Amos 5:26–27 and Numbers 24:17 is said to be "the interpreter of the law who came to Damascus."

Two passages mention those "who entered the new covenant in the land of Damascus." Rabinowitz argues that the phrase "in the land of Damascus" here modifies not the verb "entered" but the noun "covenant"; in other words, the meaning is "those who entered the new covenant (made) in the land of Damascus." This is quite possible, but even so it is implied that those who first made the new covenant were at the time in "the land of Damascus"; in fact, that is explicitly stated in a passage denouncing those who "spoke error against the statutes of righteousness and rejected the firm covenant which they had established in the land of Damascus, that is, the new covenant."

Ever since the first publication of the Damascus Document the prevailing interpretation of these passages has been that the followers of the teacher of righteousness, compelled by persecution to leave Judah, emigrated to the region of Damascus, and there under his leadership established a new covenant. In the Manual of Discipline there is a reference to going into the wilderness, which might conceivably be connected with this departure from Judah. In that case, since the Manual of Discipline can hardly have been composed later than about 100 B.C., the emigration would have to be dated in the second century B.C. If the withdrawal from Judah has any connection with the abandonment of the manuscripts in the caves, however, it cannot be referred to in the Damascus Document, because the fragments found in the caves show that the community already possessed the Damascus Document. The Manual of Discipline, in fact, clearly defines the going into the wilderness as a withdrawal for the study of the law. It may very well mean the establishment of the community in the neighborhood of Khirbet Qumran, which is "wilderness enow." It may even, for that matter, refer to the withdrawal of individuals from society to devote themselves to the study of the law.

Those scholars who date the origin of the community of the new covenant in the pre-Maccabean period see references to events of that period in the statements of the Damascus Document about departing from the land of Judah. It is suggested, for example, that the origin of the Dead Sea community is illuminated by I Maccabees 2:29–38, which says that in the time of Antiochus Epiphanes "men who set at nought the king's command" went into hiding in the wilderness. Even the flight of Onias III to Daphne has been mentioned as throwing light, at least by analogy, on the emigration of the covenanters to the land of Damascus; the analogy, however, is at best remote.

The hypothesis of a flight to Damascus in the time of Antiochus Epiphanes encounters the objection that men seeking refuge from his wrath would not go to Damascus, which was in his territory. To this Rowley replies that during the period of confusion after the death of Antiochus, when Jonathan and Simon were playing off one contender for the Seleucid throne against another, a group persecuted by Jonathan or Simon might find refuge at Damascus under a ruler hostile to the Jewish government. Perhaps it was at the time when the Hasmoneans assumed civil power, Rowley sug gests, that the group organized and led by "the star" migrated to Damascus. The accession of Simon in 142 B.C. has been thought by Vermès to be the time when the persecution of the group, after the disappearance of the teacher of righteousness, and the installation of the sect in the more hospitable region of Damascus probably took place.

Others identify the flight from Judah with a later incident in the reign of Alexander Janneus (103–76 B.C.). At that time, Josephus says, eight hundred of the Pharisees were crucified, and eight thousand members of the party fled by night and lived in exile. So long as it was supposed that the pottery found in the first cave was Hellenistic, a date in the time of Alexander Janneus seemed entirely probable for the abandonment of the region, and it was reasonable to connect this with the flight to Damascus. The subsequent excavation of Khirbet Qumran and the exploration of the other caves has made any such hypothesis untenable. The scarcity of coins from the reign of Herod at Khirbet Qumran suggests that there was an interruption in the occupation of the site at that time, between its first and second periods.

If the flight of the Pharisees in the time of Alexander Janneus had anything at all to do with the Qumran community, it would seem to have been the occasion for the establishment of the settlement at that place, because it was at about that time, as the coins show, that the first period of the occupation of the site began. Any theory connecting the persecution of the Pharisees by Alexander Janneus with the covenanters, however, implies the questionable assumption that the covenanters were Pharisees. The validity of that assumption we consider in Chapter XIII.

Dupont-Sommer holds that the sect of the new covenant probably migrated to Damascus in 63 B.C., about six months after the conquest of Jerusalem by the Romans. Since, as he believes, the teacher of righteousness had been put to death by Aristobulus II, the group fled from Judea under a new leader known as the "star." Rabinowitz objects that this would put the sect at Damascus during the time when DuPont-Sommer himself supposes that the

Habakkuk Commentary was written, although the commentary makes no reference at all to Damascus.

Any connection between the flight to Damascus and the abandonment of the caves was made very doubtful by the discovery of fragments of the Damascus Document in the caves. Rowley suggests that perhaps only a part of the sect migrated to Damascus; or, if the migration included the whole group, a part or all of it returned later. The library of scrolls, he adds, may have been left in the caves when the sect migrated to Damascus, recovered when they returned, and finally deposited again at some later time of peril.

The War of the Sons of Light with the Sons of Darkness speaks of the conflict as taking place when the sons of light returned from "the desert of the peoples to encamp in the desert of Jerusalem." Conceivably the desert of the peoples might be the land of Damascus, and the desert of Jerusalem might then be the desolate region overlooking the Dead Sea. It should also be noted, however, that "the desert of the peoples" would be an appropriate designation for the Diaspora, the dispersion of Jews in gentile lands; "the desert of Jerusalem" might also be a figurative expression of the spiritual condition of Jerusalem from the point of view of the covenanters.

There is no necessary connection between the time of the migration and the time of the return. Vermès, who believes that the migration took place as early as 142 B.C., thinks that the first opportunity to return did not come until the end of the Hasmonean dynasty in 37 B.C. Dupont-Sommer, while placing the migration much later than Vermès does, agrees with him as to the time of the return, but suggests that while the main body of covenanters returned to Palestine in the reign of Herod, a group of them still remained at Damascus. He believes that the Damascus Document was written at about the same time as the Habakkuk Commentary, a little before 40 B.C., when the return had not yet taken place.

The whole idea of a migration of the sect to Damascus, as well as the interpretation of the 390 and 20 years in terms of the history of the covenanters, is rejected by Isaac Rabinowitz. He points out that the Damascus passages are based on the prediction of exile "beyond Damascus" in Amos 5:26f, which is quoted in the Damascus Document, though as a matter of fact the manuscript does not read "beyond Damascus" but "from the tents of Damascus." The passage about the 390 years indicates the destruction of Jerusalem by Nebuchadnezzar as the time of the divine visitation; the prophecy of Amos, which was actually fulfilled by the Assyrian conquest of the kingdom of Israel in 721 B.C., must have been applied by the writer of the Damascus Document to the Babylonian conquest of the kingdom of Judah more than a century later. In any case, "the land of Damascus," Rabinowitz believes, means the whole area of Assyria and Babylonia, in which the exiles were dispersed. From the standpoint of Palestine, it was all "beyond Damascus." The dispersed exiles were regarded as the righteous remnant to whom the new covenant promised in Jeremiah 31:31ff had been vouchsafed.

But if the sojourn in the land of Damascus means the existence of the exiles in Babylonia and Assyria, who was "the interpreter of the law who came to Damascus"? To this question Rabinowitz does not give a satisfying answer. He takes the reference to the "interpreter of the law" to mean merely that there were among the exiles experts in the art of combining texts so as to bring out hidden meanings. Such an expounder of Torah, he remarks, was Ezra. The connection with the "star out of Jacob," however, in which Rabinowitz sees a reference to the Davidic Messiah, implies at least that the interpreter of the law was an individual, and one highly honored by the covenanters. Who could have been meant if the time of the Babylonian exile was in view is a difficult question. Here, it seems to me, is the weakest point in the argument of Rabinowitz. On the general question of a migration to Damascus and a later return, however, he has made a very strong case. He has at least shown that all attempts to reconstruct the history of the sect on the assumption that there was such a migration are decidedly precarious.

There are other historical allusions in the Damascus Document, but they help very little. The condemnation of marriage with a niece is understood by some scholars as an allusion to the marriage of Joseph the son of Tobias with his own niece in the pre-Maccabean period. The validity of this interpretation, of course, stands or falls with all the other supposed references to the same period. Of itself, while fairly plausible, it is not very cogent. In connection with a quotation of Deuteronomy 32:33 there is a reference to "the kings of the peoples" and "the head of the kings of Greece, who comes to take vengeance on them." Here, if anywhere, one might suspect a specific historical reference, but where one scholar sees a clear reference to the Seleucid Antiochus Epiphanes another recognizes the Roman Pompey. One is reluctantly driven to agree with Chaim Rabin, the latest editor of the Damascus Document, that it is still "much too early to come to any conclusions" concerning the date of the composition of its component parts.

As for the Dead Sea Scrolls themselves, we have already observed that none of the other manuscripts approaches the Habakkuk Commentary in the richness of its historical allusions. The one that comes nearest to it in this respect is The War of the Sons of Light with the Sons of Darkness. This contains a brief reference to "the Kittim of Assyria and Egypt." Sukenik identified these with the Ptolemies and Seleucids. Such a use of the term Kittim would be thoroughly appropriate, because both the Ptolemies and the Seleucids were Macedonians.

The designation of Syria as Assyria, however, has aroused considerable discussion. H. L. Ginsberg calls attention to the use of Numbers 24:24 in Daniel 11:30, where the words of Balaam, "But ships shall come from Kittim and shall afflict Assyria and Eber," are quoted in part and applied to the coming of the Romans to Egypt in 168 B.C., when they compelled Antiochus Epiphanes to give up his campaign against Ptolemy VI. The word Assyria is not included in the quotation, but the application of the verse shows that the writer of Daniel 11:30 understood the term in Numbers 24:24 to mean the Seleucid kingdom of Syria. Ginsberg considers this a "bold reinterpretation" on the part of the writer of Daniel 11:30. There have been modern scholars who believed that the original intention of Numbers 24:24 was to indicate the

Seleucid kingdom by the term Assyria, but few would take that position now. The point is that it was so understood by the writer of Daniel 11:30 in the late pre-Maccabean period.

H. L. Ginsberg notes also that in several verses of Daniel 11 the language of Isaiah 8:8, which refers to Assyria, "is applied to the victorious sweep of the Seleucid armies." Here again it is not implied that the Seleucids were meant by the term Assyria in Isaiah, though some modern scholars have actually seen such a reference in several passages in the book of Isaiah and have accordingly regarded these passages as late additions to the book.

There is one Old Testament passage in which the name Assyria is taken by many scholars to refer to the Seleucids. This is Psalm 83:8. There is a striking resemblance between this psalm and a few passages in The War of the Sons of Light with the Sons of Darkness. Not all commentators, of course, agree that Psalm 83 refers to Syria in the Hellenistic period. The meaning of Assyria here depends on the date of the psalm, which is not certain. Some commentators, in fact, question any reference to a particular military campaign. The significance of the psalm, they maintain, is not historical but cultic, and the curse on the hostile nations is meant to include all possible enemies of Israel in any period, past as well as present or future. The relevance of this psalm with regard to the use of the term Assyria for the Seleucid kingdom is therefore somewhat uncertain, but the possibility that Assyria here means Syria is not to be ignored.

The following passage from the book of Jubilees (13:1) has been cited in this connection: "And Abram journeyed from Haran, and he took Sarai his wife and Lot his brother Haran's son to the land of Canaan; and he came to Assyria, and proceeded to Shechem, and dwelt near a lofty oak." Charles considers the name Assyria in this place a mistake in the text. As he punctuates the sentence, Assyria seems to be a place or region in the land of Canaan. It is possible, however, to suppose that the words "and he came" begin a new sentence, which summarizes the whole journey. In that case Assyria would be somewhere on the way from Haran to Canaan and might very well mean Syria.

The expression "Kittim of Assyria" in the War scroll is undoubtedly a cryptic reference to some power of the writer's own time. This would not be the Assyrian empire unless the book was composed before the end of the seventh century B.C. Like the word "Kittim" itself, Assyria is doubtless a disguised designation for a much later nation. The opening sentences of the book of Judith present a curiously anachronistic and probably deliberate mixture of historical periods that is worth recalling in this connection. If the reference to Assyria in the War scroll is a cryptic allusion to a later nation, it affords no clue to the date of the composition but must itself be interpreted in the light of other evidence.

The term Kittim need not have the same meaning in the War scroll that it has in the Habakkuk Commentary. Several scholars have argued that the War scroll, the Habakkuk Commentary, and the Damascus Document are so much alike that they must belong to the same period, and have therefore used the apparent reference to the Ptolemies and the Seleucids in the War scroll as an argument against the interpretation of the Kittim as the Romans in the commentary. Others, however, who believe that the commentary refers to the Romans, find no difficulty in recognizing the Ptolemies and Seleucids in the Kittim of the War scroll, and consequently in accepting a date in the Hellenistic period for that document.

Along with the Kittim, the scroll names the troops of Edom, Moab, Ammon, and Philistia as the sons of darkness who constitute the army of Belial. Hostility to Ammon and Moab is characteristic of much of the Old Testament, especially the books of Chronicles. The nations mentioned in the War scroll are all included also, together with others, in Psalm 83. The region in which they lived, east of the Jordan and the Dead Sea, was occupied in Hellenistic times by other peoples equally hostile to the Jews, and sometimes also by Jewish factions, whose opponents might have designated them by the names of Israel's ancient foes. It has been said that Psalm 83 becomes clear only when one recognizes that "the children of Lot" mentioned in it are the Tobiads of the pre-Maccabean period. Some have been tempted to associate the War scroll with the same period and situation.

Some scholars have identified the war described in the War scroll with the one referred to in Daniel 11:14: "In those times many shall rise against the king of the south; and the men of violence among your own people shall lift themselves up in order to fulfill the vision; but they shall fail." This is commonly supposed to refer to the time of Ptolemy V (203–181 B.C.), when the conflict between the Tobiad Hyrcanus and his brothers divided the Jewish nation. Reicke puts it slightly later, in the time of Antiochus Epiphanes (175–164 B.C.), when the brothers of Hyrcanus, after his death, appealed to Antiochus for help.

Eissfeldt also places the war of the War scroll in the early years of the reign of Antiochus Epiphanes, before his desecration of the temple. He interprets Edom as meaning Idumea, Moab and Ammon as meaning the Nabatean and Hellenistic cities of Transjordan, and Philistia as meaning the Hellenistic cities of the coastal plain. Rowley remarks that the mottoes inscribed on the banners in the War scroll recall the battle slogans of the Maccabees. Rabinowitz considers the War scroll a "document of triumph" and therefore feels that it cannot have been written before the Maccabean achievement of religious freedom in 164 B.C. or after Alcimus became high priest in 162. Reflecting particularly the victories of the Maccabees against neighboring peoples, it must probably be dated, he concludes, in 162 B.C.

Katz claims, however, that the use of trumpets in battle was unknown in the Hasmonean period. Josephus, he recalls, says of the followers of Judah the Galilean and Zadok the Pharisee, in the early first century A.D., that they passionately loved freedom and recognized no ruler but God. This seems to Katz to be explained and confirmed by the War scroll, which he therefore thinks may have been written in the reign of Caligula (37–41 A.D.), perhaps at the time of that emperor's demand that his statue be set up in the temple at Jerusalem.

It must not be taken for granted that there is any specific historical reference at all in the War scroll. Sukenik himself believed that an actual war was envisaged, but many who read the first published excerpts felt that the meaning was not historical but eschatological, with no more definite historical reference than any prediction of the future. The elaborate directions for the army were thought to represent either a purely apocalyptic vision or a liturgical religious drama. Driver regarded these directions as intended merely for the edification of the reader. An intermediate position was taken by Hempel, who thought that the document reflected dreams of a real, heroic war, but not one immediately contemplated. It represented, he said, "the Utopian world of Chronicles." Among those who believed that the document is apocalyptic in nature, some thought that if any historical peoples or events were referred to they could not be identified; others thought that, as in the book of Daniel, a real historical situation, that of the conflict between the Hellenists and the Maccabees, could be recognized.

A brief summary of the contents of the scroll may be helpful at this point. The "sons of light" are depicted as fighting a war against the "sons of darkness." Apparently the children of light win three battles, the army of Belial wins three, and the perfect number of seven is then completed (or soon to be completed) by the final and decisive victory of the hosts of light. Detailed prescriptions are given concerning such matters as tribal organization, the composition of the army, the selection and age limits of the warriors, the weapons and other equipment, and the conduct of the fighting. Prayers, blessings, and an exhortation which is to be delivered by the high priest before the battle, are given in full, with elaborate liturgical directions. Whether historical or eschatological, this is definitely a holy war. If it is a war on the plane of history, it is undoubtedly idealized, though perhaps no more so than the directions for warfare in Deuteronomy 20 or the narrative in such a chapter as II Chronicles 20, which the War scroll forcibly recalls. The extremely formal procedure, however, with the enemy doing nothing but flee or fall dead at the proper moment, seems more like a ballet than a battle.

Even if there is no reference to a specific war, already in progress or regarded as imminent, the writer's conception of military procedures might reflect the practices of his own time, if he was acquainted with them. Thus Février sees in this document evidence that the Jews were acquainted with the art of warfare, and that their fighting was not a matter of irregular guerrilla operations but was directed by officers trained in Hellenistic military tactics. The army was drawn up in several parallel lines, one behind another, and these were divided into separate groups so that the mobile forces might move freely back and forth between them. This disposition of troops, Février says, was customary in the Hellenistic armies of the second century B.C.

Whether the same evidence will bear a different interpretation remains to be seen. It is reliably reported, as the journalists say, that an intensive study of the War scroll from this point of view has led Yigael Yadin to date the composition in the early Roman period. Until his work is published, however, I can say nothing more definite about his conclusions or his arguments. Meanwhile it is best to suspend judgment. No specific historical allusion to any recognizable event, in any case, appears in this document.

Historical allusions have been detected or imagined in the Thanksgiving Psalms. A passage that has been especially fruitful in this regard is a section of one of the psalms which speaks of "the torrents of Belial" as an overflowing, continuing stream of fire that covers the earth and even inundates the infernal regions. Katz sees in these "torrents of Belial" a reference to the waterworks constructed in the first century A.D. under Pontius Pilate to bring water to Jerusalem. Del Medico feels that the passage alludes to the eruption of Vesuvius in 79 A.D., which was regarded in Palestine as a warning of the coming day of the Lord. These examples may suffice to show that the historical allusions in the Thanksgiving Psalms, if there are any such, are of no use for dating the document.

References to recognizable events are not to be expected in a document like the Manual of Discipline. From the lack of a militant note, however, and the assumption that the wicked are in power, Rabinowitz infers that the Manual was written in the late pre-Maccabean or early Maccabean period, between 175 and 167 B.C. Whatever force this argument may have depends on its relation to the development of ideas in the Dead Sea Scrolls, which we must now consider.

X

Ideas, Vocabulary, and Literary Relations

⎍⎍⎍⎍⎍⎍⎍⎍⎍⎍⎍⎍⎍⎍⎍⎍⎍⎍⎍⎍⎍⎍⎍⎍⎍⎍⎍⎍⎍

Together with references to persons and events, the religious ideas and practices presented in an ancient document afford some points of attachment for estimating the period in which it was written. We shall attempt later to form a comprehensive picture of the religious ideas and practices of the Qumran community. In considering some of them here, we are for the present looking only for any indications of date that can be found in them.

A word of caution may not be out of place at this point. It is not to be assumed that a belief or custom necessarily originated at the time when it is first attested in our literary sources. Newly discovered material may at any time refute such assumptions. In other words, the appearance of an idea, institution, or practice is not by itself conclusive proof of the date when a document was written. Along with all the other evidence, however, the stage of religious development reflected by our manuscripts is one of the things that must be taken into account.

The evidence of ideas and practices is often too general to afford a specific point of attachment. It is said, for example, that the Dead Sea Scrolls and the Damascus Document evince a high regard for the sabbath, and many of the Maccabees had the same feeling. Obviously, while such a point may have some significance as part of a general picture, strict observance of the sabbath is

not distinctively characteristic of any one period. The devotion of
the Qumran community to the sons of Zadok as constituting the
true priesthood is another case in point. Together with other points
of contact, it may show a general affinity with this or that group
in a particular period, but it cannot be taken as evidence of any
date, whether late or early. An origin in the time of early Christianity has been inferred from what is taken to be a Gnostic or
quasi-Gnostic polemic against the doctrine of the incarnation of
Christ, but the reference is by no means so clear or so certain as to
be of any evidential value.

From the idea of the destruction of the world by fire, which
appears in one of the Thanksgiving Psalms, Vermès formerly inferred that the psalms were written between 79 and 90 A.D.,
because other sources seemed to indicate that this idea became
known in Judaism at about that time but was soon abandoned.
The burning of the temple in 70 A.D. and the eruption of Vesuvius
in 79, he thought, might have had some part in promoting it. The
archeological evidence has since shown that such a late date is
impossible, as Vermès himself recognizes. Here again it is clear
that arguments of this sort may support other and more concrete
evidence to the same effect, but they cannot outweigh contrary
evidence of a more specific character. The idea of a destruction of
the world by fire may have been known in the Qumran community
long before it became familiar in other Jewish circles, and it may
have been widely known in Judaism at large before the first
century A.D.

Other beliefs concerning the end of the world and the coming
of the Messiah have been cited as evidence of a relatively late
date. Ideas concerning the coming of the Messiah based on
Habakkuk 2:3 are mentioned in the Talmud, and this fact has
been taken to indicate that the Dead Sea Scrolls originated in the
Talmudic period. The Habakkuk Commentary, however, while
obviously expecting the end of the world very soon, offers no cal-
culations concerning the coming of the Messiah such as are found
in rabbinic literature. Contacts with medieval Messianic speculation have been cited as evidence of a still later date for the Dead

Sea Scrolls; similar ideas, however, have been found also in earlier writings.

The use made of the Old Testament in the non-biblical scrolls and the way it is interpreted are important for the history of both Judaism and Christianity. Their significance as indicating the time when these documents were written, however, is questionable. Sonne has argued that the use of Scripture in the Dead Sea Scrolls reflects the type of interpretation practiced by the second-century Jewish exegetes called the Doreshe Reshumot ("seekers of marks"). He even sees in the scrolls a polemic against the use of the Old Testament by Christians. W. D. Davies points out, however, that the book of Habakkuk, which evidently meant much to the Qumran community, was not much used by the early Christians. He adds that very little is actually known of the biblical interpretations of the Doreshe Reshumot, while the type of interpretation found in the Dead Sea Scrolls has many parallels in other Jewish sources.

The method of interpreting Scripture is connected with the question of whether the Habakkuk Commentary should properly be called a commentary or a "midrash." Too much has been made of this question, it seems to me, but it must be mentioned because it has been linked up with the dating of this document. A midrash may be defined as a homiletical expansion of a biblical book, or part of a book, for the purpose of edification. From the time of our first acquaintance with the Habakkuk scroll, I called it a commentary because of its form. As the portions already quoted show, it quotes the biblical text bit by bit, giving after each quotation an explanation of what the author believes to be its meaning. A midrash does not follow quite this method; it follows the order of the biblical text as a commentary does, but its method of exposition is more like that of a popular expository lecture, or even the telling of a Bible story by a Sunday-school teacher. It frequently cites the opinions of various authorities and discusses problems of exegesis, but the manner of presentation is not that of a formal commentary.

Some scholars, however, have questioned the legitimacy of calling our document a commentary, not because of its form but because of the manner in which the text is applied to the writer's own time. The interpretation of the Bible is of course not like what one finds in a scholarly commentary of our day. It would be all too easy, however, to cite commentaries published even now that are quite uninhibited by sound philological and historical principles from applying prophecy to our own times, though in form and procedure they are commentaries and are so called.

As it happens, the term "commentary" has been preferred by some of the scholars who have maintained a late date for the Dead Sea Scrolls. Driver, for example, says that the Habakkuk scroll is "a true commentary . . . of a type similar in form if not in substance to those of the Middle Ages." Zeitlin even suggests that the designation of the scroll as a midrash instead of a commentary was inspired by the desire to ascribe it to the Hasmonean period. Insisting that it is a commentary, he infers that therefore it cannot be ancient, "since the Jews did not write commentaries on the Bible during the Second Commonwealth. . . . As long as Hebrew was a living tongue, there was no need for a translation or a commentary." This is not a necessary assumption. We now have the Bible in English, and English is a living language, but we still need commentaries. But the Habakkuk Commentary was intended not to explain a text that was otherwise unintelligible, but to propound a particular sectarian interpretation. Commentaries have often been written, and are still sometimes written, for that purpose.

The appearance of such a commentary from a time before the destruction of the temple was unquestionably surprising. To rule out the antiquity of the document, however, on the ground that compositions of the sort were not written in ancient times is anything but scientific procedure. How, one may ask, is our knowledge of the history of biblical interpretation to be improved if we refuse to recognize new evidence?

An arrangement of the Dead Sea Scrolls and the successive strata of the Damascus Document in chronological order on the basis of the development of ideas has been proposed by Isaac Rabinowitz. Such a development seems to him to be evident in the ideas concerning two subjects, the expected end of the world and the persecution endured by the group. As Gottstein presupposes a normal order of sociological development in the history of a group, so Rabinowitz assumes a normal succession of four stages in the evolution of ideas concerning the end of the world: (1) the end is believed to be in preparation; (2) it is believed to be at hand and actually taking place; (3) it is felt to have been delayed, and explanations of the delay are sought; and (4) the conclusion that the expectation was mistaken is accepted, and a new attempt is made to calculate the time of the end.

In the Manual of Discipline, Rabinowitz finds that the end is still thought of as in the future; in the earliest stratum of the Damascus Document, and in a "fragment of an unknown document" discovered and published by de Vaux, he finds the belief that the end of the world is at hand; in one of the Thanksgiving Psalms and in The War of the Sons of Light with the Sons of Darkness the consummation seems to be "in progress and about to reach a great climax"; in another of the Thanksgiving Psalms, in the Habakkuk Commentary, and in the rest of the Damascus Document the delay of the climax seems to be felt as a problem.

A similar process is observed with regard to the persecution of the group. In the Manual of Discipline no severe persecution has yet emerged; in the earliest stratum of the Damascus Document and in two of the Thanksgiving Psalms persecution has broken out, but the group is resisting it with confidence; in The War of the Sons of Light with the Sons of Darkness and in two other Thanksgiving Psalms the persecution has spent its force, and the saints can "blueprint" the final victory.

On the basis of these developments Rabinowitz constructs the following "sequence table" of the composition of the documents: (1) the Manual of Discipline; (2) de Vaux's fragments, the earliest stratum of the Damascus Document, and the first two Thanksgiving Psalms; (3) the War scroll and two of the Thanksgiving

Psalms; (4) another of the Thanksgiving Psalms; (5) the Habakkuk Commentary; and (6) the second and third strata of the Damascus Document.

Having thus established a relative order on the basis of ideas, Rabinowitz attempts to fix the dates of the successive stages by the historical allusions. This procedure recalls the way archeologists date their discoveries by means of pottery, establishing first a relative chronology by the sequence of pottery types in the successive levels of their excavations, and then attempting to convert this into an absolute chronology by "pegging" as many points in the sequence as possible with the aid of inscriptions, coins, and the like.

Rabinowitz finds any date after 70 A.D. excluded by the references to the temple and its cult. Eliminating, because of what seem to him insuperable objections, all the periods preceding that date except the time just before and during the early Maccabean period, Rabinowitz accepts this, without really considering the difficulties that may be raised against it, as the period in which all the documents were written. Within the period, he infers from the historical allusions in each group of documents the following dates for the six stages of his "sequence table": (1) 175–167 B.C.; (2) 167–165 B.C.; (3) 164–162 B.C.; (4) 162–160 B.C.; (5) 159–157 B.C.; (6) 157–152 B.C.

The argument developed by Rabinowitz shows at least that historical references cannot yield solid results if each document is considered only by itself. After examining each of them separately, as we have done, we must check our conclusions by comparing each one with all the others. Dating by historical allusions, if they are definite and unmistakable, is undoubtedly more satisfactory than dating by ideas, though that too must be considered. The main question is whether the references in any of the Dead Sea Scrolls or the Damascus Document can be regarded as sufficiently explicit to establish definite dates. Whether the chronological sequence for all these documents worked out by Rabinowitz is correct or even probable may be questioned. I doubt that we can even determine the order of composition so exactly, to say nothing of the exact dates.

Closely related to the development of ideas is the emergence of an appropriate vocabulary. One of Zeitlin's major arguments against an early dating of the Dead Sea Scrolls has been that they use many terms and expressions that did not come into use before the Middle Ages. He claims, for instance, that the word for "order" in the Manual of Discipline was a medieval term. A word that ordinarily means "end" is often used in the Dead Sea Scrolls with the meaning "time"; this usage too Zeitlin pronounces medieval. Distinctive terms used to designate the community in the Dead Sea Scrolls are explained by him as inventions of the medieval Karaites. Curiously enough, the argument here consists of explaining a term that does not actually appear in Karaite literature by other words derived from the same root, which are used in Karaite writings but do not appear in the Dead Sea Scrolls! The title "teacher of righteousness" also is supposed by Zeitlin to have been "coined" by the Karaites. What the argument actually amounts to is simply that these terms were not used in pre-medieval writings known before the discovery of the Damascus Document and the Dead Sea Scrolls. A position that was justifiable before this material appeared is no longer defensible. Furthermore, as Teicher remarks in this connection, the absence of the terms in question from Talmudic and apocryphal literature is not significant, because the Dead Sea Scrolls represent a quite different literary category.

Sukenik regarded the term "the head priest" in the War scroll as evidence that the document was written before the Hasmonean period, because the term regularly used for the high priest in that period was "the great priest." Zeitlin replied that this argument would require dating as early as the fifth century B.C., because the designation "head priest" was not used at all after the Babylonian exile. It came back into use, he added, in medieval Jewish literature. Some scholars believe that the term "head priest" in the War scroll does not refer to the high priest at all, but to a priest especially anointed for war, according to a rabbinic interpretation of Deuteronomy 20:3. Sukenik's argument must be taken into account, however, by those who date the War scroll later than the Hasmonean period.

Many other terms in the Dead Sea Scrolls play a part in arguments against a pre-Christian date. The use of the word "Israel" instead of "Jerusalem" is said by Zeitlin to be "contrary to the terminology of all Second Commonwealth literature known to us." Birnbaum considers this merely a matter of style. The usage of the scrolls in this particular may, however, be a result of the belief that the covenanters' community was the true Israel. The term Israel is used in much the same way in the New Testament for the Christian church.

The use of the Hebrew noun *El*, meaning God, instead of the divine name *YHWH* or the word *Adonai* (Lord), is adduced by Zeitlin as another indication of medieval date. The fact that the word God is frequently used in the apocryphal literature is dismissed as insignificant. The question, Zeitlin says, is not why *El* is used, but why the divine name is not used. Weis stresses the fact that this use of the word *El* is foreign to rabbinic literature; it would be natural, he says, for Jews living in Arab countries and accustomed to the designation of God as *Allah* in Arabic. In reply to these arguments Teicher adduces three points: (1) the practice of the Qumran community need not have been in accordance with common Jewish usage; (2) the word *El* is used in very old Jewish prayers; (3) it is actually used "only very sporadically" in medieval Jewish literature. With regard to this and other terms Zeitlin claims to be distinctly medieval, it is sufficient to repeat that the Dead Sea Scrolls come from a different group and represent a quite different literary type from the rabbinic sources.

Weis offers an ingenious explanation of the term "the simple ones of Judah" in the Habakkuk Commentary. He connects the word translated "simple" with an Arabic word meaning "youth" or "child," and so takes the expression to mean "children of Judah." He cites rabbinic sources that associate the Hebrew and Arabic words in question. This suggests an acquaintance with Arabic on the part of the rabbis at a surprisingly early time, for Weis says that even Rabbi Akiba, in the second century A.D., used the same play on words. It is not impossible, of course, that Jews of this period knew something of the Arabic language; but if so it is not inconceivable that the usage in question was known to the Qumran community somewhat earlier. Teicher observes that the same Hebrew word is used in a favorable sense in Psalm 116:6, where the Septuagint actually translates it "little children." There is no need, however, to read the meaning "children" into the Habakkuk Commentary. The meaning "simple ones" is thoroughly appropriate.

Comments on the biblical text are introduced regularly in the Habakkuk Commentary and once in the Damascus Document by the word *pishro*, "its meaning." Zeitlin attributes this expression to the medieval Karaites, and Weis again gives an elaborate and impressive argument to show that it was a result of the Arabic influence. The usage of the Damascus Document and the Habakkuk Commentary is in fact convincingly shown to be closer to that of medieval writings than to anything hitherto known from earlier periods. Since the origin of these documents before or at the latest very early in the Christian era has now been demonstrated, one can only conclude that the usage in question was either revived in a later period or preserved in a line of tradition different from that of the rabbinic literature.

The difference of usage may be taken to indicate that the commentary and the Damascus Document were not later but earlier than the rabbinic sources. Reversing the argument of Weis, Teicher suggests that later Arabic writers may have been influenced by the usage of the Dead Sea Scrolls. It is not necessary to go that far, but some relationship between the community of the Dead Sea Scrolls and the medieval Karaites is indubitable. What the relation was we must consider in another chapter. The Karaites were also familiar with the Arabic language and the terminology of Arab writers. Some kind of three-cornered relationship, of which the term *pishro* is only one example, may be involved here. All that needs to be said for the purpose now in hand is that the relationship does not and in fact cannot involve a medieval origin of the Dead Sea Scrolls.

Since our only means of telling when ideas arose is their expression in literature, the attempt to place our documents in the history of ideas and terminology is connected with the problem of literary relationships. Similarity in ideas and language may indicate merely that two documents belong to approximately the same period; it may, however, show that one of them has been influenced by the other and is therefore later. The study of literary relationships seeks to detect instances of such influence, especially the quotation of one writing by another.

Unless the source of the quotation is named, it is often very difficult to tell which document is dependent upon the other, or whether both are dependent upon a common source. A familiar example is the famous peace prophecy of Isaiah 2:2–4 and Micah 4:1–4. Does Isaiah quote Micah here, does Micah quote Isaiah, or do both quote an earlier book that has been lost?

Even a clear literary relationship is not usually sufficient by itself to establish the priority of one document or the other. It can only show that there is some connection between them, leaving the chronological relationship to be determined on other grounds. Only occasionally is there any clear indication of the relationship in time.

No other writing known to us exhibits such close affinities with the Dead Sea Scrolls as those found in the Damascus Document, but there are some indications of connection in ideas, if not direct literary dependence, in other books. The apocryphal literature of the period between the Old and New Testaments naturally calls for examination from this point of view. Hempel has remarked that the Thanksgiving Psalms appear to be later than the latest psalms and wisdom literature of the Old Testament, but that no dependence on the apocryphal book of Sirach is apparent. Such a lack of clear literary dependence is of course no indication of date. Even a later work of the same type of literature would not necessarily show dependence on Sirach, and there is actually nothing in the Dead Sea Scrolls that belongs to the category of wisdom literature.

The relationship between the Dead Sea Scrolls and the book of Sirach has proved to be an intriguing problem. Kahle has suggested that both the manuscripts of the Damascus Document and the fragments of the Hebrew text of Sirach found in the Old Cairo genizah were copies of older scrolls that had been brought from one of the caves in the Wady Qumran at about 800 A.D., at the time of the discovery related by Timotheus (see page 41). Following out the suggestion, Dupont-Sommer adds that perhaps the covenanters of Qumran inherited the book of Sirach from an earlier group and added something to it. J. Trinquet notes a possible instance of such addition. The Hebrew text of Sirach found in the Cairo genizah inserts a psalm between Chapters 50 and 51 of the Greek text. It includes the line, "Praise him who chose the sons of Zadok to be priests." There is no other reference to the sons of Zadok in the book. The whole psalm may have been inserted, Trinquet suggests, by the members of a sect; or, if it was a part of the original text, it may have been suppressed by the Greek translator because the Zadokite priests had betrayed Judaism in the time of Antiochus Epiphanes and had been replaced by the Hasmoneans.

Authentic or not, the presence of the psalm in the Hebrew text shows that the book of Sirach had been at some time in the hands of people who glorified the sons of Zadok, and these, Trinquet believes, were the covenanters who produced the Dead Sea Scrolls and the Damascus Document. He suggests that the Hebrew fragments of Sirach, the Habakkuk Commentary, the Damascus Document, and the original nucleus of the Manual of Discipline all come from the first half of the third century B.C. and express the reaction of a priestly group, the sons of Zadok, against the wrongs inflicted upon Onias III by Jason and Menelaus. The expression "sons of Zadok" as used by the sect is therefore "a protestation of fidelity to the authentic priestly tradition."

Here Trinquet obviously combines considerations of related

ideas with the interpretation of historical allusions. He believes that the Habakkuk Commentary reflects the complex history of the pre-Maccabean period, and the Kittim are the Seleucids. The one reference to the sons of Zadok, he has to admit, establishes only a very fragile connection between Sirach and the Dead Sea Scrolls. He explains the lack of any stronger connection by supposing that Sirach was merely adopted by the group without modification, while the documents reflecting their own history and distinctive tenets were produced later within the community.

The net result of the whole inquiry is that there is still no clear connection between our documents and the book of Sirach. Such a relationship as Dupont-Sommer and Trinquet postulate is not improbable, but it has not been demonstrated. What were at first thought to be fragments of the Hebrew text of Sirach were found in one of the Qumran caves; on closer examination they turned out to be Hebrew and Aramaic fragments of the book of Tobit, but other fragments of Sirach are now said to have been identified.

None of the documents with which we are concerned is an apocalyptic work in any strict sense, but there is a strong interest in the "last days," which shows a spiritual connection with the apocalyptic literature and encourages a search for indications of literary relationship. Delcor argues that there is definite affinity of vocabulary and thought between the Dead Sea Scrolls and the book of Enoch, the longest and most elaborate of all the apocalyptic works. Not all the items he mentions to support this contention are convincing. Most of them, if not all, demonstrate only a general similarity of spiritual atmosphere. Such terms as "the elect" and "mystery" are used much too widely in Jewish literature to afford any indication of a literary relationship.

One book among those commonly known as the "pseudepigrapha" is mentioned by name in the Damascus Document, and a fragment of it in Hebrew was found when the first Qumran cave was excavated. This is the Book of Jubilees, sometimes called the "Little Genesis." It is believed by most scholars to have been written in the second century B.C. during the Hasmonean period, though a few date it one or two centuries earlier. Many similarities in language and ideas between the book of Jubilees and the Manual of Discipline have been noted, and this is not surprising. The book of Jubilees was certainly known to the community, as the presence of a fragment of it in one of the caves conclusively demonstrates. The explicit mention of the book by name in the Damascus Document proves that the latter is of later origin than Jubilees; otherwise the contacts between Jubilees and the Dead Sea Scrolls seem to indicate that both it and they come from the same general period and situation, without any clear dependence one way or the other.

Both Jubilees and the Testaments of the Twelve Patriarchs contain passages commonly interpreted as references to a Messiah from the tribe of Levi. These have often been regarded as Christian additions to an early Jewish document; Dupont-Sommer, however, suggests that the Messiah referred to by the Testaments of the Twelve Patriarchs is the teacher of righteousness of the Habakkuk Commentary and the Damascus Document. Comparing the Testament and Jubilees with these documents, he finds evidence that belief in a suffering and redeeming Messiah was known in Judaism in the first century B.C., and in the light of that conclusion he calls for a re-examination of many passages in the Old Testament. C. C. Torrey has argued for many years that the texts cited by Dupont-Sommer, with other passages in the Old Testament, demonstrate the idea of a suffering Messiah in pre-Christian Judaism.

Whatever may be the nature of the relationship between the Dead Sea Scrolls and the Testaments of the Twelve Patriarchs, there is no clear indication of direct literary dependence. As Reicke has said, Jubilees and the Testaments of the Twelve Patriarchs themselves are not literary units composed at one time, but results of a long literary process; and agreements between contemporary or nearly contemporary writings may prove nothing more than a common milieu.

Contacts have been noted between the Habakkuk Commentary and the Psalms of Solomon, a collection of poems written, in part at least, not long after 63 B.C. None of them, it must be said, is close enough to indicate a direct literary relationship. Much of the similarity lies in the use of a common terminology, which is largely biblical, for very widespread ideas. The situation in the two cases, however, is similar if not the same, and in their attitudes and the points of view the Psalms of Solomon and the Dead Sea Scrolls have much in common. Delcor stresses the contrast between the saints and sinners, the condemnation of the priests' love of riches, the sympathy expressed for the poor, the condemnation of the rapacity of the priests, and the references to a flight into the desert to escape persecution. He concludes that the Psalms of Solomon and the Dead Sea Scrolls all come from the same general milieu, but not from the same period, the scrolls being somewhat earlier. Schoeps feels that the parallels between the Habakkuk Commentary and the Psalms of Solomon show that both came from groups who denied the right of the Hasmoneans to the high priesthood and were deeply impressed by the judgment visited upon the last Hasmonean king by the Romans.

To summarize our discussion of the dates of composition of the Dead Sea Scrolls, we may say that the latest possible date for any of them is the time when the manuscripts found in the caves were made; this was some time before the manuscripts were left in the cave, which has now been archeologically established as the time of the first Jewish revolt against Rome (66–70 A.D.). The earliest possible date for the composition of any of the books cannot be fixed. The excavation of Khirbet Qumran reveals an occupation beginning in the Hasmonean period, but some of the manuscripts may have been made before the community settled there. The paleography of the scrolls and fragments shows that some are much older than others. It is quite possible that the oldest manuscripts were already in existence when the books contained in some of the later manuscripts were first composed. It would be equally possible, of course, theoretically, that the latest manuscripts were only new copies of books even older than those contained in the oldest manuscripts.

With the biblical manuscripts all this is clear enough. In the case of the book of Daniel the manuscripts represented by the fragments in the caves may have been made very soon after the original compositon of the book, but such books as Isaiah and Leviticus were unquestionably older by centuries than the earliest date that can reasonably be assigned to any of the scrolls and fragments. The chief problem is that of the non-biblical writings. Here we are dependent upon the internal evidence of language, historical allusions, ideas, terminology, and literary relations.

Some of the biblical fragments have been thought by some scholars to be the remains of manuscripts from the fourth or fifth century B.C., but no scholar would date any of the non-biblical documents earlier than the late pre-Maccabean period. Several would place some of the books at that time, while others argue for later dates. There is general agreement that the Manual of Discipline is one of the earliest of the writings. It has been thought by a number of scholars that The War of the Sons of Light with the Sons of Darkness also was early, but that is not at all certain. While the Habakkuk Commentary is assigned by some to the pre-Maccabean period, there is a fairly clear tendency to move it down to the end of the Hasmonean or the beginning of the Roman period, and the arguments for this seem to me to be convincing. Whether the date should be set before or after 63 B.C. is less clear. The Thanksgiving Psalms, like the Psalms of the Old Testament, cannot be assigned to specific times. Some have suggested that they were written by the teacher of righteousness himself, but the evidence for this is not impressive. More probably they were composed at different times throughout the period. In any case, it now seems to be fairly well established that the non-biblical writings in the scrolls and fragments from the Wady Qumran were all composed within a period of about 135 years, from the accession of Antiochus Epiphanes in 175 B.C., or shortly before that, down to about 40 B.C.

PART FOUR

THE COMMUNITY OF QUMRAN

XI

Origin, History, and Organization

⎍⎍⎍⎍⎍⎍⎍⎍⎍⎍⎍⎍⎍⎍⎍⎍⎍⎍⎍⎍⎍⎍⎍⎍⎍⎍⎍⎍⎍⎍⎍

Who were these peoples who produced the Dead Sea Scrolls?
They were evidently a sectarian group, off to one side from the
main current of official Judaism represented by the temple and its
priesthood. This was evident at once when we first examined
Archbishop Samuel's scrolls at Jerusalem. For a while we spoke
of the Manual of Discipline in particular as "the sectarian document." This was of course only a tentative designation, used for
lack of one that seemed better. I have explained how the term
"Manual of Discipline" came to my mind as I read the scroll.
Meanwhile the term "sectarian document" was criticized on the
obvious ground that all the scrolls were sectarian documents.

But should the term "sect" and "sectarian" be used at all for these
texts? Before the destruction of the temple no particular type of
Judaism was "standard" or "orthodox" in such a sense that any
other tendency could be considered heretical. The words "sectarian" and "heretical," however, are not synonymous. The community of Qumran was an organized group, with definite beliefs
and strict rules, and with an attitude of condemnation toward
the practices of the official priestly leaders of Judaism at the time. If
the word "sect" is not appropriate for such a group, it is hard to
think of a better term. At any rate, that is all that we have in mind
when we speak of the community as a sect and its writings as
sectarian.

What the sect was, what name should be used for it, and what was its relation to any of the other groups known to us, we cannot say until we have found what the manuscripts tell us about its origin, history, and characteristic beliefs and practices. We shall therefore consider these before we try to identify and name the sect. Meanwhile we must continue to use some vague, noncommittal designation. That is better than putting a definite label upon the group prematurely, and then letting this influence our interpretation of the data. For convenience we may continue to use such terms as "Judean covenanters," "Qumran covenanters," or "the Qumran sect."

Concerning the origin of the community, including the lifetime and possible identity of its founder, we have already encountered many theories in our attempt to fix the dates of the documents. We have noted the suggestion that some of the Thanksgiving Psalms may have been written by the teacher of righteousness, whether he was the founder of the group or a later reformer. If this could be proved, and if we could establish the date when these psalms were composed, we should know when the teacher of righteousness lived. Unfortunately neither of these conditions can be realized. We have found that no attempt to identify either the wicked priest or the teacher of righteousness with any known historical person is wholly convincing. Several possibilities must be recognized, including even the possibility that more than one wicked priest and more than one teacher of righteousness are involved. It remains possible also that the teacher of righteousness was an individual unknown to history.

Assuming that there was only one teacher of righteousness, we cannot be sure that he was the founder of the movement. This depends partly on the relationship between the Dead Sea Scrolls and the Damascus Document. The teacher of the community (or teacher of unity) mentioned in the Damascus Document may or may not be the same as the teacher of righteousness who appears in the Habakkuk Commentary as the recipient of revelation. It has been suggested that the teacher of righteousness reformed and reorganized a movement previously founded by the teacher of the community.

One thing can be considered certain: if the teacher of righteousness and the wicked priest were individuals, they were contemporaries. Even if there were several wicked priests and several teachers of righteousness, one of the former persecuted one of the latter. The career of the teacher of righteousness, however, may have begun somewhat before or after the accession of the wicked priest. A convincing identification of the wicked priest would therefore give us only a general indication of the time when the teacher of righteousness appeared, and it would still be uncertain whether the group was organized by him.

The net result of all the searching for an anchorage in history for the Damascus Document and the Dead Sea Scrolls is disappointing. With many possibilities in view, no certainty has yet been attained. The group was obviously well organized by the time the Manual of Discipline was written; indeed, the rules of the community as compiled in that document show already a considerable development of tradition. This, more plainly than any of the historical allusions in the other texts, points to an origin of the group well back in the Hasmonean period, hardly later than the time of Alexander Janneus. This agrees with the results of the excavation of Khirbet Qumran.

Subsequent developments, however, including perhaps the career of the teacher of righteousness and his relation to the teacher of unity, the identity of the wicked priest (or priests), and all the stages of organization reflected in the Dead Sea Scrolls and the Damascus Document, are still very obscure. Rabinowitz, assuming that Jews from the Dispersion returned to Palestine during the time of the Maccabees, proposes a reconstruction of the whole history of the covenanters' community in connection with the terms "council of the community of Israel" in the Damascus Document, "council of the community" in the Manual of Discipline and the Habakkuk Commentary, and "congregation of the Jews" on early Maccabean coins. In the Manual of Discipline, he suggests, the community is in the first place the new society constituted by reuniting Israel, including the returned exiles, in Palestine. Mattathias, the inaugurator of the Maccabean revolt, and his son

Judas, its first leader, were accepted as "guides of righteousness" by the Hasidim of the Maccabean period, and the "camps" of the Damascus Document represent the effort of Judas Maccabeus to gather together the Jews who had returned from the Dispersion. After the death of Judas the reconstituted Jewish community under Jonathan (160–142 B.C.) was called the "congregation of Israel," and it is so named on his coins. Under Simon (142–134 B.C.) it was called the "congregation of the Jews," and each local unit was known as a "congregation of the city." Later the "community" reappeared among the Essenes, and the "congregation of the city" became a Pharisaic institution. This elaborate reconstruction is suggestive as a working hypothesis, but it is open to question at many points.

On these matters wisdom would seem to dictate a suspension of judgment until all the texts have been published and can be examined and compared. Even then it may never be possible to connect the beginnings of the group with any specific individuals or events known to us from other sources. In the meantime we can examine the forms of organization and the beliefs reflected in these documents. This will give us a picture of the group that will enable us to compare it with the parties and sects of Judaism already known to us. In that way it may be possible to determine which, if any, of these groups can be identified with the Qumran covenanters.

The form of the organization and its rules are found in the Damascus Document and the Manual of Discipline. We have seen that these two documents have a great deal in common, though there are sufficient differences to show that they do not come from exactly the same group. They may represent different branches of the same movement or different stages in its history, if not both. In spite of the statement of the Manual of Discipline that the sons of Aaron are to govern the community according the the first ordinances until the coming of a prophet and the Messiahs of Aaron and Israel, there were certainly changes and developments in the sect; in fact, this statement itself may have originated as a

protest against innovations. A thorough discussion would have to
treat the two documents, and the different strata within each one,
separately. For our present purpose, however, we may be content
to discuss them together, merely noting occasional differences as
we encounter them.

While the community had its own separate organization and
held itself strongly apart from the Jewish nation as a whole, it did
not regard itself as merely one group within Judaism. The texts
frequently read as though they were directed to the whole people
of Israel, though this may only reflect a tendency, not unknown
in other religious bodies, to regard all those outside of the group
as heretics and apostates. The sect considered itself, as sects
usually do, the only true people of God.

The community includes "Aaron and Israel," meaning probably
the priesthood and the laity. The Manual of Discipline mentions
priests, Levites, and "all the people," to whom the Damascus Document adds the proselytes. In another passage the place of the
Levites is taken by the elders. The organization seems to be
divided also into smaller groups, each consisting of not less than
ten men, like the *minyan* of the orthodox synagogue. Both the
Manual of Discipline and the Damascus Document speak also of
thousands, hundreds, and fifties, as well as tens. Unless the group
was, for some time at least, very large, these figures can hardly
be anything more than a rather wistful echo of scriptural language. It has been estimated that the total population of the
community in the Wady Qumran numbered not much more than
two hundred.

Although the manuscripts, with the exception of the Damascus
Document, were all found within a limited area near the Dead
Sea, there are some indications that the group was not limited
to a single locality. The expression "all their dwellings" in the
Manual of Discipline does not necessarily imply widely separated
settlements, but the Damascus Document clearly implies the
existence of many different local groups. Conceivably this might
be merely an expression of wishful thinking, but the detailed

regulations and the fact that there are indications of development in the rules themselves point to the actual existence of a number of local settlements.

At the head of each small group stands a priest. His age and other qualifications are stated in the Damascus Document. The decision of all matters in the administration of the community belongs to the sons of Aaron. The priests, the sons of Zadok, are the guardians of the covenant. A group of twelve laymen and three priests is mentioned in connection with the council of the community. Whether this is meant to specify a separate body or the quorum for a meeting of the council is not clear. The stated qualification of the fifteen members, or perhaps of the three priests only, is perfection "in all that is revealed of the whole law, through practicing truth and righteousness and justice and loving devotion, and walking humbly each with his neighbor." The purpose for which the group exists is "to maintain faithfulness in the land" and "to expiate enmity." The exposition of the law and exemplary conduct are thus the main responsibilities of the council of fifteen. Priests play a prominent part in the life of the community. They pronounce the blessing at the common meals and in the ceremony of entering the covenant. In the War scroll the chief priest plays a leading role in the war against the sons of darkness.

Both the Manual of Discipline and the Damascus Document mention an official who is designated by a term rather hard to translate satisfactorily. It may be rendered "examiner" or "investigator," but the functions prescribed for this official are fairly well indicated by the term "superintendent." Apparently the man known by this title is the same one who is called the "inspector" in the same context. The Damascus Document speaks of a superintendent of the camp and also a superintendent of all the camps. According to the Manual of Discipline, judicial decisions are reached by the assembled members of the group; at least there is no reference to judges. In the Damascus Document, however, there is a group of judges selected from the congregation, four from "Levi and Aaron" and six from "Israel." They must be between fifty-five and sixty years old, and must have a perfect knowledge of the law.

Women are not mentioned in the portions of the Manual of Discipline bought by Archbishop Samuel. The first line of the first column originally contained a word of which only the last three letters are now left. Brownlee conjectures that this was the Hebrew word for women; it might equally well, however, have been a word meaning men, or any one of a number of other words. In the last column there is an expression which at first sight seems to mean "holy daughters," and a few scholars have actually supposed this to be the meaning. There is no place for these devout ladies in the context, however, and the words should undoubtedly be read as "building of holiness" or "holy building."

Brownlee sees a reference to marriage in the statement that the "sons of truth" are "to bear seed with all everlasting blessing," but few are likely to accept that interpretation. The Damascus Document, on the other hand, clearly contemplates a group of married men with families, and the additional columns from the Manual of Discipline or a closely related document, which were acquired by the Palestine Museum, mention explicitly women and children. Skeletons of women were found in some of the graves in the cemetery of Qumran. Probably the sect included both communities of celibates and settlements of families. It is possible also that a few women of eminent saintliness were buried in the cemetery of the order even if no women were admitted as members.

Several passages in the Manual of Discipline indicate that the sect practiced community of goods. At the same time it is said that one who has inadvertently destroyed any of the property of the order shall repay it in full. One naturally wonders how a member who had turned over his private possessions to the order would have anything left with which to pay for such damage. It has been suggested that this requirement probably applied only to postulants or novices, not to those who had attained full membership in the community. The Damascus Document puts some restrictions on the ownership of property but does not deny the right of private possession. Members of the group who work for wages pay to the superintendent and the judges for community purposes the wages of two days out of each month. This is one of the most conspicuous differences between the Manual of Discipline and the Damascus Document.

A strict oath of complete allegiance to the law is required of every candidate for membership in the order, according to the Manual of Discipline. Admission is not granted at once; there is a period of probation in two stages of a year each. Only at the end of this process, and after strict examinations at the end of each stage of it, can the candidate be admitted to full membership. The Damascus Document has similar rules, but the process seems to have been less complicated.

Corresponding more or less to the stages of initiation, the community is divided into different groups. The fully initiated members are called the *rabbim*. This word may mean "many." It is frequently used in that sense in the Old Testament. The way it is used in the Manual of Discipline seems to have some association with Daniel 12:2–4, 10, where it probably reflects Isaiah 53:11. Perhaps the choice of the word to designate the members of the group was influenced by these passages in the Old Testament; if so, however, it seems to have been given a different meaning from the one it has there.

In the Habakkuk Commentary it is used in the interpretation of Habakkuk 1:10, which speaks of kings and rulers. In this place, at least, it must mean something like "great ones." In Job 32:9 the same word is a term of honor associated with "elders." In Aramaic it means "masters" or "teachers," and this seems to me to be its meaning as applied to the members of the sect in the Manual of Discipline. One is reminded of the "masters" of the medieval guilds. I have therefore adopted the word "masters" to translate *rabbim*.

The "perfect" or fully initiated members of the Hellenistic mystery cults come to mind also, and the Hebrew word for "perfect" is often applied to the *rabbim*. These "masters" participate in the direction of all the community's affairs. They vote on the admission of new members and judge the cases of offenders against the rules of the order.

Once admitted to full membership, the individual is assigned to a regular rank or place. Attendance at the meetings of the group is compulsory, and the procedure is strictly regulated. It is quite clear that the group believes in the principle enunciated by the Apostle Paul, that "all things should be done decently and in order" (I Corinthians 14:40). The order of seating as well as of speaking in the assembly is prescribed, and each member is expected to present his views in turn. He is not allowed to speak out of turn or to interrupt another member who is speaking.

Obedience to the rules of the community is strictly enforced. Infringements are punished by various penalties, ranging from a reduction of the food allowance to suspension for various periods, or even expulsion from the order. In the Damascus Document provision is made, under stated limitations, for the restoration of repentant offenders. One who breaks the sabbath and repents is to be watched for seven years, and then readmitted to the organization if his conduct has been consistently worthy. Turning over a member to a pagan court for capital punishment is itself regarded as a capital offense. The feeling here is evidently the same as was expressed by Paul in I Corinthians 6:1–8.

Much of the time of the members is given to the study of the law. This must be carried out continuously, day and night, throughout the year. In every group of ten there must always be at least one man studying or interpreting the law. The membership is divided into three shifts, in order to keep the reading and exposition of the law going throughout the night.

In accordance with the basic desire to fulfill all the demands of the law, there is a rigid insistence on ritual purity. The punishment for offenses usually includes exclusion from what is called, literally, the "purity" of the order. The word "purity" here is a technical term for objects, and especially foods, that are ritually pure and therefore to be used only by those who are in a state of ritual purity . In my translation of these documents, accordingly, I adopt the rendering "sacred food." A man who is sentenced to punishment for two years is not allowed to touch "the purity of the holy men" during the first year, and cannot touch "the drink of the masters" even in the second year. This is in accord with rabbinic regulations, by which the use of sacred liquids is more strictly limited than the use of solid substances that are sacred. Before touching the "purity," the repentant offender must be immersed in water, but such immersion is unavailing if one is not a member of the order, or if one is unworthy. Various forms of ritual ablution are prescribed; the idea of washing in a spiritual sense is characteristic also.

One of the major ritual observances of the group was the annual ceremony of entering and renewing the covenant. The liturgy of this rite is given in some detail in the Manual of Discipline. It includes the pronouncement of blessings by the priests and curses by the Levites in the manner of the ceremony described in Deuteronomy 27. The blessings, as we have seen, are based on the Aaronic blessing of Numbers 6:24–26, while the curses consist largely of the opposites of the blessings. Brownlee has pointed out that a similar annual ceremony of renewing the covenant appears in the book of Jubilees (6:17).

The closing psalm of the Manual of Discipline speaks of prayer at sunrise, at sunset, at the new moons, at the festivals, and at the beginning of the year. Whether these were periods of common prayer by the group or periods of private prayer is not clear. The intimate devotional tone of the passage makes the latter alternative somewhat more probable.

Two public prayers in connection with warfare are mentioned in the War of the Sons of Light with the Sons of Darkness. One is the "prayer of the appointed time of war," which is recited by the priest before a battle; the other is the "prayer of the return," which is sung by the whole army after a victory. On the morning following the battle, also, the warriors are told to return to their stations and "bless the God of Israel." Another reference to congregational prayer has been seen in the obscure words of one of the Thanksgiving Psalms: "who array [i.e., set themselves in array?] to thee in the assembly of the saints."

The members of the group "eat, bless, and consult together." At the beginning of the common meal the priest blesses the bread and the wine. The directions for the common meals become vivid when one recalls that the excavation of Khirbet Qumran has uncovered the refectory of the order. No mention is made of the common meal in the Damascus Document. This fact has been taken as an indication that the Manual of Discipline is of later origin than the Damascus Document, the institution of the common meal having developed in the meantime. On the other hand, the "two columns" in the Palestine Museum, which Barthélemy regards as representing an earlier phase of the movement than the Manual of Discipline, already speak of a sacred meal. Here, however, it seems to have an eschatological character, for the "Messiah of Israel" is present, having a place lower than the priest and receiving the bread only after the priest has blessed it.

The attitude of the group toward the temple and its sacrifices is somewhat confusing. The Manual of Discipline makes no reference at all to the temple or to sacrifice except in obviously figurative expressions. The community itself is "a holy house for Israel, a foundation of the holy of holies for Aaron." Its life and worship are regarded as having power to expiate sin. Prayer is called "the offering of the lips." Such expressions have been thought to indicate that the group had broken all connection with the worship of the temple. Aside from the fact that the manuscript of the Manual is incomplete, however, the absence of laws concerning sacrifice does not necessarily imply a withdrawal on principle from the temple worship. In the Damascus Document, although the priesthood of the temple is condemned for not observing the law, there are actually regulations concerning offerings that are to be sent to the temple. The Habakkuk Commentary denounces "the wicked priest" and "the last priests of Jerusalem," but this severe condemnation of priests for profaning the sanctuary, like the cleansing of the temple by Jesus, shows a high respect for it and its institutions.

In the Damascus Document the sect is called a "house of division" because it withdrew from the holy city when Israel defiled the sanctuary. The lawfulness of animal sacrifice as such, however, is not questioned. Prayer is preferred to unworthy sacrifice, but so is it in the Old Testament. There is no evidence that sacrifice was practiced elsewhere than in the temple. It has been suggested that the rules concerning sacrifice in the Damascus Document are survivals from the period before the separation from temple worship, and that they were retained because the group expected later to resume worship at the temple. This seems quite probable. The later rabbis who produced the Talmud studied minutely the laws concerning the temple and its ritual long after the temple was destroyed. Orthodox Jews have continued to do so ever since, believing that when the Messiah comes he will restore the temple.

Both the Manual of Discipline and the Damascus Document emphasize the observance of the festivals at the proper times. The religious calendar was, in fact, an object of concern for all branches of Judaism. One of the crimes of Antiochus Epiphanes was that he undertook "to change the times and the law" (Daniel 7:25). The Judean covenanters committed themselves "not to advance their times nor postpone any of their appointed festivals." The Damascus Document mentions sabbaths and festivals among the "hidden things in which all Israel went astray."

The Habakkuk Commentary changes the text of Habakkuk 2:15, making it read, "to gaze on their festivals." The following lines interpret this as a reference to the appearance of the wicked priest on the Day of Atonement, "to confound them and to make them stumble on the day of fasting, their sabbath of rest." There is a close parallel to this, at least in language, in one of the Thanksgiving Psalms:

> so that God beheld their error,
> going mad at their festivals.

In another connection we have noted S. Talmon's interpretation of the passage in the commentary on the assumption that the sect followed a calendar different from that of the temple priesthood. The wicked priest, Talmon suggests, appeared before the group on the day it observed as the Day of Atonement. Is was "their sabbath of rest," but not his. The verbs "to confound" and "to make stumble" mean that he undertook to prevent them from keeping their Day of Atonement. Talmon recalls a striking parallel to this incident: at about the end of the first century A.D. Rabban Gamaliel ordered Rabbi Joshua, whose view of the calendar he considered unorthodox, to appear before him with staff and purse on the day which Rabbi Joshua believed to be the Day of Atonement.

A few lines in the Manual of Discipline are of particular interest in this connection. The closing psalm contains the expression, "at the coming of seasons to the days of a new moon." Dupont-Sommer connects this with a calendar prescribed in the book of Jubilees and I Enoch. The Damascus Document, as a matter of fact, explicitly refers to the book of Jubilees for an explanation of the sacred times. The calendar of Jubilees and Enoch, which was later adopted by the Maghariya and the Karaites, clearly represents a reaction against the official calendar.

The prevalent system of fixing the festivals by the first appearance of the new moon, and trying to adjust the lunar cycle of months to the solar cycle of seasons, was discarded by the author of Jubilees. By his calendar the year was divided into four seasons, beginning on the first day of the first, fourth, seventh, and tenth months respectively. Each season consisted of 91 days (two months of 30 days each and one of 31). Thus the year had 364 days, exactly 52 weeks. This had the advantage of making the festivals fall always on the same day of the week.

But the lunar month has only twenty-eight days; consequently the first of the month by this sectarian calendar would fall back more and more into the phase of the waxing moon. By the end of a year the observance of the new moon would come ten days after the real new moon. Dupont-Sommer sees an allusion to this, and so an indication that this was the calendar of the sect, in the words, "at the coming of seasons to the days of a new moon." Two lines later we read of "holy days in their ordered sequence as a memorial in their seasons." Dupont-Sommer takes this to refer particularly to the sabbath, emphasizing the fact that in this calendar the sabbaths are determined by reference to the seasons because each season contains exactly thirteen sabbaths. An expression in the next line, "at the beginning of years and in the circuit of their seasons," indicates, Dupont-Sommer believes, that the sect began its year in the spring. In that case the New Year was observed on the first day of the first month, whereas orthodox Judaism then, as now, observed the New Year in the autumn, on what by the spring calendar was the first day of the seventh month.

Most readers will probably feel that Dupont-Sommer's inferences are acute but by no means obvious. The general conclusion that the Qumran sect accepted the 364-day calendar, however, seems to be well established. Some connection between the calendar of Jubilees and that of the covenanters is clearly evident in the passage already cited from the Manual of Discipline. The "day of remembrance" recalls the language of Jubilees 6:24, 28, 29. The year is divided into four seasons as in Jubilees, the years are grouped in weeks, and a time of liberation corresponding to the year of jubilee is mentioned.

This calendar was probably not a new invention but followed an old tradition. Barthélemy argues that it was the calendar in general use at the beginning of the Hellenistic period. The lunar calendar, adjusted to the solar year by the occasional "intercalation" of an extra month, was itself an innovation, adopted under Hellenistic influence. This argument is taken up and developed by Miss A. Jaubert. The book of Jubilees, she points out, insists that the feast of weeks must fall on the fifteenth day of the third month. If the year begins on the first day of the week, and each month contains thirty days, the fifteenth day of the third month will fall on Friday; but Leviticus 23:15f and Deuteronomy 16:9 require that it come on Sunday, the day after the sabbath.

The later Magharians met this difficulty by beginning the year on Wednesday. The dates given for the travels of the patriarchs in the book of Jubilees show that here too the beginning of the year on Wednesday is presupposed. Miss Jaubert demonstrates this by a table which shows that there is only one day of the week on which the patriarchs are never said to set out on a journey or to arrive anywhere. If this day is assumed to be Saturday, each of the four seasons begins on Wednesday. The fifteenth day of the third month then falls on Sunday, as the law requires; and the Day of Atonement, the tenth day of the seventh month, falls on Friday. The four new moons, the Passover, and the Feast of Tabernacles come on Wednesday also, as do all the main events in the history of the patriarchs. This works out much too neatly to be explained by mere coincidence. The full application of the theory involves some arithmetical complications, but they need not detain us here.

Barthélemy, we have seen, believes that this calendar was in general use before the Hellenistic period. Miss Jaubert raises the question whether it may have been an even more ancient Israelite calendar. By a detailed investigation she reaches the conclusion that the calendar of Jubilees was that of the priestly school of historians that edited the Hexateuch, and from which the work of the Chronicler came. According to her theory, it originated not later than the Babylonian exile and was the religious calendar of post-exilic Israel, though for civil purposes the calendar prevalent in the Persian empire was used. After the Macedonian conquest and the spread of Hellenism the religious calendar was threatened even in its own domain, the festivals. Hence arose a bitter struggle within the priesthood itself between Hellenists and anti-Hellenists. Even the Maccabean rising may have had some connection with this controversy. Later, however, even the descendants of the Maccabees seem to have renounced the old priestly calendar. Their desertion of the ancient tradition is what is condemned in the books of Enoch and Jubilees. It finally resulted, Miss Jaubert suggests, in the division and persecution reflected by the Habakkuk Commentary.

Beginning where Miss Jaubert leaves off, J. Morgenstern reaches quite different results, but he agrees that the calendar of Jubilees was an ancient one. He argues, indeed, that it was a somewhat modified survival of a "pentecontad" calendar originally of Amorite or Canaanite origin and adopted by the Israelites at the time of the conquest of Canaan. Through various vicissitudes, which we cannot follow here, it survived among the farming people, especially in the north, and in sectarian groups. Traces of it appear in the Gospels and even in the practice of Palestinian peasants to this day. To examine this thesis in detail would take us much too far afield, but it must be mentioned as an instance of the ramified associations of the religious institutions reflected in the Dead Sea Scrolls.

There is still more to be said about the intriguing tenth column of the Manual of Discipline. The first five lines contain three mysterious letters in which Brownlee has discerned an acrostic on the three consonants of the Hebrew word *amen* (*'mn*). The aleph (*'*) is attached in the manuscript to the end of the verb "decreed" (if it is a verb); Brownlee takes this letter, however, as the initial consonant of the Hebrew word for God, *'elohim,* though he mentions also other possible explanations. The *m* appears in the obscure statement, "the M is large"; the *n* in the equally mysterious statement, "the letter N is for the unlocking of his eternal mercies." Noting that the shape of the *n* in this script is like that of an ancient key, Brownlee sees in the passage a probable reference to the Messiah, who with the "key of David" will unlock "the sure mercies" (Isaiah 55:3) of "the God of Amen" (Isaiah 65:16).

Dupont-Sommer rejects Brownlee's interpretation and asks what a reference to the Messiah would be doing in the midst of an enumeration of sacred times. He regards the aleph of Brownlee's acrostic as an Aramaic form of the feminine ending of a noun meaning "decree." What Brownlee takes to mean "the M" is thought by Dupont-Sommer to be either a mistake in the text or the pronoun "they," emphasizing the suffix in the preceding "their renewing themselves." Not very likely at best, this explanation involves two or three grammatical difficulties.

For the "letter N" Dupont-Sommer offers a striking and attractive explanation of his own. The letters of the alphabet in the Hebrew, as in the Greek, alphabet were used as numerals, and the letter *n* stood for the number 50. Among the Pythagoreans and various Gnostic groups the number 50 was considered especially sacred. Dupont-Sommer quotes two passages from Philo, pointing out that in a right-angled triangle with sides measuring 3 and

4 the hypotenuse measures 5, and the sum of the squares of these three numbers is 50. The number 50 was therefore regarded as the perfect expression of the right-angled triangle, the symbol of "the supreme principle of the production of the world," as Philo says.

In the passage in the Manual of Discipline, Dupont-Sommer connects "the letter N" with the preceding words, the "holy of holies," reading "the holy of holies and the letter N." This he takes to be a hendiadys, indicating not two things but one, like "this day and age." The expression "holy of holies and the letter N" means therefore "the supreme sacredness of the number 50." Brownlee, more plausibly I think, construes "the holy of holies" with the preceding words and supposes that a new clause begins with the words "and the letter N." Dupont-Sommer's explanation of the *n*, however, does not stand or fall with this particular detail of interpretation.

For the expression "the key of his eternal mercies" also Dupont-Sommer finds an explanation in the statement of Philo, for if the number 50 has the supreme sacredness Philo attributes to it, it may well be called the key to God's eternal mercies. Since the whole passage deals with the observance of the festivals, the reference to the number 50 implies that the calendar embodies all the sacredness of the right-angled triangle.

It may be that there is truth in the ideas of both Brownlee and Dupont-Sommer concerning this passage, which is at best extremely obscure and perhaps deliberately so. Barthélemy points out that the three letters in Brownlee's acrostic have a total numerical value of 91 (1 + 40 + 50), the number of days in each of the four seasons of the calendar of Jubilees. This indicates, Barthélemy thinks, that the author of the closing psalm of the Manual of Discipline meant the three letters to be understood as an acrostic. This may well be so, but it does not exclude the particular significance seen by Dupont-Sommer in the *n*. Not only the total value of the three letters in the acrostic but also each letter by itself may have had a mystical meaning for the poet.

The covenanters were not wholly preoccupied with matters of

ritual purity and the observance of sacred times. Their devotion to the law included moral and social righteousness also. In considering the organization and discipline of the community we have already seen something of their moral ideals. The problem concerning their attitude to war, for example, has been mentioned. While the War scroll is animated by the idea of a holy war, the Manual of Discipline makes no reference to warfare, and its studious sons of light seem different from those of the War scroll, though it is true that they swear to hate all the sons of darkness. All the more striking is the fact that in the two columns of a document like the Manual there are references to armies and to war. This, in fact, is one of the reasons for believing that the two columns do not belong to the Manual of Discipline. The latter not only does not mention war; it counsels the members of the community to leave the punishment of the wicked to the final judgment. The two columns, however, regard war as ordained for the destruction of the gentiles.

The attitude of the sect toward material possessions has already been mentioned. The reading "wealth" instead of "wine" in Habakkuk 2:5, as quoted in the commentary, may be recalled. It will be remembered also that while the Manual of Discipline permits no private ownership of property, at least among the full members of the group, there is a rule requiring restitution for any destruction of the property of the order, while the Damascus Document allows the members of the group to earn wages and retain them, delivering to the superintendent of the camps only the wages of two days out of each month.

The difference between these two compositions concerning marriage also has been mentioned in connection with the organization of the community, together with the references to women and children in the two columns in the Palestine Museum and the presence of some skeletons of women in the cemetery at Khirbet Qumran. Whatever these facts may mean, Hempel remarks that women clearly played no such part in the community as they did in the early Christian church. Marriage with a niece is strongly condemned in the Damascus Document. Whatever attitude to marriage the group or any branch of it may have had, all the texts emphasize a strict ideal of purity. Even lustful glances are condemned. The rules for the meetings of the group emphasize also modesty and seriousness.

In general it may be said that the moral ideals of the covenanters of Qumran are much like those of similar monastic groups in other religions, but quite unlike those of orthodox Judaism at many points. They are the ideals of a group that has withdrawn from the world into a separate life of rigid discipline and purity, going into the desert to prepare the way of the Lord by the study of the law.

XII

Beliefs

¶¶¶¶¶¶¶¶¶¶¶¶¶¶¶¶¶¶¶¶¶¶¶¶¶¶¶¶¶

Religious beliefs, as well as forms of organization and moral ideals, are reflected in the Dead Sea Scrolls, though of course not completely or in any systematic way. Enough may be discerned, at any rate, to afford a basis for comparison with other Jewish sects and parties of the same period. Such a comparison may enable us to identify the covenanters of Qumran with one of these; if identity cannot be established in any instance, more or less close relations or affinities between the covenanters and some other sect or sects may be discernible.

The covenanters obviously held the Scriptures in high esteem, as did all Jewish parties and sects. They apparently possessed and accepted all the books that were finally retained in the Jewish canon of the Old Testament when it was fixed after the destruction of the temple. The law and the prophets are extensively quoted in the Dead Sea Scrolls and used as authoritative expressions of God's will. The covenanters undertake, as the Manual of Discipline says, "to do what is good and right before him as he commanded through Moses and through all his servants the prophets." All three parts of the Old Testament canon—law, prophets, and "writings"—are quoted in the scroll of Thanksgiving Psalms. Portions of almost all the books of the Old Testament have been identified among the fragments discovered in the caves of the Wady Qumran.

How far what was accepted by the community as sacred literature included books other than those of our Hebrew Bible cannot yet be determined. Whether the covenanters had any conception of what we call a canon is uncertain; in any case their library included much more than our Old Testament. The Damascus Document quotes by name the book of Jubilees, and the unknown book of HGW is mentioned as an authoritative work both in the Damascus Document and in one of the fragments acquired by the Palestine Museum. Many works that did not find a place in the Jewish canon were obviously copied and cherished by the covenanters, as the large number of books represented by the manuscript fragments abundantly attests. How their attitude to these works compared with their attitude to the books of our Old Testament we cannot yet say.

The interpretation of Scripture plays a large part in the literature of the sect. It is hardly too much to say, with Brownlee, "The sect had its birth in biblical interpretation." It is interesting to compare the way in which the covenanters use and interpret the Old Testament with the way other Jewish writers and the writers of the New Testament interpret it. Direct quotations followed by explanations appear in the Damascus Document, the Habakkuk Commentary, and to a lesser extent the Manual of Discipline. Sometimes statements are supported by quotations with the introductory formula, "as it is written."

The authority for the interpretation is found in a new revelation given to the leader of the sect, the teacher of righteousness, who is called "the priest into whose heart God put wisdom to explain all the words of his servants the prophets, through whom God declared all the things that are coming upon his people and his congregation." This new revelation goes beyond what the prophets themselves were able to see; for example, "God told Habakkuk to write the things that were to come upon the last generation, but the consummation of the period he did not make known to him"; what the prophet himself did not see, however, was revealed to "the teacher of righteousness, to whom God made known all the mysteries of the words of his servants the prophets."

The interpretation put upon the Scriptures is primarily historical, not in the sense that it corresponds to modern conceptions of historical criticism and interpretation, but in the sense that everything is supposed to refer directly to the history of the group itself. Not only are events of the writers' own times interpreted in the light of Scripture; it is even more characteristic that the Scriptures themselves are interpreted in the light of recent events. A rapid perusal of the Habakkuk Commentary and the Damascus Document will show how freely texts are combined, interpreted, and applied to present conditions and events in a way quite foreign to their real meaning.

If such a use of Scripture appears strange to the modern reader, innumerable examples of exactly the same practice can be found in popular expositions of prophecy today. To give just one example, a very recent book makes the ridiculous statement that the "ships of Kittim" in Daniel 11:30 are the British ships that were sent from Cyprus in the First World War to attack the coasts of Syria and Palestine, and that verses 40–42 of the same chapter refer to the British occupation of the Middle East; and this is followed by an ominous conclusion regarding Egypt's effort to throw off British control! The covenanters of Qumran never went to greater extremes of absurdity than that.

When biblical material is used in the scrolls for the life and worship of the community, there is a good deal of free adaptation and modification. An excellent example is the benediction prescribed for the priests in the Manual of Discipline, which is an adaptation of the "Aaronic benedicton" of Numbers 6:24–26. Borrowing a device used by Brownlee, the translation that follows uses italics for the words that are drawn from the ancient benediction.

May he *bless you* with all good *and keep you* from all evil;
May he *give light* to your heart with living wisdom *and be gracious to you* with eternal knowledge;
May he *lift up his* loving *countenance* to *you* for eternal *peace*.

A similar use of biblical language with free expansion may sometimes be observed today in the non-liturgical Protestant churches. Closing a service of worship with Paul's benediction at the end of II Corinthians 13, for example, ministers often are not content to stop where the apostle stopped, but seem impelled by a craving for liturgical sonority to add "both now and for evermore."

The way in which the Old Testament is interpreted in the Habakkuk Commentary involves a curious fact which we noted in discussing the text of the Old Testament as it appears in the Dead Sea Scrolls. The text of Habakkuk as quoted in the commentary sometimes appears in one form, while the explanation that follows the quotation seems to presuppose a different form of the text. In Habakkuk 1:11, for example, where the standard text reads "guilty man, whose might is his god," the quotation in the commentary reads, "and he makes his might his god"; yet the interpretation that follows seems to reflect the idea of guilt, for it mentions a "guilty house." The quotation of Habakkuk 2:15 reads "their festivals" where the standard text has "their nakedness"; yet the verb in the ensuing explanation, at least as understood by some scholars, means "uncover him." (In this case the interpretation of the passage in the commentary is questionable; see pp. 153–56.) The quotation of Habakkuk 2:16 reads "stagger" instead of "be uncircumcised"; yet the explanation includes the clause, "because he did not circumcise the foreskin of his heart." Some scholars believe that in these places the commentator was acquainted with two different readings of the text, both the one he quoted and the one presupposed by his interpretation. Delcor suggests that he may have used a manuscript of Habakkuk in which the readings of the Masoretic text were noted in the margin. Another possibility is that the commentary was originally composed on the basis of a text that followed the Masoretic readings, but a scribe who later copied the commentary altered the quotations to agree with what he considered a superior text.

The interest of the covenanters in the Old Testament was legal as well as historical. The correct interpretation of the law was very important for them. The very purpose of the group's existence, in fact, was to prepare the way of the Lord by the study of the law. The passage in the Damascus Document that speaks of the leader of the covenant as the "star" that Balaam had said would "arise out of Jacob" describes him and his associates as interpreters of the law. The Habakkuk Commentary calls the followers of the teacher of righteousness "doers of the law." Their adversaries are accused of despising the law and opposing God's commandments. One of the Thanksgiving Psalms calls the teachings of false interpreters "smooth things," borrowing this term from Isaiah 30:10. The Hebrew word is *ḥalaqot;* the Pharisees called their legal precepts *halakot,* and perhaps, as Brownlee suggests, the writer of the psalm may have intended a pun on that term by his use of the word *ḥalaqot,* subtly implying that the Pharisaic interpretation of the law was false.

A candidate for admission into the community had to be examined "with regard to his understanding and his deeds in the law." Entering the covenant involved taking an oath to return wholeheartedly to the law of Moses. So important was the study and interpretation of the law for the community that a special place was set aside for the purpose, and at every hour during the day and night it was required that members of the group be present and engaged in this pursuit. Since the same Hebrew verb means both "to study" and "to interpret," Brownlee supposes that what was done in this place was not so much individual or group study as "oral exegesis." The procedure was perhaps a good deal like that of the rabbis and their disciples in their discussions of the law.

The Manual of Discipline prescribes that the sons of Aaron shall govern the community according to the "first ordinances" until the expected coming of "a prophet and the Messiahs of Aaron and Israel." The expression "first ordinances" suggests an unalterable set of regulations, perhaps the laws of Moses themselves, which are to be the constitution for the government of the community until the end of the age. I have already suggested that this passage may be a protest against innovation in the organization and rules of the sect itself. It may equally well be a hostile allusion to the oral traditions of the Pharisees, which applied the law of Moses in ways that often involved rather bold interpretations. Jesus criticized these traditional interpretations of the Pharisees, charging that the scribes made God's law of no effect by their traditions; he interpreted the law freely, however, according to its inner intent, and did not consider it, as the covenanters did, a code to be preserved without change and strictly enforced.

The interpretations of the law in the Dead Sea Scrolls and the Damascus Document, and their relation to the rabbinic interpretations later crystallized in the Talmud, should be thoroughly investigated. This can be done only by specialists in rabbinic law. Such a comparison might contribute much to the understanding of both the scrolls and the rabbinic literature, illuminating the development of the legal traditions of the rabbis before they attained final form in the Talmud.

Vermès remarks that the return to the law of Moses involved a legalistic type of piety, culminating in a scrupulous concern for ritual purity, but he adds that all this stress on the law did not produce a merely mechanical, external observance. The Manual of Discipline emphasizes also the necessity of sincere, wholehearted devotion. Obedience to the law, as Vermès rightly says, meant for the covenanters a response to a divine revelation, not a revelation of truth to be believed but a revelation of duties to be done. Acceptance of this revelation and obedience to it implied confidence in God's promise; thus obedience was an expression of faith. This, one may add, is fully in accord with the basic Jewish conception of religion as "obedience to the revealed will of God." At the same time, the piety of the covenanters was a sectarian piety. Only within the community was true obedience to the law supposed to be possible.

In addition to the devotion of the covenanters to the Hebrew Scriptures, there are elements in their thinking that have suggested various kinds of gentile influence. In particular, many scholars see in the Dead Sea Scrolls reflections of the religious movement known as Gnosticism. Others find no trace of Gnosticism in them. The question whether the covenanters were Gnostics is important for the understanding of the sect of Qumran and its place in the history of religion. We must therefore devote some attention to it.

To some degree it is a question of definition. What is meant when one speaks of Gnosticism? In the strictest sense the term refers to a heretical form of Christianity that arose in the second century A.D. This Christian heresy, however, was not an entirely new or unique phenomenon; it was a strange amalgam of ideas both new and old, some of them going back all the way to ancient Babylonian religion. It is possible therefore to think of Gnosticism as a general movement of thought affecting other religions as well as Christianity. The Christian or pseudo-Christian Gnosticism of the second century was undoubtedly only one phase of this movement, which was essentially more pagan than Christian. Many scholars believe that there was a pre-Christian type of Jewish Gnosticism; others deny this. Those who believe it see in the Dead Sea Scrolls new evidence for their contention.

When we speak of Gnosticism in the Dead Sea Scrolls, therefore, the question is not whether the covenanters were Gnostics in the strictest sense, defined in terms of the Christian heresy, but whether they belonged to the general movement or tendency known as Gnosticism in a broader sense. At the same time the terms Gnostic and Gnosticism should not be used in such a broad way that their meaning becomes vague and confusing. They should be reserved for forms of religion, whether Christian or non-Christian, that exhibit at least the most characteristic features of Gnosticism as represented by the second-century Christian heresy.

To judge on its merits the question of Gnostic influence in the scrolls, let us consider in turn the most characteristic features of Gnosticism and ask what evidence for each of them can be found in the Dead Sea Scrolls. In so doing we shall of course remember that these documents do not represent all the beliefs of the Qumran covenanters. We cannot assume that all of their beliefs were ever committed to writing at all. If any idea does not appear in the scrolls, we shall not fall into the fallacy of an "argument from silence," supposing that we have proved that the sect had no such belief. We shall conclude merely that, since no evidence of the belief in question has survived, its existence cannot be assumed.

The first and most essential of the characteristic features of Gnosticism is the conception of salvation by knowledge, not achieved by learning but received by mystical illumination, either through lonely contemplation or through participation in sacramental rites, though an element of instruction is involved also. This basic idea is indicated by the very name Gnosticism, derived from the Greek word *gnosis,* which means knowledge.

There is undoubtedly a strong emphasis on knowledge in the Dead Sea Scrolls and the Damascus Document. A few typical passages may be quoted by way of illustration. "God loves the knowledge of wisdom; and sound wisdom he has set before him; prudence and knowledge minister to him." Dupont-Sommer calls this a characteristic statement of Gnosis. Again, ". . . and in the heat of God's anger against the inhabitants of the earth he commanded that their knowledge should depart from them before they completed their days." This is perhaps an allusion to Genesis 6:3, and what is meant may be merely the general confusion of mind characteristic of senility. Commenting on Habakkuk 2:14—"For the earth will be filled with the knowledge of the glory of YHWH as the waters cover the sea"—the Habakkuk Commentary says, "And afterward knowledge will be revealed to them like the waters of the sea in abundance." Dupont-Sommer speaks of this as the revelation of the divine Gnosis. The Manual of Discipline says that the members of the sect must bring their knowledge as well as their wealth and their strength into the community. A man who refuses to enter the covenant has "refused instruction and knowledge of righteous laws." The "sons of truth" are those who "walk humbly with prudence in all things and love for the truth of the mysteries of knowledge."

The most frequent and perhaps most significant references to knowledge in the Manual of Discipline are in the concluding psalm, which calls God the "source of knowledge and fountain of holiness." Later in the same passage the writer makes these statements:

> With wise counsel I will conceal knowledge,
> and with knowing prudence I will put a hedge about [wisdom].
>
> .   .   .
>
> For from the source of his knowledge he has opened up my light.
>
> .   .   .
>
> My eye has gazed on sound wisdom,
> which has been hidden from the man of knowledge,
> and prudent discretion from the sons of man.
>
> .   .   .
>
> Blessed art thou, my God,
> Who openest to knowledge the heart of thy servant.
>
> .   .   .
>
> Thou hast taught all knowledge.

The verb "know" is used in the Thanksgiving Psalms in ways that have been thought to reflect Gnostic ideas: e.g., "I know that there is hope for him whom thou hast formed from the dust for the eternal assembly," and "I know that man has no righteousness." These expressions recall a statement in the Manual of Discipline: "I know that in his hand is the judgment of every living thing." In such contexts this verb has no more Gnostic significance than it has in such a biblical passage as Job 19:25: "I know that my Redeemer lives."

The same thing may be said of the way the noun "knowledge" is used. One of the Thanksgiving Psalms includes the words, "to open the fountain of knowledge to all who understand." Another psalm says of the "babblers of lies and seers of deceit" that "they withheld the draught of knowledge from the thirsty." Dupont-Sommer, quoting this passage, asserts that Gnosis is one of the essential concepts of the sect; but again a close biblical parallel may be cited: "Woe to you lawyers! for you have taken away the key of knowledge; you do not enter yourselves, and you hindered those who were entering" (Luke 11:52).

Not only the word "knowledge" but also such synonyms as

"wisdom," "prudence," "understanding," "insight," and the like appear often in the scrolls. The vocabulary in this respect is much the same as that of the Old Testament book of Proverbs. The fact that knowledge is emphasized does not of itself indicate Gnostic influence. A reflection of such influence may perhaps be seen in the degree of emphasis, but actually the stress on knowledge is no greater in the Dead Sea Scrolls than it is in the wisdom litera-ture of the Old Testament.

The saving knowledge of the Gnostics was believed to be given by revelation. In the Dead Sea Scrolls also knowledge is thought of as having been revealed. The following lines from one of the Thanksgiving Psalms afford a typical expression of this idea:

> For thou wilt make me wise in wonders like these,
> and in the company . . . thou wilt give me knowledge.

In keeping with this is the frequent reference to divine mysteries. The Habakkuk Commentary declares that "the mysteries of God are marvelous," and again a little later: "For all the periods of God will come to their fixed term, as he decreed for them in the myster-ies of his wisdom." Similar expressions appear in the Thanksgiving Psalms; for example, "for thou hast caused me to know thy mar-velous mysteries." The same expression, "thy marvelous mysteries," occurs in the War scroll, which speaks also of the "dominion of Belial and all the mysteries of his enmity," recalling the Apostle Paul's expression, "the mystery of lawlessness." The mysteries of God's understanding and his "marvelous mysteries" are mentioned also in the Manual of Discipline and the Damascus Document.

A few other typical statements from the Manual of Discipline may be quoted in this connection. The section on the two spirits says that the sins of the sons of righteousness are caused by the angel of darkness "according to the mysteries of God, until his time." The spirit of truth gives men "understanding, and insight, and mighty wisdom, . . . and a spirit of knowledge in every thought of action, . . . walking humbly with prudence in all things, and concealing the truth of the mysteries of knowledge." A later section of the Manual says that "those who choose the way" must be admonished in order "to guide them in knowledge and so to give them understanding in the marvelous mysteries and the truth." The closing psalm contains these lines:

> For there is no other beside thee
> to oppose thy counsel,
> to understand all thy holy purpose,
> to gaze into the depth of thy mysteries,
> or to comprehend all thy marvels.

The idea of knowledge as the revelation of a divine mystery, entrusted to a limited group, is characteristic of Gnosticism. Salvation is attained by knowledge, but knowledge of what? It is not knowledge in general, or learning, or practical wisdom that brings redemption. The Gnostic idea is that salvation comes through a comprehension of the nature of reality, of the soul's origin, nature, and predicament in this world, and of the way of salvation from that predicament. The idea of what is known by "the man of truth" that is expressed in the Dead Sea Scrolls is quite different from this Gnostic conception. What is meant by knowledge in the scrolls has to do with the wonders of God's creation, the fulfillment of prophecy, and the meaning of the divine laws man must obey.

Insistence on a knowledge of the law as necessary for salvation is not characteristic of Gnosticism. It is an essential part of the legal tradition of the Old Testament, carried on and developed by rabbinic Judaism. The Pentateuch itself stresses the importance of a knowledge of the law for the priests. Knowledge was exalted by Judaism in general. Vermès remarks that those who speak of non-Jewish elements in the Dead Sea Scrolls may be thinking of Judaism too exclusively in terms of the Talmud, ignoring the prayers of the synagogue. For the place of knowledge in Jewish piety he cites one of the "Eighteen Benedictions," as given in the old Palestinian form represented by a manuscript from the Old Cairo genizah: "Deign to grant us, our Father, a knowledge coming from thee, a knowledge and a wisdom coming from the law. Blessed be thou, O Lord, who dost deign to grant us knowledge."

The sons of Aaron in the Dead Sea Scrolls are heirs to this tradition. The central place of the law in what is meant by knowledge in the Dead Sea Scrolls is unmistakable. Those who "have offered themselves for his truth" are required by the Manual of Discipline to "bring all their knowledge and strength and wealth into the community of God, to purify their knowledge in the truths of God's ordinances." The wicked man is condemned because "his soul has abhorred the discipline of knowledge." It is stipulated that "the counsel of the law must be concealed among the men of error; but there must be admonition of true knowledge and righteous judgment for those who choose the way." Such an association of knowledge with the law is as alien to Gnosticism as it is characteristic of Judaism.

The Gnostic conception of reality and of the soul is expressed in the form of an elaborate mythology. Reality is conceived as pure spirit, uncontaminated by matter. The material world is derived from the pure realm of spirit by a series of emanations or generations like the successive pairs of gods and goddesses of the pagan cosmogonies. The spiritual world of reality is often referred to in terms of light, the material world of delusion in terms of darkness.

In the Dead Sea Scrolls there is a dualism of light and darkness that strikingly recalls this Gnostic dualism. The great warfare with which the War scroll deals is called "the war of the sons of light with the sons of darkness." In the Manual of Discipline those who "enter the covenant" are required "to love all the sons of light" and "to hate all the sons of darkness." The most interesting and significant passage in this connection tells how God "created man to have dominion over the world and made for him two spirits, that he might walk by them until the appointed time of his visitation." These two spirits are called "the spirits of truth and perversion," "the spirits of light and darkness," and also "the prince of lights" and "the angel of darkness." Not only are "the sons of error" completely under the rule of "the angel of darkness"; even "the sons of righteousness" are led astray by him and suffer affliction "in the dominion of his enmity," but "the God of Israel and his angel of truth have helped all the sons of light." All men are under the dominion of one or the other of the two spirits, which struggle for mastery even within the individual soul. But this is only for the duration of the present world order. God has ordained an "appointed time of visitation," when he will destroy evil and "make the upright perceive the knowledge of the Most High and the wisdom of the sons of heaven."

H. J. Schoeps, who had previously denied that there was a pre-Christian form of Gnosticism within Judaism, announced recently that this account of the two spirits in man had constrained him to change his mind. But there is nothing here like the "endless genealogies" of Gnosticism. The doctrine of the two spirits of light and darkness has other non-Jewish affinities, as we may see presently, but to call these ideas Gnostic seems to me to necessitate stretching the term until it loses all specific meaning. Dualism is here, yes; but it is a dualism of good and evil, not of spirit and matter.

Another basic feature of Gnosticism is not found in this passage or elsewhere in the Dead Sea Scrolls or the fragments thus far published. This is the conception of the soul as a spark of the divine light that has become imprisoned in the dark world of matter. This is not the belief of the Qumran covenanters. To call the righteous "sons of light" and the wicked "sons of darkness" is quite a different matter. The idea of an angel of darkness, who not only owns and dominates the "men of Belial's lot" but also has some power over the "men of God's lot" during the present age, is very different from the Gnostic conception of the soul. Gnosticism regarded the soul as essentially pure, temporarily imprisoned in the world, but needing only the knowledge of its origin, nature, and true destiny to be freed from the bonds of the flesh and to ascend through one sphere after another to its native abode.

This saving knowledge, according to the Gnostics, is given by a divine Redeemer, who has descended from above to release the souls of men and lead them back to the realm of light. It would be difficult to find anything in the Dead Sea Scrolls even faintly reminiscent of such conceptions. One thinks of the teacher of righteousness and his revelation of the true meaning of prophecy, but only by reading a great deal into what is said of him could one imagine any connection with the heaven-descended Redeemer of Gnosticism. The expectations concerning the Messiahs of Aaron and Israel, of which more will be said later, come no nearer to the Gnostic idea.

Points of contact between the Dead Sea Scrolls and Gnosticism in other respects have been noted. Some, though not all, groups of Gnostics followed a strictly ascetic life, as did the covenanters of Judea. Here again, however, the similarity is not such as to establish a relationship. Undoubtedly the scrolls contain ideas and ideals resembling those of the Gnostics at various points. Some indirect and indefinable historical connection is not impossible. On the whole, however, it seems unnecessary and only confusing to apply the term Gnosticism to the form in which such ideas appear in the Dead Sea Scrolls.

Above all it must be emphasized that knowledge is not in itself, according to the scrolls, the way of salvation. Knowledge of the law is important, because only by obedience to the law can judgment be averted. Knowledge of prophecy is important for comfort and encouragement to persevere in obedience. Knowledge of God's mysteries induces praise of and humble dependence upon God. But knowledge has no saving power in itself; it is not the immediate vehicle of deliverance. It is rather the answer to the question, "What must I do that I may inherit eternal life?"

If Gnosticism did not directly influence the Judaism of the Qumran sect, both may have drawn water from the same well. The ideas in which a kinship between them has been seen were especially at home in Zoroastrianism, the religion of ancient Iran. Perhaps, as Kuhn puts it, the Dead Sea Scrolls show us the point at which the stream of Zoroastrian influence poured into the stream of Jewish tradition and united with it. The combined stream then flowed on, he says, into the New Testament on one side and into

Gnosticism on the other. Iranian influence in Judaism has long been recognized, but perhaps, as Dupont-Sommer observes, no Jewish document exhibits this influence quite so clearly as the section of the Manual of Discipline containing the account of the two spirits, which has been summarized above. Dupont-Sommer quotes passages from the Zoroastrian Scriptures concerning the spirits of good and evil that determine the lives of men. Here, however, the good man chooses for himself the good spirit, and the bad man chooses the evil spirit. We must come back later to the "determinism" of the Dead Sea Scrolls.

The theme of the two armies of light and darkness is especially characteristic of Zoroastrianism. The evil power called Angra Mainyu or Ahriman in Zoroastrianism is called Belial in the Dead Sea Scrolls. Once in the War scroll and three times in the Manual of Discipline "the dominion of Belial" is mentioned. The Manual of Discipline calls the wicked "the men of the lot of Belial." In the Damascus Document also Belial plays a prominent part. This opposition of God and Belial is much closer to the Iranian dualism of good and evil than it is to the dualism of spirit and matter in Gnosticism, but it is still closer to the opposition between God and Satan in the Bible. The name Belial itself, in fact, is derived from the Bible. The Jewish ideas of the kingdoms of God and Satan had undoubtedly some historical connection with the Zoroastrian idea of the cosmic war between Ahura Mazda and Angra Mainyu, though the nature of the relationship is a much debated and very complicated problem. In any case it seems more accurate to call the ideas of the Manual of Discipline Iranian than to call them Gnostic.

Iranian influence in Judaism appears particularly in the apocalyptic literature, including the book of Daniel in the Old Testament and the non-canonical books of Enoch. Fragments of these apocalyptic works have been found in the Qumran caves, and the scrolls have affinities at several points with the apocalyptic literature. Several writers have observed that the idea of divine mysteries expressed in the Dead Sea Scrolls is related to the apocalyptic type of thinking. The book of Daniel uses the same word for "mystery" that appears in the Dead Sea Scrolls, and the fragments of several manuscripts of Daniel found in the caves prove that the Judean covenanters were well acquainted with this book. Similar expressions have been noted in the books of Enoch and in the Testaments of the Twelve Patriarchs. The mysteries referred to in the Dead Sea Scrolls, however, are different from those most typical of the apocalyptic literature. Unlike the latter, they do not consist of entirely new revelations, but rather of a true understanding of the revelation given long ago in the law and the prophets. This conception also, to be sure, occurs sometimes in the apocalyptic books; witness Daniel's explanation of the seventy weeks of Jeremiah.

Another point at which a spiritual kinship between the Dead Sea Scrolls and the apocalyptic literature may be seen is the belief concerning angels and demons. Some of the same terminology used in the Dead Sea Scrolls is found in the apocalyptic writings. The scrolls seem to have no special term for demons or evil spirits, but the word "angel" is applied to them—more often, in fact, than it is to good spirits. The "angel of darkness" is a case in point; "angels of darkness" are mentioned both in the Manual of Discipline and in the Damascus Document. The latter speaks also of the "angel of enmity." Only once, so far as I have observed, is the word "angel" used in the Manual of Discipline for a good spirit; that is the reference to God's "angel of truth." Usually other terms seem to be preferred for angels or good spirits. It is said that the upright are given insight "into the wisdom of the sons of heaven," and that they receive "an inheritance in the lot of the holy ones." Both of these expressions probably refer to angels.

The War of the Sons of Light with the Sons of Darkness says that there are holy angels with the army of the righteous; in fact, it uses the names of the archangels Raphael, Michael, and Gabriel.

In the Thanksgiving Psalms "the army of the holy ones," "the congregation of the sons of heaven," "the eternal assembly," "the assembly of the holy ones," and "thy marvelous assembly" are mentioned. Dupont-Sommer takes all these to mean the celestial assembly of the angels. He argues that the "holy ones" and the "sons of heaven" include both angels and the souls of the righteous, and he cites a widespread belief that associated the angels and the souls of the righteous with the stars. One may fairly doubt, however, that an assembly including both men and angels is here contemplated. The word which Dupont-Sommer and others translate "assembly" has a rather broad meaning, indicating in general a group or company.

In one of the Thanksgiving Psalms, God is addressed as "the Prince of the gods and the King of the venerable ones, and the Lord of every spirit, and the Master of every work." Dupont-Sommer, in commenting on this passage, recalls the fact that God is called "the Lord of spirits" in the book of Enoch. Dupont-Sommer is also probably right in taking the "gods" and the "venerable ones" to mean angels.

These questions of affinity with Gnosticism, Zoroastrianism, and Jewish apocalyptic thought have already introduced us to some of the most characteristic ideas in the Dead Sea Scrolls. Whatever foreign influences may have affected the ideas of the Qumran covenanters, their basic point of view and major doctrines were thoroughly Jewish, derived primarily from the Old Testament. The importance of the law and the prophets for them is enough to prove this. They never doubted that Israel was God's chosen people.

They believed strongly in the doctrine of divine election—so strongly, indeed, that their belief has even been called fatalistic. A favorite word of the Manual of Discipline is the one used in the Old Testament for the lot that was cast to determine matters of dispute or doubt, such as the territory to be occupied by a tribe. This term occurs fourteen times in the Manual and three times in the Damascus Document, but with a special meaning. It is used for the destiny allotted by God to each man, somewhat as we commonly speak of a man's lot in life. It also means the division of mankind in which each man's lot is cast. The righteous are called "the men of the lot of God"; the wicked are called "the men of the lot of Belial." The "lot of Belial" and the "people of God's lot" are named also in The War of the Sons of Light with the Sons of

Darkness. One of the Thanksgiving Psalms says, "thou hast caused to fall on man an eternal lot." Dupont-Sommer recalls in connection with this passage the statement of Josephus that the Essenes believed everything that happened to be determined by destiny.

In all this it is clear that for the covenanters election had to do not merely with the chosen people as a whole but with individuals. The conception of man's nature expressed in the section on the two spirits has been called by L. Rost a deterministic theology. Similar ideas appear in the Damascus Document, where, as Rost points out, men seem to be divided into four groups according to their assigned destinies. Such a division of individuals into groups is quite different from the old Hebrew conception of the whole nation as God's elect. The way had been prepared for a belief in individual election, however, by the Old Testament ideas of the righteous remnant and the new covenant. Vermès points out that in the Damascus Document the history of mankind is divided into five periods, in each of which God has set apart a saved remnant under the leadership of his chosen servants. Since the coming of the teacher of righteousness, the law can be rightly kept only within the community of his followers. Membership in the community is therefore a sign of the divine election. The election of the nation is of course still presupposed, but the stress is now on an election of individuals who have joined the community. In other words, the idea of the chosen people has become in effect the idea of a church. Whether the conception of the community made any place for Gentiles is another question. The only hint that this may have been so is the mention of the "sojourner" or "proselyte" in the Damascus Document, and this may possibly refer only to candidates for membership who are undergoing probation.

Belief in election or predestination is not, as commonly supposed, an expression or source of pride, but rather the reverse. Certainly this is true of the covenanters of Qumran. Their assurance that they possessed the true revelation of what the law and the prophets meant was accompanied by an acute sense of sinfulness. The writers of the Dead Sea Scrolls regarded man as weak and utterly dependent upon God. This is expressed by the term, "thing formed from clay." Being helpless and weak, man must depend upon God for both wisdom and righteousness. Perhaps the most impressive expression of humble reliance on God in the scrolls is the closing hymn of the Manual of Discipline.

Having considered the sect's belief concerning man's present condition and the meaning of salvation, we turn now to its ideas concerning God's agents of salvation. These include the bearers of revelation in the past and any Messianic bringer of redemption expected in the future. Moses was of course revered as the first giver of the law; indeed, the law of Moses was so highly esteemed that even the mention of it in an oath is forbidden in the Damascus Document. Second only to Moses was Zadok, the high priest of the time of David, because he reopened the books of the law, which had been sealed up since the death of Eleazar and Joshua.

Our word "Messiah" is an Anglicized form of the Hebrew word meaning "anointed." It is commonly applied to the king as "the Lord's anointed," and it is from this usage that we get the term Messiah as a designation of the future king promised by the prophets. In the Old Testament, however, the same term is also applied to the high priest; therefore when the Damascus Document says, "And through his anointed one he shall make them know his Holy Spirit," the reference may be not to the coming king but to Zadok. The reference to God, the anointed one, and the Holy Spirit together in this passage seems to Dupont-Sommer to foreshadow the doctrine of the Trinity. Any such inference, however, is unwarranted, because the anointed one here is probably not the Messiah at all in the sense of the future king.

In other passages, however, the word "anointed" or "Messiah" is clearly used for one who is to come at the end of the present age. The Manual of Discipline, in fact, speaks of not one but two coming Messiahs: "but they shall be ruled by the first laws with which the men of the community began to be disciplined, until the coming of a prophet and the Messiahs of Aaron and Israel." Several references to "the Messiah of Aaron and Israel" or "from Aaron and Israel" occur in the Damascus Document, but this use of the word in the singular may be the result of later alteration, either through misunderstanding or through a deliberate correction at a time when the idea of two Messiahs seemed inacceptable.

The two Messiahs may be supposed to represent the king and the high priest of the future. In that case it seems rather strange that the royal Messiah is expected to be from Israel instead of Judah. Possibly, however, "Israel" is used in a comprehensive sense for the whole people, and "the Messiah of Israel" means the lay Messiah, so to speak, while "the Messiah of Aaron" is the priestly Messiah. The conception of a Messiah from the priestly tribe of Levi appears in the apocryphal Testaments of the Twelve Patriarchs and in the rabbinic literature, often in perplexing combinations with other ideas.

In one of the Palestine Museum's two columns from a document related to the Manual of Discipline there is an account of a meal resembling closely that of the Manual, but including a reference to the Messiah of Israel. There is also a reference to "the prince of the whole congregation," who may be the same person. The Manual of Discipline does not mention the Messiah of Israel except where he appears with the prophet and the Messiah of Aaron. The Messiah of Israel in the "two columns" is subordinated to "the priest" in the description of the banquet. The banquet here described may be not a real meal but the eschatological banquet of the rabbinic literature.

Apart from the use of the term "anointed" there are other indications of Messianic ideas in the scrolls. A series of what Barthélemy considers Messianic variant readings in the St. Mark's Isaiah manuscript is noted when we come to the importance of the scrolls for textual criticism. A reference in the Damascus Document to "the arising of the teacher of righteousness at the end of days" suggests some connection between the teacher of righteousness and the coming Messiah.

Dupont-Sommer, in fact, believes that the writer of the Damascus Document expected the teacher of righteousness to return at the end of the world as the Messiah. To support this view he quotes the expression "from the gathering in of the unique teacher to the arising of the Messiah from Aaron and from Israel," but this implies a distinction between the unique teacher and the Messiah rather than their identification. Believing that the teacher of righteousness was put to death in 65–63 B.C., Dupont-Sommer infers that the end of the world was then expected very soon. All this is connected with his interpretation of the Habakkuk Commentary, where he finds an implication that the teacher of righteousness will return as the Messiah, though the teacher of righteousness is not actually given that title. It seems more reasonable to say with Vermès that while the Messiah would undoubtedly be a teacher of righteousness, the teacher of righteousness who founded the sect should be distinguished from the one who would come and teach righteousness at the end of days.

The place of the teacher of righteousness in the scheme of salvation has been well summarized by Vermès. The righteous are those who have listened to the teacher of righteousness, and the wicked are those who have refused to listen. What is essential for salvation is faith in the mission of the teacher of righteousness and fidelity to his teaching. In other words, his role is precisely that indicated by his title: he is a teacher of righteousness. Hempel points out that there is nothing in our documents of an incarnation of the divine Word in the teacher of righteousness, and no such hymn as that of Paul in Philippians 2 is sung about him. There is no trace of a gospel with the teacher of righteousness as its center.

A quite different line of connection between the teacher of righteousness and what may be called in a broad sense Messianic ideas has recently been suggested by Brownlee, though he does not argue that the teacher of righteousness was the Messiah. In several of the Dead Sea Scrolls he finds indications that the teacher of righteousness was identified with the servant of the Lord depicted in Isaiah 40–55. Who is meant by the servant in these chapters is still a matter of debate among Old Testament scholars. In many passages the servant is explicitly identified with Israel;

e.g., "But now hear, O Jacob my servant, Israel whom I have chosen!" (Isaiah 44:1). For centuries, however, many have believed that the servant was the Messiah, especially in chapter 53, which describes the suffering of the Lord's servant for the sins of others. From the earliest days of the church Christians have felt that Christ himself was portrayed in these chapters (see, e.g., Matthew 8:17; 12:17–21). There are many, however, who believe that in all these passages the servant was originally a collective figure, standing for the people of Israel.

In Isaiah 52:14, where the traditional text says of the servant, "his appearance was so marred," the St. Mark's manuscript reads, "so I have anointed his appearance." Brownlee considers this a deliberate alteration for the purpose of interpretation, the verb "anointed" suggesting a connection with the Messiah. We consider this variant reading of the text in Chapter XIV. Rightly understanding the expression "his elect" in the Habakkuk Commentary as plural, Brownlee sees in it a collective interpretation of the Lord's servant as the righteous people of God. The elect must undergo suffering like that of the servant, and like the servant they will be given judgment over the Gentiles. In the closing hymn of the Manual of Discipline, as Brownlee interprets it, the sect is given the threefold function of the servant of the Lord: prophetic witness (Isaiah 43:10), priestly atonement (Isaiah 53), and royal judgment (Isaiah 42:1). This conception of the community as the servant of the Lord, however, finds its realization in the person of the teacher of righteousness.

Many ingenious arguments for the identification of the teacher of righteousness with the Lord's servant are advanced by Brownlee. They are more elaborate and far-reaching than can be indicated here. To me they are not convincing, but they indicate a possibility that deserves consideration. It is interesting to observe that I. Sonne finds in the opening lines of one of the Thanksgiving Psalms "an expanded paraphrase of Isaiah 42:6." He suggests that the leader of the sect himself may have claimed to be the servant of the Lord.

Other aspects of what the covenanters looked for at the end

of the age must be mentioned. The expression "at the end of the days" is not only used in connection with the arising of the teacher of righteousness; it is also associated with the sons of Zadok, who are said to be "the elect of Israel, called by name, who are to stand at the end of the days." In the Habakkuk Commentary there is a reference to "those who will act treacherously at the end of days." In one place "the end of days" is connected with the invasion of the Kittim, for the commentator says of "the last priests of Jerusalem, who assembled wealth and booty from the spoil of the peoples," that "at the end of days their wealth with their spoil will be delivered into the hand of the army of the Kittim."

We have already discussed the possibility that the War of the Sons of Light with the Sons of Darkness refers not to any war on the plane of history but to an eschatological war. One of the fragments found in 1949 in the excavation of the first cave was from an unknown apocalyptic poem. After referring to the fact that the wicked of ancient times ignored God's warning and therefore perished, the poem promises the sure victory of light over darkness and the imprisonment of the wicked angels. Justice will then shine like the sun, and the world will be filled with knowledge, while the wicked will vanish forever.

During the present age the righteous suffer persecution. The frequent references to persecution in the Thanksgiving Psalms, together with a picture of the final catastrophe in one of them and the statements of devastation by the Kittim in the Habakkuk Commentary, are taken by Vermès to reflect the common idea of a time of great tribulation just preceding the end of the world. It is characteristic of apocalyptic thought to believe that the last time has begun. The present is that darkest of all hours which just precedes the dawn. Faith in the teacher of righteousness involves the conviction that this is so, and that the trials his followers are now enduring are a test of their perseverance and fidelity.

The future was only partially revealed to the prophets, for "the last period extends over and above all that the prophets said." But "all the periods of God will come to their fixed term as he decreed for them in the mysteries of his wisdom." Then the "doers of the law in the house of Judah" will be delivered "from the house of judgment because of their labor and their faith in the teacher of righteousness."

Later we read again of "the house of judgment, whose judgment God will set in the midst of many peoples; and thence he will bring it up for judgment, and in their midst will condemn it and punish it with fire of brimstone." Those who were enticed by the preacher of the lie will "come into judgments of fire," and "in the days of judgment God will destroy all the worshipers of idols and the wicked from the earth." The execution of judgment on both Gentiles and wicked Jews will be committed to the elect: "God will not destroy his people by the hand of the nations, but into the hand of his elect God will deliver the judgment of all the nations and by their chastisement all the wicked among his people will be punished."

A Hebrew noun that means primarily "end" is often used in the Dead Sea Scrolls and the Damascus Document in the sense of "time" or "period," as it is also in the book of Daniel and occasionally elsewhere. In the Damascus Document we read of the period of wrath, the period of wickedness, the period of office of the sons of Zadok, the period of the destruction of the land, the period of the first visitation, and the period of Israel's transgression. There is also a more general statement about periods. All these expressions refer to periods in history, but we hear also of the "consummation of the period of these years" in the future and the eschatological "period of visitation." The "period of wrath" is mentioned in the Thanksgiving Psalms. The Manual of Discipline uses the word with reference to the proper periods for the celebration of the festivals, the astronomical divisions of time, the period of the afflictions of the wicked, the "periods of recompense" of the righteous, the "periods of the ages" during which the divisions of mankind have their allotments, the period appointed for the existence of evil, and the final period when the dominion of evil will come to an end.

Many expressions containing the Hebrew word for "eternity" are used in the Manual of Discipline to indicate the destinies of the wicked and the righteous. The wicked are eternally cursed; they are under eternal hatred or eternal enmity; they will suffer in the darkness of eternal fire. Their fate will be eternal destruction. The righteous are promised eternal peace, eternal light, eternal truth, eternal glory. A description of what awaits both the wicked and the righteous is given in the Manual in the section on the two spirits in men.

How did covenanters conceive of the future life of the individual? Did they, in common with many other Jews of the time, believe in a resurrection of the body? If not, did they accept the idea of the immortality of the soul? A belief in the resurrection has been inferred from a few passages in the Dead Sea Scrolls. The curse to be pronounced by the Levites on the wicked, according to the Manual of Discipline, includes a statement that has been translated "and he will not make you live," which would mean that the wicked will not be raised from the dead. The text, however, does not say "make you live" but quite plainly "be favorable to you."

A reference to the resurrection of the body has been seen also in the statement of one of the Thanksgiving Psalms, "And I know that there is hope for him whom thou hast formed from the dust for the eternal assembly." Other scholars draw quite different inferences from these words. Vermès, for example, sees here a suggestion of the immortality of the soul, but not of the whole man. Such a Platonic conception seems strange in Judaism, but to show that it was not unknown Vermès quotes a statement of Josephus concerning the Essenes and also a Jewish tombstone inscription from Egypt. The Qumran covenanters, he suggests, expected the final judgment before the end of their own generation, and therefore were not concerned about the resurrection of the body. What they expected was neither the resurrection of the body nor the immortality of the soul alone, but the "assumption" of the whole person in a purified body.

Starting from the same passage, van der Ploeg has made a

special study of the idea of the future life in the Dead Sea Scrolls. The obvious kinship of the sect with the Essenes, he says, would lead us to expect a belief in the immortality of the soul apart from the body, and he believes that an examination of the texts turns this expectation into certainty. According to the Manual of Discipline, the men of Belial will suffer eternal punishment and the righteous will have "eternal joy in the life of eternity." There is little in the texts that suggests a renewed bodily life on earth, whereas there is much about existence in the world of light above, the world of God and the angels.

From an obscure passage near the end of the Manual of Discipline, which seems to indicate an eternal life in the company of the angels, van der Ploeg infers an interpretation of the Thanksgiving Psalm that was the starting point of his inquiry. It suggests to him "a sort of Elysian fields," with a host of angels, including the members of the sect.

Other passages in the Thanksgiving Psalms seem to imply that the souls of the righteous will dwell in the presence of God and the angels. The friends of God will enjoy his presence forever. Prayer is offered to God "in the assembly of the holy ones." Noting that these expressions recall the language of the Old Testament psalms, van der Ploeg concludes that the sect had either taken up again an old tradition concerning the future life or had received these ideas from some other source and read them into the psalms by reinterpretation.

The picture that emerges from all this is not clear in detail, but the main lines stand out fairly distinctly. By way of summary we may say that the Qumran sect was a Jewish group, devoted to the divine revelation given to their forefathers in the law and the prophets. Like other Jewish groups, however, they had their own way of interpreting the Scriptures. Unlike most other Jewish groups, they even believed that they had been granted a new revelation that made clear the true meaning of the Scriptures. In the prophets they found their own past and future prefigured. Affinities with Gnosticism can be seen in beliefs of the sect, but the covenanters did not depart so far from the ancient Hebrew traditon as to adopt the metaphysical dualism of the Gnostics or their elaborate mythology of redemption. They believed that all things were ordained by God. Even the existence of evil and the struggles between good and evil in human society and in the individual soul were part and parcel of the divine plan. At the end of the appointed period God would deliver his elect and destroy the hosts of wickedness.

Back of these ideas lie not only the ancient Hebrew tradition but also the moral dualism and the angelology and demonology of Iranian religion. Iranian influence may have been at work also in the sect's beliefs concerning salvation. Possibly no more such foreign elements need be assumed than were already embodied in the latest books of the Old Testament and the post-biblical apocalyptic writings. It is also possible, however, that new currents of thought from the general mixture of traditions and cultures we call Hellenism had made their way into the side-stream of Judaism.

Be that as it may, the covenanters firmly believed that they were God's elect, not only as members of the chosen people but also individually as sons of light, the men of God's lot. They had entered the covenant and were members of the community that believed in the teacher of righteousness as the inspired interpreter of the divine mysteries. They looked for a prophet and the Messiahs of Aaron and Israel. They confidently expected the judgment and eternal punishment of the sons of darkness, when the dominion of Belial would be brought to an end. They fervently hoped to be cleansed of all evil by the spirit of truth and to enjoy eternal felicity in the presence of God with the angelic hosts.

Whatever else may be said of the Qumran theology, this much is clear. But who were these people? What kind of Jews were they? Can we identify them with any of the groups within Judaism known to us from other sources?

XIII

Identification

Not one but several identifications of the Qumran community sect have been proposed and defended by scholars, though recently a disposition to regard the question as settled has become apparent. Using the clues provided by our survey of the characteristic features of the sect, we must now try to examine all the possibilities. The problem is by no means simple. No name for the group is given in any of the documents. In the Manual of Discipline it is apparently assumed to be "all Israel." Judah, as distinguished from Israel, is not mentioned. In the War scroll, however, the sons of light are explicitly identified as the tribes of Levi, Judah, and Benjamin; that is, the priestly tribe and the two tribes that constituted the kingdom of Judah. On the other hand, the Damascus Document reflects a hostility to Judah and a connection with the northern tribes.

Since we are dealing not with one text but with many, we cannot of course take it for granted that all the texts come from the same sect or party. All the writings contained in the scrolls and fragments found in the Qumran caves were no doubt accepted and used, but they were not all necessarily produced by the sect. Even if they represent branches or successive phases of the same general movement, one such phase or branch may prove identical with a particular group in Jewish history, while those represented by other documents cannot be so identified. It is possible to hold, for example, as Barthélemy does, that the "two columns" come from the early Hasidim, while the Manual of Discipline comes from the later sect of Essenes.

One fact is obvious, and it may serve as our point of departure. The group is evidently conservative, striving to maintain laws and traditions once and for all delivered to the ancients. Not only so, it is reactionary, in the sense that it clearly arose as a reaction against what its members considered innovations and departures from the faith of the fathers. The question before us is whether any such reactionary movement known in the history of Judaism can be confidently regarded as the movement that produced our documents.

With the spread of Hellenistic culture and customs in Palestine during the third century and early second century B.C., those Jews who were faithful to the traditions of their fathers and resisted the new ways of living came to be known as the Hasidim, the "loyal" or "devout." In the Old Testament this word is used for the righteous, godly people who are persecuted by the wicked. It is often translated "saints." Carried over into Greek in the form Asidaioi, it appears in I and II Maccabees as a designation of the devout men "who willingly offered themselves for the law," joining forces with the Maccabees in the revolt against Antiochus Epiphanes.

When Demetrius I made Alcimus high priest in 161 B.C., the Hasidim withdrew from the Maccabean revolt and tried to make peace with Alcimus, because he was "a priest of the seed of Aaron," but he treacherously killed sixty of them in a day. In general they seem to have been less militant than the Maccabees, and after the achievement of religious liberty they did not support the Maccabees or their successors, the Hasmonean rulers. They are often called the spiritual ancestors of the Pharisees, though the exact relationship is not clear.

Not a few scholars have identified the covenanters of Qumran with the Hasidim. The term Hasidim, however, seems to designate devout, conservative Jews in general rather than a definite sect or party. We may therefore say that the organized sect of the Dead

Sea Scrolls arose among the Hasidim, but this does not yet provide a specific identification.

The histories of Josephus, the New Testament, and the rabbinic literature speak of the Sadducees and the Pharisees as the two major groups within Judaism. Can the covenanters be identified with either of these? The Sadducees, though described by Josephus as one of the four Jewish "philosophies," seem not to have been in reality a party, to say nothing of a sect, but rather a class, though doubtless they stood together on political and religious issues as social classes usually do. They were in general the wealthy aristocracy, of which the temple priesthood was the most conspicuous and powerful element. They accepted only the Pentateuch as Scripture, interpreted the law very strictly, and rejected the Pharisaic system of oral tradition concerning the meaning of the law. They also rejected the new beliefs in angels and resurrection of the dead, which were espoused by the Pharisees.

The name Sadducee was probably derived from the name Zadok and is the equivalent of Zadokite. Some historians have thought that the Sadducees were so called as followers of a man named Zadok who lived in the Hasmonean period. Other explanations also have been proposed, but the most widely accepted and most probable view is that they were called Zadokites because they proudly considered themselves the descendants and successors of the Zadok who was high priest under David and Solomon. When the Damascus Document was published the prominence of the sons of Zadok in it led scholars to suspect an association between the covenanters and the Sadducees. Further study soon showed that they could hardly be identical. Dupont-Sommer points out, for example, that the covenanters highly honored the prophets, whereas the Sadducees did not accept the prophetic books as Scripture.

To account for the use of the term "sons of Zadok" in the scrolls, Dupont-Sommer suggests that before the Maccabean crisis of the second century B.C. there may have been devout priests who called themselves sons of Zadok to signify their authentic priestly lineage and their attachment to the traditional faith and cult. They were not the same group as the covenanters, but there was probably a division within the sons of Zadok, when those who felt themselves drawn to a higher religious ideal separated themselves from the rest and formed the sect of the new covenant. Such a connection with dissident members of the Zadokite priesthood is questioned by de Vaux. He suggests that in calling themselves sons of Zadok the priests of the Qumran community were reclaiming a title that had been appropriated and abused by the Sadducees. That the sect arose within the priesthood seems to me thoroughly probable. In any case, the covenanters were certainly not the group called Sadducees in the New Testament, the rabbinic literature, and the works of Josephus. The denunciation of the priests of Jerusalem in the Habakkuk Commentary would of itself be enough to prove that.

Schoeps protests against deriving a picture of Judaism in the last century B.C. and the first century A.D. from a description given by Josephus for the time of Antiochus Epiphanes. The real background for the Dead Sea Scrolls, he feels, is to be found in what is said about the Sadducees in patristic and rabbinic sources. He calls attention particularly to a group called Zadokites, who are said to have arisen among the priests in the last half-century before Christ. They called themselves righteous and condemned obeying the law merely for the sake of rewards. Their founder, Schoeps thinks, may have been a man named Zadok who was called the teacher of righteousness. One of the manuscripts of the Damascus Document actually reads at one point "teacher Zadok" instead of "teacher of righteousness," though most scholars consider this a mistake in copying.

The medieval Karaite, al-Qirqisani, includes in his history of the Jewish sects a confused but suggestive account of the Sadducees. Their leaders, he says, were two men named Zadok and Boethus, pupils of Antigonus, the successor of Simeon the Righteous. This suggests a date in the second century B.C. The Talmud, however, speaks of the family of Boethus as one of four high-priestly families in the first century A.D., and Josephus mentions a man named

Boethus as the father of Joazer, who was high priest early in that century. If the same man is referred to, this would place Boethus, and consequently Zadok, in the last century B.C.

Since the names "Zadokite" and "Sadducee" are the same in Hebrew, what al-Qirqisani says about the followers of Zadok and Boethus may not really refer to the Sadducees at all. The name Zadok is from the same root as the Hebrew word for righteousness, and it is not entirely beyond the bounds of possibility that al-Qirqisani's Zadok was really the teacher of righteousness of the Dead Sea Scrolls. In that case, of course, he was not the founder of the sect. His followers would then be Zadokites but not Sadducees; the latter would still be the dominant priestly class, who probably derived their name from the high priest of David and Solomon. All this, which seems to me possible though not very probable, would provide a theory closely resembling that of Schoeps, except that the covenanters would not be identified with the Sadducees of any period.

If the covenanters of Qumran were not Sadducees, were they Pharisees? The name Pharisee means "separated," though just what separation gave rise to it is somewhat uncertain. As devout adherents of the law, the Pharisees were separated from the Hellenists, who had deserted it. In their zeal for the observance of the law they separated themselves from all defilement and all causes of defilement. When the Hasmoneans, in their ambition to gain power, violated the law, the Pharisees separated from them. Whatever may have been the first occasion for calling them separatists, the term may have come eventually to suggest all these kinds of separation.

Devoted as they were to the observance of the law, the Pharisees were more progressive than the Sadducees in its interpretation. They applied and adapted it to changing conditions and enlarged areas of life. This was done by the development of the oral tradition, later codified and ultimately embodied in the Talmud. They also accepted as sacred the books of the prophets and the other writings, though the exact extent of the canon was not yet defined. Unlike the Sadducees, they accepted the beliefs concerning angels, and the belief in the resurrection of the dead, which seem to have come into Judaism during the Persian period and at least in part through Persian influence.

The exhortation of Isaiah 40:3 to prepare the way of the Lord in the wilderness is explained by the Manual of Discipline as meaning the study or interpretation of the law. So far the covenanters might well be Pharisees. Several scholars have argued that they were. The Pharisees also had societies somewhat resembling the organization of the covenanters. Such a society was called a *ḥaburah,* and the members were called *ḥaberim;* but they were also called *rabbim,* as the members of the sect are called in the Manual of Discipline.

A careful comparison of the Pharisaic *ḥaburah* and the community of the covenanters has been made by Saul Lieberman, who points out many similarities. Before being admitted to membership in the Pharisaic societies, candidates undertook to observe strictly the laws of ritual purity. Admission was preceded also by an investigation of the candidate's previous observance of the law, and was granted in two separate stages, with an intermediate period of probation. Some of the same terminology was used that we find in the Manual of Discipline.

The differences between the regulations of the Pharisaic societies and those of the Judean covenanters seem to Lieberman no greater than some of the differences among the Pharisees themselves. In general, the rules of the Manual of Discipline are more strict than those of the Pharisees, but there are some indications that the Pharisaic rules had once been more strict than those found in the later rabbinic literature. Some views expressed by individual rabbis, Lieberman suggests, may reflect older traditions of sectarian groups whose ideas were quite different from those of rabbinic Judaism as a whole.

Lieberman's general conclusion is that "we must be very cautious in drawing conclusions from similarities and differences between the regulations of the sects. . . . Every sect probably had its divisions and subdivisions. Even the Pharisees themselves were reported to have been divided into seven categories. It is therefore precarious to ascribe our documents definitely to any of the known three Jewish major sects."

Sensible and sound as this conclusion may be, there is one of the "three major Jewish sects," that of the Essenes, which, ever since the discovery of the Dead Sea Scrolls, has been thought of as being perhaps the group that produced them. The possibility of this identification is immediately suggested by the fact that the scrolls were found in the very region where the Essenes are said to have had their headquarters. The first person to suggest that the scrolls might have been hidden by Essenes during a period of persecution seems to have been Ibrahim Sowmy, who came with his brother Butrus to bring the scrolls to the American School at Jerusalem. My diary for March 19, 1948, says that in the afternoon I "worked on the 'Essene' manuscript," meaning the Manual of Discipline. Our first news release, dated April 10, 1948, after mentioning two of the documents, the Isaiah manuscript and the Habakkuk Commentary, continued, "a third appears to be the manual of discipline of a comparatively unknown little sect or monastic order, possibly the Essenes."

Many scholars have accepted the identification of the covenanters with the Essenes. Its first public champion was Dupont-Sommer, to whom the similarities between the Essenes and the covenanters seem so striking that he considers their identity certain. Recognizing that there were different groups among the Essenes, he insists that the Qumran sect was "a sect properly Essene and not para-Essene."

Who were these Essenes? Aside from some references in the rabbinic literature, our knowledge of them comes chiefly from the historian Josephus and the philosopher Philo. There is also a brief statement in Pliny's *Natural History*. Josephus, Philo, and Pliny all lived in the first century A.D., when the Essenes were flourishing and the community of Qumran was still studying and copying its manuscripts. Josephus was a general in the war with Rome which brought to an end the settlement of the covenanters as well as the worship at the temple. He had undoubtedly seen Essenes, and perhaps had known some of them personally. Philo, who lived in Egypt, probably had only a second-hand knowledge of them. Even the account of Josephus must be read with some caution. In his desire to make a favorable impression on his gentile readers, he describes the Essenes, like the Sadducees and Pharisees, as a school of philosophy. There is more specific and apparently reliable information, however, in his account of the Essenes than in what he says about the Sadducees and Pharisees.

Both Josephus and Philo say that there were about four thousand Essenes. Somewhat divergent statements are given, however, concerning the location of their settlement or settlements. Pliny, in connection with his description of the Dead Sea, speaks of the Essenes as living "away from the western shore, far enough to avoid harmful things, a people alone, . . . companions of palm trees." It is not clear whether the "harmful things" are the harmful qualities of the Dead Sea itself, as some think, or the evils of the world from which the Essenes have taken refuge. According to Philo the Essenes live in villages in order to avoid the lawlessness and defilements of cities, but he goes on to say that they live in many of the cities of Judea, while Josephus says that there are many of them in every city.

So long as only one cave was known, and only the first preliminary sounding had been made at Khirbet Qumran, it seemed that archeology was on the side of those who denied that the covenanters were Essenes. The dating of the pottery in the late Hellenistic period seemed to exclude the occupation of the cave during the time when the Essenes were known to have lived in that region. The later excavations removed this chronological difficulty, and the installations uncovered at Khirbet Qumran could be easily understood as belonging to a settlement of the Essenes; consequently de Vaux abandoned his previous doubts and accepted the identification of the covenanters with the Essenes. For myself I must say that the geographical connection remains the strongest reason for regarding the Qumran sectarians as Essenes. If they were not the same, there was hardly room for both Essenes and covenanters in the vicinity of the Wady Qumran.

The geographical situation, however, is by no means our only criterion for determining the relationship between the Essenes and the sect of Qumran. The accounts of Philo and Josephus contain a good deal of information about the organization and discipline, the ritual and moral practices, and the theology of the Essenes. With all this we can compare in some detail the data in the Dead Sea Scrolls and the Damascus Document.

It is apparent at once, among other things, that there are some resemblances between the Essenes and the covenanters in the titles of their officials. Both Philo and Josephus say that the Essenes honor most of all, after God himself, one whom Josephus calls "their lawgiver" and Philo "our lawgiver." This may mean a leader of the sect itself; on the whole, however, it seems more probable that the revered lawgiver was Moses. Many passages in the Dead Sea Scrolls show that Moses was held in high honor by the covenanters. Both Josephus and Philo speak also of a steward who receives the wages of the members, manages the common property, and makes all necessary purchases. The Greek word translated "steward" corresponds very well to the Hebrew title I have rendered as "superintendent" in the Manual of Discipline and the Damascus Document.

Among both Essenes and covenanters there was a period of probation preceding admission to membership. Josephus speaks of three stages of probation, each lasting a year, before a candidate was received into full membership by the Essenes. Similar stages of probation are attested by the Manual of Discipline for the covenanters. An apparent difference may be seen in the fact that the probation lasted only two years among the covenanters; but, as Brownlee points out, only the last two of the three years required by the Essenes were regarded as being spent within the fraternity. Such differences as this, he observes, may also be due to changes made in the course of time. Further parallels can be seen in the limitations imposed upon those undergoing probation, in the instruction given them, and in the examination to which they are subjected before being admitted.

The candidate for membership was required by the Essenes to

take a solemn oath. According to the summary given by Josephus, the oath included piety, justice, abstention from harming others, hatred of the wicked and helpfulness to the righteous, loyalty, obedience to those in authority, restraint in exercising authority, love of the truth, reproof of liars, refraining from theft or any kind of unlawful gain, frank disclosure of all things to fellow members, keeping secret the doctrines of the sect, preserving its books and the names of the angels.

Dupont-Sommer finds many of these items reflected in the Manual of Discipline; he even goes so far as to say that the oath of initiation there prescribed, more than any other contact, points incontestably to the identification of the sect with the Essenes. The obligation to reveal none of the secrets of the sect to outsiders is not specifically mentioned in the Dead Sea Scrolls, but there are a few possible allusions to it. The care said to have been taken by the Essenes to preserve their sacred books recalls the careful preservation and hiding of the Dead Sea Scrolls in the caves.

Josephus speaks of four divisions or classes among the Essenes. Dupont-Sommer explains these as different degrees of membership, the four classes being respectively the postulants, the novices of the first year, the novices of the second year, and the full members. Josephus says explicitly, however, that the division into four classes was made after the completion of probation. The ancient Israelite division of the people into thousands, hundreds, fifties, and tens reappears in both the Manual of Discipline and the Damascus Document, but how it actually functioned is not clear, except that it is associated with the great annual assembly for renewing the covenant. It may also have served a military purpose, as it did in ancient Israel. The War scroll presupposes a rather elaborate military organization based on the tribes and clans of Old Testament times. The regulation in the Manual of Discipline and the Damascus Document requiring the constant presence of a priest with every group of ten is connected specifically with the study of the law.

Philo tells us that when the Essenes assembled they were seated in classes according to age, and the younger members listened attentively to their elders. The order of seating in the meetings of the Qumran covenanters also was strictly prescribed, according to the Manual of Discipline. The members observed a strict rotation in speaking, and departures from the regular order were allowed only by the consent of the assembly. Similarly, Josephus tells us, when ten of the Essenes met together no member could speak without the permission of the other nine. A curious point of coincidence between the rules of the Essenes and those of the Manual of Discipline is the prohibition of spitting in the midst of the assembly.

A conspicuous feature of the life of both Essenes and covenanters was the common meal. The account of the meals of the Essenes given by Josephus contains a number of details not indicated in the Manual of Discipline or the "two columns" in the Palestine Museum, but nothing that he says is inconsistent with what appears there. In both cases it is said that a priest must pronounce a blessing before every meal; Josephus speaks also of a priestly blessing at the end of the meal.

Among both covenanters and Essenes decisions upon questions of admission and discipline were made by the assembled members, although the Damascus Document, as we have noted, contemplates also the existence of judges. According to Josephus, no sentence was passed among the Essenes by a court of less than a hundred members.

There are certain similarities in the penalties prescribed for various offenses, though they do not correspond exactly in detail. Nothing in the Manual of Discipline or the Damascus Document would prepare us for the rigor with which the Essenes, if we may believe Josephus, allowed members expelled or suspended to starve to death, or readmitted them only at the brink of death. It is not incredible, however, that such severe measures were taken on occasion by the Qumran community.

A major concern of both sects was the study and interpretation of the law, and in both sects the members studied the law in groups. Philo tells something of how this was done by the Essenes. One member, he says, read to the others from the sacred book, and what was expressed in enigmatic or allegorical form was explained by one of the most experienced men. Josephus says that some of the Essenes could foretell the future from reading the Scriptures. This may very well refer to the kind of biblical interpretation exemplified by the Habakkuk Commentary and the fragments of similar commentaries on other Old Testament books which were found in the caves of the Wady Qumran. The Habakkuk Commentary, it will be remembered, says that the teacher of righteousness was given insight surpassing that of the prophets themselves.

In theology too there are striking contacts between the Essenes and the covenanters. Both emphasize strongly the complete sovereignty of God as the source of all being. For the covenanters this is shown especially by expressions used in the Thanksgiving Psalms and in the psalm that concludes the Manual of Discipline. Josephus and Philo alike attest it for the Essenes, though Josephus, when describing the divisions of Judaism as schools of philosophy, makes belief in fate rather than in God the distinctive position of the Essenes. Philo, moreover, qualifies the Essene view by saying that they considered God the cause of good but not of evil. We have noted the idea of "the lot of God" and "the lot of Belial" in the Manual of Discipline and the account of the two spirits in man as indications of a belief in predestination among the covenanters.

The beliefs of the covenanters concerning the future life, which we have considered in Chapter XII, are quite different from those Josephus ascribes to the Essenes. "For the belief is fixed among them," he says, "that bodies are corruptible, and that the matter of which they are made is not permanent, but that souls are immortal and abide forever, and having emanated from the clearest ether they are bound to their bodies as to prisons, being dragged down by a kind of magic spell; but that when they are freed from the bonds of the flesh, they rejoice as though released from long bondage and are borne upward." Josephus adds that this resembles Greek ideas; it also recalls the basic concept of Gnosticism, for which we have looked in vain in the Dead Sea Scrolls. Hippolytus gives an account of Essene belief concerning the future life which comes closer to what we find among the covenanters and in Judaism in general. He compares the Essene idea of the abode of departed souls with the Greek idea of the isles of the blessed, but he indicates that the soul will remain in this place only until the last judgment, when the body will be raised and the flesh too will be immortal. This runs directly counter to Greek and Gnostic ideas.

At this point we encounter a difficulty that should be clearly recognized and stressed, because it affects the whole effort to compare the Essenes and the Qumran sect. We cannot tell how accurately the beliefs of the Essenes are reported in our sources. For the covenanters our evidence is sadly incomplete, but at least it is direct and trustworthy. So far as it goes, we have the actual literature written and read by the community of Qumran, even the very copies they made and used themselves. For the Essenes we have only what was said about them by outsiders writing in a different language and for people who knew nothing at all about them. The points of agreement are perhaps all the more significant on this account, while the differences may be capable of various explanations. At the same time, we cannot be so sure of our conclusions as we could be if we had the same kind of evidence for the two groups we are trying to compare. If the Essenes and the covenanters were the same sect, we do have both kinds of evidence for them, but that is just what we are trying to find out.

In matters of ritual the contacts between covenanters and Essenes do not seem to be as close as in other matters. With regard to animal sacrifice and worship at the temple there is even, apparently, a direct contradiction. According to Josephus the Essenes did not offer sacrifices when they sent gifts to the temple, but had lustrations and performed sacrifices of their own, being excluded from the temple court. Philo says that they did not practice animal sacrifice but cultivated a pure and holy state of mind. This recalls an expression used in the final section of the Manual of Discipline, "the offering of the lips." The Damascus Document, however, while putting some limitation on the number of sacrifices, presupposes the practice of offering sacrifice. Unfortunately there are obscure points in the texts of Josephus and Philo, as well as in the Damascus Document, which make a definite conclusion on this subject hazardous.

A similar lack of correspondence is to be noted in other rites and forms of worship. Essenes and covenanters alike emphasized prayer, probably public as well as private. For the Essenes our sources indicate a strict daily regimen of prayer, work, and meeting for worship as well as for meals and study. No such definite order of occupations is specified in the extant portions of the Manual of Discipline or the Damascus Document, but there are many separate references corresponding to details in the routine of the Essenes. Brownlee calls attention, for example, to the mention of prayer at dawn and during the night. The former may be the prayer before sunrise, "as if they made a supplication for its rising," mentioned by Josephus as a characteristic Essene practice. There is no connection with the sun in the Dead Sea Scrolls, but it is very doubtful that any element of sun-worship is implied by Josephus' reference to the sunrise.

Special ablutions and lustrations are stressed in the descriptions of the Essenes. The Manual of Discipline alludes to waters of purification but strictly limits their efficacy to those who are spiritually fit and worthy. The Essenes—like other Jews, for that matter— may well have had the same limitation. Certainly it is not justified to see here, as M. Gottstein does, a radical difference between the covenanters and the Essenes. He takes what is said about the impossibility of gaining atonement by water to be a polemic against baptismal rites, whereas the Essenes were a baptizing sect. There is no real reason, however, to suppose that the attitude of the Essenes was essentially different from that expressed in the Manual of Discipline.

Strict dietary regulations are attributed to the Essenes by Josephus. Because of the simplicity of their diet and the regularity of their way of living, he says, many of them lived to an age of more than a hundred years. He adds that in the war with the Romans the Essenes endured the most horrible torture rather than eat any food they considered unlawful. There is no indication of any such extraordinary concern for correct diet in the Dead Sea Scrolls.

Emphasis on the exact observance of sacred days is common to the Qumran sect and the Essenes, but the particular observances emphasized in our sources are not the same. The sanctity of the sabbath was particularly stressed by the Essenes, according to all accounts. This emphasis is not apparent in the Dead Sea Scrolls, though Brownlee points to a passage in the Damascus Document as showing that the covenanters were more strict than the Pharisees with regard to abstention from work on the sabbath.

The annual rite of entering and renewing the covenant, which the Manual of Discipline describes at length, has no counterpart in what is reported about the Essenes. Aside from the sabbath, in fact, no such stress on sacred times as we have found in the Dead Sea Scrolls is attested for the Essenes. Miss Jaubert, however, in her study of the covenanters' calendar, points out analogies between it and the calendar of the Samaritans; and in this connection she cites a statement of Epiphanius which treats the Essenes as a sect of the Samaritans. Indications of some obscure relationship with the Samaritans have been detected in the language of the Dead Sea Scrolls. If both Essenes and covenanters had some connection with the Samaritans, this may give some reason to suspect a connection between the covenanters and the Essenes.

Nötscher has remarked that the priests and Levites do not seem to have had such a prominent position among the Essenes as they have in the Manual of Discipline and the Damascus Document. Schoeps, however, suggests that the term "sons of Zadok" in these documents did not refer only to the priests but was used as an honorary designation for the whole community. This is supported by a statement in the Damascus Document: "The priests are the captivity of Israel who went forth from the land of Judah, and [the Levites] are those who joined them; and the sons of Zadok are the elect of Israel, those called by the name, who will abide at the end of days."

A different explanation is offered by Dupont-Sommer for the lack of references to priests among the Essenes. Assuming that the number of members of the sect decreased in the course of time, he suggests that this involved a proportionate decrease in the number of priests, so that by the time of Philo and Josephus there were probably very few priests left in the order. The cessation of animal sacrifice would necessarily follow; meanwhile the sacred meal had become the principal liturgical act of the community.

More than one scholar has called attention to the fact that nothing is said of the teacher of righteousness or the new covenant in the descriptions of the Essenes. The whole idea of the covenant, as a matter of fact, is conspicuous by its absence in what we are told about the Essenes. The reason for this may be that the accounts of Jewish practices and ideas given by Philo and Josephus were intended for gentile readers; consequently they minimized everything peculiar to Judaism, while emphasizing and exaggerating every resemblance to Greek and Roman ways of thinking.

Nowhere are the contacts between these sects more notable than in the area of moral and social practices. According to Philo, the Essenes were much more interested in ethics than in logic or metaphysics and devoted themselves assiduously to moral philosophy under the guidance of the divinely inspired laws of their country. This statement is a notable example of Philo's effort to be a Greek to the Greeks. It is an attempt to express in terms of Greek philosophy the devotion of the Essenes to the laws of Moses and their own sectarian regulations. So understood, it might serve as a description of the attitudes and interests manifest in the Manual of Discipline and the Damascus Document.

Both Philo and Josephus pay tribute to the high reputation of the Essenes for sanctity. They were a strictly ascetic group, putting great stress on the control of bodily appetites and passions. In the Manual of Discipline also much emphasis is placed on self-control and a serious demeanor. Humility, patience, simplicity, obedience, fidelity, and purity are among the virtues most highly prized by covenanters and Essenes alike.

Josephus mentions the great attachment of the Essenes to one another, and Philo speaks of their extraordinary spirit of equality and fellowship. This spirit of unity within the order, as often in other religious groups, was accompanied and perhaps intensified by a bitter intolerance toward all outsiders. Hippolytus says that if the Essenes even touched a member of any other sect they immediately washed themselves. One is reminded of the obligation to love all the sons of light and to hate all the sons of darkness imposed by the Manual of Discipline on those who entered the covenant.

The ideal of equality found expression among the Essenes in the repudiation of slavery. Philo says that they considered slavery a disturbance of the order of nature by covetousness. Josephus says that they regarded keeping servants as a temptation to injustice. Both authors speak of the way the Essenes ministered to one another's needs. The evidence on this point in the Dead Sea Scrolls is purely negative. Slavery, like marriage, seems to be simply ignored.

In all these particulars, without being able to point to specific parallels, one may note a general correspondence to the over-all impression given by the Dead Sea Scrolls. At least there are no striking contradictions. The same may be said with regard to the economic life of the Essenes and the covenanters. According to both Philo and Josephus, the Essenes lived primarily by agriculture. They avoided commercial dealings of all kinds, Philo says, because these gave rise to covetousness. The covenanters must have been farmers too, though one cannot but wonder what kind of agriculture was possible in the desolate vicinity of Khirbet Qumran. Philo adds that other peaceful occupations were cultivated by the Essenes. Animal husbandry, the keeping of bees, and various useful arts and crafts were practiced to keep the community supplied with the necessities of life. By all these means the Essenes managed to satisfy their frugal desires so successfully, Philo would have us believe, that they were generally and rightly considered rich, although they had no stores of silver and gold or extensive holdings of land.

Among the covenanters we have found the practice of having all things in common, though the Damascus Document reflects a less radical form of this institution than the Manual of Discipline. All authorities agree that the Essenes practiced the community of goods. Pliny says simply that they were "without money." Josephus says that they held everything in common, so that the rich enjoyed no more of their wealth than the utterly destitute. This is a somewhat puzzling statement, because it seems to imply that there were still rich and poor members; but perhaps Josephus refers only to those who had formerly been rich or poor. Philo has much to say on this subject. Housing, supplies, expenses, clothing, wages, flocks and herds—all, he says, belonged to the whole community and were equally available to every member. The aged and the sick were as well cared for as if they had had large families to look after them.

Philo's statement that the members received wages but put them into a common fund recalls the provision of the Damascus Document that a fixed portion of each man's wages must be given to the superintendent. According to Hippolytus, every man, on entering the Essene order, had to sell his property and turn over the receipts to the "ruler." The Manual of Discipline speaks of bringing one's wealth into the order together with one's strength and knowledge. In this connection de Vaux makes the interesting observation that hundreds of coins have been found in the excavation of Khirbet Qumran, but none in any of the caves. He infers from this fact that all transactions involving money were centralized at the headquarters of the community, and the individual members did not handle money.

To many scholars the similarity at this point has seemed to be a striking confirmation of their belief that the Essenes and the covenanters were the same. Others find sufficient differences to convince them—or to confirm their belief—that two different sects are represented. A. Rubinstein suggests that much of the tradition embodied in the Damascus Document was derived from the Essenes, but that the Essenism of the Damascus covenanters was decadent. Certainly we must recognize the possibility that differences in time, or variations between different branches of the same sect, may at least partially explain the apparent discrepancies.

Even more surprising to their contemporaries than the community of goods was the Essenes' abstention from marriage. Pliny says that they lived "without any women, having renounced all sexual relations." Nevertheless, he adds with wonder, "day by day the multitude joining them of its own accord is regularly renewed, since many flock together whom, wearied with life, fortune by its storms drives to their way of living. Thus through thousands of ages, incredible to relate, a people in which no one is born is eternal, so fruitful to them is the repentance of others!"

Our other sources also dwell at some length on this strange feature of the Essene sect. Josephus says that they renounced marriage but adopted young children and brought them up according to the principles of the sect, not because they condemned marriage and the propagation of the race on principle, but because they had no confidence in the faithfulness of women. Philo takes advantage of this peculiarity of the Essenes to expound at length his own low estimate of female character. The Essenes do not marry, he says, because women are selfish, jealous, and hypocritical; if they have children, they become proud, bold, and even violent. A man bound by natural affection to a woman and children, Philo concludes, is no longer a free man but a slave.

Whether or not this was the view of the main body of Essenes, certainly not all of them agreed with Philo. There was one branch of the sect, Josephus tells us, that shared the ideas and customs of the rest in other matters, but regarded the renunciation of marriage as a crime equivalent to murder. They subjected their wives to three years of probation, he continues, and required them to bathe and wear linen garments as the men did.

In our sources for the covenanters we have found some divergence with regard to marriage. The Manual of Discipline makes no reference at all to women and children, but their presence in the community is clearly attested by the Damascus Document and the Palestine Museum's "two columns." As Brownlee remarks, if the covenanters were Essenes at all, those at least of whom the Damascus Document and the two columns tell were of the marrying kind.

Perhaps the most conspicuous apparent divergence between the

Essenes and the covenanters is in their attitudes toward war. Philo particularly emphasizes the peaceful pursuits and concerns of the Essenes. None of them, he says, engaged in any occupation connected with war or liable to be exploited for military purposes. The community depicted in the Manual of Discipline and the Habakkuk Commentary seems peaceful enough, but a military organization and active warfare are presupposed by the "two columns," and the War of the Sons of Light with the Sons of Darkness, even if we suppose that the warfare of which it speaks is the eschatological struggle between the hosts of good and evil, breathes a militant spirit that would have satisfied the Maccabees or the Zealots.

As a matter of fact, even for the Essenes the testimony of our sources is not entirely unambiguous. Josephus speaks of at least one Essene who was a warrior and lauds the heroism of the Essenes in the war against the Romans. Hippolytus even says that some people called the Essenes Zealots and others called them Sicarii, because they killed any uncircumcised man who talked about God and the law. The identification of the Essenes with those extreme proponents of armed revolt against Rome known as Zealots and Sicarii renders this whole statement suspect, but it may accurately reflect some military activity on the part of Essenes. It is possible also that the attitudes of the Essenes and covenanters changed with changing circumstances.

Before we try to reach a general conclusion a few other points of similarity or difference may be mentioned. The Essenes are said to have renounced the use of oaths, except for the oath of initiation. There is no evidence of such an attitude among the covenanters, unless it is implied by a passage in the Damascus Document, where, as Brownlee points out, it is forbidden to swear "except the oath written in the oaths of the covenant."

Among the reasons adduced by Gottstein for believing that the covenanters and the Essenes were not the same is the fact that the order of the Essenes was of the type in which membership is permanent, whereas the sect of Qumran, he contends, belonged to the type in which a periodic rebirth is necessary. As evidence of this he cites the passage in the Manual of Discipline which describes the annual ceremony of renewing the covenant, but that is quite a different thing from a periodic spiritual rebirth of individuals.

Many items of practice and belief included in the accounts of the Essenes have not appeared in the Dead Sea Scrolls, but the "argument from silence" in such cases proves nothing. Aside from the possibility of error in the statements concerning the Essenes, it must be remembered that the Qumran scrolls and fragments represent only a part of the community's library. What may still appear when all the fragments have been deciphered remains to be seen. What may have been contained in the rest of the books that are only partially preserved, to say nothing of those that have not survived at all, cannot even be imagined.

But if the gaps in our knowledge and even the discrepancies do not disprove the identity of Essenes and covenanters, are the points of correspondence sufficiently close to establish it? Several scholars have contended that what the Essenes and the sect of Qumran have in common is equally characteristic of other Jewish groups. If there is to be any identification of Essenes and covenanters, it can hardly be more than an identification of a particular type of Essene with a particular group of covenanters. The term Essene does not necessarily indicate a single organization with a sharply definable set of beliefs and practices; it may designate rather a number of groups that were similar but not identical. Together with variations between different groups of the same period, we must reckon with changes from one period to another.

That being so, the possibility of some kind of historical connection with other groups as well as the Essenes must not be forgotten. We have seen that the covenanters were not identical with the Pharisees, but it does not follow that they were entirely unrelated to the Pharisees. An important suggestion in this respect has been made by R. Marcus. He considers the legal tradition of the Damascus Document essentially that of the Pharisees; consequently he argues that if the Damascus and Qumran covenanters and the Essenes were all the same sect, they were a branch of the Pharisees.

Recalling L. Ginzberg's demonstration of the existence of a conservative and a liberal wing in Pharisaism, Marcus concludes that the Essenes formed a third division, the left-wing Pharisees. Thus we get a new classification of the parties in first-century Palestinian Judaism: on the extreme right were the Sadducees and on the extreme left the Zealots; between them were the three groups of Pharisees, with the Essenes or covenanters standing next to the Zealots. Some such alignment seems quite plausible if the identification of the Essenes and the Qumran covenanters is assumed.

The general conclusion that must be drawn at this stage of investigation seems to me quite clear, and I do not believe that any more specific conclusion is justified. If several related sects are included under the term Essene, the covenanters may be called Essenes; if by Essene we mean a particular sect, which we assume to be accurately described by the ancient writers, then the covenanters were not Essenes. For the present it seems to me best not to speak of the Qumran sect as Essenes, but rather to say that the Essenes and the covenanters, with other groups of which we know little or nothing, represented the same general type. It is more important to define the extent of agreement and difference than it is to accept or reject a particular name.

A few other identifications that have been proposed for the covenanters should be at least mentioned. Josephus speaks of a "Zadok the Pharisee" who was associated with Judas of Galilee in the rebellion against the Romans in 6 A.D. Zadok and Judas, he says, founded the "fourth philosophy" of the Jews, whose adherents agreed on the whole with the Pharisees but fanatically insisted on freedom from any human ruler and cheerfully endured death rather than recognize any man as their lord. Judas the Galilean is believed by many historians to have been the founder of the group known as Zealots, though Josephus uses this term only for those who fought against Rome sixty years later.

The community of the Dead Sea Scrolls has actually been identified by an eminent historian with the most violent of the Zealots, the Sicarii. It will be remembered that Hippolytus connected the Zealots and Sicarii with the Essenes. This identification carries with it so many quite incredible implications that it need not be discussed here in any detail, but it is true that there are rather impressive points of contact between the covenanters and the followers of Judas and Zadok. Possibly some members of the community joined the Zealots in the last decades before the destruction of the temple. Any closer connection than that, however, can hardly be postulated. The community of the Dead Sea Scrolls was quite certainly much older than the movement inaugurated by Zadok and Judas.

After the account of the followers of Zadok and Boethus, which was mentioned above in connection with the Sadducees, al-Qirqisani continues: "Thereupon appeared the teaching of a sect called Magharians; they were called so because their books were found in a cave" (the Arabic word for cave being *magharah*). This statement is followed by one concerning Jesus; the Magharians may therefore have appeared shortly before the Christian era. Barthélemy and de Vaux have suggested that the Magharians may have been the Qumran covenanters. It is quite possible, as Kahle says, that the Magharians were actually Essenes, and that they were given the name Magharian by later writers because their books had been found in a cave and their real identity was unknown.

The bare possibility of suggesting that the covenanters, the Zadokites, the Essenes, the Zealots, and the Magharians were all one and the same group makes all the more pertinent the warnings of Lieberman and others against identifying the Qumran community with any known sect in Judaism. In spite of obvious similarities and obscure possibilities of some kind of relationship, the sect or sects of the Damascus Document and the Dead Sea Scrolls may have been distinct from any that have been mentioned.

Still other identifications have been seriously proposed and must not be ignored. Teicher, for example, argues vigorously that the community of the Dead Sea Scrolls was the early Jewish-Christian sect called Ebionites. For many reasons this theory is untenable. It is developed with extraordinary industry and erudition, but it is impossible on chronological grounds, if for no other reason.

Teicher recognizes that the texts presuppose a well-developed, organized sect, and concludes that their composition must therefore be dated considerably later than 70 A.D. Since the archeological evidence makes 70 A.D. the last possible date for the copying of the latest manuscripts, and the paleography compels us to date the oldest of the manuscripts much earlier than that, no further refutation of Teicher's theory is necessary.

This does not mean that there was no connection at all between the covenanters and the Ebionites. The possibility of such a connection has been explored by Oscar Cullmann. In particular he has investigated the contacts between the Qumran texts and the early Christian documents known as the pseudo-Clementine writings, which are believed to be of Ebionite origin. In spite of differences at a number of points, he finds in these two groups of texts the same theology, the same ritual practices, and the same prescribed ways of living. Taken separately, the parallels would not necessarily indicate that the covenanters and the Ebionites were directly related, but the mass of them makes this seem probable. The only essential difference is that the priesthood, which is held in high honor by the covenanters, is radically rejected by the Ebionites. Identifying the covenanters with the Essenes, Cullman finds that the opposition to the temple and its sacrifices that is apparent among the Essenes has become much sharper in the pseudo-Clementine writings. The Ebionites have also a critical attitude toward the Old Testament, which is lacking among the Essenes.

The relationship is too close, Cullman feels, to be explained by supposing that the Ebionites merely preserved features of primitive Christianity that had been derived originally from sectarian Judaism. A later, more direct Essene influence upon the Jewish Christians must be assumed. The Qumran community was destroyed during the war with Rome in 66–70 A.D., and it was at this time that the Jewish Christians left Jerusalem and withdrew across the Jordan. Cullmann concludes that the remnant of the Qumran sect must have joined these Jewish Christians. Both the resemblances and the differences, he maintains, can be understood as the result of this fusion. Pending further investigation of details, this hypothesis seems not at all improbable. In any case, Teicher's theory that the sect of Qumran and the Ebionites were the same cannot be accepted.

Still more decisively than the Ebionites, the Karaite sect is excluded by archeological evidence from being given credit for the Dead Sea Scrolls. The Karaite movement arose in the early Middle Ages in the eastern part of the Arab empire. It rejected the traditional interpretations built up by the rabbis and acknowledged only the authority of the Scriptures. Zeitlin and others have pointed out many interesting and impressive contacts between the practices and beliefs of the Karaites and those that appear in the Dead Sea Scrolls and the Damascus Document. While it is impossible that the medieval Karaites could have produced the Dead Sea Scrolls, the parallels with Karaite literature which Zeitlin and Weis have pointed out must have some significance. The Old Cairo genizah in which the medieval manuscripts of the Damascus Document were found had probably belonged originally to a Karaite synagogue, and these particular manuscripts were probably made by Karaites.

Kahle suggests that Benjamin al-Nihawandi, a leading Persian Karaite of the ninth century A.D., was acquainted with the books of the Magharians found in the cave near Jericho, and that these stimulated him to develop Karaite theology on a new basis. The manuscripts of the Damascus Document found in the Old Cairo genizah, Kahle believes, were copies of older scrolls found in the same cave at that time. Instead of supposing that the Damascus Document was composed under Karaite influence, therefore, Kahle maintains that the Karaites were influenced by the Damascus Document and the other scrolls found in the cave near Jericho at about 800 A.D.

Teicher agrees with Kahle on this point. He recalls the fact that in the ninth and tenth centuries there was a controversy between the Karaites and the "Rabbanites," the adherents of the rabbinic traditions. Quoting a Karaite writer to the effect that Zadokite books were widely known at this time, he reminds us that this was also the time when the manuscripts of the Damascus Document found in the Old Cairo genizah were made. The Rabbanites as well as the Karaites in the tenth century adopted practices alien to Talmudic law, Teicher says, and he suggests that both derived their new practices from Zadokite writings that had become known to both groups at about the same time.

If Kahle and Teicher are right, the affinities between the Dead Sea Scrolls and medieval Karaite literature are to be attributed to the influence of the manuscripts found near Jericho at the beginning of the ninth century. At first sight this theory seems romantic and far-fetched, but it is not impossible. Some kind of historical connection between the Karaites and the sect of Qumran must be recognized, and this hypothesis is as credible as any explanation that has been offered. Support for it may be seen in the fact that bits of the Damascus Document have now been found in the Qumran caves.

To sum up the net result of all the efforts to identify the covenanters, we must first of all insist that any identification must observe the chronological limits set by the established age of the documents. The sect of the teacher of righteousness and his followers was clearly one of the groups formed within Judaism during the pre-Maccabean and Hasmonean periods. It may probably be accurately included under the term Hasidim, but that does not indicate a specific sect. In many ways it was akin to the Essenes, as we know them from sources of the Roman period. If this term is used in a broad, comprehensive sense, we may legitimately call the Qumran sectarians Essenes. For the present, however, in order not to prejudge the case, it seems better to reserve that name for the group described by Philo and Josephus, which, if their reports are accurate, was not exactly identical or coextensive with the Qumran community. As a matter of convenience we may still designate the latter by the term "covenanters," which implies neither the acceptance nor the rejection of their identification with the Essenes. At any rate, it is clear that the sect of Qumran was more closely related to the Essenes than to any other group known to us.

PART FIVE

THE IMPORTANCE OF THE DEAD SEA SCROLLS

XIV

Contributions to Textual Criticism,
Historical Grammar, and Paleography

⎍⎍⎍⎍⎍⎍⎍⎍⎍⎍⎍⎍⎍⎍⎍⎍⎍⎍⎍⎍⎍⎍⎍⎍⎍⎍

Our consideration of the Dead Sea Scrolls would be quite incomplete if we failed to ask what difference they make for scholarship and for religion. Everything thus far has been merely preparing the way for the consideration of that ultimate question. Since many of the scrolls and fragments contain portions of books of the Bible, and since they are much older than any other extant Hebrew manuscript of the Old Testament, one of the first questions to be raised is what they contribute to the textual criticism of the Old Testament.

The task of textual criticism is to detect and eliminate errors in the text as it has come down to us, and so to restore, as nearly as possible, what was originally written by the authors of the books. The means available for this purpose are of three kinds. The first and most important is the comparison of different manuscripts.

This is not possible for the Old Testament as it is for the New Testament. We have an abundance of New Testament manuscripts, which differ very widely in the wording of the text at many points. It is possible to compare them, arrange them in "families" according to their agreements and differences, and so construct a family tree of the divergent types of text. Moving down the spreading branches to the trunk, so to speak, we come to the oldest form of text represented by the extant manuscripts.

With the Old Testament this can be done only to a very limited degree. For a thousand years or more it was the regular practice of the Jews to copy the text with meticulous accuracy and correct it very carefully according to the official or Masoretic text. Old, worn-out manuscripts were discarded and relegated to the genizah. The result is that no Hebrew manuscripts of the Old Testament older than the ninth century A.D. have been preserved, and all the surviving manuscripts agree almost exactly, except in very minute details.

In the Old Testament, therefore, scholars must depend very largely on the second available means of reconstructing an older form of the text. This is the comparison of the Hebrew manuscripts with the ancient versions, the translations into Greek, Aramaic, Syriac, Latin, and other languages. Having been made between the third century B.C. and the fifth century A.D., these versions were based on much older Hebrew manuscripts than those that have survived to our time. They have to be used with much caution, of course, because it is not always possible to be sure what Hebrew words are represented by a phrase in a translation. At the same time they afford a very valuable means of checking the accuracy of the traditional Hebrew text and correcting its errors.

The third means of restoring the text must be used still more cautiously and only as a last resort. It consists of what is called "conjectural emendation." This does not mean sheer guesswork without any objective basis. By a knowledge of the language, by comparison with parallel or similar passages, and sometimes by comparison with other ancient texts outside of the Bible, one can sometimes see that a word or group of words that has no intelligible meaning can, by a slight change of one or more letters, be made to yield a meaning in accord with the context. At many points in the Old Testament such conjectural emendation is the only way to make any sense at all out of the text. This fact, however, often tempts a scholar to exercise his ingenuity in making quite unnecessary and unjustified changes in the text. The only adequate protection against such unwarranted emendations is the combined judgment of competent, conservative, and at the same time open-minded scholars.

In this state of affairs the discovery of a biblical manuscript centuries older than the standard medieval manuscripts of the Old Testament is an event of major importance for textual criticism. Even though the subject is somewhat technical, therefore, we must try to assess the value of the Dead Sea Scrolls in this respect.

The St. Mark's manuscript of Isaiah is the only one of the scrolls that contains a whole book of the Bible, and, with the exception of some of the small fragments, it is the oldest of the manuscripts found in the caves. We may therefore begin our discussion by considering the importance of this manuscript for recovering the correct Hebrew text of the book of Isaiah.

The age of the manuscript, of course, does not establish its importance. An old manuscript is not necessarily a good manuscript. A copy made in the ninth or tenth century A.D. may more accurately reproduce the original text than one made in the first or second century B.C. As a matter of plain fact, the St. Mark's Isaiah manuscript is obviously inferior at a great many points to the best medieval manuscripts. This does not, however, deprive the ancient scroll of all importance.

Many of the differences between the St. Mark's Isaiah scroll and the Masoretic text can be explained as mistakes in copying. Apart from these, there is a remarkable agreement, on the whole, with the text found in the medieval manuscripts. Such agreement in a manuscript so much older gives reassuring testimony to the general accuracy of the traditional text. It does not, however, prove that the latter is the original text of Isaiah. What it shows is that any major changes that occurred in the transmission of the text had already been made before the beginning of the Christian era. In other words, a virtual standardization of the text had come about more or less automatically two or three centuries before the Masoretes made it official. As Hempel puts it, the decisive history of the text of the Old Testament had already been completed by the time of Jesus, not only in the books of the law, of which no jot or tittle should be altered, but also in the books of the prophets.

The conspicuous differences in spelling and grammatical forms between the St. Mark's manuscript and the Masoretic text makes their substantial agreement in the words of the text all the more remarkable. Considering how widely the earliest manuscripts of the New Testament vary, how radically the ancient Greek versions differ from the traditional Hebrew text, and what a long time intervened between the Dead Sea Scrolls and the oldest of the medieval manuscripts, one might have expected a much larger number of variant readings and a much wider degree of divergence. It is a matter for wonder that through something like a thousand years the text underwent so little alteration. As I said in my first article on the scroll, "Herein lies its chief importance, supporting the fidelity of the Masoretic tradition."

This statement was sharply criticized by Paul Kahle. For him the most significant fact about the scroll is that it has a large number of real variant readings, which are elsewhere practically nonexistent in Hebrew manuscripts of the Old Testament. The scroll therefore shows us for the first time what Hebrew manuscripts of the Bible were like before they had been made to conform to a standardized text. I still feel that the amount of agreement with the Masoretic text is the manuscript's most significant feature, but, having said that, I agree that the variants constitute its second point of importance.

An idea of the nature of these variant readings may be given by noting the points at which the Revised Standard Version of the Old Testament has followed the St. Mark's manuscript. When the Old Testament section of the Standard Bible Revision Committee was in session at Northfield, Massachusetts, in the summer of 1948, a man who was staying at the same hotel remarked one day, "You will have to revise your translation of Isaiah all over again now, won't you?" This was not necessary, but of course the new evidence was considered. I had then just returned from Palestine, having made on the way home a list of the variant readings in the St. Mark's manuscript. The committee had this before it while revising the translation of Isaiah.

Thirteen readings in which the manuscript departs from the traditional text were eventually adopted. In these places a marginal note cites "One ancient Ms," meaning the St. Mark's Isaiah scroll. A brief review will show that even in these thirteen places the superiority of the manuscript's reading is not always certain. For myself I must confess that in some cases where I probably voted for the emendation I am now convinced that our decision was a mistake, and the Masoretic reading should have been retained.

In eight of the thirteen instances the reading of the scroll is supported to some degree by the ancient versions. I give these instances first, and then those that are attested only by the St. Mark's manuscript. To make the essence of the matter as clear as possible, I refer only to the Greek, Aramaic, Syriac, and Latin versions, which are the most important; I also assume, though this is decidedly an artificial simplification, that there is just one version in each of these four languages. By far the most important of them is the Greek version, commonly called the Septuagint.

In three cases the Greek version and two others lend more or less support to the manuscript against the Masoretic text. I shall quote the passages as they appear in the St. Mark's scroll.

(1) Isaiah 60:19:

> The sun shall be no more your light by day,
>   nor for brightness shall the moon give light to you by night.

The traditional text here omits the phrase "by night," but it is attested by the Greek, Old Latin, and Aramaic versions as well as by the St. Mark's scroll.

(2) Isaiah 51:19:

> These two things have befallen you—
>   who will condole with you?—
> devastation and destruction, famine and sword;
>   who will comfort you?

The Masoretic text reads in the last line, "how may I comfort you?" The Greek, Syriac, and Latin versions agree with the scroll.

(3) Isaiah 14:4:

> How the oppressor has ceased,
> the insolent fury ceased!

Instead of "the insolent fury" previous translations read "the golden city." This is merely a desperate effort to give a meaning to a Hebrew word whose real meaning, if it has any, is unknown. It does not occur anywhere else. The word that replaces it in the Isaiah scroll differs from it only in having an *r* instead of a *d*. In some forms of the Hebrew alphabet these two letters look much alike and are often confused. The Greek, Syriac, and Latin in this case do not have exactly the same reading as the scroll, but they have other readings which to some degree seem to support it.

In one passage the Septuagint alone agrees with the scroll.

(4) Isaiah 45:2:

> I will go before you
> and level the mountains.

The traditional text reads "rough places" (literally "swellings") instead of "mountains." The difference in meaning is slight; the only question is which reading was more probably that of the original text.

Twice where the Greek agrees with the Masoretic text two or three other versions support the scroll.

(5) Isaiah 56:12:

> "Come," they say, "let us get wine,
> let us fill ourselves with strong drink."

The traditional text reads, "let me get wine," but the plural form fits the context better. In this case the Latin, Aramaic, and Syriac versions but not the Septuagint agree with the St. Mark's manuscript.

(6) Isaiah 49:24:

> Can the prey be taken from the mighty,
> or the captives of a tyrant be rescued?

The Masoretic text reads here, "the captives of a righteous man," which makes no sense. Previous English translations tried to make sense out of it by a free paraphrase, "the lawful captives." The scroll is supported in this instance by the Syriac and Latin versions.

Once the Latin alone agrees with the St. Mark's manuscript.

(7) Isaiah 14:30:

> but I will kill your root with famine,
> and your remnant I will slay.

The traditional text, "he will slay," does not fit the context. The King James Version and the American Standard Version boldly evade the difficulty by changing the verb to the passive, "shall be slain." The reading of the scroll seems clearly superior, in spite of the fact that only the Latin among the ancient versions supports it. The fact that it seems superior does not prove, to be sure, that it is original. Orlinsky argues that the Latin translator here and elsewhere simply took liberties with the Hebrew text. That would seem more likely if we did not have also the testimony of the St. Mark's manuscript, though of course the same rather obvious correction could have been made independently in the scroll and in the Latin version.

In one instance the Latin has partial support in the Syriac version.

(8) Isaiah 15:9:

> For the waters of Dibon are full of blood;
> yet will I bring upon Dibon even more.

The name of the city is given both times in the Masoretic text as Dimon. No such city is mentioned anywhere else, but a city named Dibon is well known. The Latin version reads Dibon in this verse, and the Syriac reads Ribon, confusing *d* and *r* but supporting the *b* instead of *m*. The St. Mark's Isaiah scroll has the same reading as the Latin.

In this case, however, Orlinsky's critique is devastating. In agreement with eminent topographers, he denies that the place here referred to is Dibon at all. Its location is unknown, though it may be the city called Madmen in Jeremiah 48:2; in any case Dibon has already been mentioned in the second verse of Isaiah 15, and no other place is named twice in the chapter. A play on the name Dimon and the Hebrew word for blood, *dam*, was probably intended by the prophet. If Dibon was the original reading and was changed to Dimon, this was done twice. As a Parthian shot Orlinsky quotes in a footnote my previous acknowledgment that the readings of the Latin version and the scroll "may of course be merely obvious and independent corrections." I am now inclined to think that they were.

The remaining five of the thirteen variants in the scroll that were adopted in the Revised Standard Version have no support in any of the ancient versions. In these cases the choice between the Masoretic text and the scroll is governed only by intrinsic probability, as indicated by the context.

(9) Isaiah 3:24:

> Instead of perfume there will be rottenness;
>   and instead of a girdle, a rope;
> and instead of well-set hair, baldness;
>   and instead of a rich robe, a girding of sackcloth;
> instead of beauty, shame.

The last word is missing in the Masoretic text. The line reads in the earlier English versions, "branding [or burning] instead of beauty." The Hebrew word translated "branding" or "burning" is the first word in the line. It occurs nowhere else with any such meaning; ordinarily it is a conjunction, meaning "for" or "that," or an adverb, meaning "surely" or the like. (The Revised Standard Version, understanding it in the latter sense, simply leaves it untranslated.) If it is used in either of these ways here, however, the line is incomplete:

> for [or surely] instead of beauty—

The word "shame" in the St. Mark's scroll completes the sentence.

(10) Isaiah 21:8:

> Then he who saw cried:
>   "Upon a watchtower I stand, O Lord . . ."

Instead of "he who saw" the Masoretic text reads "a lion." This has always made trouble for translators. The King James Version reads, "And he cried, A lion." The Revised Version and the American Standard Version say, "and he cried as a lion." What a lion would be doing here is hard to say, but the Hebrew words for "lion" and "he who saw" appear and sound somewhat alike. An inattentive scribe might easily substitute one for the other.

(11) Isaiah 23:2:

> Be still, O inhabitants of the coast,
>> O merchants of Sidon,
> your messengers passed over the sea
> and were on many waters.

The second and third lines of this verse read in the Masoretic text, translated literally, "a merchant of Sidon passing over the sea they replenished you." The Hebrew for "they replenished you" resembles quite closely the word in the St. Mark's scroll meaning "your messengers." The choice between the two readings is a matter of subjective judgment as to the appropriateness of one or the other in the context, but the Masoretic reading has compelled translators to render it rather freely.

(12) Isaiah 33:8:

> Covenants are broken,
>> witnesses are despised.

Instead of "witnesses" the Masoretic text reads "cities." This is another case of the frequent confusion between *d* and *r*.

(13) Isaiah 45:8:

> Shower, O heavens, from above,
>> and let the skies rain down righteousness;
> let the earth open, that salvation may sprout forth. . . .

Where the scroll has "that salvation may sprout forth" the traditional text reads "that they may bring forth salvation." The difference is not important; either reading is quite possible, and the choice between them is hardly more than a matter of subjective preference.

No reader will suppose that the adoption of these thirteen readings by the committee that made the Revised Standard Version proves that in these instances and in these alone the St. Mark's Isaiah scroll is superior to the Masoretic text. Each variant was discussed on its merits in the committee; the decision was taken by vote, and the result was rarely unanimous. Other scholars and some members of the committee would judge otherwise in some cases. My own misgivings have already been expressed. It must be said, however, that the choice of these readings expresses the considered judgments of the majority of a representative group of scholars.

Four of the thirteen variants we have considered are included in a list of ten readings in the St. Mark's manuscript noted by Walter Baumgartner as preferable to the Masoretic readings. Of the remaining six in his list, four were not adopted by the Revision Committee, but two were incorporated in the translation without any marginal note. It may be of some interest to note briefly the main facts concerning these two readings.

The first is of no great importance. In Isaiah 7:1 the Masoretic text says, "In the days of Ahaz the son of Jotham, son of Uzziah, king of Judah, Rezin the king of Syria and Pekah the son of Remaliah the king of Israel went up to Jerusalem for war against it, but he could not conquer it." After the compound subject one expects a plural form of the verb "could," and the Revised Standard Version reads, "but they could not conquer it." This is the reading of the St. Mark's manuscript, the Septuagint, and the Latin and Syriac versions; it is also the reading of the Masoretic text itself in the parallel narrative of II Kings 16:5. Many scholars accordingly believed, long before the discovery of the Dead Sea Scrolls, that the original text of Isaiah had the plural form of the verb at this point.

The form in the Masoretic text, as a matter of fact, can be understood as an infinitive, used idiomatically to continue the narrative, instead of a finite singular form. That is why the Revised Standard Version translates it, without a note, as plural. Orlinsky argues, however, that the verb here is in the singular, like "went up" earlier in the verse and "has devised" in verse 5, because the king of Syria took the initiative in the whole affair, and the king of Israel merely followed him. This may be true, but the singular form of "went up" and "has devised" is no evidence for it: a singular verb is regularly used with a compound subject in Hebrew when the verb comes first. The choice between the two readings in this case is almost a matter of splitting a hair. The difference is significant only as an illustration of the kind of variant readings we find in the manuscript.

The other instance of agreement with the scroll in the Revised Standard Version, with no footnote, is more instructive. In Isaiah 49:17 the Masoretic text reads "your sons," whereas the St. Mark's scroll reads, "your builders." The latter reading makes better sense in the context and has some support in the other versions. In this case, however, the difference consists only in a vowel. The same consonants can be read either way. The medieval vowel-points of the Masoretic text give the meaning "sons"; the St. Mark's manuscript, by inserting a vowel letter, gives the reading "builders." In all such cases, where preferred meanings are secured by assuming different vowels without changing the consonantal text, the Revised Standard Version has no footnotes.

The four variant readings listed by Baumgartner but not adopted in the Revised Standard Version are unimportant, though one of them comes up for consideration in another connection. Another may be mentioned, because it has been rather enthusiastically acclaimed by several scholars. In Isaiah 40:12, "Who has measured the waters in the hollow of his hand," some commentators have long felt that a slight modification of the word "waters" so as to make it mean "seas" gave a meaning more in accord with the context. The St. Mark's manuscript, by merely splitting the word into two (*my ym* instead of *mym*), makes it mean "waters of a sea." As Orlinsky points out, however, the definite article would normally be used before the word "sea" in Hebrew as in English.

For some variant readings of the St. Mark's manuscript that are not supported by the ancient versions there is support of other kinds. To Mr. E. E. Buttner of South Africa I am indebted for the information that in Isaiah 40:7–8 and 64:1 the readings of the scroll agree with quotations of these texts by the second-century church father Justin Martyr, and in the former instance by Cyprian also. Wallenstein has pointed out that in 40:10 and 56:1 the scroll agrees with quotations by the early Jewish poet Yannai. A quotation of Isaiah 52:8 in the Jewish Prayer Book, as H. L. Ginsberg has shown, agrees with the St. Mark's manuscript against both the Masoretic text and the Septuagint. On other grounds also, scholars have considered certain variants in the scroll superior to the readings of the Masoretic text. Nötscher gives a list of sixteen Hebrew expressions in the Masoretic text of Isaiah which occur nowhere else, and which he thinks the readings of the scroll prove to be unnecessary and probably incorrect.

One variant not very striking in itself is interesting because it agrees in part with a quotation of the text in the New Testament. In Isaiah 7:14 the Masoretic text reads, "she shall call his name Immanuel." The same consonants with other vowels would mean "you shall call." Where this verse is quoted in Matthew 1:23 the Greek reads literally "they shall call," the meaning being impersonal and equivalent to a passive verb, "his name shall be called." The St. Mark's scroll too has an impersonal form of the verb, but in the singular, "one shall call," or (as it may be pointed) a passive form, "shall be called."

The corrections inserted in the manuscript at a number of points have already been mentioned. For the history of the text they deserve a special study by themselves. It is significant that they are usually in the direction of conformity to the Masoretic text. The question remains how many of the readings that were corrected were merely copyist's blunders, and how many were genuine variants which the corrector altered to make them agree with what he considered a better text. A popular text like that of this manuscript would be less subject to correction than a more official text, and might therefore preserve ancient readings that were eliminated from official texts.

In some places where the scroll is supported by the ancient versions Barthélemy holds that the Masoretic reading is a deliberate modification in the interest of a particular group. An example is Isaiah 49:5, where the scroll and some of the versions read, "and Israel shall be gathered to him," while the Masoretic text reads, "and Israel shall not be gathered." The Hebrew for "not" and "to him" are spelled differently but sound alike. Barthélemy suggests that the reading "not" was introduced in opposition to the Samaritans, who were identified with Israel by the scribes who made the change. The reading "to him," preserved here by the ancient versions and by the St. Mark's manuscript, was noted by the Masoretes as a marginal reading and was adopted in the English Revised Version of 1881 and the American Standard Version of 1901. The reading "not" may have been originally a mistake made by a scribe who was writing from dictation and not paying close attention to the meaning of what he wrote.

Among the variants which Barthélemy believes to be ancient readings, deliberately eliminated from the official text, there are several which he calls Messianic variants, meaning that they express the Messianic interest and beliefs of the Judean covenanters. If it is true that they have a Messianic significance, they afford valuable evidence for the beliefs of the sect. We must still ask, however, whether the official scribes altered the text to eliminate what they considered objectionable implications, or whether the alteration was made by the covenanters to introduce their own beliefs into the text. That the latter procedure would not have been out of the question is shown by what was done with the text of Habakkuk, as we may see presently, in the commentary. Barthélemy considers it probable, however, that in some if not all of these places the scroll preserves the original reading, which was altered by the official scribes to eliminate objectionable doctrinal implications. We cannot pause here to discuss each of these variants, but anyone who carefully examines the passages in question will find that the supposed Messianic implications are decidedly questionable.

One reading cited by Barthélemy is somewhat more impressive than the others and has been the object of very lively discussion by several scholars. In Isaiah 52:14, where the Masoretic text, translated literally, reads "marred more than a man was his appearance," the St. Mark's scroll says—or seems to say—"I have anointed more than a man his appearance." Barthélemy takes this strange statement to mean, "I have anointed him, so that his appearance surpasses that of a man." Nötscher accepts this interpretation and points out that the form of the verb "was marred" used in the Masoretic text does not occur anywhere else. Brownlee also accepts Barthélemy's view at this point and argues strongly for the interpretation of the word in the scroll as "I anointed." This is certainly the most obvious way to take it, but J. Reider and Arie Rubinstein have shown that it may be an unusual form of the word meaning "marred," and the idea of anointing a person's appearance seems intrinsically unlikely even for an "Essene" scribe. Barthélemy's whole argument, to my mind, is unconvincing. His theory is worth noting, however, because it calls attention to the possibility that this unofficial, pre-Masoretic text may here and there reflect the special interests and beliefs of the sect.

Much more might be added about the St. Mark's Isaiah scroll, but what has been said may suffice to indicate its importance for establishing the best possible text of the Old Testament. By and large it confirms the antiquity and authenticity of the Masoretic text. Where it departs from the traditional text, the latter is usually preferable. In a significant number of variant readings, however, some with and some without support in the versions and other ancient witnesses, the manuscript gives very valuable help in getting back of the Masoretic text to more ancient readings, closer to the original words of the book. Both negatively and positively all this is important for the history of the text.

The other manuscript of Isaiah, which was bought from the Bedouins by Sukenik and which I will therefore call the Hebrew University's Isaiah scroll, contains only a part of the text of Chapters 10–66, and even so many lines have been lost and there are many gaps in what remains. Both in spelling and in wording this manuscript is much closer than the St. Mark's scroll to the Masoretic text. It has many slight variants, some of which agree with the St. Mark's scroll and some with the ancient versions, but they consist almost entirely of little differences in spelling and grammar. If this is, as it seems to be, another popular text from the time before the standardization of the consonantal text, the extent of its agreement which the Masoretic text is all the more impressive.

Fragments of other manuscripts of Isaiah have been found in the exploration and excavation of the caves. Professor James Muilenburg has published a few fragments of Isaiah from Cave 4. They are of about the same age as the Habakkuk Commentary and the War scroll. Like the Hebrew University's Isaiah scroll, they agree closely with the Masoretic text. Nowhere do they agree with the Septuagint when it differs from the Masoretic text.

Since the Habakkuk Commentary quotes the first two chapters of the book of Habakkuk, it too has some importance for textual criticism. Like the St. Mark's Isaiah scroll, it frequently differs from the Masoretic text. Sometimes the difference is obviously the result of a mistake in copying. In the quotation of Habakkuk 2:16, for example, one letter of the Hebrew word for "glory" has been left out. There are many differences in spelling, some of which suggest writing "by ear." Some mistakes seem to have been caused by confusion between two similar letters in a previous copy.

Apart from mere differences in spelling, van der Ploeg finds about fifty variant readings in the commentary. Most of these have little or no importance. What appears to be a real variant may in some cases be merely a mistake of copying or hearing. This explanation must not be adopted too lightly, however. In quoting Habakkuk 1:11, for example, the commentary reads "and he made" instead of "and he was guilty." Since the ensuing comment on the verses uses the word "guilty," van der Ploeg thinks that this variant may have been accidental; Elliger, however, and I think rightly, considers the reading of the commentary superior to that of the Masoretic text. It gives the meaning, "he made his might his god," whereas the Masoretic reading is at best obscure; indeed, scholars had previously proposed an emendation of the Hebrew word almost identical with the reading of the commentary.

In Habakkuk 1:17, where the Masoretic text reads "his net,"

the commentary has "his sword," so that instead of "he empties his net" the meaning becomes "he bares his sword." The reading "his sword" is presupposed also in the comment which follows. It has some slight support in the ancient versions, in fact, and scholars have proposed it as an emendation of the text. Elliger feels that the reference to merciless slaughter at the end of the verse confirms this reading.

One of the most interesting variants in the Habakkuk Commentary is attributed by van der Ploeg to mere confusion of similar letters. In Habakkuk 2:5 the Masoretic text says, "Wine is treacherous." C. C. Torrey has made a strong case for the hypothesis that the original reading was, "Greece is treacherous." The Habakkuk Commentary has a third reading, "Wealth is treacherous."

In Hebrew the word for wine is *hyyn,* the word for Greece is *hywn* (using the definite article in both cases), while the word for wealth (without the definite article) is *hwn.* The reading "wealth" may obviously be merely a mistake in copying; the change in meaning, however, has some connection with the severe condemnation of wealth by the Qumran covenanters. Either a deliberate change from "wine" to "wealth" or an unconscious assumption that this was the correct reading would express the feeling of the group that, bad as wine might be, wealth was worse.

Each of these readings, no doubt, expresses a truth. Wine and wealth are both treacherous, and in ancient times there were those who mistrusted the Greeks. Not far from the time when the Habakkuk Commentary was written the Roman poet Vergil made Laocoon say at Troy, as he hurled his spear at the wooden horse, "I fear the Greeks even when they bring gifts." What Habakkuk himself wrote or said, of course, is another question. There is no adequate reason to suppose that it was "wealth."

A choice between the two letters most frequently confused in Hebrew manuscripts, *d* and *r,* is involved in the reading of the commentary on Habakkuk 2:15—"gaze on their feasts" instead of "gaze on their nakedness." Here again the variant reading is presupposed by the interpretation which follows. Perhaps it was already present in the manuscript of Habakkuk used by the author of the commentary; or perhaps that manuscript was written in a script that did not clearly distinguish *d* and *r*. In the latter case the significance of the event the commentator saw reflected in the text may have caused him unconsciously to read "feasts" instead of "nakedness." It is also within the bounds of possibility, however, that he made the change deliberately to produce the meaning he desired. There is surely no sufficient evidence to make it probable that the Masoretic reading "nakedness" should be changed to "feasts."

For a few of its variants the commentary has some support in the ancient versions. The addition of "and" before "he drags them" in Habakkuk 1:15 is not important, but it is worth noting as a case of agreement with the Septuagint against the Masoretic text. In 1:17 the Masoretic text begins with an interrogative particle. The versions, with the exception of the Targum, do not indicate a question, and many modern scholars have accordingly emended the text so as to read an affirmative statement. The Habakkuk Commentary omits the interrogative particle. Minor departures from the traditional text at other points have at least partial support in the versions.

In Habakkuk 2:16 there is a variant which supports a very simple emendation favored by many modern scholars, with considerable support in the versions. Where the Masoretic text reads, "Drink and be uncircumcised," the commentary has, "Drink and stagger." The two Hebrew verbs differ only in the order of two consonants. The comment on the verse contains a word from the same root as "be uncircumcised," suggesting that in this case the commentator based his interpretation on the Masoretic reading. One might suppose that a copyist had made a mistake, either in this manuscript or in a previous copy made after the composition of the commentary; but the appropriateness of the variant in the context and the support which it has in the versions indicate a more substantial basis. It may be the Masoretic reading, therefore, which is the result of a mistake in copying.

In the familiar words of Habakkuk 2:3, "For the vision is yet for the appointed time," the commentary supports the Masoretic text against an emendation strongly urged by some modern scholars. H. L. Ginsberg, for instance, maintains that instead of the adverb "yet" the original text read the noun "witness." The sentence would then mean, "For the vision is a witness to the appointed time" (i.e., evidence of the ordained consummation). In a consonantal text, with no indication of vowels, the two Hebrew words would be the same. The Habakkuk Commentary, however, by inserting a vowel letter, unmistakably supports the Masoretic reading, "yet." This does not prove, of course, that the original reading was not "witness." It proves merely that the mistake, if it was such, was an ancient one.

From all these variant readings van der Ploeg concludes that the commentary represents a tradition quite different from any attested by the versions or the Masoretic text. With such exceptions as we have noted, the versions support the Masoretic text where the commentary differs from it. Like the two scrolls of Isaiah, the Habakkuk Commentary preserves a popular form of the text. Elliger, after a painstaking examination of the variants, concludes that the commentary has very little value for restoring a more correct text. In general it merely shows how old and relatively reliable the Masoretic text is. The chief difficulties in the text of Habakkuk remain, being the result of corruption of the text before the time when the commentary was written.

For the remaining books of the Bible no extensive scrolls comparable to those found in 1947 have been discovered, but in the almost innumerable fragments found in the caves almost every book of the Old Testament is represented. Even if only a small portion of a book is preserved, it may give significant evidence concerning the text. Frank M. Cross, Jr., points out that the large quantity of fragments from the caves makes possible a sampling of different textual types. The fact that so many of the books are represented provides a cross section of the whole Old Testament, which in some ways is more important for textual criticism than complete manuscripts of only two or three books.

Among the fragments found in the first cave, perhaps during the illicit operation of 1948, there were some from the book of Daniel, including the place in the second chapter where the language suddenly changes from Hebrew to Aramaic. This change appears in the ancient manuscript exactly as it is in the standard text. The fragments of Leviticus in the old Hebrew script which were found in the first cave in 1949 gave us, as Birnbaum remarked, our oldest witness to the text of any part of the Bible. It is therefore significant that they agree almost entirely with the Masoretic text of Leviticus.

The most astonishing quantity of fragments came from Cave 4. James Muilenburg has published the fragments of a beautifully written scroll of Ecclesiastes. This scroll, which was written about 150 B.C., seems to have differed from the Masoretic text to about the same degree and in much the same ways as the St. Mark's Isaiah scroll, with which it is approximately contemporary. Other fragments from this cave, however, present quite a different picture. Monsignor Patrick W. Skehan, working on the fragments from Cave 4 at the Palestine Museum, found one containing a tiny bit of the eighth verse of Deuteronomy 32 with the first evidence of any ancient Hebrew manuscript of the reading, "according to the number of the sons of God," where the Masoretic text has "sons of Israel." On the basis of the Septuagint, which reads "angels of God," scholars have long believed that the original text was "sons of God," and this is the reading adopted by the Revised Standard Version. Another fragment contained enough of the ending of the same chapter to show the astonishing fact that the text was arranged in metrical lines, as are also some fragments of the Psalms. In this fragment also there are readings that agree with the Septuagint as against the Masoretic text.

A bit of the text of I Samuel found in the fourth cave has been published by F. M. Cross. No less than twenty-seven fragments, when pieced together, were found to form a portion of two columns of manuscript containing part of the text of I Samuel 1:22–2:6 and 2:16–25. The script indicates a date in the first century B.C. The text represents the same general tradition as that which was the

basis of the Septuagint in I Samuel. This enhances the importance
of the Septuagint for the reconstruction of the Hebrew text of
Samuel. Not only so; the fragments demonstrate the importance of
a particular group of Septuagint manuscripts, the chief representative of which is the Codex Vaticanus. Fragments of other
manuscripts of Samuel attest other textual traditions. As Cross
writes, "Thus for the first time, really, we are introduced to an Old
Testament text in a state of relative fluidity."

The fragments from Cave 4 are clearly the remains of manuscripts made before the effort to standardize the text had gone
very far, though the text of the Pentateuch and perhaps that of
the book of Isaiah may have been fixed relatively early. The
process of standardization went through its most decisive phase
within a century and a half after the abandonment of the Qumran
caves, but it is clear that the rabbis of the second and subsequent
centuries did not inaugurate the process. Their work evidently
rested on ancient traditions, and the text they adopted as authoritative was one that had already been standardized to a considerable degree.

Later texts from the caves of the Wady Murabbaat illuminate
the history of the Septuagint. This, however, involves problems
with which only specialists in that field can deal competently. It
also takes us beyond the area of our present concern, the manuscripts of the Qumran community.

What has been said may be enough to indicate the importance
of the Dead Sea Scrolls and fragments for the technical study of
the text of the Old Testament. The general reader and student of
the Bible may be satisfied to note that nothing in all this changes
our understanding of the religious teachings of the Bible. We did
not need the Dead Sea Scrolls to show us that the text has not
come down to us through the centuries unchanged. Interpretations
depending upon the exact words of a verse must be examined
in the light of all we know about the history of the text. The
essential truth and the will of God revealed in the Bible, however,
have been preserved unchanged through all the vicissitudes in the
transmission of the text. Even when mistaken interpretations were

propounded, as in the commentary on Habakkuk and the fragments of other commentaries, only slight changes in minor details were made in the text itself.

Since these manuscripts are much older than any previously known, it is reasonable to ask whether they throw any light not only on the wording of the text but on the composition of the books of the Old Testament. Many people have asked, for example, whether the Isaiah scrolls contain anything bearing on the distinction between the work of the prophet Isaiah, who lived in the eighth century B.C., and a "Second Isaiah" of the sixth century or later. We could not reasonably expect, however, to find evidence of this sort. It is rather interesting, to be sure, that the division between the two halves of the St. Mark's manuscript, in which Kahle finds two different forms of the Hebrew text, comes just at the end of chapter 33; because in style and ideas chapters 34 and 35 clearly belong with chapters 40–66 rather than with chapters 1–33. (Chapters 36–39, of course, are quoted from II Kings.)

Whatever significance this division of the manuscript may have, however, no conclusion can be drawn from it concerning the composition of the book. The book of Isaiah had attained its present form long before the St. Mark's manuscript was written. There have been critics, it is true, who dated sections of the book as late as the Maccabean period. The St. Mark's manuscript is not quite old enough to make even that impossible. What its date and contents definitely prove is that the book of Isaiah was complete, with all its parts in their present order, by the end of the second century B.C.

Concerning the composition of the book of Habakkuk, it is of some interest to note that the Habakkuk Commentary omits the third chapter. The fact that the last column has only four lines of writing shows that the end of the commentary has been reached. Many scholars have long believed that the third chapter was not a part of the original book of Habakkuk. Its absence from the scroll is consistent with this theory but does not prove it. It does not even prove that the third chapter was unknown to the Judean covenanters. Being a psalm, it does not lend itself to such use as is made of the other chapters. It is even possible that the commentary was never finished. The Septuagint has all three chapters, but whether this particular part of the Septuagint is older than the Habakkuk Commentary is another question.

Indirect evidence concerning the antiquity of the psalms of the Old Testament has been seen in the differences in language, spirit, and theology between them and the Thanksgiving Psalms of the Dead Sea Scrolls. Aside from such general indications, the Dead Sea texts could hardly be expected to tell us anything about the composition of the Old Testament books. More light might be expected, perhaps, on the formation of the canon. That question we have already considered in connection with the theology of the Qumran covenanters. It cannot be said that much has been added yet to our knowledge of the subject.

Of less general interest but important for scholars is the material provided by the scrolls and fragments for the history of the Hebrew language. Their peculiarities of spelling have come to our attention in several connections. Some of these may indicate mere personal idiosyncrasies or sheer ignorance; at any rate, it is clear that Hebrew orthography was in a fluid state when the scrolls were written. The spelling of the scrolls is certainly not older than that of the Masoretes. The relative scarcity of vowel letters in the Masoretic text, for example, corresponds to a much more ancient practice than the lavish use of them in the Dead Sea Scrolls. The Masoretes either retained the orthography found in their oldest manuscripts or deliberately returned to an ancient type of spelling.

The Dead Sea Scrolls exhibit transitional phases in the development of Hebrew orthography. Perhaps the most important fact to note in this connection is that the scrolls carry farther tendencies already evident in the latest books of the Hebrew Old Testament, especially I–II Chronicles, Ezra, and Nehemiah, where the Masoretes did not so thoroughly restore the older spelling as they did in the law and the prophets.

The full and rather eccentric spelling of the scrolls is not merely a subject for study by itself; it shows also how Hebrew was pronounced at the time when the manuscripts were copied. Aside from such features as may reflect only a local or even a sectarian dialect, the scrolls and fragments represent stages in the history of the language earlier in some respects than what can be seen in the Masoretic text of the Old Testament, for while the Masoretes preserved or restored the archaic consonantal spelling, they also standardized and stereotyped the grammatical forms and pronunciation according to their own ideas of what was correct.

Emphasizing the value of the Dead Sea Scrolls from this point of view, Kahle observes that before they were discovered we had only three unsatisfactory means of determining how Hebrew was pronounced before the time of the Masoretes. Transliterations of parts of the Old Testament text in the Greek and Latin alphabets were available, but such transliterations can never indicate pronunciation exactly. The pronunciation of Hebrew by the Samaritans afforded some information, but allowance had to be made for peculiarities of their dialect. The third means of recovering a pre-Masoretic pronunciation was provided by Hebrew texts with vowel-pointing according to an older Palestinian system. In the orthography of the Dead Sea Scrolls we now have a fourth body of evidence, perhaps the most important of all. Previous discussions of pre-Masoretic Hebrew grammar must now be revised in the light of this new evidence.

Not only the pronunciation but also the formation of words is illuminated by the Dead Sea manuscripts. In syntax also the scrolls exhibit some characteristic features. Even in the biblical texts notable modifications of the language are in evidence. Yet the Hebrew of these documents is not at all the dialect of the later rabbinic literature. Scholars have remarked that the scrolls prove at least that a great deal was being written in Hebrew; indeed, there must have been a veritable renaissance of the language in the Hasmonean period. At the same time there are indications that the spoken language of the scribes and authors was Aramaic rather than Hebrew. Affinities with the slightly later Palestinian Christian Aramaic or Syriac dialect have been detected. The points of contact with the Samaritan dialect of Hebrew, however, indicate the persistence of Hebrew as a living language.

It is useless at present to speculate concerning the relative importance of time, place, and religious associations in forming the language of these manuscripts. The dialect of the Dead Sea Scrolls, if it may be so called, was not necessarily one spoken only in the region of Jericho and the eastern slope of the Judean plateau. The members of the group must have come from various parts of Palestine. Much special study is still needed on these problems.

The proportion of texts in Hebrew rather than Aramaic is significant, however it is to be explained. The mother tongue of most of the Jews of Palestine at this time was Aramaic. Hebrew may have been used more for religious literature because it was the language of Scripture and the synagogue. It must not be forgotten, however, that a sufficient quantity of Aramaic texts has been found to demonstrate the use of Aramaic also as a literary language. The Aramaic manuscripts of Qumran give us our first literary documents in a form of Aramaic used in Palestine in the time of Christ. Hitherto the only Aramaic documents known from this period were brief inscriptions.

In discussing the age of the Dead Sea Scrolls we considered the bearing of paleography on the question. Important as this line of evidence is, we were compelled to recognize the fact that comparative material for the late Hellenistic and early Roman periods is none too plentiful, and very little of it can be exactly dated. The enormous quantity of fragments and scrolls from the Wady Qumran and the Wady Murabbaat has now very substantially increased the amount of material available for the paleographer. It makes possible a more complete sequence of types of script; and when a few points in the sequence can be "fixed" by evidence of other kinds, such as the pottery and coins found in the excavations, the relative dating becomes bit by bit an absolute dating. Much has been learned from the scrolls and fragments concerning the history of the square or Aramaic script. The accumulation of almost innumerable fragments representing a long range of time has made possible a much larger picture than was afforded by the finds in the first cave.

Equally important for the paleographer are the fragments inscribed in the Old Hebrew alphabet, though they still present a problem of their own. Evidently the archaic script continued to be used for a long time at Qumran; in fact a process of development in this script itself can be seen. The manuscripts in which the archaic alphabet is used are not older, it seems, but roughly contemporary with those written in the square script. One fragment, indeed, has the old script and the square script intermingled! Students of paleography will be kept busy for many years working out all the details of these new developments. The Dead Sea cave materials also illuminate other matters connected with ancient writing and bookmaking. In them ancient Jewish methods of producing books, about which all that was previously known depended on statements in the rabbinic literature, can now be studied at first hand.

XV

Contributions to the Study of
Judaism and Christianity

⊔⊓⊓⊔⊓⊔⊓⊓⊔⊓⊓⊔⊓⊓⊔⊓⊔⊓⊓⊔⊓⊓⊔⊓⊓⊔⊓⊔⊓⊓⊔⊓⊓⊔⊓⊓⊔⊓⊓⊔⊓⊓⊔⊓⊓⊔⊓⊓⊔⊓⊓⊔⊓⊓⊔⊓⊓⊔⊓⊓⊔⊓

The matters treated in the foregoing chapter are of immediate concern only to specialists. A much broader interest attaches to the contents of the texts and their importance for the history of Judaism and Christianity.

The chief importance of the Dead Sea Scrolls for Jewish religious and cultural history has been most plainly pointed out by Kahle. In the generations following the destruction of the temple, he reminds us, authoritative norms for Jewish life and thought were codified, and the limits of the canon of Scripture was fixed. All earlier writings not in accord with the "normative" Judaism thus established were either destroyed or lost and forgotten.

It has always been clear to historians that before the destruction of the temple Judaism was much more diversified than it became in the Talmudic period; but all that was known concerning some of its varieties came from the comments of writers who looked at them from the outside and without too much sympathy. Only the apocryphal writings afforded any inside knowledge of Jewish groups other than the Pharisees; and these were preserved only by Christians, in translations (sometimes translations of translations), and often in more or less altered and Christianized editions.

In the Qumran texts and the Damascus Document we now have

a considerable quantity of literature cherished and produced by a dissident group of Jews during the time when the temple was standing, just after the composition of the latest books of the Old Testament, and just before and during the time when the New Testament was coming into being.

Our brief discussion of the beliefs of the sect has shown something of the ideas expressed in these documents, including unexpected conceptions of the meaning and way of salvation and ideas concerning the nature of the sect itself as an organized remnant within the Jewish nation. The religious vocabulary of Judaism in these periods is richly illustrated by the texts. One of the most significant aspects of pre-Christian Judaism which finds expression in them is its devotional spirit. The Thanksgiving Psalms, the concluding psalm of the Manual of Discipline, and the liturgical portions of the War of the Sons of Light with the Sons of Darkness supplement in a very important way our knowledge of this side of Judaism, for which previously we had almost no source material outside of the Prayer Book and a few of the apocryphal writings.

Everything that is important for Judaism in the last two or three centuries before Christ and in the first century A.D. is important also for Christianity. By enriching our understanding of Judaism in the period in which Christianity arose, the Dead Sea Scrolls have given us material for a better understanding of the New Testament and early Christianity. It has even been said that the discoveries will revolutionize New Testament scholarship. This may perhaps cause some alarm. There is no danger, however, that our understanding of the New Testament will be so revolutionized by the Dead Sea Scrolls as to require a revision of any basic article of Christian faith. All scholars who have worked on the texts will agree that this has not happened and will not happen.

In our review of the controversies aroused by the discovery of the Dead Sea Scrolls we have observed how much excitement was caused by Dupont-Sommer's references to anticipations of Christianity in the Habakkuk Commentary. Christians should have no reluctance to recognize anticipations of Christianity in the Dead Sea Scrolls or in other Jewish writings, if or when they really exist. The Gospel was given as the fulfillment of what was already revealed. God, who spoke in many and various ways to the fathers by the prophets, spoke more clearly and fully in his Son. Even the possibility of direct "borrowing" from the books of the covenanters by the writers of the New Testament is merely a question of historical fact. Why should not the church adopt and preserve anything which it found true and valuable, as it unquestionably adopted some of the forms of synagogue worship and later even appropriated pagan elements? Christians have never hesitated to recognize that John the Baptist had some influence on the early church.

Dupont-Sommer himself actually speaks of preparation rather than anticipation, though he does use such terms as "reincarnation" and "borrowing." Direct influence of the Qumran sect on the early church may turn out to be less probable than parallel developments in the same general situation. The question here is the same one encountered when we attempt to explain similarities between Judaism and Zoroastrianism, or between Christianity and the pagan mystery cults.

It should not be surprising to find close contacts in language and thought between the early church and the Qumran community. Jesus was baptized by John the Baptist in the Jordan during the time when the community of covenanters was flourishing not many miles away. Many scholars have suggested that John the Baptist was an Essene. Brownlee suggests that Essenes may have adopted John as a boy, as was their custom according to Josephus.

Quite apart from the question of identifying the Essenes and the Qumran covenanters, there are certainly many points at which John's ideas resemble those expressed in the Dead Sea Scrolls. Like the covenanters, he was devoted to preparing the way of the Lord in the wilderness. His baptism of repentance may have had some historical connection with the ritual bathing of the Qumran sect. He insisted, as the Manual of Discipline does, that without previous spiritual cleansing bathing in water cannot remove guilt.

Parallels have been seen between John's Messianic expectations and those of the Dead Sea Scrolls. His prediction that the one coming after him would execute judgment by fire is undoubtedly related in some way to the Zoroastrian idea of a final conflagration in which the mountains will melt and pour over the earth like a river; and this idea is vividly presented in one of the Thanksgiving Psalms in terms of the "torrents of Belial" that will consume in flame even the foundations of the mountains. The conception of a Messianic baptism by the Holy Spirit is present also in the scrolls. The statement of the Manual of Discipline that at the end of this age God will cleanse man by sprinkling upon him the spirit of truth recalls John's proclamation that the Messiah will baptize his people with the Holy Spirit.

It has been argued that John's movement originated within the priesthood but later seceded from it, as the Qumran community perhaps did. Many other common elements, more or less impressive, have been pointed out. It has even been suggested that John may have thought of himself as the returning teacher of righteousness before he transferred his hopes to Jesus. Unlike the Essenes or covenanters, however, John addressed the whole people. Another conspicuous difference between what we know of him and what we find in the Dead Sea Scrolls is that nothing corresponding to the strong organization of the community is attested concerning John's disciples.

With regard to all this it must be said that, if John the Baptist had ever been an Essene, he must have withdrawn from the sect and entered upon an independent prophetic ministry. This is not impossible, but the connection is not so close as to make it seem very probable. It is not at all unlikely, however, that John had some knowledge of the community of Qumran. The religious movement he inaugurated was certainly an expression of the same general tendency in Judaism which produced that sect and others in the period just before and after the beginning of the Christian era.

Not only John the Baptist but even Jesus himself has sometimes been thought to have been an Essene. This is quite out of the question, as all competent historians now recognize. The Dead Sea Scrolls, however, contain a number of points in language and ideas which seem surprisingly like what the New Testament reports concerning Jesus. Dupont-Sommer, after reading the Habakkuk Commentary, declared that Jesus now seemed "an astonishing reincarnation of the teacher of righteousness." Like Jesus, he said, the teacher of righteousness was believed by his disciples to be God's Elect, the Messiah, the Redeemer of the world. Both the teacher of righteousness and Jesus were opposed by the priestly party, the Sadducees; both were condemned and put to death; both proclaimed judgment on Jerusalem; both established communities whose members expected them to return and judge the world.

Many scholars hastened to point out that Dupont-Sommer's interpretation of the Habakkuk Commentary produced closer parallels with Christian faith and practice at some points than could be substantiated by exact exegesis. His statement that the teacher of righteousness was God's Elect and the Messiah, for example, is not borne out by the text of the commentary or any of the scrolls. As we have seen, the term "elect" probably refers to the community, and there is no indication that the teacher of righteousness was believed to be the Messiah or the Redeemer of the world.

There is nothing unique or new in the hostility of the priests to the teacher of righteousness—or in his martyrdom, if that is actually implied by the Habakkuk Commentary—"for so men persecuted the prophets." It is true that both Jesus and the teacher of righteousness pronounced judgment on Jerusalem; so did many of the prophets. The assertion that the teacher of righteousness was expected to return and judge the world depends upon questionable interpretations of passages in the Dead Sea Scrolls and the Damascus Document. The covenanters expected a Messiah, as all Jews did; indeed, they expected two Messiahs. They expected also a prophet, as other Jews did. That they looked for the return of the teacher of righteousness himself has not been demonstrated.

Aside from parallels, real or supposed, in the careers of Jesus and the teacher of righteousness, and in the beliefs of their followers concerning them, similarities in their own teachings have been pointed out. That ethical teachings similar to those of Jesus appear in the scrolls should not seem surprising. At best the resemblance is not as close as may be found, for instance, in the Testimonies of the Twelve Patriarchs. The contrast between the love of enemies inculcated by the Sermon on the Mount and the hatred for the sons of darkness demanded by the Manual of Discipline shows how far the covenanters were from the teaching of Jesus. Their high standards of morality in other respects are found already in the Old Testament.

The teacher of righteousness claimed, no doubt, as Jesus did, that the new revelation given to him explained and perfected the revelation in the Scriptures. The rabbis also, while claiming no such special revelation, felt that what they taught was the true meaning of the law, although, more or less consciously, they actually added much that was new. There is nothing in the Dead Sea Scrolls approaching the radical interpretation of the law given by Jesus, who made everything hang on Deuteronomy 6:5 and Leviticus 19:18. There are sayings of the rabbis, in fact, which come much closer to the teaching of Jesus at this point than anything in the scrolls.

Parallels between the Dead Sea Scrolls and the sayings of Jesus concerning the future have been noted, but there the differences are even more striking. At the same time the sharp opposition of the realms of good and evil is as central in the teaching of Jesus as it is in the Qumran literature, even though the scrolls do not speak of the kingdom of God and the kingdom of Satan as Jesus does, and he does not use the expression, "dominion of Bilial." It is at least worth noting also that Jesus speaks of the "sons of light": "for the sons of this world are wiser in their own generation than the sons of light" (Luke 16:8). In general the sayings of Jesus are related to the apocalyptic literature of Judaism more closely than to anything in the scrolls. It may fairly be questioned, indeed, whether the teachings of Jesus and the beliefs of the Qumran community have anything in common which cannot be found in other Jewish sources also.

With the early church of Jerusalem, as portrayed in the Acts of the Apostles, the situation is different. The resemblances here are much more impressive and significant. The position of Peter in the Jerusalem church has been compared with that of the "superintendent" of the Manual of Discipline and the Damascus Document. The authority of the Twelve Apostles in the early chapters of Acts is recalled by the council of twelve laymen and three priests in the Manual of Discipline. Nothing like the dominance of the priests in the Qumran community is recorded concerning the early church, but many priests are said to have joined the disciples, More important than the form of organization is what may be called the church idea, the concept of a spiritual group, the true people of God, distinct from the Jewish nation as such. In the Qumran community's concept of itself can be seen an approach to this, doubtless without a full realization of all its implications; but the Christian church itself did not at once realize the full implications of the church idea.

In the forms of worship of the church and the Qumran sect there are obvious similarities. We have found some ambiguity in the evidence concerning the attitude of the sect to the temple and its sacrifices. In this connection Sherman E. Johnson has called attention to the fact that two different tendencies developed in the early church: some of the disciples continued to worship at the temple, but the party led by Stephen preached that God did not dwell in any temple made by human hands.

Both the covenanters and the early Christians also had rites of their own that were notably similar. What has been said about baptism in connection with John the Baptist applies as well to the church of Jerusalem, and the references in the Manual of Discipline to cleansing by the spirit of truth remind us of the stress on the gift of the Spirit in the apostolic church. The regulations for the community meals in the Dead Sea Scrolls call to mind "the breaking of bread" together in the early church. Suggestions have been found in the Manual of Discipline concerning the way in which the early church observed the sacrament of the Lord's Supper, and even concerning the procedure at Jesus's last supper with his disciples, as compared with the usual way of observing the Passover. Such inferences, however, should not be drawn without caution. There is little in the Gospels to suggest that the fellowship of Jesus and his disciples had any such formal structure as that of the Qumran community. That the commemoration of the Supper by the church was patterned more or less on Jewish models is, of course, entirely probable. The meals of the covenanters give us a concrete example of one such model, but not necessarily one that particularly influenced Christian practice.

There are many points of similarity in the life and ideals of the Qumran sect and those of the early church of Jerusalem. A spirit of love and unity was cultivated in both, though their attitudes toward those outside their own number were conspicuously different. The fellowship of the members found radical expression in the Jerusalem church, as in the community of Qumran, in the sharing of property. The Manual of Discipline prescribes the punishment of "a man who lies regarding wealth," indicating that cases like that of Ananias and Sapphira were not unknown among the covenanters. The punishment, however, was relatively lenient: exclusion from "the sacred food of the masters" for a year, with a reduction of the food allowance by one fourth, instead of being struck dead. Perhaps such cases were more common in the Qumran sect than in the church.

Even the scholars who have looked most eagerly for parallels between the early Christians and the covenanters have recognized that there are equally notable differences. The church was not an exclusive, esoteric group with jealously guarded secret teachings. The gospel given to it had to be proclaimed to all the world. One of the most conspicuous differences between the church and the Qumran sect in organization and life was the entirely different status of women in the two communities.

Some of the most characteristic theological doctrines of the New Testament have parallels in the Dead Sea Scrolls. This is strikingly true of some of Paul's ideas. The "mystery of lawlessness" referred to in II Thessalonians 2:7 has been compared with the "mystery of evil" in the Thanksgiving Psalms. The dualism of the Dead Sea Scrolls recalls the opposition of flesh and spirit and of the earthly and the heavenly in Paul's letters. In II Corinthians 6:14-15 Paul sharply contrasts righteousness and iniquity, light and darkness, Christ and Belial. The name Belial, one of the most characteristic terms of the Dead Sea Scrolls, occurs only here in the New Testament. It has been suggested that Paul used at this point a bit of early Christian tradition reflecting the ideas of the Qumran sect.

Paul's utter distrust of all human righteousness is not unlike what appears in some of the scrolls. An important parallel to Romans 3:20 and Galatians 2:16 has been seen in the following passage in one of the Thanksgiving Psalms:

> I know that righteousness does not belong to a man,
> nor to a son of man blamelessness of conduct;
> to the Most High God belong all works of righteousness.

The idea that only God is righteous, and no man can claim any righteousness in his sight, appears already in very similar language in the Old Testament. But the covenanters did not stop there. Something approaching Paul's idea of justification by the righteousness of God is expressed in the concluding psalm of the Manual of Discipline:

> As for me, if I slip, the steadfast love of God is my salvation
>   forever;
> and if I stumble in the iniquity of flesh,
> my vindication in the righteousness of God will stand to eternity.

> •   •   •

> And in his steadfast love he will bring my vindication.
> In his faithful righteousness he has judged me,
> and in the abundance of his goodness he will forgive all my
>   iniquities.

The point of prime importance here is that while man has no righteousness of his own, there is a righteousness which God, in his own righteousness, freely confers. The meaning of the righteousness of God in Romans 3:21-26 is thus illustrated and shown to be rooted in pre-Christian Judaism.

Not only is salvation dependent upon God's righteousness; it is also connected in the Habakkuk Commentary with faith in the teacher of righteousness. The passage where this appears is a part of the commentary on Habakkuk 2:4, one of Paul's favorite proof-texts for his doctrine of justification by faith in Christ. What the commentator means by faith in the teacher of righteousness, however, is not the same as what faith in Christ meant to Paul. Three elements are more or less involved: fidelity to the teacher of righteousness, confidence in him, and a belief about him. Some scholars see here only the first of these three ideas, but it seems clear to me that more than this is meant. Confident acceptance of his teaching and leadership is presupposed, and this implies also the belief that he knows by revelation the true meaning of prophecy. The same three elements are included also in what Paul means by faith in Christ, but the belief about Christ which he considers necessary for salvation goes much farther than anything that was believed about the teacher of righteousness. There is no implication in the Dead Sea Scrolls that the teacher of righteousness had himself accomplished a redemptive work in any way comparable to the saving work of Christ.

Another difference must be noted also. The Dead Sea Scrolls and the Damascus Document imply that faith in the teacher of righteousness and the doing of the law constitute together the way of salvation. For Paul justification was by faith alone, and good works were not a condition but a result of salvation. The conception that righteousness can only be given by God, not achieved by man, is none the less important as a part of Paul's Jewish heritage.

Salvation included, for Paul, not only justification but also the power to overcome sin through the gift of the Spirit. The Qumran covenanters also attributed good works to God. The passage quoted above from one of the Thanksgiving Psalms, after saying that all righteous works belong to God, continues:

> A man's way is not established
> except by the Spirit which God created for him
> to make blameless a way for the sons of man.

So also the lines quoted from the last column of the Manual of Discipline are followed by these:

> And in his righteousness he will cleanse me from the impurity
> of man,
> from the sin of the sons of man.

Salvation means for the covenanters, as for Paul, not only forgiveness and cleansing from sin but also participation in a spiritual fellowship. One of the Thanksgiving Psalms speaks of "the eternal assembly," "the army of the saints," and "communion with the congregation of the sons of heaven." The prominence of this idea in the New Testament hardly needs to be emphasized. The stress on unity and mutual love in the early church and in the Qumran community has already been mentioned.

The covenanters' belief in predestination has been discussed in Chapter XII. Paul too emphasizes divine election and foreordination as the ground of man's salvation. The problem of reconciling this doctrine with commands and exhortations implying freedom of choice is left unresolved in the Dead Sea Scrolls, as it is in Paul's epistles; in fact, while the question is earnestly faced in the Epistle to the Romans, it is not even raised in the scrolls. The Qumran texts afford no examples of such theological arguments as we find in the letters of Paul.

Echoes of the Dead Sea Scrolls in the Epistle to the Ephesians and the First Epistle of Peter have led a writer to say that if the name of Christ were removed from these letters one might suppose that they came from the Wady Qumran. Here again not all the contacts are as significant as they may seem at first sight. The exhortation of the high priest before the battle in the War scroll contains the sentence: "Do not tremble or be in dread of them and do not turn back." This has been pointed out as a striking parallel with Ephesians 6:11, "that you may be able to stand against the wiles of the devil." The language of the high priest's exhortation, however, is directly based on Deuteronomy 20:3, and neither the words nor the idea have any real connection with the verse in Ephesians.

It has been said that the entire passage concerning "the whole armor of God" in Ephesians 6:11ff, even to details of formulation, is deeply rooted in the tradition of the Dead Sea Scrolls; but the basic idea and some of the details of these verses are based on Isaiah 59:17, which was of course familiar also to the writers of the Dead Sea Scrolls. An exact parallel to the reference in Ephesians 6:16 to "the flaming darts of the evil one" has been seen in one of the Thanksgiving Psalms; here the context shows that not flaming darts but lances flashing in the sun are referred to by the poet. It is true, however, that this passage in Ephesians contains ideas and terms found in the Dead Sea Scrolls.

Contacts between the scrolls and the Epistle to the Hebrews, to which several scholars have drawn attention, consist not so much in verbal parallels as in basic points of view. The writer of the epistle is interested in the ritual laws of the Pentateuch but treats them as only temporary, foreshadowing the effective and final sacrifice of Christ, the Minister of a new and better covenant. The covenanters, we have seen, had no idea of such a divine redemptive act that would supersede the sacrificial system of the old covenant, but they considered themselves the beneficiaries of a new covenant and used the language of the sacrificial cult in a figurative sense.

If the references in the Thanksgiving Psalms to "the congregation of the sons of heaven," "the eternal assembly," "the assembly of the holy ones," mean, as some believe, a celestial assembly including both angels and the souls of the righteous, there is an impressive parallel in a familiar passage of the Epistle to the Hebrews: "But you have come to Mount Zion and to the city of the living God, the heavenly Jerusalem, and to innumerable angels in festal gathering, and to the assembly of the first-born who are enrolled in heaven." This interpretation of the passage in the Thanksgiving Psalm, however, is uncertain, as we have seen.

At many points in other books of the New Testament parallels with the Qumran texts have been noted. One especially interesting example may be mentioned. The explanation given in the Habakkuk Commentary for the unexpectedly long duration of the last time recalls what is said in the third chapter of II Peter about the delay in the coming of Christ. The reader may remember that a description of the final conflagration of the world like that in the same chapter of II Peter is found in one of the Thanksgiving Psalms.

More than in any other part of the New Testament, contacts with the Dead Sea Scrolls have been noted by many scholars in the Gospel of John. Perhaps the most striking verbal parallel is in the closing psalm of the Manual of Discipline:

> Everything that is he establishes by his purpose,
> and without him it is not done.

A reader of the New Testament is reminded of what is said of the eternal Word in John 1:3: "without him was not anything made that was made."

The dualism of light and darkness is especially characteristic of this Gospel. As the War scroll says of the hosts of Belial, "In darkness are all their works," so John 3:19-21 says, ". . . the light has come into the world, and men loved darkness rather than light, because their deeds were evil. For every one who does evil hates the light, and does not come to the light, that it may be clearly seen that his deeds have been wrought in God."

This antithesis runs all through the Gospel and epistles of John. In John 12:35-36, to give only one more example, Jesus says, "The light is with you for a little longer. Walk while you have the light, lest the darkness overtake you; he who walks in the darkness does not know where he goes. While you have the light, believe in the light, that you may become sons of light." There are differences, obviously, between the Johannine ideas and those of the Qumran sect. For the evangelist the darkness has tried in vain to overcome the light; the light has already triumphed over the darkness; Christ himself is the Light of the world. These new and decisive notes, however, do not diminish the importance of the common background.

The whole manner of thinking and the literary style of the fourth Evangelist are strikingly like what we find in the Qumran texts. Whereas Paul thinks and writes more like a disciple of the rabbis, the style and thought of "the beloved disciple" are more priestly and liturgical—as though, it has been said, the Gospel was written to be read aloud in a great cathedral. Such major ideas as faith, truth, judgment, and love are equally prominent in the Dead Sea Scrolls and in the fourth Gospel.

At other points scholars have seen in John's Gospel either reflections of the beliefs of the covenanters or reactions against them. Many of the hypotheses that have been advanced seem to me more ingenious than convincing, but every theory should have its day in court and a fair hearing. I see no reason to believe, for example, that the glorification of the law by the covenanters in particular, rather than by Judaism in general, led the writer of the fourth Gospel to stress Christ's superiority to the law of Moses. That the Evangelist had the teacher of righteousness in mind when he wrote that Nicodemus addressed Jesus as "a teacher come from God," or that others hailed him as "the prophet who is to come into the world," is not even probable.

Other indications of Messianic ideas shared by the Evangelist and the writers of the scrolls have been seen or fancied, but most of them depend upon very dubious inferences from obscure passages in the texts. Equally unconvincing, to my mind, is the suggestion that the preoccupation of the covenanters with the religious calendar suggested the arrangement of Jesus's miracles and discourses in the fourth Gospel in connection with the Jewish festivals. Jesus's words to Nicodemus about being born of water and the spirit may have been intended to condemn reliance upon baptisms and ablutions, but the Qumran sect was not the only group that practiced such rites.

Even the most striking parallels between the Johannine literature and the Dead Sea Scrolls involve little that is peculiar to them. Some of the features most characteristic of both groups of writings have a wider background in the general stream of Iranian influence in Judaism and in other religions of western Asia. What may be said without any exaggeration is that the Gospel and epistles of John and the Dead Sea Scrolls reflect the same general background of sectarian Judaism. The scrolls thus show—and this has not always been recognized—that we do not have to look outside of Palestinian Judaism for the soil in which the Johannine theology grew.

Several scholars have argued that there must have been a much closer connection. The writer of the fourth Gospel, says one, must have been for some time a member, if not an officer, of the Qumran community. The link between the Evangelist and the community, says another, may have been John the Baptist and his followers; the Evangelist, whom tradition connects with Ephesus, may have been acquainted with the disciples of John the Baptist at Ephesus who are referred to in the nineteenth chapter of Acts, or perhaps the Evangelist was himself the unnamed disciple of John the Baptist who followed Jesus, according to John 1:35–40. Still another writer suggests that members of the Qumran community may have taken refuge in Syria at the time of the Jewish revolt against Rome, and the ideas they spread there by word of mouth may in that way have come to the attention of the Evangelist.

All these ideas are worth mentioning, because they at least illustrate the stimulus the Dead Sea Scrolls have given to the imagination of scholars. They are all legitimate and laudable, provided the resulting theories are subjected to calm criticism, and vague possibilities are not confused with certainties or probabilities. In general it is quite possible, though hardly demonstrable, that the Evangelist was led to a reappraisal and a new formulation of his faith through an acquaintance with this *or some similar* Jewish sect.

Far-reaching conclusions concerning the date and historical value of the Gospel of John have been drawn from its affinities with the Dead Sea Scrolls. A late date is precluded, it is argued, because the Evangelist must have known at first hand the community of covenanters, which was broken up and dispersed by 70 A.D. The possible connections with Syria or Ephesus just mentioned show that this argument is inconclusive. The historical accuracy of the account of John the Baptist in the fourth Gospel has been declared vindicated by the Dead Sea Scrolls, but the argu-

ment by which this is supported depends upon debatable interpretations of the texts.

The books that have been mentioned are not the only parts of
the New Testament in which the language and ideas of the Dead
Sea Scrolls seem to be echoed. The frequent references to "his
servants the prophets" in the Revelation of John recalls the use of
that expression in the Manual of Discipline. In the first three chapters of Revelation traces of an acrostic on the word Amen have
been detected, like the one in the tenth column of the Manual of
Discipline. An exceptionally obscure passage in the Thanksgiving
Psalms has recently been interpreted as dealing with the birth of
the Messiah, whose mother is the community itself, pictured as a
woman in the anguish of travail. In Revelation 12:1–6 there is a
mysterious account of a woman in heaven who brings forth "a
male child, one who is to rule all the nations with a rod of iron."

Aside from specific parallels between particular books of the
New Testament and the Dead Sea Scrolls, a few more general
points of contact with the New Testament as a whole may be mentioned. The attitude of the covenanters to the Old Testament is
a case in point. It has been observed that the fondness of the covenanters for some of the apocryphal writings raises the question
whether our sharp division between canonical and non-canonical
books existed for them. This has a bearing on early Christianity,
because books not contained in the canon of the Old Testament are
cited in the New Testament. The covenanters seem to have had the
same rather broad conception of Scripture as Jesus and the early
church.

We have already dealt with the sect's interpretation of the Scriptures as an item in the history of Judaism. The Habakkuk Commentary in particular invites comparison with the New Testament
in this respect. In both cases it is believed that the true meaning of
prophecy has been communicated by a new revelation. The mode
of interpretation is much the same also. The teacher of righteousness, however, is not said to have fulfilled prophecy himself as
Jesus did, though something like this is involved in what is said

about "the star." In general the ideas concerning the interpretation of the Bible that Jesus and the writers of the New Testament accepted were those which were prevalent at the time in Judaism, though some of them may have been more characteristic of such groups as the covenanters than they were of Judaism at large.

Together with the theological content of the New Testament, the vocabulary with which its doctrines are expressed is illustrated abundantly by the Qumran texts. To understand what the words used by Jesus and the Apostles would mean to their hearers or readers, one must know how the same words were used in contemporary Jewish literature. At this point the Dead Sea Scrolls substantially enrich the material at our disposal. In the Gospels particularly, the Aramaic language of Jesus and the first disciples lies just under the surface of the Greek text. Here most of all, but also in the rest of the New Testament, the associations which the words had for those who first heard and preached the gospel become clearer as we read the literature of their contemporaries, the covenanters of Qumran.

Literary forms of composition used in the New Testament, as well as theological ideas and vocabulary, are in some cases much like those exemplified by the Dead Sea Scrolls. The canticles in the first two chapters of the Gospel of Luke, which were probably first composed in Hebrew, resemble the Thanksgiving Psalms in some respects, though they have none of the obscure, perhaps deliberately cryptic allusions with which the Thanksgiving Psalms abound. In Colossians 1:12–14 a quotation of an early Christian hymn is seen by some scholars, and it has been declared similar in style and form as well as thought to the Thanksgiving Psalms. The hortatory sections of the epistles in the New Testament have been compared with the Manual of Discipline and the Damascus Document; here, however, the parallels in Greek literature are much closer.

All these parallels and contacts, and many others that have been adduced, are important for the study of the New Testament. They are no less significant because some scholars have exaggerated their importance. It is not necessary to suppose that any of the

writers of the New Testament had ever heard of the particular
sect that produced the Dead Sea Scrolls, and I see no definite evidence that they had. Why are the covenanters—or, for that matter, the Essenes—nowhere mentioned in the New Testament?
There is no reticence with regard to the Pharisees and Sadducees
or the followers of John the Baptist.

For myself I must go farther and confess that, after studying the
Dead Sea Scrolls for seven years, I do not find my understanding
of the New Testament substantially affected. Its Jewish background is clearer and better understood, but its meaning has neither been changed nor significantly clarified. Perhaps I simply cannot see what is before my eyes. When visiting archeological excavations, I have sometimes been unable, with the utmost good
will, to see things pointed out by the excavators. It is true that a
trained eye can often see what is invisible to the uninitiated. It
is also true that scholars, being human, sometimes fail to distinguish between trained perception and uncritical imagination.

But why expect too much? Is it not enough that we can interpret
the New Testament with more assurance of perfect understanding
because we know better the intellectual and spiritual setting in
which it was written? And, knowing more fully the world into
which the Gospel came, its deep devotion and high hopes as well
as its pathetic aberrations, we can the better realize what the
Gospel brought to that world. Perhaps the best thing the Dead
Sea Scrolls can do for us is to make us appreciate our Bible all the
more by contrast.

Connections between the Dead Sea Scrolls and the post-apos-
tolic Christian writings offer a fruitful field for study. One of the
French Dominican fathers at Jerusalem, J. P. Audet, has examined
the connections between the Manual of Discipline and the account
of the "Two Ways" contained in the Epistle of Barnabas and the
Teaching of the Twelve Apostles. In the second division of the
Manual of Discipline he finds a literary framework and a development of thought almost identical with those of the Two Ways,
though with great difference in detail. So close is the relationship
that he believes the author of the Two Ways may have been a

member of the Qumran covenanters, or at least may have been acquainted with them; in any case the moral teaching of the Manual of Discipline must have been well known at the beginning of the Christian era. The same scholar finds also a relationship between the Manual of Discipline and the Shepherd of Hermas so close as to suggest that Hermas goes back of the Christian apocryphal literature to the ideas presented in the Manual of Discipline. Here is an area of study calling for further exploration.

SUMMARY

Much obviously remains to be done in the investigation of the Dead Sea Scrolls. The exhaustive study that is needed will take many years and will require the attention of many scholars. Before final conclusions can be reached, all the texts must be sorted out, deciphered, and published. Meanwhile, however, much is already assured. The "battle of the scrolls" concerning their dating has been settled, and the views first advanced on the basis of paleography still hold the field, even though at one point or another the lines may have to be rectified.

The dates of composition of the individual documents are still uncertain; consequently the origin and history of the sect still need clarification. Further study of the archeological data will help in these matters, but it may leave many questions still unanswered. While the time when the site now known as Khirbet Qumran was occupied by the sect has been fixed within the decades from 100 B.C. to 70 A.D., the history of the group before the establishment of the community at that place can only be inferred from the texts. The organization and its extensive library may have been much older than the settlement in the Wady Qumran.

The relation of the community to the groups in Judaism known from other sources is still somewhat obscure. The identity of the covenanters with the Essenes in particular is largely a matter of definition. If the covenanters were not Essenes, they were in any case closely related and lived in the same region.

Like the Christian monastic orders of the Middle Ages, the

covenanters rendered a service to biblical scholars by making and preserving manuscripts of the Bible, even though most of these have survived only in small scraps. For Isaiah and for two of the three chapters of Habakkuk we have fairly complete texts. For practically all the other books of the Old Testament we have some fragments. The scrolls are therefore very important for textual criticism. For the interpretation and theology of the Old Testament they have relatively little value.

The doctrines and practices of the covenanters substantially enrich our knowledge of Judaism at the time just before and during the origin and early growth of Christianity. It is now abundantly clear that we cannot understand the Judaism of the Roman period simply in terms of the Pharisees and Sadducees. The tree whose trunk was the Old Testament had then many branches which later were lopped off or withered away.

The enlarged understanding of Judaism contributes in turn to our understanding of the New Testament in its relation to its background and derivation, and all the more so because the beliefs, ideals, organization, and rites of the covenanters, as compared with those of the early church, exhibit both impressive similarities and even more significant contrasts.

PART SIX

TRANSLATIONS

Explanatory note: In the first three of the following translations asterisks are used to indicate places where the text, if not wholly destroyed, is preserved in such a fragmentary condition that a connected translation is impossible. In the other two documents such places are so numerous and extensive that only the most fully preserved portions are here translated.

Dots indicate brief gaps in the text. Occasionally, however, where the missing text can be restored by conjecture with a reasonable degree of probability, this has been done without any indication in the translation. In two or three places repetitions that were obviously caused by a scribe's carelessness have been eliminated.

In the Damascus Document, which is here included because of its close connection with the Dead Sea Scrolls, the numbered divisions correspond to the chapters in the translation of R. H. Charles. In the Habakkuk Commentary the numbers given are those of the chapters and verses in the biblical text of Habakkuk. For the Manual of Discipline only the most obvious major divisions are indicated.

Some readers may be disappointed that translations of the Isaiah manuscripts are not included. The fact is that most of the differences between these manuscripts and the traditional Hebrew text do not involve changes of meaning that would be evident in a translation, and the differences that do involve such changes are not sufficiently frequent to justify taking the space for translations of these texts.

A. The Damascus Document

Part of this composition exists in two forms, that of Manuscript A being briefer than that of Manuscript B. Portions contained only in the latter are here enclosed in brackets and marked *Ms. B.*

History and Exhortation

I. And now listen, all you who know righteousness and understand the works of God. For he has a controversy with all flesh, and will execute judgment upon all who despise him. For when those who forsook him trespassed, he hid his face from Israel and from his sanctuary, and gave them up to the sword; but when he remembered the covenant of the ancients, he left a remnant to Israel and did not give them up to destruction. And in the period of the wrath—three hundred and ninety years, when he gave them into the hand of Nebuchadnezzar, king of Babylon—he visited them and caused to sprout from Israel and Aaron a root of planting to inherit his land and to grow fat in the goodness of his soil. Then they perceived their iniquity and knew that they were guilty men; yet they were like men blind and groping for the way for twenty years. And God observed their works, that they sought him with a perfect heart; and he raised up for them a teacher of righteousness to lead them in the way of his heart. And he made known to later generations what he did to a later generation, to a congregation of treacherous men, those who turned aside out of the way.

This was the time concerning which it was written, "Like a stubborn heifer, Israel was stubborn," when arose the man of scorn, who preached to Israel lying words and led them astray in a trackless wilderness, so that he brought low their iniquitous pride, so that they turned aside from the paths of righteousness, and removed the landmark which the forefathers had fixed in their inheritance, so making the curses of his covenant cleave to them, delivering them to the sword that wreaks the vengeance of the covenant. For they sought smooth things, and chose illusions, and looked for breaches, and chose the fair neck; and they justified the wicked and condemned the righteous, transgressed the covenant and violated the statute. And they banded together against the life of the righteous, and all who walked uprightly their soul abhorred, and they pursued them with the sword and exulted in the strife of the people. Then was kindled the wrath of God against their congregation, laying waste all their multitude; and their deeds were uncleanness before him.

II. And now listen to me, all you who have entered the covenant, and I will uncover your ears as to the ways of the wicked. God loves the knowledge of wisdom; and sound wisdom he has set before him; prudence and knowledge minister to him. Longsuffering is with him, and abundance of pardon to forgive those who turn from transgression, but power and might and great wrath with flames of fire by all the angels of destruction upon those who turn aside from the way and abhor the statute, so that they shall have no remnant or survival.

For God did not choose them from the beginning of the world, but before they were established he knew their works and abhorred their generations from of old, and he hid his face from the land and from his people until they were consumed; for he knew the years of abiding and the number and explanation of their periods for all who exist in the ages, and the things that come to pass even to what will come in their periods for all the years of eternity.

But in all of them he raised up for himself men called by name, in order to leave a remnant to the land, and to fill the face of the world with their seed. And he caused them to know by his anointed his Holy Spirit and a revelation of truth; and in the explanation of his name are their names. But those he hated he caused to go astray.

III. And now, my sons, listen to me, and I will uncover your eyes to see and understand the works of God, and to choose what he likes and reject what he hates; to walk perfectly in all his ways, and not to go about with thoughts of a guilty impulse and eyes of fornication; for many went astray in them, and mighty men of valor stumbled in them, formerly and until now. In their walking in the rebelliousness of their hearts the watchers of heaven fell; in it they were caught who did not keep the commandment of God, and their children, whose height was like the loftiness of the cedars, and whose bodies were like the mountains, fell thereby. Yea, all flesh that was on the dry land fell; yea, it perished; and they were as though they had not been, because they did their own will and did not keep the commandment of their Maker, until his anger was kindled against them.

IV. In it the sons of Noah and their families went astray; in it they were cut off. Abraham did not walk in it, and he was accounted as God's friend, because he kept the commandments of God and did not choose the will of his own spirit. And he passed on the commandment to Isaac and Jacob, and they kept it and were recorded as friends of God and possessors of the covenant forever.

The sons of Jacob went astray in them and were punished according to their error, and their sons in Egypt walked in the stubbornness of their hearts, taking counsel against the commandments of God and doing each what was right in his own eyes. They ate blood, and he cut off their males in the desert. And he said to them in Kadesh, "Go up and take possession of the land," but they hardened their spirit and did not listen to the voice of their Maker, the commandments of their Teacher, but murmured in their tents.

Then the anger of God was kindled against their congregation; their children perished by it, their kings were cut off by it, and their mighty men perished by it; and their land was made desolate by it. By it the first that entered the covenant became guilty, and they were delivered to the sword, because they forsook the covenant of God and chose their own will, and went about after the stubbornness of their heart, each doing his own will.

V. But with those who held fast to the commandments of God, those who were left of them, God established his covenant for Israel to eternity, revealing to them hidden things in which all Israel had gone astray. His holy Sabbaths and his glorious festivals, his righteous testimonies and his true ways, and the desires of his will, by which, if a man does them, he shall live, he opened up before them. And they dug a well for many waters, and he who despises them shall not live. But they defiled themselves with the transgression of man, and in the ways of the unclean woman, and they said, "That is for us." But God in his wondrous mysteries forgave their iniquity and pardoned their transgression, and he built for them a sure house in Israel, the like of which has not existed from of old or until now. Those who hold fast to it are for eternal life, and all the glory of man is theirs; as God established it for them by the prophet Ezekiel, saying, "The priests and the Levites and the sons of Zadok, who kept the charge of my sanctuary when the sons of Israel went astray from me, they shall offer to me fat and blood."

VI. The priests are the captivity of Israel who went forth from the land of Judah, and the Levites are those who joined them; and the sons of Zadok are the elect of Israel, those called by name, who will abide at the end of days. Behold the explanation of their names according to their generations, and the period of their abiding, and the number of their distresses, and the years of their sojourning, and the explanation of their works, the first saints whom God forgave, and who justified the righteous and condemned the wicked.

All who come after them must do according to the explanation of the law in which the forefathers were instructed until the completion of the period of these years. According to the covenant which God established with the forefathers to forgive their sins, so God will forgive them. And at the completion of the period to the number of these years they shall no more join themselves to the house of Judah, but every one must stand up on his watchtower. The wall has been built; the decree is far away.

And during all these years Belial will be let loose in Israel, as God spoke by the prophet Isaiah the son of Amoz, saying, "Terror and the pit and the snare are upon you, O inhabitant of the land." This means the three nets of Belial of which Levi the son of Jacob spoke, in which he caught Israel and set them before them as three kinds of righteousness. The first is fornication; the second is wealth; the third is the pollution of the sanctuary. He who gets out of one will be caught in another, and he who is rescued from one will be caught in another.

VII. The builders of the wall who follow a precept—the precept is a preacher, because it says, "They will surely preach"—they will be caught in two nets: in fornication by taking two wives during their lifetime, whereas the foundation of the creation is, "male and female he created them"; and those who went into the ark, "Two by two they went into the ark." And concerning the prince it is written, "He shall not multiply wives for himself."

But David did not read the sealed book of the law which was in the ark; for it was not opened in Israel from the day of the death of Eleazar and Joshua and the elders who served the Ashtaroth, but was hidden and not disclosed until Zadok arose. The deeds of David were overlooked, except the blood of Uriah, and God left them to him.

Moreover they defile the sanctuary, because they do not separate according to the law, but lie with her who sees the blood of her issue. And they take each his brother's daughter or his sister's daughter; but Moses said "You shall not approach your mother's sister; she is your mother's near kinswoman." And the ordinance of intercourse for males is written, and like them for the women. And if the brother's daughter uncovers the nakedness of the brother of her father; she is a near kinswoman.

Moreover they defiled their holy spirit, and with a tongue of blasphemies they opened the mouth against the statutes of God's covenant, saying, "They are not established." And abominations they speak concerning them. They "all kindle fire and set brands alight!" "The webs of spiders" are their webs, and "adders' eggs" are their eggs. He who is near them shall not be counted innocent; the more he does it, the more shall he be held guilty, unless he was forced.

But of old God punished their works, and his anger was kindled because of their doings. For "it is not a people of understanding"; "they are a nation void of counsel," because there is no understanding in them. For of old arose Moses and Aaron through the prince of lights, and Belial raised Jannes and his brother with his evil device, when Israel was delivered the first time.

VIII. In the period of the destruction of the land arose the removers of the landmark and led Israel astray. And the land became desolate, because they spoke rebellion against the commandments of God by Moses, and also by the holy anointed ones; and they prophesied falsehood to turn away Israel from following God.

But God remembered the covenant of the forefathers, and raised up from Aaron men of understanding, and from Israel wise men. And he made them listen, and they dug the well. "A well which princes dug, which the nobles of the people delved with the staff." The well is the law, and those who dug it are the captivity of Israel, who went out from the land of Judah and sojourned in the land of Damascus, all of whom God called princes, because they sought him, and their glory was not rejected in the mouth of anyone. And the staff (or legislator) is he who studies the law, as Isaiah said, "He produces an instrument for his work." And the nobles of the people are those who come to dig the well with the staves (or rules) which the staff (or legislator) prescribed to walk in during the whole period of wickedness; and without them they shall not attain to the arising of him who will teach righteousness at the end of days.

And all who have been brought into the covenant not to come into the sanctuary to kindle fire on his altar in vain shall become those who shut the door, as God said, "Who among you will shut his door, so that you will not kindle fire on my altar in vain?"—unless they observe to do according to the explanation of the law for the period of wickedness; and to separate from the sons of the pit; and to keep away from the unclean wealth of wickedness acquired by vowing and devoting and by appropriating the wealth of the sanctuary; and not to rob the poor of his people, so that widows become their spoil, and they murder the fatherless; and to make a separation between the unclean and the clean, and to make men know the difference between the holy and the common; and to keep the Sabbath day according to its explanation, and the festivals and the day of the fast, according to the decision of those who entered the new covenant in the land of Damascus; to contribute their holy things according to their explanation; to love each his brother as himself; and to hold fast the hand of the poor and the needy and the proselyte; and to seek every one the peace of his brother; for a man shall not trespass against his next of kin; and to keep away from harlots according to the ordinance; to rebuke each his brother according to the commandment, and not to bear a grudge from day to day; and to separate from all uncleannesses according to their ordinances; for a man shall not make abominable his holy spirit, as God separated for them.

For all who walk in these things in perfection of holiness, according to all his teaching, God's covenant stands fast, to make them live to a thousand generations. [*Ms. B:* As it is written, "Who keeps covenant and steadfast love for him who loves him and for those who keep his commandments to a thousand generations.]

IX. And if they dwell in camps according to the order of the earth [*Ms. B:* which was from of old] and take wives [*Ms. B:* according to the guidance of the law] and beget sons, they shall walk according to the law and according to the ordinances of the teachings, according to the order of the law, as it says, "between a man and his wife and between a father and his son."

But all who reject it when God visits the land, the recompense of the wicked is to be rendered to them, when the word comes to pass which is written in the words of the prophet Isaiah the son of Amoz, who said, "He will bring upon you and upon your people and upon your father's house such days as have not come since the day that Ephraim departed from Judah." [*Ms. B:* But all who reject the commandments and the statutes, the recompense of the wicked is to be rendered to them when God visits the land, when the word comes to pass which was written by the prophet Zechariah, "O sword, awake against my shepherd and against the man who stands next to me, says God; smite the shepherd, and the sheep shall be scattered, and I will turn my hand against the little ones." Now "those who give heed to him" are the poor of the flock.]

When the two houses of Israel separated, Ephraim departed from Judah; and all who turned back were given over to the sword, but those who stood firm escaped to the land of the north, as it says, "And I will exile the *sikkuth* of your king and the *kiyyun* of your images from the tents of Damascus." The books of the law are the booth of the king, as it says, "And I will raise up the booth of David that is fallen"; the king is the assembly; and the *kiyyun* of the images are the books of the prophets, whose words Israel despised; and the star is the interpreter of the law who came to Damascus, as it is written, "A star shall come forth out of Jacob, and a sceptre shall rise out of Israel." The sceptre is the prince of the whole congregation. And when he arises, he "shall break down all the sons of Seth."

These escaped in the period of the first visitation, but those who turned back they delivered to the sword [*Ms. B:* when comes the Messiah of Aaron and Israel; as it was during the period of the first visitation, of which he spake by Ezekiel, "to set a mark upon the foreheads of those who sign and groan," but the rest were delivered to "the sword that executes vengeance for the covenant."] And such shall be the judgment of all of those who enter his covenant that do not hold fast to the oath, being visited for destruction through Belial. That is the day on which God will visit [*Ms. B:* as he has spoken.]

The princes of Judah have become those [*Ms. B:* who remove the landmark; upon whom I will pour wrath like water] upon whom thou wilt pour wrath. For they will hope for healing, but all the rebellious will crush them, [*Ms. B:* for they entered the covenant of repentance;] because they did not turn away from the way of the treacherous, but defiled themselves in the ways of harlots and in the wealth of wickedness and revenge and bearing a grudge, each against his brother, and hating each his neighbor; and they hid themselves each against his near kin, and drew near to unchastity, and behaved arrogantly for wealth and unjust gain; and they did each what was right in his own eyes, and chose each the stubbornness of his heart; and they did not separate from the people [*Ms. B:* and their sin]; and they cast off restraint with a high hand, walking in the way of the wicked, concerning whom God said, "Their wine is the poison of serpents and the cruel venom of asps." The serpents are the kings of the peoples, and their wine is their ways, and the venom of asps is the head of the kings of Greece, who comes to take vengeance upon them.

But all these things those who built the wall and daubed it with whitewash did not understand, for a raiser of wind and preacher of lies. [*Ms. B:* one walking in wind and weighing storms and preaching to man for a lie] preached to them, because the anger of God was kindled against all his congregations, and as Moses said, "Not because of your righteousness or the uprightness of your heart are you going in to possess these nations, but because of his love for your fathers, and because of his keeping the oath." And such is the judgment of the captivity of Israel; they turned aside from the way of the people.

In God's love for the forefathers, who stirred up after him [*Ms. B:* who testified against the people after God], he loved those who came after them, for theirs is the covenant of the fathers. But in his hatred of the builders of the wall [*Ms. B:* But God hates and abhors the builders of the wall] his anger was kindled [*Ms. B:* against them and against all who follow them].

And such is the judgment of every man who rejects the commandments of God and forsakes them; and they turn away in the stubbornness of their hearts. This is the word that Jeremiah spoke to Baruch the son of Neriah, and Elisha to his servant Gehazi. All the men who entered the new covenant in the land of Damascus, [*Ms. B:* but turned back and acted treacherously and departed from the well of living water, shall not be reckoned in the company of the people, and in its book they shall not be written, from the day of the gathering in of the unique teacher until arises a Messiah from Aaron and from Israel. And such is the judgment for all who enter the congregation of the men of perfect holiness, and he abhors doing the precepts of upright men. He is the man who is melted in the furnace. When his deeds become known, he shall be expelled from the congregation as one whose lot has not fallen among those who are taught of God. According to his trespass the men of knowledge shall rebuke him until the day when he comes back to stand in the meeting of the men of perfect holiness. And when his deeds become known, according to the interpretation of the law in which the men of perfect holiness walk, no man shall agree with him in wealth and service; for all the holy ones of the Most High have cursed him.

And such shall be the judgment of every one who rejects the former ones and the latter ones; those who have taken idols into their hearts and walked in the stubbornness of their hearts. They have no share in the house of the law. According to the judgment of their fellows who turned back with the men of scorn shall they be judged, for they spoke error against the statutes of righteousness and rejected the firm covenant which they had established in the land of Damascus, that is, the new covenant. And neither they nor their families shall have a share in the house of the law.

From the day of the gathering in of the unique teacher until the annihilation of all the men of war who returned with the man of the lie will be about forty years; and in that period will be kindled the anger of God against Israel, as it says, "There is no king and no prince and no judge, and none who rebuke in righteousness." Those who repented of the transgressions of Jacob have kept the covenant of God.

Then each will speak to his neighbor, to strengthen one another, that their steps may hold fast to the way of God; and God will listen to their words and hear, and a book of remembrance will be written before him for those who fear God and think of his name, until salvation and righteousness are revealed for those who fear God. Then you shall again discern between the righteous and the wicked, between him who serves God and him who does not serve him. And he will show kindness to thousands, to those who love him and keep his commandments, to a thousand generations, after the manner of the house of Peleg, who went out from the holy city and leaned upon God during the period when Israel transgressed and polluted the sanctuary; but they turned to God. And he smote the people with few words. All of them, each according to his spirit, shall be judged in the holy council. And all who have broken through the boundary of the law, of those who entered the covenant, at the appearing of the glory of God to Israel shall be cut off from the midst of the camp, and with them all who condemn Judah in the days of its trials.

But all who hold fast to these ordinances, going out and coming in according to the law, and who listen to the voice of a teacher and confess before God, "We have sinned, we have done wickedly, both we and our fathers, in walking contrary to the statutes of the covenant; right and true are thy judgments against us"; all who do not lift a hand against his holy statutes and his righteous judgments and his true testimonies; who are instructed in the former judgments with which the men of the community were judged; who give ear to the voice of a teacher of righteousness and do not reject the statutes of righteousness when they hear them—they shall rejoice and be glad, and their hearts shall be strong, and they shall prevail over all the sons of the world, and God will forgive them, and they shall see his salvation, because they have taken refuge in his holy name.]

Community Regulations

X. Any man who dedicates anything which is the property of the camp, according to the statutes of the Gentiles he must be put to death: And as for what it says, "You shall not take vengeance or bear a grudge against the sons of your own people," any man of those who enter the covenant who brings a charge against his neighbor without having rebuked him before witnesses, and brings it in the heat of his anger, and tells his elders, in order to bring him into contempt, he is an avenger and grudge-bearer; but nothing is written except, "He takes vengeance on his adversaries and bears a grudge against his enemies." If he kept silence about him from day to day, but in the heat of his anger against him spoke against him concerning a capital offense, he has wronged him, because he did not confirm the commandment of God, who said to him, "You shall reprove your neighbor, lest you bear sin because of him."

Concerning the oath: as it says, "Let not your own hand deliver you," if a man makes one take an oath in the open field, not in the presence of the judges or at their command, his own hand has delivered him.

When anything is lost, and it is not known who stole it from the property of the camp in which it was stolen, one shall make its owners take the oath of the curse, and he who hears, if he knows and does not tell, shall be guilty.

When any restitution for guilt is made of something which has no owners, he who makes restitution shall confess to the priest, and it shall all go to him in addition to the ram of the guilt-offering. And so everything lost which is found and has no owner shall go to the priests, because he who found it does not know the right of it. If no owners are found for it, they shall keep it.

When a man trespasses in any matter against the law and his neighbor sees it and he is alone; if it is a capital offense, he shall tell it in his presence with an accusation to the superintendent, and the superintendent shall write it down with his own hand, until he does it again before one witness; then he shall return and make it known to the superintendent. If he is caught again before one witness, the case against him is complete. But if there are two and they testify concerning one offense (*or*, but they testify concerning a different offense), the man shall be separated from the sacred food by himself, if they are trustworthy, and on the day that they see the man they shall tell it to the superintendent.

And concerning the statute: They shall accept two trustworthy witnesses, and concerning one offense, to separate the sacred food. And there shall not be accepted a witness by the judges, to have a man put to death on his testimony, whose days have not been fulfilled so as to pass over to those who are numbered, one who fears God. No man shall be believed against his neighbor as a witness who transgresses a word of the commandment with a high hand, until he is cleansed so that he can return.

XI. And this is the order for the judges of the congregation: There shall be as many as ten men chosen by the congregation according to the time, four of the tribe of Levi and Aaron and six from Israel, instructed in the book of *hgw* and in the teachings of the covenant, from five and twenty years to sixty years old. But no one shall take the position from the age of sixty years and upward to judge the congregation; for when man transgressed, his days were diminished, and in the heat of God's anger against the inhabitants of the earth he commanded that their knowledge should depart from them before they completed their days.

XII. Concerning purification with water: Let not a man wash in water that is filthy or not enough for covering a man. Let him not purify in it any vessel. And any pool in a rock in which there is not enough covering, which an unclean person has touched, its water is unclean like the water of a vessel.

XIII. Concerning the Sabbath, to observe it according to its ordinance: Let not a man do work on the sixth day from the time when the sun's disk is its full width away from the gate, for that is what it says: "Observe the Sabbath day to keep it holy." And on the Sabbath day let not a man utter anything foolish or trifling. Let him not lend anything to his neighbor. Let them not shed blood over wealth and gain. Let him not speak of matters of work and labor to be done on the morrow. Let not a man walk in the field to do the work of his business on the Sabbath. Let him not walk out of his city more than a thousand cubits. Let not a man eat on the Sabbath day anything but what is prepared. And of what is perishing in the field let him not eat. And let him not drink anything except what is in the camp. If he is on the way and is going down to battle let him drink where he stands, but let him not draw water into any vessel. Let him not send the son of a foreigner to do his business on the Sabbath day. Let not a man put on garments that are filthy or that were put in storage unless they have been washed in water or rubbed with frankincense. Let not a man go hungry of his own accord on the Sabbath. Let not a man walk after an animal to pasture it outside of his city more than two thousand cubits. Let him not lift his hand to strike it with his fist. If it is stubborn, let him not take it out of his house. Let not a man take anything from the house out-of-doors, or from out-of-doors into the house, and if he is in a booth, let him not take anything out of it or bring anything into it. Let him not open a sealed vessel on the Sabbath. Let not a man take on him ointments to go out and come in on the Sabbath. Let him not lift up in his dwelling house rock or earth. Let not the nurse take up the sucking child to go out and come in on the Sabbath. Let not a man provoke his male or female slave or his hired servant on the Sabbath. Let not a man help an animal to give birth on the Sabbath day; and if she lets her young fall into a cistern or a ditch, let him not raise it on the Sabbath. Let not a man rest in a place near to Gentiles on the Sabbath. Let not a man profane the Sabbath for the sake of wealth or gain on the Sabbath. And if any person falls into a place of water, or into a place, let not a man come up by a ladder or rope or instrument. Let not a man bring up anything to the altar on the Sabbath except the burnt offering of the Sabbath, for thus it is written, "beside your Sabbaths."

XIV. Let not a man send to the altar burnt offering or meal offering or frankincense or wood by the hand of a man who is unclean with any of the uncleannesses, allowing him to make the altar unclean; for it is written, "The sacrifice of the wicked is an abomination, but the prayer of the righteous is like an acceptable offering." And when anyone enters the house of worship, let him not enter while unclean, requiring washing. And when the trumpets of assembly sound, let him act before or afterward, or so that they shall not stop the whole service on the Sabbath; it is holy. Let not a man lie with a woman in the city of the sanctuary making unclean the city of the sanctuary with their impurity.

Any man in whom the spirits of Belial rule, and who speaks rebellion, shall be judged according to the judgment of the medium and wizard. And every one who goes astray so that he profanes the Sabbath and the feasts shall not be put to death, but the sons of man shall be responsible for taking charge of him; and if he is healed of it, they shall have charge of him seven years, and after that he shall come into the assembly.

Let no one stretch out his hand to shed the blood of a man of the Gentiles on account of wealth and gain; moreover let him not take any of their wealth, lest they blaspheme, unless it is by the counsel of the society of Israel. Let not a man sell animals or birds that are clean to the Gentiles, lest they sacrifice them. And from his threshing-floor or his winepress let him not sell them anything among all his possessions. And let him not sell them his male or female slave who entered with him into the covenant of Abraham.

Let not a man make himself abominable with any living creature or creeping thing by eating of them, from the larvae of bees to any living creature that creeps in the water. And let not fish be eaten unless they have been split alive and their blood has been poured out. And all the locusts according to their kinds shall be put into fire or into water while they are still alive, for this is the law of their creation. And all wood and stones and dust which are polluted by the uncleanness of men shall be considered like them as polluting: according to their uncleanness he who touches them shall be unclean. And every instrument, nail, or peg in the wall which is with the dead in the house shall be unclean with the uncleanness of an implement for work.

XV. The order of the session of the cities of Israel: According to these ordinances separation is to be made between the unclean and the clean, and the difference between the holy and the common is to be made known. And these are the statutes for the wise man, that he may walk in them with every living being according to the law of one time and another. And according to this ordinance the seed of Israel shall walk, and they shall not be cursed.

And this is the order of the session of the camps: Those who walk in these ways during the period of wickedness, until arises the Messiah of Aaron and Israel, must be as many as ten men at least, by thousands and hundreds and fifties and tens. And in a place having ten there shall not be absent a priest learned in the book of *hgw*. According to his word shall they all be ruled. And if he is not qualified in all these ways, but a man of the Levites is qualified in these ways, the decision to go out or come in for all who enter the camp shall be made according to his direction. And if there is a judgment against a man concerning the law of disease, then the priest shall come and stand in the camp, and the superintendent shall instruct him in the explanation of the law. And if he is simple, he shall lock him up; for theirs is the judgment.

XVI. And this is the order for the superintendent of the camp: He shall instruct the many in the works of God and make them understand his wondrous mighty acts; and he shall recount before them the things that have been done of old in their divisions. And he shall have mercy on them as a father on his sons, and shall bring back all their erring ones as a shepherd does with his flock. He shall loose all the ties that bind them, so that there shall be none oppressed and crushed in his congregation. And every one who is added to his congregation he shall examine him as to his works, his understanding, his strength, his might, and his wealth. And they shall register him in his place according to his being in the lot of the truth. No man of the sons of the camp shall have authority to bring a man into the congregation without the word of the superintendent of the camp. And no man of all those who enter the covenant of God shall do business with the sons of the pit except hand to hand. And no man shall make an agreement for buying and selling unless he has told the superintendent who is in the camp.

*　　　*　　　*

For all who walk in these ways the covenant of God stands fast, to rescue them from all snares of the pit; for the simple go on and are punished.

XVII. And this is the order of the session of all the camps: They shall all be enrolled by their names; the priests first, the Levites second, the sons of Israel third, and the proselyte fourth. And so they shall sit, and so they shall ask concerning everything. And the priest who is appointed at the head of the many shall be from thirty to sixty years old, instructed in the book of *hgw* and in all the ordinances of the law, so as to speak them rightly. And the superintendent who is over all the camps shall be from thirty years old to fifty years old, proficient in every secret counsel of men and in every tongue according to their number. According to his direction those who enter the congregation shall enter, each in his turn. And any word which any man has to speak he shall speak to the superintendent concerning any controversy and decision.

XVIII. And this is the order of the many, for settling all their affairs: The wages of two days for every month at least—and they shall put it into the hand of the superintendent, and the judges shall give from it for orphans, and from it they shall support the poor and the needy, and for the aged man who dies, and for the wanderer, and for him who goes into captivity to a foreign people, and for the virgin who has no redeemer, and for the slave for whom nobody seeks any work of the association.

* * *

XIX. He shall not swear either by *aleph* and *lamed* or by *aleph* and *daleth*.

* * *

If he swears and transgresses, he profanes the Name. And if by the curses of the covenant he has sworn before the judges, and has transgressed, he is guilty; and he shall confess and make restitution, that he may not bear sin and die. The sons of those who enter the covenant for all Israel for an eternal decree, when they attain to passing into the number of those enrolled, shall be obligated by the oath of the covenant.

And such is the ordinance during the whole period of wickedness for every one who turns from his corrupt way. On the day that he speaks with the superintendent of the many they shall enroll him with the oath of the covenant which Moses made with Israel, the covenant to return to the law of Moses with the whole heart and with the whole soul, to what one finds to do during the whole period of wickedness. But no man shall tell him the ordinances until he stands before the superintendent, lest he prove simple when he examines him.

* * *

Therefore the man shall obligate himself to return to the law of Moses, for in it everything is specified.

XX. The explanation of their periods, for the blindness of Israel to all these, is specified in the *Book of the Divisions of the Times according to their Jubilees and in their Weeks*. And on the day that the man obligates himself to return to the law of Moses the angel of enmity will depart from behind him if he makes good his words. Therefore Abraham was circumcised on the day that he received knowledge. And as for what it says, "What has passed your lips you shall keep," to perform it; no binding oath which a man takes upon himself, to do anything according to the law, shall he redeem even at the cost of death. If a man takes anything upon himself contrary to the law, let him not, even at the cost of death, perform it. As for any oath of a woman, of which it says, "Her husband must annul her oath," let not a man annul an oath of which he does not know whether it should be confirmed or annulled. If it is to transgress the covenant, he shall annul it and not confirm it. And such is the ordinance for her father. Concerning the law of the free will offerings, a man shall not vow for the altar anything taken by force.

*   *   *

B. The Habakkuk Commentary

~~~~~~

Quotations from Habakkuk are in italics.

* * *

(*Chapter 1:4*) *So the law is slacked.* This means that they rejected the law of God. *And justice never goes forth, for the wicked man encompasses the righteous man.* This means that the wicked man is the wicked priest, and the righteous man is the teacher of righteousness.

* * *

(5) *Look among the nations, and see; Wonder and be astounded. For I am doing a work in your days that you would not believe if it were told.* This means those who acted treacherously together with the man of the lie, for they did not heed the words of the teacher of righteousness from the mouth of God, and those who acted treacherously against the new covenant, for they did not believe the covenant of God but profaned his holy name. And truly the saying refers to those who will act treacherously at the end of days: that is, those who are ruthless against the covenant, who do not believe when they hear all the things that are coming upon the last generation from the mouth of the priest into whose heart God put wisdom to explain all the words of his servants the prophets, through whom God declared all the things that are coming upon his people and his congregation.

(6) *For lo, I am rousing the Chaldeans, that bitter and hasty nation.* This means the Kittim, who are swift and men of valor in battle, overthrowing rulers and subduing them in the dominion of the Kittim. They

take possession of many lands and do not believe in the statutes of God.

*　　*　　*

Over smooth ground they go, smiting and plundering the cities of the earth, for that is what it says: *to seize habitations not their own.*

(7) *Dread and terrible is he; from himself his justice and his exaltedness proceed.* This means the Kittim, the dread and terror of whom are on all the nations. And with deliberation all their planning is to work evil, and with cunning and deceit they proceed with all the peoples.

(8) *Swifter than leopards are his horses, and more fierce than evening wolves. His horsemen advance proudly, they spread out; from afar they fly like a vulture swift to devour.* (9) *They all come for violence; the aspect of their faces is an east wind.* This means the Kittim, who trample the earth with their horses and with their animals; and from afar they come, from the coasts of the sea, to devour all the peoples like a vulture without being satisfied. And with wrath and indignation, with hot ire and furious anger they deal with all the peoples; for that is what it says: *the aspect of their faces is an east wind. They gather captives like sand.*

*　　*　　*

(10) *At kings he scoffs, and of rulers he makes sport.* This means that they mock at great ones and despise honored men; of kings and princes they make sport, and scoff at a multitude of people. *He laughs at every fortress, and heaps up earth and captures it.* This means the rulers of the Kittim, who despise the fortresses of the peoples and with mockery laugh at them, and with a multitude of people they surround them to seize them, and in terror and dread they are delivered into their hands; and they overthrow them because of the iniquity of those who dwell in them.

(11) *Then the wind changes and passes on, and he makes his might his god.* This means the rulers of the Kittim, who by the counsel of a guilty house pass on, each before his fellow: their rulers come, one after another, to destroy the earth. *And he makes his might his god:* this means . . .

*　　*　　*

(12) *Art thou not from everlasting, O LORD my God, my Holy One? We shall not die. O LORD, thou hast ordained him for judgment, and thou, O Rock, hast established him to chastise him,* (13) *having eyes*

too pure to behold evil; and thou canst not look on wrong. This saying means that God will not destroy his people by the hand of the nations, but into the hand of his elect God will deliver the judgment of all the nations and by their chastisement all the wicked among his people will be punished; because they kept his commandments when they were in distress. For as for that which it says, *having eyes too pure to behold evil,* this means that they did not follow the lust of their eyes in the period of wickedness. *Why do ye look on faithless men, but thou art silent at the swallowing by the wicked man of one more righteous than he?* This means the house of Absalom and the men of their party, who kept silence at the chastisement of the teacher of righteousness, and did not help him against the man of the lie, who rejected the law in the midst of their whole congregation.

(14) *And thou madest man like the fish of the sea, like crawling things, to rule over them.* (15) *All of them with a hook he brings up, and drags them out with his net; he gathers them in his seine. Therefore he sacrifices to his net; therefore he rejoices and exults,* (16) *and burns incense to his seine; for by them fat is his portion, and his food is rich.*

* * *

the Kittim, and they gather their wealth with all their booty like the fish of the sea. And as for what it says, *therefore he sacrifices to his net and burns incense to his seine,* this means that they sacrifice to their standards, and their weapons of war are the object of their worship. *For by them fat is his portion, and his food is rich:* this means that they parcel out their yoke and their tribute, their food, upon all the peoples year by year, laying waste many lands.

(17) *Therefore he bares his sword continually, slaying nations, and has no pity.* This means the Kittim, who cause many to perish by the sword—youths, men, and old men; women and little children—and on the fruit of the womb they have no mercy.

(*Chapter 2:1*) *At my post I will take my stand, and station myself on my tower, and look forth to see what he will say to me, and what he will reply concerning my reproach.* (2) *And the LORD answered me and said, "Write the vision and make it plain upon the tablets, so that he may run who reads it.*

* * *

And God told Habakkuk to write the things that were to come upon the last generation, but the consummation of the period he did not make known to him. And as for what it says, *that he may run who reads it,* this means the teacher of righteousness, to whom God made known all the mysteries of the words of his servants the prophets.

(3) *For still the vision is for an appointed time; it hastens to the period and does not lie.* This means that the last period extends over and above all that the prophets said; for the mysteries of God are marvelous. *If it tarries, wait for it, for it will surely come; it will not delay.* This means the men of truth, the doers of the law, whose hands do not grow slack from the service of the truth, when the last period is stretched out over them. For all the periods of God will come to their fixed term, as he decreed for them in the mysteries of his wisdom.

(4) *Behold, puffed up, not upright is his soul in him.* This means that they make double the judgment upon themselves; they do not win acceptance when they are judged, for their souls are not upright. *But the righteous shall live by his faith.* This means all the doers of the law in the house of Judah, whom God will rescue from the house of judgment because of their labor and their faith in the teacher of righteousness.

(5) *Moreover wealth is treacherous, an arrogant man, and will not abide. His greed is as wide as Sheol; and he like death has never enough. To him are gathered all the nations, and to him are assembled all the peoples.* (6) *Shall not all of them take up their taunt against him, in scoffing derision of him, and say, "Woe to him who heaps up, but it is not his own! How long will he load himself with pledges?"* This means the wicked priest, who was named according to the truth when he first took office; but when he had begun to rule in Israel, his heart was lifted up, and he forsook God and betrayed the statutes because of wealth. He plundered and assembled the wealth of men of violence who rebelled against God. He took the wealth of peoples, adding to himself iniquity and guilt; and ways of abominations he wrought, in all impurity of uncleanness.

(7) *Will they not suddenly arise, those who torment you; will they not awake, those who torture you? Then you will be booty for them.* (8) *Because you have plundered many nations, all the remainder of peoples will plunder you.* This means the priest who rebelled . . .

* * *

his scourge with judgments of wickedness; and horrors of sore diseases they wrought in him, and vengeance in his body of flesh. And as for what it says, *Because you have plundered many nations, all the remnant of peoples will plunder you;* this means the last priests of Jerusalem, who assembled wealth and booty from the spoil of the peoples, but at the end of days their wealth with their spoil will be delivered into the hand of the army of the Kittim, for they are the remainder of the peoples. *For the blood of men and violence to the earth, to the city and all who dwell in it:* this means the wicked priest, whom, for the wrong done to the teacher of righteousness and the men of his party, God delivered into the hand of his enemies, afflicting him with a destroying scourge, in bitterness of soul, because he acted wickedly against his elect.

(9) *Woe to him who gets evil gain for his house, to set his nest on high, to be safe from the reach of harm!* (10) *You have devised shame to your house by cutting off many peoples; and you sin against yourself.* (11) *For the stone will cry out from the wall, and the beam from the woodwork respond.*

❖   ❖   ❖

so that its stones are in oppression and its wooden beam in robbery. And as for what it says, *by cutting off many peoples; and you sin against yourself;* this means it is the house of judgment, of which God will set the judgment in the midst of many peoples; and thence he will bring it up for judgment, and in their midst will condemn it and punish it with fire of brimstone.

(12) *Woe to him who builds a town in blood and founds a city in iniquity!* (13) *Is it not, behold, from Yahweh of hosts that peoples labor only for fire, and nations weary themselves for naught?* This saying means the preacher of the lie, who enticed many to build a city of delusion in blood and to establish a congregation in falsehood for the sake of its honor, making many grow weary of the service of delusion and making them pregnant with works of falsehood, that their toil may be in vain, to the end that they may come into judgments of fire, because they reviled and insulted God's elect.

(14) *For the earth will be filled with the knowledge of the glory of the LORD as the waters cover the sea.* This saying means that when they repent

❖   ❖   ❖

the lie. And afterward knowledge will be revealed to them like the waters of the sea in abundance.

(15) *Woe to him who makes his neighbors drink, who pours out his*

wrath; yea, he has made them drunk, to gaze on their festivals! This means the wicked priest, who persecuted the teacher of righteousness in order to confound him in the indignation of his wrath, wishing to banish him; and at the time of their festival of rest, the day of atonement, he appeared to them to confound them and to make them stumble on the day of fasting, their Sabbath of rest.

(16) *You are sated with ignominy instead of glory. Drink, you yourself, and stagger! The cup in the LORD's right hand will come around to you, and shame will come upon your glory!* This means the priest whose ignominy was greater than his glory, because he did not circumcise the foreskin of his heart, but walked in the ways of drunkenness, that his thirst might be removed. But the cup of the wrath of God will confound him, increasing his confusion. And the pain . . .

❋　❋　❋

(17) *For the violence done to Lebanon will overwhelm you; the destruction of the beasts will terrify you, for the blood of men and violence to a land, to a city and all who dwell in it.* This saying means the wicked priest, that to him may be paid his recompense, as he recompensed the poor; for Lebanon is the council of the community, and the beasts are the simple ones of Judah, the doers of the law. God will execute judgment upon him and destroy him, as he plotted to destroy the poor. And as for what it says, *for the blood of a city and violence to a land,* this means the city, that is Jerusalem, in which the wicked priest wrought abominable works and defiled God's sanctuary; *and violence to a land,* these are the cities of Judah, because he plundered the wealth of the poor.

(18) *What profit is a graven image when he who forms it has graven it, a molten image, a teacher of falsehood? For he who forms it relies on what he has formed, making dumb idols!* This saying means all the graven images of the nations, who formed them to worship them and bow down to them, yet they cannot rescue them on the day of judgment.

(19) *Woe to him who says to a wooden thing, Awake; to a dumb stone, Arise! Can this give revelation? Behold, it is overlaid with gold and silver, and there is no breath at all in it. But the LORD is in his holy temple; let all the earth keep silence before him!* This means all the nations who worship stone and wood; and in the day of judgment God will destroy all the worshipers of idols and the wicked from the earth.

C. The Manual of Discipline

~~~~~~

I—*Entering the Covenant*

*   *   *

. . . the order of the community; to seek God . . . ; to do what is good and upright before him as he commanded through Moses and through all his servants the prophets; to love all that he has chosen and hate all that he has rejected; to be far from all evil and cleave to all good works; to do truth and righteousness and justice in the land; to walk no longer in the stubbornness of a guilty heart and eyes of fornication, doing all evil; to bring all those who have offered themselves to do God's statutes into a covenant of steadfast love; to be united in the counsel of God and to walk before him perfectly with regard to all the things that have been revealed for the appointed times of their testimonies; to love all the sons of light, each according to his lot in the counsel of God, and to hate all the sons of darkness, each according to his guilt in vengeance of God.

And all who have offered themselves for his truth shall bring all their knowledge and strength and wealth into the community of God, to purify their knowledge in the truth of God's statutes, and to distribute their strength according to the perfection of his ways and all their property according to his righteous counsel; not to transgress in any one of all the words of God in their periods; not to advance their times or postpone any of their appointed festivals; not to turn aside from his true statutes, going to the right or to the left.

And all who come into the order of the community shall pass over into the covenant before God, to do according to all that he has commanded, and not to turn away from following him because of any dread or terror or trial or fright in the dominion of Belial. And when they pass into the covenant, the priests and the Levites shall bless the God of salvation and all his works of truth; and all those who are passing into the covenant shall say after them, "Amen! Amen!"

The priests shall recount the righteous acts of God in his mighty works and tell all the acts of steadfast love and mercy upon Israel; and the Levites shall recount the iniquities of the sons of Israel and all their guilty transgressions and sin in the dominion of Belial. Then all those who are passing into the covenant shall confess after them, saying, "We have committed iniquity, we have transgressed, we have sinned, we have done evil, we and our fathers before us, in walking contrary to the statutes of truth; but righteous is God, and true is his judgment on us and on our fathers; and the mercy of his steadfast love he has bestowed upon us from everlasting to everlasting."

Then the priests shall bless all the men of God's lot, who walk perfectly in all his ways, and shall say: "May he bless you with all good and keep you from all evil; may be enlighten your heart with life-giving prudence and be gracious to you with eternal knowledge; may he lift up his loving countenance to you for eternal peace." And the Levites shall curse all the men of Belial's lot and shall answer and say: "Accursed may you be in all your wicked, guilty works; may God make you a horror through all those that wreak vengeance and send after you destruction through all those that pay recompense; accursed may you be without mercy according to the darkness of your works, and may you suffer wrath in the deep darkness of eternal fire. May God not be gracious to you when you call, and may he not pardon, forgiving your iniquities; may he lift up his angry countenance for vengeance upon you, and may there be no peace for you at the mouth of all those that hold enmity!" And all who are passing over into the covenant shall say after those who bless and those who curse, "Amen! Amen!"

And the priests and Levites shall continue and say: "Accursed for passing over with the idols of his heart may he be who comes into this covenant and sets the stumbling block of his iniquity before him, turning back with it, and when he hears the words of this covenant blesses himself in his heart, saying, 'May I have peace, because I walk in the stubbornness of my heart!' But his spirit will be swept away, the thirsty together with the sated, without pardon. The wrath of God and the jealousy of his judgments will burn in him to eternal destruction; and all the curses of this covenant will cleave to him; and God will set him apart for evil; and he will be cut off from the midst of all the sons of light, when he turns away from following God with his idols and the stumbling-block of his iniquity. He will put his lot in the midst of those accursed for ever." And all who are coming into the covenant shall answer and say after them, "Amen! Amen!"

So shall they do year by year all the days of the dominion of Belial. The priests shall pass over first in order, according to their spirits, one after another; and the Levites shall pass over after them, and all the people shall pass over third in order, one after another, by thousands and hundreds and fifties and tens, so that every man of Israel may know his appointed position in the community of God for the eternal council. And none shall be abased below his appointed position or exalted above his allotted place; for they shall all be in true community and good humility and loyal love and righteous thought, each for his fellow in the holy council, and they shall be sons of the eternal assembly.

Everyone who refuses to enter God's covenant, walking in the stubbornness of his heart, shall not attain to his true community. For his soul has abhorred the discipline of knowledge, the judgments of righteousness he has not confirmed because of his apostasies; and with the upright he will not be reckoned. His knowledge and his strength and his wealth shall not come into the council of community, because in the traffic of wickedness is his devising, and there is pollution in his plans. He will not be justified while giving free rein to the stubbornness of his heart. In darkness he looks at the ways of light, and with the perfect he will not be reckoned. He will not be purified by atonement offerings, and he will not be made clean with the water for impurity; he will not sanctify himself with seas and rivers or be made clean with any water for washing. Unclean, unclean he will be all the days that he rejects the ordinances of God, not being instructed in the community of his counsel.

But in a spirit of true counsel for the ways of a man all his iniquities will be atoned, so that he will look at the light of life, and in a holy spirit he will be united in his truth; and he will be cleansed from all his iniquities; and in an upright and humble spirit his sin will be atoned, and in the submission of his soul to all the statutes of God his flesh will be cleansed, that he may be sprinkled with water for impurity and sanctify himself with water of cleanness. And he will establish his steps, to walk perfectly in all the ways of God, as he commanded for the appointed times of his testimonies, and not to turn aside to right or left, and not to transgress against one of all his words. Then he will be accepted by pleasing atonements before God; and this will be for him a covenant of eternal community.

II—*The Two Spirits in Man*

The instructor's duty is to make all the sons of light understand and to teach them in the history of all the sons of man as to all their kinds of spirits with their signs, as to their works in their generations, and as to the visitation of their afflictions together with the periods of their recompense. From the God of knowledge is all that is and that is to be; and before they came into being he established all their designing. And when they come into being for their testimony according to his glorious design, they fulfill their work; and nothing is to be changed. In his hand are the ordinances of all; and he provides for them in all their affairs.

He created man to have dominion over the world and made for him two spirits, that he might walk by them until the appointed time of his visitation; they are the spirits of truth and of error. In the abode of light are the origins of truth, and from the source of darkness are the origins of error. In the hand of the prince of lights is dominion over all sons of righteousness; in the ways of light they walk. And in the hand of the angel of darkness is all dominion over the sons of error; and in the ways of darkness they walk. And by the angel of darkness is the straying of all the sons of righteousness, and all their sin and their iniquities and their guilt, and the transgressions of their works in his dominion, according to the mysteries of God, until his time, and all their afflictions and the appointed times of their distress in the dominion of his enmity. And all the spirits of his lot try to make the sons of light stumble; but the God of Israel and his angel of truth have helped all the sons of light. For he created the spirits of light and of darkness, and upon them he founded every work and upon their ways every service. One of the spirits God loves for all the ages of eternity, and with all its deeds he is pleased forever; as for the other, he abhors its company, and all its ways he hates forever.

And these are their ways in the world: to shine in the heart of man, and to make straight before him all the ways of true righteousness, and to make his heart be in dread of the judgments of God, and to induce a spirit of humility, and slowness to anger, and great compassion, and eternal goodness, and understanding and insight, and mighty wisdom, which is supported by all the works of God and leans upon the abundance of his steadfast love, and a spirit of knowledge in every thought of action, and zeal for righteous judgments, and holy thought with sustained purpose, and abundance of steadfast love for all the sons of truth, and glorious purity, abhorring all unclean idols, and walking humbly with prudence in all things, and concealing the truth of the mysteries of knowledge.

These are the counsels of the Spirit for the sons of the truth of the world and the visitation of all who walk by it, for healing and abundance of peace in length of days, and bringing forth seed, with all eternal blessings and everlasting joy in the life of eternity, and a crown of glory with raiment of majesty in everlasting light.

But to the spirit of error belong greediness, slackness of hands in the service of righteousness, wickedness and falsehood, pride and haughtiness, lying and deceit, cruelty and great impiety, quickness to anger and abundance of folly and proud jealousy, abominable works in a spirit of fornication and ways of defilement in the service of uncleanness, and a blasphemous tongue, blindness of eyes and dullness of ears, stiffness of neck and hardness of heart, walking in all the ways of darkness and evil cunning. And the visitation of all who walk by it is for abundance of afflictions by all destroying angels, to eternal perdition in the fury of the God of vengeance, to eternal trembling and everlasting dishonor, with destroying disgrace in the fire of dark places. And all their periods to their generations will be in sorrowful mourning and bitter calamity, in dark disasters until they are destroyed, having no remnant or any that escape.

In these two spirits are the origins of all the sons of man, and in their divisions all the hosts of men have their inheritance in their generations. In the ways of the two spirits men walk. And all the performance of their works is in their two divisions, according to each man's inheritance, whether much or little, for all the periods of eternity. For God has established the two spirits in equal measure until the last period, and has put eternal enmity between their divisions. An abomination to truth are deeds of error, and an abomination to error are all ways of truth. And contentious jealousy is on all their judgments, for they do not walk together.

But God in the mysteries of his understanding and in his glorious wisdom has ordained a period for the ruin of error, and in the appointed time of punishment he will destroy it forever. And then shall come out forever the truth of the world, for it has wallowed in the ways of wickedness in the dominion of error until the appointed time of judgment which has been decreed. And then God will refine in his truth all the deeds of a man, and will purify for himself the frame of man, consuming every spirit of error hidden in his flesh, and cleansing him with a holy spirit from all wicked deeds. And he will sprinkle upon him a spirit of truth, like water for impurity, from all abominations of falsehood and wallowing in a spirit of impurity, to make the upright perceive the knowledge of the Most High and the wisdom of the sons of heaven, to instruct those whose conduct is blameless. For God has chosen them for an eternal covenant, and theirs is all the glory of man; and there shall be no error, to the shame of all works of deceit.

Thus far the spirits of truth and of error struggle in the heart of a man; they walk in wisdom and folly; and according to each man's inheritance in truth he does right, and so he hates error; but according to his possession in the lot of error he does wickedly in it, and so he abhors truth. For in equal measure God has established the two spirits until the period which has been decreed and the making new; and he knows the performance of their works for all the periods of eternity. And he causes the sons of men to inherit them, that they may know good and evil, making the lots fall for every living man according to his spirit in the world until the time of visitation.

III—*Rules of the Order*

And this is the order for the men of the community who have offered themselves to turn from all evil and to lay hold of all that he commanded according to his will, to be separated from the congregation of the men of error, to become a community in law and in wealth, answering when asked by the sons of Zadok, the priests who keep the covenant, and when asked by the majority of the men of the community, who lay hold of the covenant. At their direction the regulation of the lot shall be decided for every case regarding law, wealth, or justice, to practice truth, unity, and humility, righteousness and justice and loyal love, and to walk humbly in all their ways, that each may not walk in the rebelliousness of his heart or go astray after his heart and his eyes and the thought of his guilty impulse; to circumcise in unity the uncircumcision of impulse and the stiff neck, to lay a foundation of truth for Israel for the community of an eternal covenant, to atone for all who offer themselves for holiness in Aaron and for a house of truth in Israel, and those who joined with them for community and for controversy and for judgment, to condemn all who transgress the statute.

And as for these, this is the regulation of their ways concerning all these ordinances. When they are gathered together, every one who comes into the council of the community shall enter into the covenant of God in the sight of all who have offered themselves; and he shall take it upon himself by a binding oath to turn to the law of Moses, according to all that he commanded, with all his heart and with all his soul, to all that is revealed of it to the sons of Zadok, the priests who keep the covenant and who seek his will, and to the majority of the men of their covenant, who have offered themselves together to his truth and to walking in his good will; and that he will take it upon himself in the covenant to be separated from all the men of error who walk in the way of wickedness. For these are not reckoned in his covenant, for they have not sought or searched for him in his statutes, to know the hidden things in which they have gone astray, incurring guilt, and the things revealed which they have done with a high hand, arousing anger leading to judgment and the wreaking of vengeance by the curses of the covenant, bringing upon themselves great judgments to eternal destruction without remnant.

They shall not enter the water, in order to touch the sacred food of the holy men, for they will not be cleansed unless they have turned from their evil. For there is something unclean in all who transgress his word. And he shall not be united with him in his work and in his wealth, lest he bring upon him guilty transgression, but shall keep far from him in everything, for thus it is written: "From everything false you shall keep far." And no man of the men of the community shall answer when asked by them regarding any law or ordinance. And he shall not eat or drink anything from their wealth, and shall not take from their hand anything at all except for a price, as it is written: "Cease from man, whose breath is in his nostrils, for of what worth is he reckoned?" For all who are not reckoned in his covenant are to be separated with all that is theirs; and a holy man shall not lean upon any works of vanity; for vain are all those who do not know his covenant, and all those who despise his word he will destroy from the world, and all their works are but impurity before him; and there is something unclean in all their wealth.

When he enters the covenant to do according to all these statutes, to be united for a holy congregation, they shall investigate his spirit in the community, between a man and his neighbor, according to his understanding and his works in the law, as directed by the sons of Aaron, who have offered themselves in unity to establish his covenant and to have charge of all his statutes which he commanded men to do, and as directed by the majority of Israel, who have offered themselves to turn in unity to his covenant. They shall be registered in order, each before his neighbor, according to his understanding and his works, so that every one of them shall obey his neighbor, the lesser obeying the greater; and so that they shall have an investigation of their spirits and their works year by year, so as to elevate each one according to his understanding and the perfection of his way or put him back according to his perversions, so that each one may reprove his neighbor in truth and humility and loyal love for each one.

One shall not speak to his brother in anger or in resentment, or with a stiff neck or a hard heart or a wicked spirit; one shall not hate him in the folly of his heart. In his days he shall reprove him and shall not bring upon him iniquity; and also a man shall not bring against his neighbor a word before the masters without having rebuked him before witnesses.

In these ways they shall walk in all their dwellings, every living man, each with his neighbor. The lesser shall obey the greater with regard to wages and property. Together they shall eat, and together they shall worship, and together they shall counsel.

In every place where there are ten men of the council of the community there shall not be absent from them a priest. Each according to his position, they shall sit before him; and thus they shall be asked for their counsel regarding everything. And when they set the table to eat, or the wine to drink, the priest shall stretch out his hand first to pronounce a blessing with the first portion of the bread and the wine. And from the place where the ten are there shall never be absent a man who searches the law day and night, by turns, one after another. And the masters shall keep watch together a third of all the nights of the year, reading the book and searching for justice, and worshiping together.

This is the order for the session of the masters, each in his position. The priests be seated first and the elders second; then all the rest of the people shall be seated, each in his position. And thus they shall be asked concerning justice and every council and matter which comes to the masters, so that each may render his opinion to the council of the community. A man shall not speak in the midst of his neighbor's words, before his brother finishes speaking. And further he shall not speak before his position which is written before him. The man who is asked shall speak in his turn; and in the session of the masters a man shall not speak a word which is not to the liking of the masters. And when the man who is the superintendent over the masters—or any man who has a word to speak to the masters but who is not in the position of the one asking the community's counsel—the man shall stand on his feet and say, "I have a word to speak to the masters." If they tell him, he shall speak.

Everyone who has offered himself from Israel to be added to the council of the community shall be examined by the man appointed at the head of the masters as to his understanding and his works. If he comprehends instruction, he shall bring him into the covenant, to turn to the truth and to turn away from all error; and he shall explain to him all the ordinances of the community. Then later, when he comes in to stand before the masters, they shall all be questioned about his affairs; and as the lot determines, according to the counsel of the masters, he shall be admitted or depart. On being admitted to the council of the community, he shall not touch the sacred food of the masters until they examine him as to his spirit and his deeds when he has completed a whole year; moreover he shall not participate in the wealth of the masters.

When he has completed a year within the community, the masters shall be questioned about his affairs, as to his understanding and his deeds in the law; and if the lot determines that he shall be admitted to the assembly of the community, as directed by the priests and the majority of the men of their covenant, his wealth and his wages shall be put at the disposal of the man who has supervision over the wages of the masters, and he shall enter it in the account at his disposal, but shall not spend it for the masters.

The new member shall not touch the sacred drink of the masters until he has completed a second year among the men of the community; but when he has completed a second year, he shall be examined with questioning by the masters. If the lot determines that he is to be admitted to the community, he shall be registered in the order of his position among his brethren, for law and for judgment and for the sacred food and for the sharing of his property; and the community shall have his counsel and his judgment.

These are the ordinances by which they shall judge when investigating together concerning cases. If there is found among them a man who lies about his wealth, and knows it, he shall be excluded from the sacred food of the masters for a year, and shall be deprived of a fourth of his food ration. One who answers his neighbor with a stiff neck, or speaks with impatience, breaking the foundation of his fellowship by disobeying his neighbor who is registered before him, his own hand has delivered him; therefore he shall be punished for a year. Any man who mentions anything by the Name which is honored above all shall be set apart. If one has cursed, either when frightened by trouble or for any reason he may have, he shall be set apart and shall not return again to the council of the community. If he spoke in wrath against one of the priests registered in the book, he shall be punished for a year and set apart by himself from the sacred food of the masters. But if he spoke unintentionally, he shall be punished six months.

One who lies about what he knows shall be punished six months. A man who without justification knowingly denounces his neighbor shall be punished for a year and set apart. One who speaks craftily with his neighbors, or knowingly perpetrates a fraud, shall be punished six months. If he commits a fraud against his neighbor, he shall be punished three months; if he commits a fraud against the wealth of the community, causing its loss, he shall repay it in full. If he is not able to pay it, he shall be punished sixty days.

One who bears a grudge against his neighbor without justification shall be punished six months [*inserted above this line:* a year]; so also he who takes vengeance for himself for anything. One who speaks with his mouth the word of a fool shall be punished three months. For one who speaks while his neighbor is speaking the punishment shall be ten days. One who lies down and goes to sleep during a session of the masters, thirty days. So also a man who leaves during a session of the masters unadvisedly and without cause as many as three times at one session shall be punished ten days; but if they object and he leaves, he shall be punished thirty days.

One who walks before his neighbor naked when he does not have to do so shall be punished six months. A man who spits into the midst of the session of the masters shall be punished thirty days. One who brings his hand out from beneath his robe when it is torn, so that his nakedness is seen, shall be punished thirty days. One who laughs foolishly, making his voice heard, shall be punished thirty days. One who brings out his left hand to gesticulate with it shall be punished ten days.

A man who gossips about his neighbor shall be separated for a year from the sacred food of the masters, and he shall be punished; and a man who gossips about the masters is to be dismissed from among them and shall not come back again. A man who murmurs against the institution of the community shall be dismissed and shall not come back; but if he murmurs against his neighbor without justification he shall be punished six months.

If a man's spirit wavers from the institution of the community, so that he becomes a traitor to the truth and walks in the stubbornness of his heart; if he repents he shall be punished two years. During the first he shall not touch the sacred food of the masters, and during the second he shall not touch the drink of the masters; and he shall be seated after all the men of the community. When his two years are completed, the masters shall be asked about his case. If they admit him, he shall be registered in his position; and after that he shall be asked for judgment. If any man is in the council of the community for ten full years, and his spirit turns back so that he becomes a traitor to the community and goes out from before the masters to walk in the stubbornness of his heart, he shall not come back again to the council of the community. If any man of the men of the community partakes with him of his sacred food, or of his wealth which he has delivered to the masters, his sentence shall be like his; he shall be dismissed.

There shall be in the council of the community twelve men, and there shall be three priests who are perfect in all that has been revealed of the whole law, to practice truth and righteousness and justice and loyal love and walking humbly each with his neighbor, to preserve faithfulness in the land with sustained purpose and a broken spirit, and to make amends for iniquity by the practice of justice and the distress of tribulation, and to walk with all by the standard of truth and by the regulation of the time.

When these things come to pass in Israel, the council of the community will be established in the truth for an eternal planting, a holy house for Israel, a foundation of the holy of holies for Aaron, true witnesses for justice and the elect by God's will, to make atonement for the land and to render to the wicked their recompense—this is the tested wall, a precious cornerstone; its foundations will not tremble or flee from their place—a most holy dwelling for Aaron with eternal knowledge for a covenant of justice and to offer a pleasing fragrance, and a house of perfection and truth in Israel to establish a covenant for eternal statutes. And they shall be accepted to make atonement for the land and to decide the judgment of wickedness, and there shall be no error. When these men have been prepared in the foundation of the community for two years with blameless conduct, they shall be separated in holiness in the midst of the council of the men of the community; and when anything which has been hidden from Israel is found by the man who is searching, it shall not be hidden from these men out of fear of an apostate spirit.

When these things come to pass for the community in Israel, by these regulations they shall be separated from the midst of the session of the men of error to go to the wilderness to prepare there the way of the LORD; as it is written, "In the wilderness prepare the way of the LORD; make straight in the desert a highway for our God." This is the study of the law, as he commanded through Moses, to do according to all that has been revealed from time to time, and as the prophets revealed by his Holy Spirit.

Any man of the men of the community, of the covenant of the community, who wilfully takes away a word from the whole commandment shall not touch the sacred food of the holy men; he shall not know any of their counsel until his works are cleansed from all error, so that he conducts himself blamelessly. Then he shall be admitted to the council as directed by the masters, and afterward he shall be registered in his position. According to this law shall it be done for every one who is added to the community.

These are the ordinances by which the men of perfect holiness shall walk, each with his neighbor, every one who enters the holy council, those who conduct themselves blamelessly as he commanded. Any man of them who transgresses a word of the law of Moses overtly or with deceit shall be dismissed from the council of the community and shall not come back again; and none of the holy men shall participate in his wealth or in his counsel concerning anything. But if he acts unintentionally, he shall be separated from the sacred food and the council; and they shall interpret the ordinance that he shall not judge a man or be asked concerning any counsel for two years. If his conduct is perfect in the meeting, in interpretation, and in counsel as directed by the masters; if he has not again sinned unintentionally by the completion of his two years—because for one unintentional sin he shall be punished for two years—as for him who acts deliberately, he shall not come back again; only he who sins unintentionally shall be tested for two years, that his conduct and his counsel may be perfected under the direction of the masters—after that he shall be registered in his position for the holy community.

When these things come to pass in Israel according to all these regulations, for a foundation of a holy spirit, for eternal truth, for a ransom for the guilt of transgression and sinful faithlessness, and for acceptance for the land more than the flesh of whole burnt offerings and the fats of sacrifice, and an offering of the lips for justice like the pleasing quality of righteousness, and perfect conduct like a willing gift of an acceptable offering; at that time the men of the community shall be set apart, a house of holiness for Aaron, to be united as a holy of holies and a house of community for Israel, those who conduct themselves blamelessly.

Only the sons of Aaron shall administer judgment and wealth, and as they direct the lot shall determine for every regulation of the men of the community. As for the wealth of the holy men, who conduct themselves blamelessly, their wealth shall not be combined with the wealth of the men of deceit, who have not purified their conduct by separating themselves from error and conducting themselves blamelessly. They shall not depart from any counsel of the law, walking in all the stubbornness of their hearts; but they shall judge by the first judgments by which the men of the community began to be disciplined, until there shall come a prophet and the Messiahs of Aaron and Israel.

These are the statutes for the wise man, that he may walk in them with every living being, according to the regulation of one time and another and the weight of one man and another; to do the will of God according to all that has been revealed for each time at that time; and to learn all the wisdom that has been found, according to the times, and the statute of the time; and to set apart and weigh the sons of Zadok according to their spirit; and to hold firmly to the elect of the time according to his will, as he commanded. According to each man's spirit he is to be given his due; according to the cleanness of each man's hands he is to be admitted; and according to his understanding he is to be accepted; so too his love together with his hate.

There must be no admonitions or contention with the men of the pit, for the counsel of the law must be concealed among the men of error; but there must be admonition of true knowledge and righteous judgment for those who choose the way; each according to his spirit, according to the regulation of the time, to guide them in knowledge and so to give them understanding in the marvelous mysteries and truth among the men of the community, that they may conduct themselves blamelessly, each with his neighbor, in all that has been revealed to them— that is the time of clearing the way to the wilderness--to give them understanding of all that has been found to be done at this time; and to be separated from every man, and not to pervert his way because of any error.

These are the regulations of the way for the wise man in these times, for his love together with his hate, eternal hate for the men of the pit in a spirit of concealment, leaving to them wealth and manual labor like a slave for the man who rules over him, and humility before the man who has the mastery over him. Each one must be zealous for the statute and its time, for the day of vengeance, to do what is acceptable in everything he puts his hands to, and in all his dominion as he commanded; and everything done in it will be accepted freely.

IV—*The Closing Psalm*

With nothing but the will of God shall a man be concerned,
but with all the words of his mouth shall he be pleased;
he shall not desire anything which he did not command,
but to the ordinance of God he shall look always.
In every period that is to be he shall bless his Maker,
and in whatever state he is he shall tell of his righteousness.
With an offering of the lips he shall bless him
throughout the periods which A has decreed:
at the beginning of the dominion of light, through its circuit,
and at its ingathering to its decreed dwelling;
at the beginning of the watches of darkness,
when he opens his treasury and appoints it for a time;
and at its circuit, together with its ingathering before the light,
when lights appear from the holy habitation,
together with their ingathering to the glorious dwelling;
at the coming in of seasons in days of the new moon,
both their circuit and their connection one with another.
When they renew themselves, the M is large for the holy of holies;
and the letter N is for the key of his eternal, steadfast love.

At the heads of seasons in every period to be,
at the beginning of months for their seasons
and holy days in their fixed order,
for a memorial in their seasons,
with an offering of the lips I will bless him
as a decree engraved forever.
At the heads of years and in the circuit of their seasons,
when the circle of their fixed order completes the day ordained for it,
one leading to another: the season of reaping to summer,
the season of sowing to the season of vegetation,
seasons of years to weeks of them,
and at the head of their weeks for a season of emancipation;
as long as I exist a decree engraved shall be on my tongue
for fruit of praise and for a gift of my lips.
I will sing with knowledge,
and all my music shall be for the glory of God;
my lyre and harp shall be for his holy fixed order,
and the flute of my lips I will raise
in his just circle.

With the coming of day and night
I will enter the covenant of God;
and with the outgoing of evening and morning
I will speak his decrees;
and while they exist I will set my limit
so that I may not turn back.

His judgment I will pronounce, according to my perversity—
for my transgression is before my eyes—
   like a statute engraved.
And to God I will say, "My righteousness";
to the Most High, "Foundation of my goodness,
Source of knowledge and Fountain of holiness,
Height of glory and Strength of all,
to eternal majesty!"
I will choose as he teaches me,
And I will be pleased as he judges me.

When I begin to put forth my hands and my feet,
I will bless his name;

when I begin to go out or come in,
when I sit down or stand up,
and as I lie on my couch, I will sing aloud to him;
I will bless him with an offering of the utterance of my lips
more than the oblation spread out by men.
Before I raise my hand to satisfy myself
with the delights of what the world produces,
in the dominion of fear and terror,
the place of distress with desolation,
I will bless him, giving special thanks.
On his might I will meditate,
and on his steadfast love I will lean all the day;
for I know that in his hand is the judgment of every living man,
and all his works are truth.
When distress is let loose I will praise him,
and when I am delivered I will sing praise also.

I will not render to a man the recompense of evil;
with good I will pursue a man;
for with God is the judgment of every living man;
and he will repay to a man his recompense.
I will not be jealous of an evil spirit;
wealth got by violence my soul shall not desire;
and the abundance of a man of the pit I will not seize
until the day of vengeance;
but my anger I will not turn back from men of error,
and I will not be pleased until he has established judgment.
I will not remain angry with those who turn from transgression,
but I will not have mercy on any who turn aside from the way,
and I will not show favor to those who are smitten until their conduct
     is blameless.

I will not keep baseness in my heart,
and folly shall not be heard in my mouth;
iniquitous falsehood, deceits, and lies
shall not be found on my lips;
but the fruit of holiness shall be on my tongue,
and abominable things shall not be found on it.

With thanksgivings I will open my mouth,
the righteous acts of God shall my tongue recount always
and the faithlessness of men until their transgression is complete.
Empty words I will banish from my lips,
unclean things and perversions from the knowledge of my mind.
With wise counsel I will conceal knowledge,
and with knowing prudence I will hedge about wisdom
with a firm limit, to preserve fidelity
and strong justice according to the righteousness of God.
I will exalt the decree with the measuring-line of times,
and will teach the practice of righteousness,
loyal love for the humble,
and strengthening of hands for the fearful of heart;
for the erring in spirit understanding;
to instruct the fainting with doctrine,
to answer humbly before the haughty of spirit,
and with a broken spirit to men of injustice,
who point the finger and speak wickedly
and are envious of wealth.

But as for me, my judgment belongs to God,
and in his hand is the blamelessness of my conduct
together with the uprightness of my heart;
and in his righteousness my transgression will be wiped out.
For from the source of his knowledge he has opened up my light;
my eye has gazed into his wonders
and the light of my heart penetrates the mystery that is to be.
That which is eternal is the staff of my right hand;
on a strong rock is the way I tread;
before nothing will it be shaken.
For the faithfulness of God is the rock I tread,
and his strength is the staff of my right hand.
From the source of his righteousness is my judgment.
A light is in my heart from his marvelous mysteries;
my eye has gazed on that which is eternal,
sound wisdom which is hidden from the man of knowledge,
and prudent discretion from the sons of man,
a source of righteousness and reservoir of strength

together with a spring of glory hidden from the company of flesh.
To those whom God has chosen he has given them for an eternal
    possession;
he has given them an inheritance in the lot of the holy ones
and with the sons of heaven has associated their company
for a council of unity and a company of a holy building,
for an eternal planting
through every period that is to be.

But I belong to wicked mankind,
to the company of erring flesh;
my iniquities, my transgression, my sin,
with the iniquity of my heart
belong to the company of worms and those who walk in darkness.
For the way of a man is not his own,
a man does not direct his own steps;
for judgment is God's,
and from his hand is blamelessness of conduct.
By his knowledge everything comes to pass;
and everything that is he establishes by his purpose;
and without him it is not done.
As for me, if I slip,
the steadfast love of God is my salvation forever;
and if I stumble in the iniquity of flesh,
my vindication in the righteousness of God will stand to eternity.
If he lets loose my distress,
from the pit he will deliver my soul;
he will direct my steps to the way.
In his mercy he has brought me near,
And in his righteousness he will cleanse me from the impurity of man,
from the sin of the sons of man.
Thanks be to God for his righteousness,
to the Most High for his majesty!

Blessed art thou, O my God,
who openest to knowledge the heart of thy servant.
Direct in righteousness all his works
and establish the son of thy handmaid,
as thou didst accept the elect of mankind

to stand before thee forever.
For without thee conduct will not be blameless,
and apart from thy will nothing will be done.
It is thou that hast taught all knowledge;
and everything that has come to pass has been by thy will.
And there is no other beside thee
to oppose thy counsel,
to understand all thy holy purpose,
to gaze into the depth of thy mysteries,
or to comprehend all thy marvels,
together with the strength of thy power.
Who is able to bear thy glory,
and what then is he,
the son of man, among thy marvelous works;
what shall one born of woman be accounted before thee?
As for him, he was kneaded from dust,
and the food of worms is his portion.
He is an emission of spittle, a cut-off bit of clay,
and his desire is for the dust.
What will clay reply, a thing formed by hand?
What counsel will it understand?

D. Selections from The War of the Sons of Light with the Sons of Darkness

I (i.1–7)

At the beginning of the undertaking of the sons of light, they shall start against the lot of the sons of darkness, the army of Belial, against the troop of Edom and Moab and the sons of Ammon, against the people of Philistia, and against the troops of the Kittim of Assyria, and with them as helpers the violaters of the covenant. The sons of Levi, the sons of Judah, and the sons of Benjamin, the exiles of the desert, shall fight against them and their forces with all their troops, when the exiles of the sons of light return from the desert of the peoples to encamp in the desert of Jerusalem. And after the battle they shall go up from there against the king of the Kittim in Egypt; and in his time he shall go forth with great wrath to fight against the kings of the north; and his wrath shall destroy and cut off the horn of their strength. That will be a time of salvation for the people of God, and a period of dominion for all the men of his lot, but eternal destruction for all the lot of Belial. And there shall be a great tumult against the sons of Japheth; and Assyria shall fall with none to help him. And the dominion of the Kittim shall come to an end, so that wickedness shall be laid low without any remnant; and there shall be no survivor of the sons of darkness.

II (ii.1–13)

The chiefs of the priests they shall arrange in rank behind the chief priest and second to him, twelve chiefs to minister continually before God. Twenty-six chiefs of the assignments shall minister in their assignments; and after them the chiefs of the Levites to minister continually, twelve, one to a tribe; and the chiefs of their assignments shall minister, each in his position. The chiefs of the tribes and the fathers of the congregation shall be always in their places in the gates of the sanctuary; and the chiefs of their assignments with their officers shall be in their places at their appointed times, for new moons and for sabbaths and for all the days of the year. From fifty years old and upward, they shall be in their places over the burnt offerings and over the sacrifices, to set out the fragrant incense for God's acceptance, to make atonement for all his congregation, and to make acceptable offerings before him always with an honored table. All these they shall set in order in the appointed time of the year of release. During the thirty-three years of war that are left the men of renown, those acclaimed in the assembly, and all the chiefs of the fathers of the congregation shall choose for themselves men of war for all the lands of the Gentiles from all the tribes of Israel; men of valor shall be equipped for them, to go out for warfare, according to the testimonies of war, year by year. But in the years of release they shall not be equipped to go out for warfare, for that is a sabbath of rest for Israel. During thirty-five years of service the battle shall be set in array six years, and those who set it in array shall be the whole congregation together. And as for the war of the divisions during the twenty-nine years that are left, in the first year they shall fight against Mesopotamia, and in the second against the sons of Lud; in the third they shall fight with the remnant of the sons of Syria, with Uz and Hul, Togar and Mashsha who are across the Euphrates; in the fourth and fifth they shall fight with the sons of Arpachshad; in the sixth and seventh they shall fight with all the sons of Assyria and Persia and the people of the east as far as the great desert; in the eighth year they shall fight against the sons of Elam; in the ninth they shall fight against the sons of Ishmael and Keturah; and in the ten years after these the war shall be distributed against all the sons of Ham.

III (iii.1–11)

. . . the ranks of battle, and the trumpets of their assembling when the war gates are opened for the champions to go forth, the trumpets of the war-blast over the slain, the trumpets of ambush, the trumpets of pursuit when the enemy is smitten, and the trumpets of reassembly when the battle turns back. On the trumpets of the assembly of the congregation they shall write "The Called of God"; on the trumpets of the assembly of the commanders they shall write "The Princes of God"; on the trumpets of the connections they shall write "The Order of God"; on the trumpets of the men of renown they shall write "The Chiefs of the Fathers of the Congregation." When they are gathered together to the house of meeting they shall write "The Testimonies of God for the Holy Council." On the trumpets of the camps they shall write "The Peace of God in His Holy Camps"; on their trumpets of breaking camp they shall write "The Powers of God for Scattering the Enemy and Putting to Flight Those Who Hate Righteousness and Turning Back Kindness against Those Who Hate God." On the trumpets of the ranks of battle they shall write "The Ranks of the Banners of God for the Vengeance of His Anger against All the Sons of Darkness." On the trumpets of assembly of the champions, when the war gates are opened to go forth to the array of the enemy, they shall write "Memorial of Vengeance in the Assembly of God"; on the trumpets of the slain they shall write "The Mighty Hand of God in Battle to Cast Down all the Faithless Slain"; on the trumpets of ambush they shall write "The Mysteries of God for the Destruction of Wickedness"; on the trumpets of pursuit they shall write "God's Smiting of All the Sons of Darkness— His Anger Will Not Turn Back until They Are Destroyed." When they return from the battle to come to the array, they shall write on the trumpets of return "The Gathering of God"; on the trumpets of the way of return from the battle of the enemy to come to the congregation of Jerusalem they shall write "The Rejoicings of God at the Return of Peace."

IV (iv.1–14)

On the standard of Merari they shall write "The Offering of God," and the name of the prince of Merari and the names of the commanders of its thousands; on the standard of the thousand they shall write "The Anger of God with Fury against Belial and All the Men of His Lot without Remnant," and the name of the commander of the thousand and the names of the commanders of its hundreds; on the standard of the hundred they shall write "The Hundred of God, a Hand of War against All Erring Flesh," and the name of the commander of the hundred and the names of the commanders of its tens; on the standard of the fifty they shall write "The Position of the Wicked Has Ceased by the Power of God," and the name of the commander of the fifty and names of the commanders of its tens; on the standard of the ten they shall write "Songs of God with a Harp of Ten Strings," and the name of the commander of the ten and the names of the nine men of his command.

When they go to the battle they shall write on their standards "The Truth of God," "The Righteousness of God," "The Glory of God," "The Justice of God," and after these the whole order of the explanation of their names. When they draw near to the battle they shall write on their standards "The Right Hand of God," "The Assembly of God," "The Panic of God," "The Slain of God," and after these the whole explanation of their names. When they return from the battle they shall write on their standards "The Extolling of God," "The Greatness of God," "The Praises of God," "The Glory of God," with the whole explanation of their names.

The order of the standards of the congregation: when they go out to the battle they shall write on the first standard "The Congregation of God," on the second standard "The Camps of God," on the third "The Tribes of God," on the fourth "The Families of God," on the fifth "The Banners of God," on the sixth "The Assembly of God," on the seventh "The Called of God," on the eighth "The Armies of God," and they shall write the explanation of their names with their whole order. When they draw near to the battle they shall write on their standards "The War of God," "The Vengeance of God," "The Strife of God," "The Reward of God," "The Strength of God," "The Peace-Offerings of God," "The Power of God," "The Destruction of God on Every Nation of Vanity," and the whole explanation of their names they shall write on them. When they return from the battle they shall write on their standards "The Deliverances of God," "The Victory of God," "The Help of God," "The Staff of God," "The Comfort of God," "The Praises of God," "The Lauding of God," "The Peace of God."

V (vi.1–14)

. . . seven times, and they shall return to their position. And after them three troops of champions shall go out and stand between the ranks. The first troop shall hurl at the rank of the enemy seven war-darts. On the blade of the dart they shall write "The Lightning of a Lance for the Power of God"; and on the second weapon they shall write "Shootings of Blood to make the Slain Fall in the Anger of God"; and on the third dart they shall write "Flashing of a Sword Consuming the Iniquitous Slain in the Judgment of God." All these shall cast seven times and return to their position. After them two troops of champions shall go out and stand between the two ranks, the first troop, holding lance and shield, and the second troop, holding shield and javelin to make the slain fall in the judgment of God and to lay low the rank of the enemy in the power of God, to pay the recompense of their evil to every nation of vanity. And the God of Israel shall have the kingdom; and among the saints of his people he will display might.

And seven lines of horsemen also shall stand on the right and left of the rank; on this side and that shall their lines stand: seven hundred horsemen on one side and seven hundred on the other side. Two hundred horsemen shall go out with a thousand of the rank of the champions, and so they shall stand on all sides of the camp. The whole shall be four thousand six hundred and a thousand and four hundred chariots for the men of the line of the ranks, fifty to a rank. And the horsemen shall be beside the chariots, men of the line, six thousand five hundred to a tribe. All the chariots that go out to the battle with the champions shall have stallions, swift-footed and tender-mouthed, gentle, and mature, in middle life, trained for battle and able to hear sounds and to see all imaginable sights. The men who ride on them shall be men of valor for war, trained in chariotry, and in middle life, from thirty to forty-five years old. And the horsemen of the line shall be from forty to fifty years old.

VI (vii.1–15)

The men of the line shall be from forty to fifty years old; and those who set up the camp shall be from fifty to sixty years old; the officers also shall be from forty to fifty years old. And all those who strip the slain and those who take the spoil and those who cleanse the earth and those who keep the weapons and he who sets out the food—all of them shall be from twenty-five to thirty years old. And no youth or woman shall enter their camps when they go forth from Jerusalem to go to battle until they return. No lame or blind man or halt man, or one with a permanent blemish in his flesh, or a man afflicted with the uncleanness of his flesh—none of these shall go with them to battle; they shall all be volunteers for war, blameless in spirit and flesh, and ready for the day of vengeance. And no man who is not clean from his issue on the day of battle shall go down with them; for holy angels are together with their armies. And there shall be a space between all their camps for the place of the hand, about two thousand cubits. And no indecent, evil thing shall be seen in the vicinity of any of your camps.

When the ranks of battle are drawn up over against the enemy, rank over against rank, there shall go forth from the middle gate to the space between the ranks seven priests of the sons of Aaron wearing garments of white linen, tunics and trousers of linen, and girt with girdles of fine twined linen, blue and purple and scarlet stuff, a varied pattern, the work of a designer, and caps on their heads—garments of war, not to be brought to the sanctuary. One priest shall go before the men of the rank to strengthen their hands in the battle; and in the hands of the other six shall be the trumpets of assembly, the memorial trumpets, the trumpets of the war-blast, the trumpets of pursuit, and the trumpets of reassembly. And when the priests go forth to the space between the ranks there shall go with them seven Levites holding in their hands the seven rams' horns of jubilee, and three officers of the Levites before the priests and the Levites. Then the priests shall sound the two trumpets of assembly.

VII (viii.1–14)

The trumpets shall continue to sound to direct the slingers until they have finished throwing seven times. After that the priests shall sound for them the trumpets of return, and they shall come beside the first battle line to take their positions. The priests shall sound the trumpets of assembly, and three troops of champions shall come out from the gates and stand between the ranks, and beside them the charioteers to right and left. Then the priests shall sound on the trumpets a prolonged note, the signal for putting the battle in array, and the leaders shall spread out to their lines, each to his position. When they are standing in three lines, the priests shall sound for them a second call, a quiet and sustained note, the signal for advancing until they are near the rank of the enemy. Then they shall take hold of their weapons, and the priests shall sound on the six trumpets of the slain a sharp and agitated note to direct the battle; and the Levites and all those who have the rams' horns shall sound in unison a great war-blast, so that the enemy's heart shall melt. At the sound of the blast, the war-darts shall be let fly to make the slain fall. The sound of the rams' horns shall be accelerated, while with the trumpets the priests are sounding a sharp and agitated note to direct the hands of battle until they have thrown at the rank of the enemy seven times. After that the priests shall sound for them on the trumpets of return a quiet, prolonged, and sustained note. According to this order the priests shall sound for the three troops.

VIII (ix.1–9)

They shall begin with their hands to make some fall among the slain; and all the people shall make haste with the sound of the war-shout, and the priests shall continue sounding on the trumpets of the slain to direct the battle until the enemy is smitten and they turn their backs. The priests shall sound to direct the battle, and when they are smitten before them the priests shall sound on the trumpets of assembly, and all the champions shall go out to them from the midst of the ranks of persons. Then six troops shall stand, and the troop which is brought near, all of them seven ranks, twenty-eight thousand men of war, and the charioteers six thousand. All these shall pursue to destroy the enemy in the war of God, to eternal destruction. Then the priests shall sound for them on the trumpets of pursuit, and they shall gird themselves against all the enemy, for a pursuit to destruction. And the chariots shall turn them back into the battle until they are utterly destroyed. And while the slain are falling the priests shall keep sounding from afar, but they shall not come in among the slain lest they be defiled by their unclean blood, for they are holy; they shall not profane the anointing oil of their priesthood with the blood of a nation of vanity.

IX (x.1–10)

. . . our camps, and to be on guard against every indecent, evil thing; and what he made known to us, that thou art in the midst of us, a great and terrible God, to despoil all our enemies before us. And he taught us of old for our generations, saying, "When you draw near to the battle, the priest shall stand and speak to the people, saying, 'Hear, O Israel, you draw near this day to battle against your enemies: do not fear, and let not your heart faint; do not tremble or be in dread of them; for your God goes with you to fight for you against your enemies to save you.'" And our officers shall speak to all those ready for the battle, willing volunteers, to make them strong in the power of God and to turn back all the fainthearted; to make them strong together with all mighty men of valor. And what he spoke through Moses, saying, "When you go to war in your land against the adversary who oppresses you, you shall sound a war-blast on the trumpets, and you shall be remembered before your God and shall be saved from your enemies." Who is like thee, O God of Israel, in heaven or on earth, who hast wrought such great works as thine and such mighty power as thine; and who is like thy people Israel, whom thou didst choose for thyself from all the peoples of the lands, the people of the saints of the covenant?

X (xi.1–12)

For thine is the battle, and by the strength of thy hand their corpses were scattered without burial. Goliath the Gittite, a mighty man of valor, thou didst deliver into the hand of thy servant David, because he trusted in thy great name and not in sword and spear, for thine is the battle; and he subdued the Philistines many times in thy holy name. Moreover by our kings thou didst save us many times, because of thy mercy and not according to our works, in which we acted wickedly, and the evil deeds of our transgressions. Thine is the battle, and from thee is power, and it is not ours; nor has our strength or the might of our hands done valiantly, but it is by thy strength and by the power of thy great might; as thou didst make known to us of old, saying, "A star shall come forth out of Jacob, and a scepter shall arise out of Israel, and it shall crush the forehead of Moab and break down all the sons of

Sheth; and he shall go down from Jacob and destroy the remnant of Seir, and the enemy shall be dispossessed, and Israel shall do valiantly." By thy anointed ones, seers of testimonies, thou hast made known to us the ordering of the battles of thy hands, to fight *[interlinear correction: to get glory]* against our enemies, to make the troops of Belial fall, seven nations of vanity, by the poor whom thou hast redeemed with strength and with peace, for marvelous power, and a melted heart, for a door of hope. And thou didst to them as to Pharaoh and the officers of his chariots at the Red Sea. The stricken in spirit thou wilt consume like a flaming torch among sheaves, consuming wickedness; thou wilt not turn back until guilt is destroyed. Of old thou didst cause us to hear the appointed time of the power of thy hand against the Kittim, saying, "And Assyria shall fall by a sword, not of a man; and a sword, not of man, shall devour him."

XI (xii.10–15)

Rise, mighty one; bring back thy captives, man of glory!
Seize thy plunder, thou who doest valiantly!
Lay thy hand on the necks of thy enemies
and thy foot on the heaps of the slain;
smite the nations, thy adversaries,
and let thy sword consume guilty flesh!
Fill thy land with glory,
thy inheritance with blessing!
Let there be an abundance of cattle in thy territories,
silver and gold and precious stones in thy palaces.
Rejoice greatly, O Zion;
appear with glad shouts, O Jerusalem;
and exult, all ye cities of Judah!
Open the gate continually,
that the wealth of nations may be brought in to thee;
that their kings may minister to thee,
and all that have afflicted thee may bow down to thee
and lick the dust of thy feet.
O daughters of my people, cry aloud with the sound of a glad shout;
Adorn yourselves with glorious ornaments!

XII (xiii.1–6)

. . . and his brethren the priests and the Levites, and all the elders of the order with him; and they shall bless in their places the God of Israel and all his faithful works, and his indignation which he has directed against Belial and all the spirits of his lot. And they shall answer and say, "Blessed be the God of Israel with all his holy purpose and all his faithful works. And blessed be all his hosts in righteousness, who know him by faith.

"But cursed be Belial with his hostile purpose, and may he be an object of indignation in his guilty dominion; and cursed be all the spirits of his lot in their wicked purpose, and may they be objects of indignation in all their unclean service of defilement; for they are the lot of darkness, but the lot of God belongs to eternal light."

XIII (xiv.2–5)

After they have gone up from the slain to come to the camp, they shall all sing the psalm of returning. And in the morning they shall wash their garments and be cleansed of the blood of the corpses of guilt; and they shall return to their positions where they set the rank in array before the slain of the enemy fell. There they shall all bless the God of Israel and exalt his name together with joy. And they shall answer and say, "Blessed be the God of Israel, who maintains loyalty to his covenant and testimonies of salvation for the people he has redeemed."

XIV (xvii.5–9)

Today is his appointed time to lay low and to make fall the prince of the dominion of wickedness; and he will send eternal help to the lot he has redeemed by the power of the angel he has made glorious for rule, Michael, in eternal light, to give light in joy to all Israel, peace and blessing to the lot of God, to exalt among the gods the rule of Michael and the dominion of Israel over all flesh. Righteousness shall rejoice in the high places, and all the sons of his truth shall be joyful in eternal knowledge. And you, sons of his covenant, be strong in the crucible of God until he waves his hand and fills his crucibles with his mysteries that you may stand.

E. Selections from the Thanksgiving Psalms

Figures in parentheses indicate columns and lines of the manuscript.

I (i.21–30)

These things I know from thy understanding,
for thou hast uncovered my ear for marvelous mysteries.
But I am a thing formed of clay, and kneaded with water,
the company of nakedness and source of uncleanness,
a furnace of iniquity and frame of sin,
a spirit of error and one perverted, without understanding,
and terrified by righteous judgments.
What shall I say without being instructed,
or declare without observing?
Everything is engraved before thee with a pen of remembrance
for all the everlasting periods
and the circuits of the number of the years of eternity,
with all their appointed times;
and they are not hidden or lacking from thy presence.
How then shall a man recount his sin,
or how argue concerning his iniquities?
What can he reply concerning righteous judgment?
Thine, O thou who art the God of knowledge,
are all works of righteousness, the counsel of truth;
but to the sons of man belong the service of iniquity

and works of deceit.
Thou didst create breath with the tongue;
thou knewest its words and didst establish the fruit of the lips
before they existed.
Thou didst place words on a line,
and the utterance of the breath of the lips in measure;
thou didst bring forth lines for their mysteries
and utterances of spirits for their reckoning,
to make known thy glory, and to tell thy wonders
in all the works of thy truth.

II (ii.8–13, 16–19)

I was a trap for transgressors,
but healing for all who repented of transgression;
prudence for the simple,
and a sustained purpose for all those of a fearful heart.
Thou didst make me a reproach and derision to the treacherous,
a counsel of truth and understanding to those whose way is straight.
I became, against the iniquity of the wicked,
an evil report on the lips of oppressors;
scorners gnashed their teeth,
and I was a song to transgressors.
Against me the assembly of the wicked made a tumult;
they roared like the gales of the seas,
when its waves make a tumult
and toss up mire and dirt.
Thou didst make me a banner for the righteous elect,
an interpreter of knowledge in wondrous mysteries.
The men of deceit roared against me
like the sound of the roar of many waters.
Devices of Belial were their plans;
they turned to the pit the life of a man
whom thou didst establish by my mouth, and didst teach him;
understanding thou didst put in my heart
to open the fount of knowledge to all who understand.
But they exchanged them for the uncircumcised lips and alien tongue
of a people without understanding,
that they might come to ruin in their error.

III (ii.20–30)

I thank thee, O Lord,
because thou hast put my soul in the bundle of life;
thou hast fenced me off from all the snares of the pit.
Oppressors sought my life,
while I laid hold on thy covenant.
But they are a worthless company,
a congregation of Belial.
They do not know that thou hast made me stand,
and in thy steadfast love thou wilt save my life,
for from thee are my steps.
As for them, it is from thee that they gather against my life,
that thou mayest be glorified by the judgment on the wicked.
Thou wilt work mightily in me before the sons of man,
for by thy steadfast love I stand.
But I said, "Mighty men have encamped against me;
they have surrounded me with all their weapons of war;
they have loosed arrows for which there is no healing,
and the flashing of a spear with fire that consumes trees.
Like the tumult of many waters is the roar of their voices,
a tempestuous cloudburst, destroying many;
nought and worthlessness break through to the stars
when their waves are lifted up."
But though my heart melted like water,
my soul took hold of thy covenant.
The net they spread for me caught their own feet;
they fell into the traps they had hid for my soul.
But my foot stands on level ground;
in the assembly I will bless thy name.

IV (ii.31–36)

I thank thee, O Lord,
because thine eye watches over my soul;
thou hast rescued me from the jealousy of the interpreters of lies,
from the congregation of those who seek smooth things.
Thou hast redeemed the soul of the poor,

whom they planned to destroy,
shedding his blood for thy service.
But they knew not that from thee are my steps.
They made me an object of contempt and reproach
in the mouth of all who seek deceit.
But thou, my God, didst succor the soul of the humble and poor
from the hand that was too strong for him;
thou didst redeem my soul from the hand of the mighty,
and didst not let me be frightened by their taunts
into forsaking thy service for fear of destruction by the wicked.

V (iii.6–15)

. . . they made my life a ship on the deep,
and like a fortified city before them.
I am in distress
like a woman in travail with her firstborn,
when her pangs come,
and grievous pain on her birth-stool,
causing torture in the crucible of the pregnant one;
for sons have come to the waves of death,
and she who conceived a man suffers in her pains;
for in the waves of death she gives birth to a man-child;
with pains of Sheol he bursts forth
from the crucible of the pregnant one,
a wonderful counselor with his power;
yes, a man comes forth from the waves.
In her who conceived him, all the waves came quickly,
swift pains also when they were born
and horror for those who conceived them.
When he was born all the pangs came in the crucible of the pregnant
one.
She who conceived nought had grievous pain,
and waves of the pit with all horrors.
The foundations of the wall are broken
like a ship on the face of the waters;
the clouds sound with a noise of tumult,
the dwellers on earth are like those who go down to the seas,
terrified by the noise of the waters.

All their wise men are like sailors on the deep,
for all their wisdom is confounded by the noise of the seas,
when the depths boil above the springs of water.

VI (iii.19–36)

I thank thee, O Lord,
because thou hast redeemed my soul from the pit;
from the Sheol of Abaddon
thou hast brought me up to an eternal height,
and I walk in an unsearchable plain.
I know that there is hope
for him whom thou hast formed from the dust
for an eternal company.
Thou hast purified the perverse spirit of a great sin,
to stand in his place with the army of the holy ones,
and to come together with the congregation of the sons of heaven.
Thou hast cast for man an eternal lot
with the spirits of knowledge,
to praise thy name together in joyful song
and to recount thy wonders in the presence of all thy works.
But I, a thing formed of clay, what am I?
A thing kneaded with water, for whom have I value,
and what strength have I?
For I took my stand in the border of wickedness,
and with the hapless in their lot;
but the poor man's soul was in dread, with great confusion;
engulfing destruction accompanied my steps;
when all the snares of the pit were opened,
and all the nets of wickedness were spread,
the seine of the hapless also on the face of the water;
when all the arrows of the pit flew, not turning aside,
and were loosed beyond hope;
when the line fell on judgment,
and the lot of anger on those who were forsaken;
a molten mass of wrath on dissemblers,
and a period of wrath for all worthlessness.
The cords of death surrounded me inescapably;
the torrents of Belial flowed over all the high banks.

Like a fire eating into all their springs,
destroying every green or dry tree in their channels,
it rushes about with flashes of flame,
until all who drink of them are no more;
into the walls of clay it eats,
and into the platform of the dry land.
The foundations of the mountains are given to the flames;
the roots of flint become torrents of pitch.
It devours to the great abyss;
the torrents of Belial burst into Abaddon;
the sentient beings of the abyss roar
with the noise of the eruptions of mire.
The earth cries aloud at the ruin
which has been wrought in the world;
all its sentient beings shout;
all who are upon it go mad
and melt in utter ruin.
For God thunders with the noise of his might,
and his holy dwelling re-echoes with his glorious truth;
the host of heaven utter their voice;
the eternal foundations melt and shake;
and the war of the mighty ones of heaven
rushes about in the world and turns not back
until the full end decreed forever;
and there is nothing like it.

VII (iv.8–37)

For they have become loathsome to themselves,
and do not regard me when thou dost work mightily in me;
for they drive me from my land like a bird from its nest,
and all my neighbors and friends are driven far from me;
they have regarded me as a broken vessel.
But they are interpreters of lies and seers of deceit;
they devised baseness against me,
exchanging thy law, which thou didst cut into my heart,
for smooth things for thy people.
They withheld the draught of knowledge from the thirsty,
and for their thirst made them drink vinegar;

so that God beheld their error,
going mad at their feasts,
being taken in their nets.
But thou, O God, dost despise every purpose of Belial;
it is thy counsel that will stand,
and the purpose of thy heart that is established forever.
But they are hapless, they plan devices of Belial;
they seek thee with a double heart,
and are not established in thy truth.
A root bearing poisonous and bitter fruit is in their plans,
and with the stubbornness of their hearts they go about.
They have sought thee among idols,
and have set the stumbling block of their iniquity before their faces.
They have come to seek thee
following the directions of false prophets, enticed by error.
But they with strange lips
and an alien tongue speak to thy people,
making foolish by deceit all their works.
For they did not heed thy instruction;
they did not listen to thy word;
for they said of the vision of knowledge, "It is not right,"
and of the way of thy heart, "It is not that."
But thou, O God, wilt answer them,
judging them in thy power
according to their idols and their many transgressions,
that they may be taken in their plans,
in which they are estranged from thy covenant.
Thou wilt cut off in judgment all men of deceit,
and seers of error will be found no more;
for there is no foolishness in all thy works
or deceit in the devices of thy heart.
Those who please thee will stand before thee forever;
those who walk in the way of thy heart will be established to eternity.
As for me, while leaning upon thee
I will rise and stand up against those who despise me,
and my hand will be against all who scorn me;
for they do not regard me,
though thou didst work mightily in me
and didst appear to me in thy strength to enlighten them;

thou didst not plaster with shame
the faces of all those who consulted me,
who assembled for thy covenant and heard me,
those who walk in the way of thy heart
and present themselves to thee in the company of the holy ones.
But thou wilt bring forth their judgment forever,
and truth with equity.
Thou wilt not mislead them by the hand of the hapless,
according to their plotting against them;
but wilt put the fear of them on thy people,
a shattering for all the peoples of the lands,
to cut off in judgment all transgressors of thy words.
By me thou hast enlightened the faces of many,
and hast made them strong until they were numberless;
for thou hast given me knowledge of thy wondrous mysteries,
and in thy wondrous company thou hast wrought powerfully with me;
thou hast wrought wondrously in the presence of many,
for the sake of thy glory
and to make known to all the living thy mighty works.
Who that is flesh could do aught like this,
what thing formed of clay could do such wonders?
For man lives in iniquity from the womb,
and in faithless guilt to old age.
I know that righteousness does not belong to a man,
nor to a son of man blamelessness of conduct;
to the Most High God belong all works of righteousness.
A man's way is not established
except by the spirit which God created for him,
to make blameless a way for the sons of man,
that they may know all his works
in the might of his power and the greatness of his mercy
to all the sons of his good pleasure.
As for me, shaking and trembling have seized me,
and all my bones are broken;
my heart melts like wax before the fire,
and my knees go like water falling on a slope.
For I remember my guilty deeds,
together with the faithlessness of my fathers,
when the wicked rose against thy covenant,

the hapless against thy word.
Then I said, "For my transgression
I am left outside of thy covenant."
But when I remembered the strength of thy hand,
together with the abundance of thy mercy,
I rose and stood up, and my spirit became strong,
standing firm before affliction;
for I leaned on thy steadfast love
and thy abundant mercy.

VIII (v.7–15)

Thou didst put me in a dwelling with many fishermen,
spreaders of nets on the face of the water,
and hunters for the sons of error;
and there for judgment thou didst establish me.
A counsel of truth thou didst make strong in my heart,
and water of the covenant for those who seek it.
Thou didst shut the mouth of lions,
whose teeth are like swords
and their fangs like sharp spears;
the poison of serpents, all their thoughts are to seize;
they are many, but they do not open their mouths against me.
For thou, my God, hast hidden me
before the sons of man.
Thy law is hidden in my heart,
until the time when thy salvation will be revealed to me.
For when my soul was in distress thou didst not forsake me,
but didst hear my cry in the bitterness of my soul.
Thou hast judged my sorrow; thou hast regarded my groaning;
and thou hast rescued the life of the afflicted man in the den of lions,
who sharpened their tongues like a sword;
for thou, my God, didst shut their teeth,
lest they tear the life of the afflicted and poor man;
thou didst gather in their tongue, like a sword into its scabbard,
so that the life of thy servant was not destroyed.

IX (vi.7–10)

I am comforted concerning the tumult of the people
and concerning the uproar of kingdoms,
when they assemble against my counsel,
which thou wilt exalt for a little while,
a reviving among thy people
and a remnant in thy inheritance;
and thou didst purify them, cleansing them of guilt.
For all their works are wrought in thy truth,
and in thy steadfast love thou wilt judge them,
in wealth of mercy and abundance of pardon,
directing them according to thy words
and according to the uprightness of thy truth,
establishing them in thy counsel for thy glory.

X (vii.2–5)

My foot sank in the mire;
my eyes turned away from seeing evil,
my ears from hearing of blood;
my heart was appalled at the thought of evil;
for the worthlessness of a people is shown by the impulse of their being.
All the walls of my building were broken;
my bones were out of joint;
they were shaken like a ship in the raging of a storm;
my heart was utterly distraught;
and a spirit of confusion confounded me
because of the ruin wrought by their transgression.

XI (vii.6–9, 11–15)

I thank thee, O Lord, because thou hast sustained me with thy strength
and hast shed abroad thy Holy Spirit in me;
I shall not be moved.
Thou hast strengthened me in the face of the battles of wickedness;
in all the ruin they wrought thou didst not turn in dismay from thy
    covenant.

Thou hast made me like a strong tower,
like a high wall;
thou hast established my building on a rock,
with eternal bases as my foundation,
and all my walls as a tested wall
that will not be shaken.
For the lying lips shall be dumb;
for all who attack me for judgment thou wilt condemn,
separating by me the righteous from the wicked.
For thou knowest every purpose of action
and perceivest every answer of the tongue.
Thou hast established my heart in thy teachings and in thy truth,
to direct my steps to the paths of righteousness,
that I might walk before thee in the region of life,
to the path of glory and peace.

XII (vii.26–32)

I thank thee, O Lord, because thou hast made me wise in thy truth
and in thy wondrous mysteries hast given me knowledge;
in thy steadfast love for a sinful man,
in the abundance of thy mercy for one whose heart is perverted.
Who is like thee among the gods, O Lord?
Who is like thy truth?
Who will be justified before thee when he is judged?
There is no spirit that can reply to thy accusation,
and none is able to stand before thy wrath.
But all the sons of thy truth thou wilt bring in pardon before thee,
cleansing them from their transgressions
in the abundance of thy goodness and the greatness of thy mercy,
to make them stand before thee to the ages of eternity.
For the Eternal God art thou,
and all thy ways are established forever and ever,
and there is none besides thee.
What is a man of nought, who has only a breath,
to consider thy wondrous works?

XIII (viii.4–12)

I thank thee, O Lord, because thou hast put me
at a source of flowing streams in dry ground,
a spring of water in a land of drought,
channels watering a garden of delight,
a place of cedar and acacia,
together with pine for thy glory,
trees of life in a fount of mystery,
hidden amid all trees that drink water.
They shall put forth a branch for an eternal planting,
taking root before they sprout.
They shall send out their roots to the stream;
its stump shall be exposed to the living water;
and it shall become an eternal source.
When there is a branch on it,
all the beasts of the forest will feed on it;
its stump will be trampled by all that pass by,
its branches by every winged bird;
and all the springs of water shall rise against it.
For in their planting they go astray,
and do not send out a root to the stream.
But he who causes a holy branch
to sprout for a planting of truth
is hiding his mystery, without its being thought of;
without its being known, he is sealing it up.
And thou, O God, hast put a hedge about its fruit
in the mystery of mighty men of valor and holy spirits;
and a flame of fire turning every way.

XIV (ix.6–13)

As for me, from ruin to devastation,
from pain to wounding, from pangs to breaking,
my soul is bowed down among thy wonders,
and thou hast not rejected me in thy steadfast love;
from period to period my soul delights
in the multitude of thy mercies.

I will reply with a word to those who would confound me,
with a rebuke to those cast down because of me;
I will condemn his decision, but thy judgment I will vindicate.
For I know of thy truth, and I will choose my judgment;
I accept my afflictions, because I hope for thy steadfast love.
Thou hast put a supplication in the mouth of thy servant,
and hast not rebuked my life;
my peace-offerings thou hast not rejected,
and hast not forsaken my hope;
and before the stroke thou hast made my spirit stand.
For thou hast established my spirit and knowest my thought;
in my distress thou hast comforted me,
and in pardon I delight;
and I repent of former transgression.

XV (ix.31–36)

From my youth thou hast appeared to me in thy just wisdom,
and with firm truth thou hast sustained me.
With thy Holy Spirit thou dost delight me,
and to this day thou dost lead me.
Thy righteous rebuke is with my thoughts,
and the guarding of thy peace to deliver my soul;
abundance of pardon with my steps,
and a multitude of mercies when thou dost enter into judgment with
    me;
and to old age thou wilt support me.
For my father does not know me,
and my mother against thee has forsaken me;
but thou art a Father to all the sons of thy truth;
thou rejoicest over them
like her who has compassion on her sucking child;
and like a foster father thou wilt sustain in thy bosom
all that thou hast made.

XVI (x.3–14)

For what is man? He is earth,
a cut-off bit of clay, and to dust is his return;

but thou dost make him wise in wonders like these,
and of thy true counsel thou wilt give him knowledge.
But I am dust and ashes.
What can I plan unless thou hast desired it,
and what can I think apart from thy will?
What can I accomplish unless thou hast established me,
and how can I be wise unless thou hast planned for me?
What shall I speak unless thou openest my mouth,
and how should I reply if thou didst not make me wise?
Behold, thou art Prince of gods and King of the honored ones,
Lord of every spirit and Ruler over every work.
Apart from thee nothing is done;
it is not known without thy will.
There is none besides thee,
and there is none with thee in strength;
there is nothing over against thy glory,
and thy power has no price.
Who among all thy wondrous, great works
is able to stand before thy glory?
What then is he who returns to his dust,
that he should prevail against thee?
For thy glory alone thou hast made all these.
Blessed art thou, my Lord, God of mercy!

XVI (xi.3–12)

I thank thee, O Lord, because thou hast done wondrously with dust;
with a thing formed of clay thou hast done powerfully.
Confessing, confessing, what am I?
For thou hast given me knowledge of thy true counsel
and hast made me wise by thy wondrous works.
Thou hast put praises in my mouth
and on my tongue rejoicing,
and the circumcising of my lips in a place of loud praise,
that I may sing of thy steadfast love
and meditate on thy power all the day.
Continually I will bless thy name
and tell of thy glory among the sons of man;
in the abundance of thy goodness my soul shall delight;

for I know that what thou sayest is truth,
and in thy hand is righteousness;
in thy purpose is all knowledge,
and in thy strength all power;
and all glory is with thee.
In thy wrath are all judgments of affliction;
in thy goodness is abundance of pardon
and mercy for all the sons of thy good pleasure.
For thou hast given them knowledge of thy true counsel
and made them wise in thy wondrous mysteries.
For thy glory's sake thou hast cleansed man from transgression,
to consecrate himself to thee
from all unclean abominations and guilt of unfaithfulness;
to unite himself with the sons of thy truth
and to be in the same lot with thy holy ones.

XVII (xii.4–12)

I will praise thy name among those who fear thee,
with songs of thanksgiving and prayer,
lying prostrate and making supplication
continually from period to period;
with the coming in of light from its dwelling,
in the circuits of day in its fixed order,
according to the decrees of the great luminary,
at the turn of evening and the outgoing of light,
at the beginning of the dominion of darkness,
at the appointed time of night in its circuit,
at the turn of morning, and the period of its ingathering
to its dwelling before the light,
at the outgoing of night and the coming in of day,
continually in all the generations of time,
the foundations of a period and the circuit of seasons
in their fixed order and with their signs for all their dominion,
in a fixed order made firm by the mouth of God,
by the testimony of him who is.
And it shall be, and there is no other,
and besides it there has not been,

and shall not ever be;
for the God of knowledge established it,
and there is no other with him.
But I am wise; I know thee, my God;
by the spirit thou didst put in me, which is trustworthy,
I have listened to thy wondrous counsel.

BIBLIOGRAPHY

Bibliography

~~~~~~

Note: While this bibliography is selective, many significant contributions have undoubtedly been omitted. Among these are reviews, which are sometimes quite important. Many relatively unimportant items are here included because reference is made to them in one way or another in this book. A few very recent publications that were not available in time to be used in the preparation of the book are noted in order to make the bibliography as up to date as possible.

ABBREVIATIONS

AER	*American Ecclesiastical Review*
ALBO	*Analecta Lovaniensia Biblica et Orientalia*
AO	*Archiv Orientální*
B	*Biblica*
BA	*Biblical Archaeologist*
BARB	*Bulletin de la classe des lettres et des sciences morales de l'Académie Royale de Belgique*
BASOR	*Bulletin of the American Schools of Oriental Research*
BASOR—SS	*Bulletin of the American Schools of Oriental Research—Supplementary Studies*
BHT	*Beiträge zur historischen Theologie*
BIES	*Bulletin of the Israel Exploration Society*
BJRL	*Bulletin of the John Rylands Library*
BO	*Bibliotheca Orientalis*
CBC	*Catholic Biblical Quarterly*
CRAIBL	*Comptes rendus des séances de l'Académie des Inscriptions et Belles-Lettres*
CS	*Cahiers Sioniens*
ET	*Evangelische Theologie*
ETL	*Ephemerides theologicae Lovanienses*
FF	*Forschungen und Fortschritte*

HTR	*Harvard Theological Review*
HUCA	*Hebrew Union College Annual*
IEJ	*Israel Exploration Journal*
ILN	*Illustrated London News*
JBL	*Journal of Biblical Literature*
JJS	*Journal of Jewish Studies*
JQR	*Jewish Quarterly Review*
JTS	*Journal of Theological Studies*
NC	*La Nouvelle Clió*
NRT	*Nouvelle revue théologique*
NTS	*New Testament Studies*
PAAJR	*Proceedings of the American Academy for Jewish Research*
PEQ	*Palestine Exploration Quarterly*
RB	*Revue biblique*
RHR	*Revue de l'histoire des religions*
RSR	*Recherches de science religieuse*
S	*Scripture*
ThLZ	*Theologische Literaturzeitung*
TR	*Theologische Rundschau*
TZ	*Theologische Zeitschrift*
VD	*Verbum Domini*
VT	*Vetus Testamentum*
ZAW	*Zeitschrift für die alttestamentliche Wissenschaft*
ZDMG	*Zeitschrift der Deutschen Morgenländischen Gesellschaft*
ZRG	*Zeitschrift für Religions- und Geistesgeschichte*
ZTK	*Zeitschrift für Theologie und Kirche*

Albright, W. F. "On the Date of the Scrolls from 'Ain Feshkha and the Nash Papyrus." BASOR, October 1949, pp. 10–19.

———. "Comments on Dr. Lacheman's Reply and the Scrolls." BASOR, December 1949, pp. 16–17.

———. "Are the 'Ain Feshkha Scrolls a Hoax?" JQR, 1949, pp. 41–49.

———. "The Chronology of the Dead Sea Scrolls." BASOR—SS, 1951, pp. 57–60.

———. "The Dead Sea Scrolls." *The American Scholar*, 1952–53, pp. 77–85.

Arbez, E. P. "Notes on the New Hebrew Mss." CBC, 1950, pp. 173–89.

———. "The New Hebrew Manuscripts." AER, 1950, pp. 25–36, 137–45, 196–206.

Audet, J. P. "Affinités littéraires et doctrinales du 'Manuel de Discipline.'" RB, 1952, pp. 219–38; 1953, pp. 41–82.

Avi-Yonah, M. "The 'War of the Sons of Light and the Sons of Darkness' and Maccabean Warfare." IEJ, 1952, pp. 1–5.

Bardtke, H. *Die Handschriftenfunde am Toten Meer*. Berlin: Evangelische Haupt-Bibelgesellschaft, 1952.

———. "Bemerkungen zu den beiden Texten aus dem Bar Kochba-Aufstand." ThLZ, 1954, cols. 295–303.

Barthélemy, D. "Le grand rouleau d'Isaïe trouvé près de la Mer Morte." RB, 1950, pp. 530–49.

———. "Notes en marge de publications récents sur les manuscrits de Qumran." RB, 1952, pp. 187–218.

———. "Redécouverte d'un chaînon manquant de l'histoire de la Septant." RB, 1953, pp. 18–29.

Bauchet, J. M. P., and Sutcliffe, E. F. "The Sectarian Document." S, 1949, pp. 76–79.

———. "Note sur les variantes de sens d'Isaïe 42 et 43 dans le manuscrit du désert de Juda." NRT, 1949, pp. 305f.

———. "Notes on the Recently-Found Hebrew Manuscripts." S, 1949, pp. 115-17.

———. "The Newly Discovered Scrolls of the Judean Desert." CBC, 1949, pp. 308–15.

———. "A Note on the Orthography of the Dead Sea MSS." CBC, 1950, p. 68.

———. "Transcription and Translation of Megilloth Genuzoth B. Plate VI." CBC, 1950, pp. 458–59.

———. "Transcription and Translation of a Psalm from Sukenik's Dead Sea Scroll." CBC, 1950, pp. 331–35.

———. "A Note on the Scroll of Thanksgiving Songs." S, 1951, pp. 277f.

Baumgarten, J. M. "Sacrifice and Worship among the Jewish Sectarians of the Dead Sea (Qumrān) Scrolls." HTR, 1953, pp. 141–59.

Baumgartner, W. "Der palästinische Handschriftenfund." TR, 1948/49, pp. 329–46.

———. "Die hebräischen und armäischen Handschriften aus Palästina." TZ, 1951, pp. 391–94.

———. "Der Palästinische Handschriftenfund." TR, 1951, pp. 97–154.

———. "Die Bedeutung der Hohlenfunde aus Palästina für die Theologie." *Schweizerische Theologische Umschau*, 1954, pp. 49–63.

Beegle, D. "Proper Names in the New Isaiah Scroll." BASOR, October 1951, pp. 26–30.

Bellinger, L. "Report upon a Fragment of Cloth from the Dead Sea Scroll Cave." BASOR, April 1950, pp. 9–11.

Birnbaum, S. A. "The Date of the Isaiah Scroll." BASOR, February 1949, pp. 33–35.

———. "The Date of the Habakkuk Cave Scroll." JBL, 1949, pp. 161–68.

———. "The Date of the Covenant Scroll." PEQ, 1949, pp. 140–47.

———. "The Dates of the Cave Scrolls." BASOR, October 1949, pp. 20–22.

———. "The Leviticus Fragments from the Cave." BASOR, April 1950, pp. 20–27.

———. "How Old Are the Cave Manuscripts? A Palaeographical Discussion." VT, 1951, pp. 91–109.

———. "Notes on the Internal and Archaeological Evidence Concerning the Cave Scrolls." JBL, 1951, pp. 227–32.

———. "The Date of the Hymns Scroll." PEQ, 1952, pp. 94–103.

———. "A Fragment of an Unknown Script." PEQ, 1952, pp. 118–20.

Black, M. "The Dating of the New Hebrew Scrolls on Internal Evidence." JJS, 1949, p. 199.

Bonsirven, J. "Révolution dans l'histoire des origines chrétiennes?" *Etudes*, 1951, pp. 213–18.

Braun, F. M. "L'arrière-fond judaïque du quatrième évangile et la Communauté de l'Alliance." RB, 1955, pp. 5–44.

Brownlee, W. H. "The Jerusalem Habakkuk Scroll." BASOR, December 1948, pp. 8–18.

——. "Further Light on Habakkuk." BASOR, April 1949, pp. 9–10.

——. "Further Corrections of the Translation of the Habakkuk Scroll." BASOR, December 1949, pp. 14–16.

——. "The Original Height of the Dead Sea Habakkuk Scroll." BASOR, April 1950, pp. 7–9.

——. "A Comparison of the Covenanters of the Dead Sea Scrolls with Pre-Christian Jewish Sects." BA, 1950, pp. 50–72.

——. "Excerpts from the Translation of the Dead Sea Manual of Discipline." BASOR, February 1951, pp. 8–13.

——. "Light on the Manual of Discipline (DSD) from the Book of Jubilees." BASOR, October 1951, pp. 30–32.

——. "The Dead Sea Manual of Discipline." BASOR—SS, 1951.

——. "The Text of Isaiah VI 13 in the Light of DSIa." VT, 1951, pp. 296–98.

——. "Biblical Interpretation among the Sectaries of the Dead Sea Scrolls." BA, 1951, pp. 54–76.

——. "Benediction from the Dead Sea Manual of Discipline." *Duke Divinity School Bulletin*, 1952, p. 2.

——. "The Historical Allusions of the Dead Sea Habakkuk Midrash." BASOR, April 1952, pp. 10–20.

——. "The Manuscripts of Isaiah from which DSIa was Copied." BASOR, October 1952, pp. 16–21.

——. "The Cross of Christ in the Light of Ancient Scrolls." *The United Presbyterian*, November 20, 1953, pp. 6, 7, 11; December 7, p. 11; December 14, pp. 7–8; December 21, pp. 12–13; December 28, pp. 10–11.

——. "The Servant of the Lord in the Qumran Scrolls." BASOR, December 1953, pp. 8–15.

——. "Emendations of the Dead Sea Manual of Discipline and Some Notes Concerning the Habakkuk Midrash." JQR, 1954, pp. 141–58.

——. "The Servant of the Lord in the Qumran Scrolls. II." BASOR, October 1954, pp. 33–38.

Burrows, M. "The Contents and Significance of the Manuscripts." BA, 1948, pp. 57–61.

——. "Variant Readings in the Isaiah Manuscript." BASOR, October 1948, pp. 16–24; February 1949, pp. 24–32.

——. "Orthography, Morphology, and Syntax of the St. Mark's Isaiah Manuscript." JBL, 1949, pp. 195–211.

———. "A Note on the Recently Discovered Manuscripts." JQR, 1949, pp. 51–56.

———. "The Discipline Manual of the Judaean Covenanters." *Oudtestamentische Studien*, 1950, pp. 156–92.

———. *The Dead Sea Scrolls of St. Mark's Monastery*. New Haven: American Schools of Oriental Research, volume I, 1950; volume II, fascicle 2, 1951.

———. "The Dating of the Dead Sea Scrolls." BASOR, April 1951, pp. 4–6.

———. "Concerning the Dead Sea Scrolls." JQR, 1951, pp. 105–32.

———. "*Waw* and *Yodh* in the Isaiah Dead Sea Scroll (DSIa)." BASOR, December 1951, pp. 18–20.

———. "The Meaning of '*śr 'mr* in DSH." VT, 1952, pp. 255–60.

Chamberlain, J. V. "Another Qumran Thanksgiving Psalm." JNES, 1955, pp. 32–41.

Collier, D. "New Radiocarbon Method for Dating the Past." BA, 1951, pp. 25–28.

Coppens, J. "Découverte de nouveaux manuscrits de la Bible." ETL, 1949, pp. 309–12.

———. "Où en est le problème des manuscrits récemment découverts dans le désert de Juda?" ALBO, 1951, pp. 14–18.

———. "Les manuscrits du désert de Juda." ALBO, 1951.

———. "Les manuscrits du désert de Juda." ETL, 1950, pp. 326–29, 580–582; 1952, pp. 399–403.

———. "Découverte de nouveaux manuscrits." ETL, 1952, pp. 207f.

Cross, F. M. "The Newly Discovered Scrolls in the Hebrew University Museum in Jerusalem." BA, 1949, pp. 36–46.

———. "A New Qumran Biblical Fragment Related to the Original Hebrew Underlying the Septuagint." BASOR, December 1953, pp. 15–26.

———. "The Manuscripts of the Dead Sea Caves." BA, 1954, pp. 2–21.

Crowfoot, G. M. "Linen Textiles from the Cave of Ain Feshkha in the Jordan Valley." PEQ, 1951, pp. 5–31.

Cullmann, O. "Die neuentdeckten Qumrantexte und das Judenchristentum der Pseudoklementinen." *Neutestamentliche Studien für Rudolf Bultmann* (*Zeitschrift für die neutestamentliche Wissenschaft*, Beiheft 21), Berlin: Töpelman, pp. 35–51.

Davies, W. D. " 'Knowledge' in the Dead Sea Scrolls and Matthew 11:25–30." HTR, 1953, pp. 113–39.

Delcor, M. *Les Manuscrits de la Mer Morte. Essai sur le Midrash d'Habacuc* (*Lectio Divina* 7). Paris: Cerf, 1951.

———. "Le Midrash d'Habacuc." RB, 1951, pp. 521–49.

———. "Le Sacerdoce, les lieux de culte, les rites et les fêtes dans les documents de Qumrân." RHR, 1953, pp. 5–41.

del Medico, H. E. "La Découverte d'apocryphes de l'Ancien Testament dans le Désert de Judée." RSR, 1948, pp. 589–92.

———. *Deux Manuscrits hébreux de la Mer Morte*. Paris: Geuthner, 1951.

del Medico, H. E. "Peut-on dater les Manuscrits de la Mer Morte?" *Dieu Vivant*, 1951, pp. 119–26.

———. "Les Esséniens dans l'oeuvre de Flavius Josèphe." *Byzantinoslavica*, 1952–53, pp. 1–45, 189–226.

Detaye, C. "Le Cadre historique du Midrash d'Habacuc." ETL, 1954, pp. 323–43.

de Vaux, R. "Les Manuscrits hébreux du désert de Juda." *La Vie Intellectuelle*, 1949, pp. 583–95.

———, with G. L. Harding. "La Cachette des anciens manuscrits hébreux." CRAIBL, 1949, pp. 99–102.

———. "Post-scriptum. La cachette des manuscrits hébreux." RB, 1949, pp. 234–37.

———. "La Grotte des manuscrits hébreux." RB, 1949, pp. 586–609.

———. "A propos des manuscrits de la Mer Morte." RB, 1950, pp. 417–429.

———. "Les Manuscrits de la Mer Morte et les origines chrétiennes." *La Vie Intellectuelle*, 1951, pp. 60–70.

———. "Fouille au Khirbet Qumrân." RB, 1953, pp. 83–106.

———. "Les Grottes de Murabba'at et leurs documents." RB, 1953, pp. 245–267.

———. "Quelques Textes hébreux de Murabba'at." RB, 1953, pp. 268–275.

———. "Exploration de la région de Qumrân." RB, 1953, pp. 540–61.

———. "Fouilles de Khirbet Qumran. Rapport préliminaire sur la deuxième campagne." RB, 1954, pp. 193–236.

Diringer, D. "Early Hebrew Script Versus Square Hebrew Script" (in *Essays and Studies Presented to Stanley Arthur Cook*). London: Taylor, 1950, pp. 35–49.

———. "Early Hebrew Writing." BA, 1950, pp. 74–95.

Driver, G. R. "The Hebrew Manuscripts." JQR, 1949, pp. 127–34.

———. "New Hebrew Manuscripts." JQR, 1950, pp. 359–72.

———. New Hebrew Scrolls. *Hibbert Journal*, 1950, pp. 11–21.

———. "Hebrew Scrolls." JTS, 1951, pp. 17–30.

———. *The Hebrew Scrolls from the Neighbourhood of Jericho and the Dead Sea*. London: Oxford University Press, 1951.

———. "Once Again the Judaean Scrolls." JQR, 1953, pp. 1–20.

Dupont-Sommer, A. *Observations sur le Commentaire d'Habacuc découvert près de la Mer Morte*. Paris: Adrien-Maisonneuve, 1950.

———. "Le 'Commentaire d'Habacuc' découvert près de la Mer Morte: Traduction et notes." RHR, 1950, pp. 129–71.

———. "La 'Règle' de la Communauté de la Nouvelle Alliance: extraits traduits et commentés." RHR, 1950, pp. 5–21.

———. "Le Commentaire d'Habacuc découvert près de la Mer Morte." CRAIBL, 1950, pp. 196–99.

———. "Lumières nouvelles sur les Manuscrits découverts près de la Mer Morte." NC, 1950, pp. 330–35.

———. *Observations sur le Manuel de Discipline découvert près de la Mer Morte.* (*Communication lue devant l'Académie des Inscriptions.*) Paris: Adrien-Maisonneuve, 1951.

———. "Le 'Manuel de Discipline' découvert près de la Mer Morte. CRAIBL, 1951, pp. 189–200.

———. "Le Maître de Justice fut-il mis à mort?" VT, 1951, pp. 200–215.

———. "Contribution à l'exégèse du Manuel de Discipline x 1–8." VT, 1952, pp. 229–43.

———. "Encore sur le mot *'bwt* dans DSH xi 6." VT, 1952, pp. 276–78.

———. "La Sainteté du signe "noun" dans le Manuel de Discipline." BARB, 1952, pp. 184–93.

———. "Le Testament de Levi (XVII–XVIII) et la secte juive de l'Alliance." *Semitica,* 1952, pp. 33–53.

———. "Découvertes nouvelles dans le Désert de Juda." *Revue de la Pensée Juive,* 1952, pp. 66–77.

———. *Aperçus préliminaires sur les Manuscrits de la Mer Morte.* Paris: Adrien-Maisonneuve, 1950. (English translation, *The Dead Sea Scrolls,* Oxford: Blackwell, 1952.)

———. *Nouveaux aperçus sur les Manuscrits de la Mer Morte.* Paris: Adrien-Maisonneuve, 1953. (English translation: *The Jewish Sect of Qumran and the Essenes, New Studies on the Dead Sea Scrolls,* London: Vallentine, Mitchell & Co., 1954.)

———. "Quelques remarques sur le *Commentaire d'Habacuc,* à propos d'un livre récent." VT, 1955, pp. 113–29.

Eissfeldt, O. "Die Bedeutung der 1947 in Palästina aufgefundenen alten hebräischen und aramäischen Handschriften." FF, 1949, pp. 196–200.

———. "Nachtrag zu dem Aufsatz über die 1947 gefundenen hebräischen Handschriften." FF, 1949, p. 302.

———. "Zahl und Art der in den Rollen enthaltenen Schriftwerke; ihre Entstehungszeit und ihre religionsgeschichtliche Einordnung." ThLZ, 1949, cols. 95–98.

———. "Varianten der Jesaia-Rolle." ThLZ, 1949, cols. 221–26.

———. "Ansetzung der Rollen nach paläographischen Kritèrien." ThLZ, 1949, cols. 226–28.

———. "Vorläufige Ergebnisse einer im Frühjahr 1949 vorgenommenen Untersuchung der Fundhöhle." ThLZ, 1949, col. 228.

———. "Neue Nachrichten über die im Frühjahr 1949 vorgenommenen Untersuchung der Fundhöhle." ThLZ, 1949, cols. 595–97.

———. "Der Anlass zur Entdeckung der Höhle und ihr ähnliche Vorgänge aus älterer Zeit." ThLZ, 1949, 2 cols. 597–600.

———. "Die Bestimmung der aramäisch geschriebenen Rolle als das apokryphe Lamech-Buch." ThLZ, 1950, cols. 23–26.

———. "Hauptmann Philippe Lippens' Bericht über die Wiederentdeckung der Fundhöhle." ThLZ, 1950, cols. 145–51.

———. *"Variae lectiones rotulorum manu scriptorum anno 1947 prope Mare Mortuum repertorum ad Jes 1–66 et Hab 1–2 pertinentes."* Stuttgart, 195ㅗ

Eissfeldt, O. "Zeilenfüllung." VT, 1952, pp. 87–92.

Elliger, K. "Studien zum Habakuk-Kommentar vom Toten Meer." BHT 15, 1953.

Février, J. G. "La Tactique hellénistique dans un texte de 'Ayin Fashkah." *Semitica*, 1950, pp. 53–61.

———. "La Date des textes de 'Ayin Fashkah en écriture paléohébraïque." *Journal Asiatique*, 1951, pp. 275–82.

Filson, F. V. "New Fragments of the Dead Sea Scrolls." BA, 1949, pp. 99–100.

———. "Some Recent Study of the Dead Sea Scrolls." BA, 1950, pp. 96–99.

Flusser, D. "The Connection Between the Apocryphal Execusio Isaiae and the Dead Sea Scrolls." BIES, 1952, pp. 28–46.

———. "The Apocryphal Book of Ascensio Isaiae and the Dead Sea Sect." IEJ, 1953, pp. 30–47.

Freedman, D. N. "The 'House of Absalom' in the Habakkuk Scroll." BASOR, April 1949, pp. 11–12.

Ginsberg, H. L. "The Hebrew University Scrolls from the Sectarian Cache." BASOR, December 1948, pp. 19–23.

———. "Notes on the Two Published Letters to Jeshua Ben Galgolah." BASOR, October 1953, pp. 25–27.

Goossens, R. "Onias le Juste, le Messie de la Nouvelle Alliance, lapidé à Jérusalem en 65 av. JC." NC, 1950, pp. 336–53.

———. "L'Etat actuel des recherches sur les Manuscrits de la Mer Morte et sur la Secte de la Nouvelle Alliance." NC, 1950, pp. 634–71.

———. "Les Eléments messianiques des traditions sur Onias le Juste, chez Josèphe et dans le Talmud." BARB, 50, pp. 440–69.

———. "La Secte juive de la Nouvelle Alliance et les origines chrétiennes." *Revue de l'Université de Bruxelles*, 1951, pp. 399–435.

———. "Du Nouveau sur les origines chrétiennes." *Le Flambeau*, 1951, pp. 1–20.

———. "La Secte de la Nouvelle Alliance et les Esséniens." *Le Flambeau*, 1952, pp. 145–54.

———. "Les Kittim du Commentaire d'Habacuc." NC, 1952, pp. 137–70.

———. "Le Vocabulaire du Manuel de Discipline." NC, 1952, pp. 297–99.

Gottstein, M. H. "Bible Quotations in the Sectarian Dead Sea Scrolls." VT, 1953, pp. 79–82.

———. "A DSS Biblical Variant in a Medieval Treatise." VT, 1953, pp. 187–88.

———. "Studies in the Language of the Dead Sea Scrolls." JJS, 1953, pp. 104–107.

———. "Die Jesaia-Rolle im Lichte von Peschitta und Targum." B, 1954, pp. 51–71.

———. "Anti-Essene Traits in the Dead Sea Scrolls." VT, 1954, pp. 141–47.

Grossouw, W. "The Dead Sea Scrolls and the New Testament." *Studia Catholica*, 1951, pp. 289–99; 1952, pp. 1–8.

Guillaume, A. "Mt. 27, 46 in the Light of the Dead Sea Scrolls." PEQ, 1951, pp. 78–80.

———. "Les Manuscrits hébreux." RB, 1952, pp. 182–86.

Guindon, W. G. "Radio-active Carbon and the Dead Sea Scrolls." CBQ, 1951, pp. 268–75.

Habermann, A. M. *'Edah we-'Eduth.* Jerusalem: Mahbaroth le-Siphruth, 1952.

Harding, G. L. "The Dead Sea Scrolls." PEQ, 1949, pp. 112–16.

———. "The Dead Sea Scrolls." ILN, 1949, pp. 493–95.

———. "Khirbet Qumran and Wady Murabba'at." PEQ, 1952, pp. 104–109.

Hempel, J. "Beobachtungen an der 'syrischen' Jesajarolle vom Toten Meer (DSIa)." ZDMG, 1951, pp. 138–73.

Janssens, H. F. *Vocabulaire du "Manuel de Discipline."* Brussels: privately published, 1952.

Johnson, S. E. "The Dead Sea Manual of Discipline and the Jerusalem Church of Acts." ZAW, 1954, pp. 106–20.

Kahle, P. "Die Auffindung der Rollen und ihr Ankauf. Die textkritische Bedeutung der Jesaia-Rolle. Der Anlass für das Verbergen der Rollen." ThLZ, 1949, cols. 91–94.

———. "Die Zeit der Bergung der hebräischen Handschriften in der Höhle." ThLZ, 1950, cols. 537–42.

———. "The Age of the Scrolls." VT, 1951, pp. 38–48.

———. *Die Hebräischen Handschriften aus der Höhle,* Stuttgart: Kohlhammer, 1951.

———. "Zu den Handschriftenfunden aus der Höhle." ThLZ, 1951, cols. 161–66.

———. "Die Gemeinde des Neuen Bundes und die hebräischen Handschriften aus der Höhle." ThLZ, 1952, pp. 401–12.

———. "The Karaites and the Manuscripts from the Cave." VT, 1953, pp. 82–84.

———. "Die im August 1952 entdeckte Lederrolle mit dem griechischen Text der kleinen Propheten und das Problem der Septuaginta." ThLZ, 1954, cols. 81–94.

Kanael, B. "Notes on the Ancient Hebrew Script in the Judaean Scrolls." BIES, 1954, pp. 46–52.

Katz, B. Z. *glwy swd hmgylwt hgnwzwt bm'rt yryhw.* Tel Aviv: N. Tvarski, 1950.

Kraeling, C. H. "A Dead Sea Scroll Jar at the Oriental Institute." BASOR, February 1952, pp. 5–7.

Kuhl, C., "Schreibereigentümlichkeiten. Bemerkungen zur Jesajarolle (DSIa)." VT, 1952, pp. 307–33.

Kuhn, K. G. "Zur Bedeutung der neuen palästinischen Handschriftenfunde für die neutestamentliche Wissenschaft." ThLZ, 1950, cols. 81–86.

———. "Die in Palästina gefundenen hebräischen Texte und das Neue Testament." ZTK, 1950, pp. 192–211.

Kuhn, K. G. "Die Schriftrollen vom Toten Meer—zum heutigen Stand ihrer Veröffentlichung." ET, 1951, pp. 72ff.

———. "Über den ursprünglichen Sinn des Abendmahls und sein Verhältnis zu den Gemeinschaftsmahlen der Sektenschrift." ET, 1951, pp. 508–27.

———. "Πειρασμός im Neuen Testament und die damit zusammenhängenden Vorstellungen." ZTK, 1952, pp. 200–22.

———. "Die Sektenschrift und die iranische Religion." ZTK, 1952, pp. 296–316.

———. "Les Rouleaux de Cuivre de Qumrân." RB, 1954, pp. 193–205.

———. "Die beiden Messias Aarons und Israels." NTS, 1955, pp. 168–79.

Lacheman, E. R. "A Matter of Method in Hebrew Paleography." JQR, 1949, pp. 15–39.

———. "Reply to the Editor." BASOR, December 1949, pp. 16–17.

———. "Can Hebrew Palaeography Be Called 'Scientific'?" JQR, 1951–52, pp. 377–85.

———. "Hebrew Palaeography Again." JQR, 1953, pp. 116–22.

Lambert, G. "Les Manuscrits découverts dans le désert de Juda." NRT, 1949, pp. 286–304, 414–16, 620–37.

———. "La Grotte aux manuscrits du désert de Juda." *Revue Générale Belge*, 1950, pp. 405–24.

———. "Les Manuscrits du désert de Juda." NRT, 1950, pp. 53–65, 199–202, 493–515; (with G. Vermès) 1951, pp. 385–98.

———. "Le Manuel de Discipline de la grotte de Qumrân." NRT, 1951, pp. 938–75, and ALBO, 1951.

———. "Les Manuscrits hébreux de la grotte de Qumrân." *Les Etudes Classiques*, 1951, pp. 217–66.

———. "Le Maître de justice et la Communauté de l'Alliance." NRT, 1952, pp. 259–83.

———. "Traduction de quelques 'psaumes' de Qumrân et du 'pêsher' d'Habacuc." NRT, 1952, pp. 284–97.

Lehmann, O. H. "Materials Concerning the Dating of the Dead Sea Scrolls—I, Habakkuk." PEQ, 1951, pp. 32–54.

———. "A Third Dead Sea Scroll of Isaiah." JJS, 1953, pp. 38–40.

———, with S. M. Stern. "A Legal Certificate from Bar Kochba's Days." VT, 1953, pp. 391–96.

Lieberman, S. "Light on the Cave Scrolls from Rabbinic Sources." PAAJR, 1951, pp. 395–404.

———. "The Discipline in the So-Called Dead Sea Manual of Discipline." JBL, 1952, pp. 199–206.

Lindblom, J. "Die Jesaja-Apokalypse in der neuen Jesajahandschrift (DSIa)." *Bulletin de la Société Royale des Lettres de Lund*, 1950–51, pp. 87–97.

———. "Die Ebed Jahwe-Orakel in der neuentdeckten Jesajahandschrift (DSIa)." ZAW, 1951, pp. 235–48.

Loewinger, S. "New Corrections to the Variae Lectiones of O. Eissfeldt." VT, 1954, pp. 80–87.

———. "The Variants of DSI II." VT, 1954, pp. 155–63.

Mansoor, M. "Two More New Psalms as Translated from the Dead Sea Scrolls." *Commentary*, 1955, pp. 368–69.

Marcus, R. "Philo, Josephus and the Dead Sea *yaḥad.*" JBL, 1952, pp. 207–209.

———. "Textual Notes on the Dead Sea Manual of Discipline." JNES, 1952, pp. 205–11.

———. "A Note on the Bar Kokeba Letter from Murabba'at." JNES, 1954, p. 51.

Martin, W. J. *The Dead Sea Scroll of Isaiah* (The Sixth Campbell Morgan Memorial Lecture). London: The Bookroom, Westminster Chapel, 1954.

Meyer, R. "Zur Sprache von 'Ain Feschcha." ThLZ, 1950, pp. 721–26.

Michaud, H., "Un Mythe zervanite dans un des manuscrits de Qumrân." VT, 1955, pp. 137–47.

Michel, A. *Le Maître de Justice d'après les documents de la Mer Morte, la littérature apocryphe et rabbinique.* Avignon: Aubanel Père, 1954.

Milik, J. T. "Note sui manoscritti di 'Ain Fešha." B, 1950, pp. 73–94, 204–20.

———. "Il Rotolo frammentario di Isaia." B, 1950, pp. 246–49.

———. "Le Giarre di manoscritti della grotta del Mar Morto e dell'Egitto Tolemaico." B, 1950, pp. 504–508.

———. Duo cantici ex volumine hymnorum nuper inventum ad Mare Mortum." VD, 1950, pp. 362–71.

———. "Manuale Disciplinae." VD, 1951, pp. 129–58.

———. "Nota ad volumen hymnorum Mss. Maris Mortui." VD, 1951, pp. 231–32.

———. "Ex discussione de Manuscriptis Maris Mortui." VD, 1951, pp. 362–65.

———. "The Dead Sea Scrolls Fragment of the Book of Enoch." B, 1951, pp. 393–400.

———. "Elenchus textuum ex caverna Maris Mortui." VD, 1952, pp. 34–45, 101–109.

———. "Fragments d'un midrasch de Michée dans les manuscrits de Qumran." RB, 1952, pp. 412–18.

———. "Une Lettre de Siméon bar Kokheba." RB, 1953, pp. 276–94.

———. "Une Inscription et une lettre en araméen christo-palestinien (pl. XVIII–XIX)." RB, 1953, pp. 526–39.

———. "Un Contrat juif de l'an 134 après Jesus-Christ." RB, 1954, pp. 182–190.

Molin, G. "Die Rollen von en Fešha und ihre Stellung in der jüdischen Religionsgeschichte." *Judaica*, 1951, pp. 161–213.

———. *Die Söhne des Lichtes, Zeit und Stellung der Handschriften vom Toten Meer.* Vienna and Munich: Herold, 1954.

Morgenstern, J. "The Calendar of the Book of Jubilees, Its Origin and Its Character." VT, 1955, pp. 34–76.

Moscati, S. *I Manoscritti ebraici del deserto di Giuda.* Rome: Instituto per L'Oriente, 1955.

Mowinckel, S. "Handskriftfunnet ved Dødehavet og dets betydning for teksthistorien." *Norsk teologisk tidsskrift*, 1951, pp. 145–77.

Mowry, L. "The Dead Sea Scrolls and the Gospel of John." BA, 1954, pp. 78–97.

Muilenburg, J. "A Qoheleth Scroll from Qumran." BASOR, October 1954, pp. 20–28.

———. "Fragments of Another Qumran Isaiah Scroll." BASOR, October 1954, pp. 28–32.

Noth, M. "Eine Bemerkung zur Jesajarolle vom Toten Meer." VT, 1951, pp. 224–26.

Nötscher, F. "Der Handschriftenfund am Toten Meer vom Jahre 1947." *Palästinahefte*, 1950, pp. 7–22.

———. "Entbehrliche Hapaxlegomena in Jesaia." VT, 1951, pp. 299–302.

———. "Jüdische Mönchsgemeinde und Ursprung des Christentums nach den jüngst am Toten Meer aufgefundenen hebräischen Handschriften." *Bibel und Kirche*, 1952, pp. 21–38.

O'Callaghan, R. T. "The Scrolls Newly Discovered in Palestine." S, 1949, pp. 41–46.

Orlinsky, H. M. "Studies in the St. Mark's Isaiah Scroll." I, JBL, 1950, pp. 149–66; II, JNES, 1952, pp. 153–56; III, JJS, 1951, pp. 151–54; IV, JQR, 1953, pp. 329–40; V, IEJ, 1954, pp. 5–8; VI, HUCA, 1954, pp. 85–92.

Rabin, C. *The Zadokite Documents*. Oxford: Clarendon Press, 1953.

———, with J. L. Teicher. "Material Evidence of the Christian Origin of the Dead Sea Scrolls." JJS, 1952, pp. 128–32.

———. "Notes on the Habakkuk Scroll and the Zadokite Documents." VT, 1955, pp. 148–62.

Rabinowitz, I. "The Second and Third Columns of the Habakkuk Interpretation-Scroll." JBL, 1950, pp. 31–49.

———. "The Existence of a Hitherto Unknown Interpretation of Psalm 107 among the Dead Sea Scrolls." BA, 1951, pp. 50–52.

———. "The Authorship, Audience and Date of the de Vaux Fragment of an Unknown Work," JBL, 1952, pp. 19–32.

———. "Sequence and Dates of the Extra-Biblical Dead Sea Scroll Texts and 'Damascus Fragments.'" VT, 1953, pp. 175–85.

———. "A Hebrew Letter of the Second Century from Beth Mashko." BASOR, October 1953, pp. 21–25.

———. "A Reconsideration of 'Damascus' and '390 Years' in the 'Damascus' ('Zadokite') Fragments." JBL, 1954, pp. 11–35.

Rabinowitz, J. J. "Note sur la lettre de Bar Kokheba." RB, 1954, pp. 191–92.

———. "The Legal Document from Murabba'at." B, 1954, pp. 198–206.

———. "Some Notes on an Aramaic Contract from the Dead Sea Region." BASOR, December 1954, pp. 15–16.

Ratzaby, Y. "Remarks Concerning the Distinction between *Waw* and *Yodh* in the Habakkuk Scroll." JQR, 1950, pp. 155–57.

Reed, William L. "The Qumran Caves Expedition of March, 1952." BASOR, October 1954, pp. 8–13.

Reicke, B. "Die Ta'āmire-Schriften und die Damaskus-Fragmente." *Studia Theologica,* 1948, pp. 45–70.

———. *Handskrifterna fran Qumrân (eller 'Ain Feschcha) I–III (Symbolae Biblicae Upsalienses* XIV). Uppsala: Wretman, 1952.

———. "Traces of Gnosticism in the Dead Sea Scrolls?" NTS, 1954, pp. 137–40.

Reider, J. "The Dead Sea Scrolls." JQR, 1950, pp. 59–70.

Roberts, B. J. "The Jerusalem Scrolls." ZAW, 1950, pp. 224–45.

———. "Some Observations on the Damascus Document and the Dead Sea Scrolls." BJRL, 1952, pp. 366–87.

———. "The Dead Sea Scrolls and the Old Testament Scriptures." BJRL, 1953, pp. 75–96.

Rost, L. "Die Sektenrolle." ThLZ, 1950, cols. 341–44.

———. "Bemerkungen zum neuen Habakkuktext." ThLZ, 1950, cols. 477–482.

———. "Neue Handschriften vom Toten Meer." ThLZ, 1952, cols. 117–18.

———. "Der von Père de Vaux in der Académie des Inscriptions et Belles Lettres erstattete Bericht über Ḥirbet Qumrām." ThLZ, 1952, cols. 277–80.

———. "Der von Père de Vaux über die neue Höhle und ihren Inhalt erstattete Bericht." ThLZ, 1952, cols. 317–20.

———. "Das Verhältnis von 'Damaskusschrift' und 'Sektenroll.' ThLZ, 1952, cols. 723–26.

———. "Der 'Lehrer der Einung" und der 'Lehrer der Gerechtigkeit.' " ThLZ, 1953, cols. 143–48.

Rowley, H. H. *The Zadokite Fragments and the Dead Sea Scrolls.* Oxford: Blackwell, 1952.

———. "The Covenanters of Damascus and the Dead Sea Scrolls." BJRL, 1952, pp. 111–54.

——— "The Historical Background of the Dead Sea Scrolls." *Expository Times,* 1952, pp. 378–84.

———. "The Internal Dating of the Dead Sea Scrolls." ETL, 1952, pp. 257–276, and ALBO, 1952.

Rubinstein, A. "Urban Halakhah and Camp Rules in the 'Cairo Fragments of a Damascene Covenant.' " *Sefarad,* 1952, pp. 283–96.

———. "Isaiah LVII 17—and the DSIa Variant." VT, 1954, pp. 200–201.

——— "Singularities in Consecutive-Tense Constructions in the Isaiah Scroll." VT, 1955, pp. 148–62.

Samuel, A. Y. "The Purchase of the Jerusalem Scrolls." BA, 1949, pp. 26–31.

Schoeps, H. J. "Der Habakuk-Kommentar von 'Ain Feshkha—ein Dokument der Hasmonäischen Spätzeit," ZAW, 1951, pp. 249–58.

———. "Handelt es sich wirklich um ebionitische Dokumente?" ZRG, 1951, pp. 322–36.

———. "Das Gnostische Judentum in den Dead Sea Scrolls." ZRG, 1954, pp. 1–4.

Schubart, W. "Zu dem Funde hebräischer Handschriften in Palästina." ThLZ, 1951, pp. 533–36.

Schubert, K. "Die Texte aus der Sektiererhöhle bei Jericho." *Bonner Biblische Beiträge,* 1950, pp. 224–45.

———. Die jüdischen und judenchristlichen Sekten im Lichte des Handschriftenfundes von En Fešcha. *Zeitschrift für katholische Theologie,* 1952, pp. 1–62.

———. "Bemerkungen zum Verständnis einiger Termini in den Handschriften von En Fešha und im Damaskusdokument." ThLZ, 1952, pp. 329–36.

Scott, R. B. Y. "Acquisition of Dead Sea Scroll Fragments by McGill University." BASOR, October 1954, p. 8.

Seeligmann, I. L. "The Epoch-making Discovery of Hebrew Scrolls in the Judean Desert." BO, 1949, pp. 1–8.

Segal, M. H. *"lb'ywt šl mgylwt hm'rh."* *Eretz Israel,* 1949–50, pp. 39–44.

———. *"ltwldwt kt hyhd."* *Tarbiz,* 1950–51, pp. 136–52.

———. "The Habakkuk Commentary and the Damascus Fragments." JBL, 1951, pp. 131–47.

———. "The Promulgation of the Authoritative Text of the Hebrew Bible." JBL, 1953, pp. 35–39.

Segert, S. "Zur Habakuk-Rolle aus dem Funde vom Toten Meer I." AO, 1953, pp. 218–39.

———. "Ein Alter Bericht über den Fund Hebräischer Handschriften in einer Höhle." AO, 1953, pp. 263–69.

———. "Zur Habakuk-Rolle aus dem Funde vom Toten Meer III." AO, 1954, pp. 444–59.

Sellers, O. R. "Excavation of the 'Manuscript' Cave at Ain Fashkha." BASOR, April 1949, pp. 5–9.

———. "Archaeological News from Palestine." BA, 1949, pp. 54–57.

———. "Date of Cloth from the Scrolls Cave." BA, 1951, p. 29.

———. "Radiocarbon Dating of Cloth from the 'Ain Feshkha Cave." BASOR, October 1951, pp. 24–26.

Silberman, L. H. "The two 'Messiahs' of the Manual of Discipline." VT, 1955, pp. 77–82.

Skehan, P. W. "A Fragment of the 'Song of Moses' (Deut. 32) from Qumran." BASOR, December 1954, pp. 12–14.

Sonne, I. "A Hymn against Heretics in the Newly Discovered Scrolls and Its Gnostic Background." HUCA, 1950–51, pp. 275–313.

———. Final Verdict on the Scrolls? JBL, 1951, pp. 37–44.

———. "The Newly Discovered Bar Kokeba Letters." PAAJR, 1954, pp. 75–108.

———. "The X-Sign in the Isaiah Scroll." VT, 1954, pp. 90–94.

Starcky, J. "Un Contrat nabatéen sur papyrus." RB, 1954, pp. 161–81.

Stauffer, E. "Zur Frühdatierung des Habakukmidrasch." ThLZ, 1951, cols. 667–74.

Stenzel, M. "Habakkuk II 15–16." VT, 1953, pp. 97–99.

Stern, S. M. "Notes on the New Manuscript Find." JBL, 1950, pp. 19–30.

Sukenik, E. L. *mgylwt gnwzwt.* Jerusalem: Bialik Foundation, I, 1948; II, 1950.

——. *nḥmw nḥmw 'my.* Jerusalem, 1949.

——. "The Scrolls: A reply to Dr. Zeitlin." *Jewish Chronicle*, November 17, 1950, p. 13.

——. *'wṣr hmgylwt hgnwzwt.* Jerusalem: Bialik Foundation and Hebrew University, 1954.

Syszsman, S. "A Propos du Karaïsme et des textes de la Mer Morte." VT, 1952, pp. 343–48.

——. "Sur la Geniza du Caire." VT, 1953, pp. 411–13.

Talmon, S. "Yom hakkippurim in the Habakkuk-Scroll." B, 1951, pp. 549–563.

——. "Notes on the Habakkuk Scroll." VT, 1951, pp. 33–37.

——. "The Sectarian *yhd*—A Biblical Noun." VT, 1953, pp. 133–40.

Teicher, J. L. "The Dead Sea Scrolls—Documents of the Jewish-Christian Sect of Ebionites." JJS, 1951, pp. 67–99.

——. "The Damascus Fragments and the Origin of the Jewish Christian Sect." JJS, 1951, pp. 115–43.

—————— "Method in Hebrew Palaeography." JJS, 1951, pp. 220–202.

——. "Jesus in the Habakkuk Scroll." JJS, 1952, pp. 53–55.

——. "The Teaching of the Pre-Pauline Church in the Dead Sea Scrolls." JJS, 1952, pp. 111–18; 1953, pp. 1–13, 93–103, 139–53.

——. "Documents of the Bar-Kochba Period." JJS, 1953, pp. 132–34.

——. "Jesus' Sayings in the Dead Sea Scrolls." JJS, 1954, p. 38.

——. "Are the Bar Kokhba Documents Genuine?" JJS, 1954, pp. 39–40.

——. "The Habakkuk Scroll." JJS, 1954, pp. 47–59.

——. "The Christian Interpretation of the Sign X in the Isaiah Scroll." VT, 1955, pp. 189–98.

Torrey, C. C. "A Hebrew Fragment of Jubilees." JBL, 1952, pp. 39–41.

Tournay, R. P. R. "Les Anciens manuscrits hébreux récemment découverts." RB, 1949, pp. 204–33.

Trever, J. C. "The Discovery of the Scrolls." BA, 1948, pp. 46–57.

——. "Preliminary Observations on the Jerusalem Scrolls." BASOR, October 1948, pp. 3–16.

——. "A Paleographic Study of the Jerusalem Scrolls." BASOR, February 1949, pp. 6–23.

—————— "Identification of the Aramaic Fourth Scroll from 'Ain Feshkha." BASOR, October 1949, pp. 8–10.

——. "The 'Suppressed' Scroll of the Haftarot." JQR, 1950, pp. 71–81.

——. "Some Comments on the Palaeography of the Dead Sea Scrolls." JJS, 1951, pp. 195–99.

——. "Studies in the Problem of Dating the Dead Sea Scrolls." *Proceedings of the American Philosophical Society*, 1953, pp. 184–93; and *Smithsonian Report* for 1953, pp. 425–35.

Trinquet, J. "Les Liens 'sadocites' de l'écrit de Damas, des manuscrits de la Mer Morte et de l'Ecclésiastique." VT, 1951, pp. 287–92.

Tur-Sinai, N. H. "The Development of the Letters and the Date of the Dead Sea Scrolls." BIES, 1951, pp. 5–13.

van der Ploeg, J. "De in 1947 in de Woestijn van Juda gevonden oude Handschriften in het kader van gelijktijdige schriftelijke Documenten." *Ex Oriente Lux,* 1949–50, pp. 41–71.

———. "Le Rouleau d'Habacuc de la grotte de 'Ain Fešha." BO, 1951, pp. 2–11.

———. "De in 1947 bij de Dode Zee gevonden oude Handschriften." *Ex Oriente Lux,* 1951–52, pp. 221–48.

———. "Quelques traductions du 'Manuel de discipline' de la Mer Morte." BO, 1952, pp. 127–33.

———. "L'Immortalité de l'homme d'après les textes de la Mer Morte." VT, 1952, pp. 171–75.

Van 't Land, F. A. W. and Van der Woude, A. S. *De Habakuk-rol van 'Ain Fašha.* Assen: Van Gorcum, 1954.

Vermès, G. "Nouvelles lumières sur la Bible et sur le Judaïsme." CS, 1949, pp. 224–33.

———. "La Secte juive de la Nouvelle Alliance." CS, 1950, pp. 25f.

———. "La Secte juive de la Nouvelle Alliance d'après ses hymnes récemment découverts." CS, 1950, pp. 178–202.

———. "Le 'Commentaire d'Habacuc' et le Nouveau Testament." CS, 1951, pp. 337–49.

———. "La Communauté de la Nouvelle Alliance d'après ses écrits récemment découverts." ETL, 1951, pp. 70–80, and ALBO, 1951.

———. *Les Manuscrits du Désert de Juda.* Tournai: Desclée, 1953.

———. "Où en est la question des Manuscrits de la Mer Morte?" CS, 1953, pp. 3–16.

———. "Le Cadre historique des Manuscrits de la Mer Morte." RSR, 1953, pp. 5–29, 203–30.

Vincent, A. "Où en est la question des Manuscrits de la Mer Morte? Nouvelles découvertes." *Revue des Sciences Religieuses,* 1952, pp. 258–64.

Wallenstein, M. *Hymns from the Judean Scrolls.* Manchester, Eng.: Manchester University Press, 1950.

———. "Some Lexical Material in the Judean Scrolls." VT, 1954, pp. 211–14.

Wechsler, T. *"hgnyzh hglwyh whgnyzh hgnwzh."* *Haolam,* December 1, 1949, pp. 156–57.

———. "The 'Hidden Geniza' Once More, or Mr. Trever *versus* Mr. Trever. JQR, 1951, pp. 247–50.

———. "The Origin of the So-Called Dead Sea Scrolls." JQR, 1952, pp. 121–39.

Weis, P. R. "The Date of the Habakkuk Scroll." JQR, 1950, pp. 125–54.

Wernberg-Møller, P. "Notes on the Manual of Discipline (DSD) I 18, II 9, III 1–4, 9, VII 10–12, and XI 21–22." VT, 1953, pp. 195–202.

Wieder, N. "The Habakkuk Scroll and the Targum." JJS, 1953, pp. 14–18.

———. "The 'Law-Interpreter' of the Sect of the Dead Sea Scrolls: The Second Moses." JJS, 1953, pp. 158–75.

Wright, G. E. "The Cave Excavated; Fragments of the Book of Daniel Found; The Extent of the Total Discovery; Photographs of the Jerusalem Scrolls." BA, 1949, pp. 32–36.

———. "Additional Comments on the Scroll Cave." BA, 1949, pp. 64–65.

———. "Some Radio-carbon Dates." BA, 1951, pp. 31f.

——— "More Cave Manuscripts." BA, 1952, 44f.

Yadin, Y. "A Note on DSD IV:20." JBL, 1955, pp. 40–43.

Yalon, H. *"gdmwtn whšwbwtn šl hmgylwt hgnwzwt."* Haṣopheh, March 25 and April 13, 1949.

——— *"llšwn hmgylwt hgnwzwt."* Sinai, 1950, pp. 260–94.

Yeivin, S. "The Date and Attribution of the Leviticus Fragments from the Cache in the Judaean Desert." BASOR, April 1950, pp. 28–30.

Zeitlin, S. "The Hoax of the 'Slavonic Joseph.'" JQR, 1948, pp. 171–81.

———. "'A Commentary on the Book of Habakkuk' Important Discovery or Hoax?" JQR, 1949, pp. 235–47.

———. "Scholarship and the Hoax of the Recent Discoveries." JQR, 1949, pp. 337–63.

———. "The Alleged Antiquity of the Scrolls." JQR, 1949, pp. 57–78.

———. "The Mystery of the Hebrew Scrolls." *Crozer Quarterly*, 1950, pp. 35–42.

———. "Where Is the Scroll of the Haftarot?" JQR, 1950, pp. 291–96.

———. "When Were the Hebrew Scrolls 'Discovered,' in 1947 or in 1907?" JQR, 1950, pp. 373–78.

———. "The Hebrew Scrolls: Once More and Finally." JQR, 1950, pp. 1–58.

———. "The Hebrew Scrolls: A Challenge to Scholarship." JQR, 1951, pp. 251–75.

———. "The Hebrew Scrolls and the Status of Biblical Scholarship." JQR, 1951, pp. 133–92.

———. *The Zadokite Fragments.* (JQR Monograph Series, No. 1), Philadelphia: Dropsie College, 1952.

———. "Bar Kokba and Bar Kozeba." JQR, 1952, pp. 77–82.

———. "The Hebron Pogrom and the Hebrew Scrolls." JQR, 1952, pp. 140–52.

———. "The Fiction of the Recent Discoveries Near the Dead Sea." JQR, 1953, pp. 85–115.

———. "The Mishna in Yadaim IV.8, and 'The Sectarians.'" JQR, 1953, pp. 297–300.

———. "The Antiquity of the Hebrew Scrolls and the Piltdown Hoax: A Parallel." JQR, 1954, pp. 1–29.

———. "The Essenes and Messianic Expectations." JQR, 1954, pp. 83–119.

———. "A Note on the Fiction of the 'Bar Kokba' Letter." JQR, 1954, pp. 174–80.

The following appeared after this book went to press:

Barthélemy, D., and Milik, J. T., *Qumran Cave I* (*Discoveries in the Judaean Desert I*). Oxford: Clarendon Press, 1955.